D0873998

RED BARBER

RED BARBER

THE LIFE AND LEGACY OF
A BROADCASTING LEGEND

JUDITH R. HILTNER AND JAMES R. WALKER

UNIVERSITY OF NEBRASKA PRESS • LINCOLN

The University of Nebraska Press is part of a land-grant
institution with campuses and programs on the past, present,
and future homelands of the Pawnee, Ponca, Otoe-Missouria,
Omaha, Dakota, Lakota, Kaw, Cheyenne, and Arapaho
Peoples, as well as those of the relocated Ho-Chunk, Sac and
Fox, and Iowa Peoples.

Library of Congress Cataloging-in-Publication Data
Names: Hiltner, Judith R., author. | Walker, James Robert,
author.
Title: Red Barber: the life and legacy of a broadcasting legend /
Judith R. Hiltner and James R. Walker.
Description: Lincoln: University of Nebraska Press, [2022] |
Includes bibliographical references and index.
Identifiers: LCCN 2021045242
ISBN 9781496222855 (hardback)
ISBN 9781496231857 (epub)
ISBN 9781496231864 (pdf)
Subjects: LCSH: Barber, Red, 1908–1992. | Sportscasters—
United States—Biography. | BISAC: SPORTS & RECREATION /
Baseball / History | BIOGRAPHY & AUTOBIOGRAPHY /
Entertainment & Performing Arts
Classification: LCC GV742.42.B34 H55 2022 | DDC 796.092
[B]—dc23/eng/20211020
LC record available at https://lccn.loc.gov/2021045242

Set in Arno Pro by Laura Buis.

CONTENTS

ILLUSTRATIONS

ACKNOWLEDGMENTS

We are most profoundly grateful to Carl Van Ness and Michele Wilbanks of the Special and Area Studies Collections at the George A. Smathers Libraries at the University of Florida in Gainesville. Van Ness and Wilbanks responded to our every request (and there were many) and helped us navigate the enormous collection of documents, photographs, and memorabilia in the Walter Lanier "Red" Barber Papers and Book Collection. They allowed us to use their facilities to photograph or scan over ten thousand letters, article clippings, and scrapbook pages, enabling us to examine and absorb the bulk of their Barber holdings in our home offices in Chicago. In addition, we were able to listen to over forty hours of audio recordings and view several thousand slides in their collection. They arranged to digitalize more than twenty audio recordings and several of Barber's home movies and made them available online. These digital offerings included the original recordings of Red sharing his recollections, the oral text from which Robert Creamer crafted Barber's memoir, *Rhubarb in the Catbird Seat*. Complete and convenient access to this collection, curated by the George A. Smathers Libraries for the last four decades, provided many of our most valuable sources and much of the primary content of our book.

We offer our deepest thanks to the many folks who granted us interviews for this biography and provided valuable insights into Red, Lylah, and Sarah Barber. Red's niece, E. V. E. Joy, provided generous access to family photos, letters, and documents and shared detailed and delightful memories of Red, his father William Barber, his brother Billy, and his sister Effie Virginia. She even gave us a fabulous roof over our heads when we visited her in Florida. Much of what we learned about Sarah Barber derives from stimulating interviews with Ellie Edelstein, Margie Edwards, Liz Bremner, Leslie Rich, and Judy Gomez, who knew Red's daughter during her years as an educator in New York and/or after her retirement to Santa Fe. Their memories, reflections, and candor were invaluable since, sadly, Sarah passed away in 2005. Glenn Lautzenhiser, who organized a spectacular 2008 celebration of Red's one hundredth birthday in Columbus, Mississippi, provided a wealth of information and insight into Red's hometown and its many famous citizens. With true hospitality he arranged for us to meet, during the weekend before Christmas 2019, with experts on Columbus and their town's celebrated broadcaster: Dixie Butler, Nancy Carpenter, Birney Imes, Jerry Jones, Derek Rogers, Harry Sanders, Slim Smith, Mona Vance-Ali, Rufus Ward, and Chuck Yarborough. Glenn also gave us access to his personal files and a video of the Red Barber celebration. Mona Vance-Ali, archivist at Mississippi's Columbus-Lowndes Public Library System, provided access to files on Red Barber and directed us to documents that provided crucial insights into the Columbus that Red knew as a young boy.

Others with rich insights into Red Barber's career also took time to talk with us. Marty Appel told us about Red's impact on Phil Rizzuto during his Yankees years and directed us to the amazing Tom Villante, who worked closely with Red during the early 1950s in Brooklyn. Tom's spicy memories of Red are sprinkled throughout our biography. George Vecsey and Steve Jacobson provided both critical insights into Red's later days with the Yankees and much encouragement for our project, while Walker

Lundy told us about Red's work as a columnist for the *Tallahassee Democrat*. Bob Edwards, who wrote his own excellent Barber book—*Fridays with Red*—was incredibly generous with his insights into his "radio friend" for more than a decade. Bob read an earlier and much rougher draft of our biography, and his many comments helped us sand off some rough edges. It was his call for a fuller biography of Red Barber that inspired our effort. Steve Gietschier, an expert reader of our earlier draft, helped us focus our text more sharply, showing us where we could effectively contract our first effort. He also found several errors and offered corrections. Readers will never know how much they benefitted from his pointed suggestions, but Steve's efforts have enriched their experience. Our third reader was our friend Stuart Shea. Stu magnanimously shared his polished skills as editor and his encyclopedic baseball knowledge to improve our text. We also thank Vin Scully for his welcomed support of our project, his many valuable letters to Red, and comments about his mentor's influence on his own amazing career.

We were generously and ably assisted by the staffs of the Giamatti Research Center at the National Baseball Hall of Fame and Museum; the Library of Congress; the Sanford Museum; the Anson County, North Carolina, Historical Society; and the Department of Archives and Special Collections at Rollins College. Special thanks to Alicia Clarke and Brigitte Stephenson of the Sanford Museum for guiding us through the museum's Red Barber materials, including his high school yearbooks. Similarly, Darla Moore, who oversees the Department of Archives and Special Collections at Rollins College, helped us move quickly but carefully through the archive's materials on both Red and Sarah Barber. Many thanks to Brent Shyer, Vice President of Special Projects at O'Malley-Seidler Partners LLC, for sharing with us interesting correspondence between Walter O'Malley and Red Barber.

We gratefully acknowledge Andrew Zimbel, photographer George Zimbel's son, for granting us permission to use three wonderful never-before-published photographs of Red that his father shot for a 1957 *Look* magazine photo essay on Barber. Similarly, John Horne, Coordinator of Rights and Reproductions at the National Baseball Hall of Fame and Museum, located and relayed to us four of the photographs used in this book.

We give a special thank you to the folks at the University of Nebraska Press. It has been a pleasure to work once again with Rob Taylor, senior acquisitions editor, and Courtney Ochsner, associate acquisitions editor, at the Press. They are models for the professional editor, responding to all our queries while processing our shortcomings with good grace. Finally, we acknowledge our debt to Bojana Ristich, our expert copyeditor, and Elizabeth Zaleski, senior project editor, for their many contributions. Their careful attention to detail made our biography of Red Barber a much better experience for the reader.

THREE SCENES

Scene 1: Dressed in a new white linen suit, Red Barber walks out of the Gothic-inspired Tribune Tower in 1933. His fine Florida duds provide little insulation from the frigid winds blowing off Lake Michigan, reinforcing the chilly reception he just received from WGN, the fifty-thousand-watt voice of the *Chicago Tribune*. Radio royalty in his college town, he has not even been granted an interview here. Gazing across Pioneer Court, he catches a glimpse of the skyscraper at 333 North Michigan Avenue, home to the office of Kenesaw Mountain Landis, the first commissioner of Major League Baseball. Although Chicago rejects the young man, Landis's instruction will become a cornerstone in his career.

Scene 2: Lylah Barber sits in the last row of the Music Hall balcony, deaf to the performance emanating from the distant stage. It was the Barbers' first opportunity to enjoy the cultural delights of Cincinnati, their new home. The couple had purchased better tickets but abruptly headed up to the empty back row when they noticed an African American couple sitting next to the seats they had purchased. All she can think about during the symphony is the mindless prejudice that triggered their shabby retreat. This "daughter of the south" now longs to become "a citizen of the world."

Scene 3: Sarah Barber opens the door to her parents' comfortable ranch home in Tallahassee. She has flown down for the holidays from New York City. Her memories of family at Christmas are sweet: wonderful presents, a multitude of holiday cards, and dinner parties with their friends. She hears Lylah announce, "Sarah's here—it's time for cocktails." Sarah's mood dims. She fears that holiday martinis may soon open unhealed wounds. Red is less and less able to cope with Lylah's worsening Alzheimer's symptoms. In a private moment, Sarah pleads with him to accept that he can no longer care for the love of his life alone. Her father removes the hearing aid in his one functioning ear, ending that conversation.

PROLOGUE

Walter Lanier "Red" Barber

The dominant strands of Red Barber's complex personality align with the first three components of his four-name signature: "Walter Lanier 'Red' Barber."

Walter is the ambitious striver, aiming to win but competing only by strictly following "the rules of the game." He is dedicated to self-discipline, self-improvement, and hard work, frequently relying upon gifted mentors who will challenge him to "up his game." He commits himself to excellence in the work he has chosen but bristles when he cannot be his own boss or dictate the terms of his employment. Walter can be prickly and expects colleagues to share his own rigorous ideal of professionalism. Despite his gifted verbal skills, Walter is a shy man who wants nothing more at the end of the day than to retreat to his lovely, well-appointed home, where his time is his own.

Lanier is a name he's inherited from his paternal grandmother's distant relationship to Sidney Lanier, acclaimed nineteenth-century "poet of the Old South." Lanier is the lover of literature, symphony, opera, the visual arts, history, and international travel who, after his first few English classes in college, entertained the prospect of becoming a university literature professor. Lanier is the humanist whose mother, a middle school English teacher, read to him from Greek mythology and the English classics when he was a child. He enjoys the challenge of mulling life's deepest questions and formulating tentative answers. He is repulsed by brutish masculine tendencies and crass commercialism when they manifest themselves in the world of competitive sports. The soft-spoken Lanier champions the cause of the weak and the vulnerable. He loves the blossoms of spring and the grace of well-proportioned human bodies.

Finally, *Red* is the fun-loving performer, giving his all playing his part in a minstrel show, singing on air with an old-time string band, and telling stories to Dodgers radio audiences during lulls in the game. He delights in surprising his listeners by integrating colorful, homespun "Barberisms" into the world of sport. Red rarely turns down an invitation for public performances on stages, in auditoriums, or in front of church congregations. He loves making playful appearances on television and radio quiz shows and, on special occasions, leading the witty colloquy at his country club.

On a midsummer evening in 1942, Red Barber stood near home plate at an Ebbets Field that had been converted into a blood donor recruiting contest between the Dodgers and the Braves. The popular radio play-by-play announcer was officiating a ceremony in which all members of both teams lined up to pledge Red Cross blood donations to save the lives of American troops. Periodically during the play of the game, Barber gently but urgently summoned his radio listeners at home to schedule their appointments at the local Red Cross blood donation center—that is, until phone lines were flooded, and the upcoming scheduling cycle was overbooked with volunteers.

Barber later officiated a more dramatic ceremony on Wall Street before a crowd of five thousand. A World War I veteran who had been wounded on the Hindenburg Line lay on a hospital bed on a platform in front of the sub-Treasury Building to give his twelfth blood donation. Over a loudspeaker the crowd heard its favorite broadcaster announce a play-by-play of medical staff as they collected blood from the veins of a war hero. In 1942 most Americans had never been asked to let strangers draw blood from their arms. Barber's calm and authoritative narration explaining the simple process both soothed and inspired his listeners. Later in his career Red frequently claimed that his Red Cross blood donor drives on radio were the most satisfying broadcasts of his life. He realized on that wartime evening at Ebbets Field that this was what the mass media were made for.

The image of the talented Red Barber announcing play-by-play bloodletting for the sake of his country was one source of our decision to undertake the first complete biography of the broad-caster's life. The story of his eighty-four years on earth, exactly centered in the twentieth century, contains compelling and timely resonance for twenty-first-century readers. Barber's radio and television broadcast career was animated by a rigorous ideal of media's civic responsibility, a vision that has been compromised so persistently since his time that most Americans today cannot fully appreciate the implications of what our culture has lost. Also contributing to his compelling story was his life-changing "near death" experience in 1948 that forced the forty-year-old Barber to ask himself the challenging questions that both troubled his con-science and motivated his pursuits for the rest of his life: What am I here for? What should I be doing with my gifts and talents?

The same values that propelled Barber as a broadcaster also ani-mated the second and third stages of his professional life after his forced retirement from full-time sports broadcasting at fifty-eight. This book examines, for the first time, Red's subsequent career as an author, journalist, public speaker, and lay preacher. Bob Edwards's *Fridays with Red*, a lively account of the final years of Barber's career, when he had a four-minute Friday spot on NPR's *Morning Edition*, skillfully captures how Red's final radio job intro-duced a new generation of listeners to the man that the octoge-narian had become. He had settled himself into talking sports and home-grown philosophy for public radio, which he may have

regarded at the time as the last remaining bastion of civically ori-
ented media. Near the end of his book, Edwards acknowledges
that his account is "not a biography" but "the story of our twelve
years together." He urges future authors who truly appreciate the
significance of Barber's role as a compelling and influential voice
of the twentieth century and who are curious about this "very private man who lived a public life" to research and produce a full
biography of Red Barber.[1]

In our response to Edwards's call, we chronicle Red Barber's
first twenty-six years in the Deep South, as he absorbed the values
of his culture. We trace the trajectory of his influential although
sometimes controversial broadcasting career; his significant civic
engagements; his rich and productive "retirement" years; and the
challenges, setbacks, and insights that shaped his personal journey through the twentieth century. Our account of his life is the
first to tap fully the massive Red Barber archives maintained at the
University of Florida. It places insights from the wealth of published literature on Barber's career and from his own published
and broadcast texts into the context of the twentieth-century
sports broadcast industry. Red narrated highlights of his life up
until 1966 with the help of sportswriter Robert Creamer, and Red's
wife, Lylah, also wrote her own less widely cited memoir, recalling significant episodes and speaking candidly about issues Red
never mentioned. Consequently, we began our project with two
rich but incomplete narratives on which to build.

After he graduated from high school in Sanford, Florida, Barber
aspired to a career as a blackfaced star of a minstrel show troupe.
But by his thirties he had become one of New York City's most
influential citizens as the voice of Brooklyn when the Dodgers were
breaking racial barriers for the first time in Major League Baseball history. During his "expatriation" from the South, his understanding of what it means to be an American evolved, sometimes
painfully, as he absorbed increasingly diverse cultural influences.
The trajectory of his story provides readers with one compelling narrative of the dynamics of tolerance and the influences

that can nurture it. Barber's story also traces the career of a radio and television pioneer who believed his most important role was engaging his audience, telling the truth, and promoting public well-being. He condemned and resisted the increasing pressure of media commercialization and the demands that would subordinate responsible reporting to the exigencies of entertainment and partisanship.

Finally, speaking to twenty-first-century readers, this book documents Barber's family story, which played a crucial role in the formation of his values, his life choices, and his own rigorous self-examinations. Red's personal story movingly dramatizes the strains that single-minded professional ambition imposes upon family life, physical health, and psychic well-being. Barber's primary family role during the closing years of life was the caretaking of his wife in her decline from Alzheimer's disease, when the ailment still was a condition that many families concealed. He also was challenged to navigate long-time family tensions triggered after his only child, Sarah, came out as a lesbian. In this regard Red Barber's story is also a narrative of cultural change in family roles and expectations familiar to readers today.

The steepest challenge in pursuing an accurate life of Red Barber is one that any biographer of a prolific speaker and writer faces. Much has been written about him in books, newspapers, and magazines—or presented in documentaries, films, and radio and television interviews—from the 1930s until today. However, most of what has been printed, broadcast, or filmed are stories that Barber himself originally composed because he so loved writing, talking, and teaching about the work that he did. Until now, even from the grave, he has been chief editor of the story of his life. One of our objectives is to integrate into our narrative meaningful episodes in his life that he did not originally supply or author.

We do justice to the most well-known story in his biography: his public career as a sports broadcaster. But we also place his broadcasting career in the context of cultural changes in twentieth-century American life and his own personal journey, including the evolution of his values, his social and political views, and his religious persuasions. We trace the sources of his midlife disaffection with television broadcasting, which triggered his pursuit of authorship to maintain his "control over the message." We document how his baseball broadcast career triggered his life-long work as promoter and dauntless fund-raiser for social and civic projects, as progressive Episcopal lay reader, and as book author and newspaper columnist. We demonstrate that Red Barber's life was fueled by his uncommon commitment to keep growing and acting effectively to impact and change people with his words. He often insisted that what mattered most to him, beyond human love, was his love of the English language.

RED BARBER

PART 1

FOUNDATIONS IN THE OLD SOUTH

"I Was Carefully Taught"

Cultured Roots

During the third week of February 1908, the Columbus, Mississippi, *Weekly Dispatch* reported that Samuel Kaye, the owner of an ice plant in nearby West Point, was moving his factory to Columbus, nearly doubling the amount of ice that would be produced in the town. Mr. Kaye was convinced that Columbus would supply a much larger market for his ice because of its central location in the region and its many rail connections. The newspaper also reported, "Dreary Weather Brings Discomfort," as excessive rainfall had converted streets in Columbus to "veritable sloughs of mud."[1] On the brighter side, the paper assured readers that Columbus's team in the Cotton States Baseball League promised to be a "real bunch of hustlers" this coming season. Even more impressive, the home team would soon play an exhibition game with the "champions of the world" in Columbus; readers were invited to "just imagine the Chicago Cubs frisking about the diamond in Columbus's own Lake Park!"[2] One thing the paper *did not* report was that Walter Lanier Barber, son of Mr. William Lanier Barber and his wife Selena Martin Barber, was born on February 17, 1908.

A week before Red Barber came into the world, a Black Mississippian, Eli Pigot, was violently torn out of it. On February 10,

1908, a mob of two thousand white people in Brookhaven, Mississippi, lynched Pigot as police deputies and armed military guards were taking him to the Lincoln County Courthouse to stand trial for allegedly assaulting a white woman. After a brief skirmish with the military guards, members of the lynch mob seized Pigot, kicked and beat him, and then hanged him from a telephone pole in front of the courthouse, after which mob members fired their bullets into his corpse as it swung from the pole.[3] The *Weekly Dispatch* published its account of Pigot's death, focusing on minor injuries suffered by the military officers who declined to save him and urging readers to honor the principled and brave townspeople of Brookhaven for "disposing" of the "wild beast who has forfeited his right to live because he has ceased to be a human being," regardless of the "ill-conceived laws" that protected him.[4]

"My Memories of Columbus, Mississippi, Are Those of a Child"

Red Barber lived the first ten years of his life in Columbus, a decade in the town's history marked by growth in commerce and in the town's rich literary, educational, and architectural heritage—developments that made lasting impressions upon him. Throughout his adult life we also see his reactions against episodes of violence and bigotry that, in his formative years in Columbus, always threatened to burst through the fragile social controls supplied by legal statutes and the unwritten codes of Southern decorum. Columbus had been spared from the ravages of the Civil War, according to local legend, because General Ulysses Grant detested Confederate general Nathan Bedford Forrest, who had a warm spot in his heart for the beautiful antebellum mansions that lined the town streets and crowned the nearby plantations. Whenever Union troops threatened to attack Columbus, Forrest would rush in his forces, a weakness that Grant fully exploited by staging a fake attack that triggered the expected massive defensive response by Forrest, enabling Union troops to ravage, uncontested, surrounding towns in the region.[5] As a result, even today, visitors are stunned by the beauty of the antebellum architecture still intact in Columbus.

However apocryphal the story of General Grant's unwitting role in the preservation of Columbus plantations, it is a testament to powerful oral traditions that have forged Columbus's local history. Uncluttered with news streams from radio and television, turn-of-the-century citizens of Columbus shared their stories with one another so that the remembered past filtered into the daily lives of youngsters like Red Barber. Consequently, a child born near the turn of the century, imaginatively at least, lived in *both* centuries. It is not surprising that we can identify in the broadcasting, writing, and public-speaking careers of Red Barber, and in his substantial civic contributions, a compelling synthesis of late nineteenth-century values and early twentieth-century aspirations.

Today citizens of Columbus enjoy telling stories about the outstanding achievers born in their town, whose lives they have memorialized by planting historical plaques in public spaces near the site of their childhood homes. Columbus is proud of two members of the same Lanier family line who were born there just three years apart: Walter Lanier "Red" Barber and Thomas Lanier (Tennessee) Williams, both lovers of literature and gifted storytellers. Both Barber and Williams descend from the same family line as Sidney Lanier, the nineteenth-century poet, born in Macon, Georgia, who was praised for his metrical innovations and his lyrical poems in *Hymns of the Marshes*, celebrating the vast, open landscape along the Georgia coast. Historical plaques in Columbus also memorialize gifted athletes and artists who, like Barber, were born there in the early years of the twentieth century, including Henry Armstrong, the African American world champion boxer, and Josh Meador, famed special effects film animator for Walt Disney Studios.

Red Barber was influenced by Columbus's firm commitment to public education, reflected in his lifetime passion for learning and his conviction that the formal education of youngsters was a crucial imperative in their upbringing. Columbus housed the first public school in Mississippi, the Franklin Academy, built in 1821, which Barber attended from 1914 to 1918. In addition to its educational mission, the founders of the school, who consulted with Thomas Jefferson in forging its curriculum, emphasized "character building and strong moral training."[6] Red Barber's mother, Selena, was trained as an educator in Mississippi's first college for women, established in Columbus in 1884 as the Mississippi Industrial Institute and College for the Education of White Girls, which included a normal school to educate prospective teachers. The groundbreaking college's three-tiered curricular design for educating women was reported in newspapers all over the country and in Europe.[7] Red's mother matriculated at the college when she was only sixteen and, after graduating four years later, became a teacher at Franklin Academy. She co-authored a textbook on English grammar used in Mississippi schools, and according to Barber, she patiently corrected her young children's speech whenever it deviated from proper syntax.[8]

Barber's hometown was well situated to succeed in its forward-looking pursuits during the decade of his birth by its geographic location as the hub of the "golden triangle," comprised of three towns: Columbus, West Point, and Starkville. Residents of West Point and Starkville flocked to Columbus for shopping. The Southern Railroad, the Columbus and Greenville Railroad, and the Mobile and Ohio Railroad all had company offices and stations in Columbus and transported goods and passengers to and from destinations in all four directions. The town's location on the Tombigbee River was also vital to its growth and prosperity; the waterway supplied active trade and transportation throughout the period of Barber's residence, supporting the growth of its key businesses, including brickworks, lumber mills, cotton oil mills, dairies, and garment plants. One local historian has documented that food and services on steamboats transporting travelers up the Tombigbee "were considered as fine as any you would enjoy in a Paris hotel."[9] Streetcars came to Columbus in 1905, running at a speed of 6–12 miles per hour, costing five cents per ride, and carrying passengers across town all the way to baseball games at Lake Park.[10]

Despite the progressive energies of Columbus, the town during Red's childhood was deeply engaged in the nostalgic post-Reconstruction era mythology, known today as the "lost cause," which pervaded the Deep South. During these years statues honoring Confederate leaders and sagas memorializing the courage of brave Civil War heroes proliferated. Klan violence was conducted openly, and accounts of lynchings, like Eli Pigot's, were widely reported by the press in grisly detail to intimidate Blacks from crossing clearly articulated social lines. All schools and churches, of course, were segregated. Blacks worked and sometimes lived on the property of white citizens but were forbidden from violating engrained racial taboos. A massive 1936 WPA profile of Columbus's history and culture up to the 1920s provides a powerful and unsettling record of the assumptions about Black people held by many whites who lived in Barber's hometown during his formative years. The publication is a "peoples' history," compiled by integrating interviews with residents who shared their knowledge of Columbus's past. In the section devoted to "The Negro," the authors record the prevailing assessments of the substantial Black population in the county since the end of Reconstruction, as articulated by long-time white residents. They report the following:

> [Black Americans had begun] to emerge from the state of servitude, a condition with which they were perfectly contented. . . . They are deeply religious but lack a moral standard—amoral, not immoral. . . . Fundamentally dishonest, they can be intimidated into honest courses through one controlling motive . . . fear. They lack initiative and are uncommunicative, but they seem satisfied with their social and economic status. They have no care for sanitation, health or living conditions, and are satisfied to huddle up with several others in one room. But they are important in this county to supply needed farm labor . . . and necessary for household work and as porters for stores.[11]

Fifty years after he moved from Columbus to north-central Florida, Red Barber recorded in his memoir that he was raised in the Deep South and was "carefully taught" its prevailing values. Barber employs the phrase "carefully taught" repeatedly in his writing and public speeches to explain how he absorbed assumptions about race during his childhood. The phrase is from the song "You've Got to Be Carefully Taught," in his favorite Rogers and Hammerstein musical, *South Pacific*. The song's message is that children are schooled by their culture to hate and fear people who look different, like the native South Pacific islanders in the musical's story. Hammerstein said in interviews that the musical's plot was designed around the theme of "race prejudice."[12] During the geographic, professional, and personal journeys of his life, Barber would be forced to confront, interrogate, and transcend some primal teachings of his youth, but the process was never an easy one.

"My Father Was My First Hero ... My Mother Gave Me My Ear for Language"

Red Barber was born in Columbus because his father, William Barber, had moved there in search of a job in railroading, a career he had followed right out of high school in Browns Creek, North Carolina, where he was born in 1879 and where he was buried in his family's plot in 1945. Like Columbus, Mississippi, Anson County, North Carolina, was also a railroad hub: the busy Charlotte-Rutherford Railroad had expanded after the Civil War into the Carolina Central, which by 1892 had merged with the Seaboard Air Railroad Line, operating among Baltimore, Portsmouth, Abbeville, and Atlanta.[13] Its trains moved through the county in all directions, pulling the young William Barber toward Mississippi.[14] At the turn of the century, railroad jobs were plentiful, and any worker displeased by conditions on one line could simply walk off a locomotive and procure for himself what might be better prospects on another line. Barber tells us that his father was one of these traveling railroad "boomers" for a few years, at one point passing through Florida during the winter and enjoying the mild weather while working as a locomotive fireman, completely exposed to the elements. But eventually the trains transported him toward a job as a locomotive engineer for the Southern Railroad and a future wife in Columbus, Mississippi. The only disadvantage of the promotion from fireman to engineer in Columbus was that it robbed him of the seniority he had earned, triggering a significant reduction in his wages and draining the resources of a soon-to-be husband and father.[15]

Barber wrote and spoke to public audiences extensively about his father throughout his life; his "first and favorite hero" was both a powerful role model and a teacher of valuable lessons. His father taught him the value of self-respect and the difference between it and the "sin" of pride. William Barber loved spinning humorous yarns while relaxing with friends and family on his front porch swing after a hard day's work, imprinting on his young son's memory the craft and the tricks of storytelling, such as how to integrate a pithy insight into an engaging anecdote by including a provocative twist at the end of the tale. "I didn't know then," Red later wrote, "that I was in school when listening to him weave his stories and making people come alive." Although it rarely happened, Red loved to hear other people call him "Walter" because that is what his father called him.[16] In a piece he wrote in 1970 for *Reader's Digest*, the engineer's son invokes his anticipation as a five-year-old in Columbus as he sits on the front steps of the family home:

> [I was] waiting until I saw him coming down the road, with a slight roll to his gait . . . not big or particularly handsome, but with a strong bearlike chest, shoulders and arms. When I went to meet him, he would put down his battered metal suitcase and swing me up in his arms. My job would be to help him out of his overalls, caked with grease, oil and coal dust. Then he would scrub his blackened hands for a long time, until they became the cleanest, gentlest hands I ever saw. He'd read good books by good authors or ask me to wind up the gramophone and listen to selections from his favorite opera or symphony.[17]

Throughout his public career and in his private life, Barber was powerfully influenced by both his father's compassion for the poor and the self-discipline that fueled his work ethic. He tells his readers that his father did not talk about religion but that he truly lived it—that is, "if religion is the living community of mankind with his fellows and his Maker." Red recalls that "whenever tramps came to our door, they always got fed. 'You can't let a man go hungry,' my father would tell my mother, 'and you can't take a chance that he *isn't* hungry.'"[18]

Among all the virtues that Red admired in his father, however, it was William Barber's approach to his work that appears to have influenced his son most forcibly. In describing his father at work, all alone and in complete control of his locomotive, Barber emphasizes the man's expertise on the job and his delight in mastering the toughest of skills by his capacity for complete concentration:

> With a deft, sure hand on the throttle, he could get the longest train under way, not with a thunderous jerk up and down the line, but with a silken smooth *click-click-click* of couplings that was his trademark. He could run any kind of train but, he explained to me, "Walter, there is nothing like the big freighters." Passenger trains, with their swift "through" times were too easy for Dad. He preferred the rumbling power of a huge string of boxcars—the challenge of pitting his will against a mile-long monster of steel. Railroading in those days was largely on single track roadbeds. This required exact schedules to avoid head on collisions. Dad was completely reliable, and so was his watch. Generous as he was, he wouldn't let anyone else touch his watch.[19]

Readers of this description who are familiar with Red's performance in the broadcast booth might see William Barber's son at work with his three-minute egg timer reminding him to announce the score, his "silken smooth" voice, and the passion for perfection in his craft, all of which he shared with his father. Red also remembers his father counseling him when he was an adolescent that he should not be afraid to leave a job that no longer satisfied or challenged him. "Don't ever let a man make you afraid for your job," his father advised. "Don't ever let him tell you the job you have is the only one you *can* have."[20] Barber may have recalled his father's words during his deliberations and decisions to "move on" throughout his professional career, especially when he could imagine bigger and better options for his talents. Shortly before he died, William Barber gave that watch, which "he wouldn't let anyone else touch," to his son, a symbol of one man's satisfaction and commitment to excellence in his work.

When William Barber arrived in Columbus in 1905, he found rooming in a boarding house inhabited by an accomplished young woman, Selena Martin, and her three younger siblings, two sisters and a brother. Their parents had died, and Selena was teaching school at Franklin Academy. She and William fell in love and were married in 1906 at the boarding house. A notice of the wedding in the local paper informed readers that the bride was "unusually intelligent, but with a pretty face and a sweet disposition."[21] William Barber married a woman who was more highly educated than himself and who was also uncommonly literate and intellectually curious. Twenty-five years later his son, Walter Lanier "Red" Barber, would do the same.

Selena Martin descended from wordsmiths who made their living in printing, writing, and publishing. Selena's grandfather, J. A. Martin, a job printer, moved from Ohio to Columbus with his brother and two sons, one of whom, Charles C. Martin, was Selena's father. The elder Martin founded and printed one of the oldest newspapers in the state, the *Columbus Index*, and in time, Martin's sons continued the publication as a weekly and semiweekly known as the *Columbus Dispatch*.[22] According to one client, S. Newton, who hired Charles C. Martin to print his book, *Backwoods Poems*, Mr. Martin had "a true artist's eye for beauty in the typographic art."[23] Selena was born in 1879, the same year as Red's father. Her mother died after the birth of her four children, and her father reared them "with the help of a black woman who was a strict and upright nurse."[24] According to Barber, his generous father welcomed his new wife's younger siblings into their home, even helping Selena's brother John with the price of a ticket to Tampa, where he got a job selling advertisements for the *Tampa Tribune*.[25] William and Selena had three children within the first ten years of their marriage: Red in 1908, (Effie) Virginia in 1910, and William (Billy) on Christmas Day, 1914. According to town records, they moved one time from their initial address, as the family grew, before they moved to Florida in 1918.[26]

In his public speeches, newspaper columns, and books, Red Barber credited his mother with cultivating his love of language. She stopped teaching school while raising her toddlers in Columbus, but she continued to exercise her pedagogic prowess with her children, particularly by reading to them. Barber recalls her passion for ancient mythology: "I knew all the Greek and Roman gods and goddesses before I knew many living people."[27] He tells us that Selena had a lovely speaking voice and read beautifully, evoking vivid images in his mind's eye that made Zeus and Apollo seem more alive than his neighbors. Barber believed his mother helped her children absorb the power of language by letting them hear the structures, cadences, and rhythms of wonderful storytellers. He claimed that her nurturing of his speaking skills contributed significantly to his success as a broadcaster: "When your job is to ad lib for hours upon hours, day after day, you must have an ear for language."[28]

"I Was Lying Right in There with the Puppies"

Although Red insisted in a 1974 interview that he did not have a strong recollection of the first ten years of his life in Columbus, his books, newspaper columns, public speeches, and interviews contain some vivid anecdotes and images from his Mississippi childhood, primarily associated with his nuclear family.[29] His recollections reveal that the family could afford no luxuries, a reality that he ascribed to his father's loss of seniority when he was "promoted" to engineer and to the federal control of railroads during the World War I. The federal government prioritized which tracks could be used to satisfy wartime demands; federal control meant that in some parts of the country railroad jobs could be frozen or laborers, lacking strong union support, could be furloughed for weeks. Barber says as a child he was conscious of the "hardness of the times" and knew that his family could not afford to live in those huge white mansions just a short walk from his home: "We had enough to eat, but never any extra clothes. Water pipes froze during cold spells and the family would live in the kitchen in front of the big wood range." Most of the presents he received for Christmas during those years, he says, came in a big box from his Aunt Virginia, William Barber's sister in North Carolina. It was wonderful "to get an orange and tangerine in your Christmas stocking."[30]

We know that during Red's time in Columbus there were public venues and gala events that could entertain a young child. The year he was born the world-renowned Ringling Brothers Circus came to Columbus. The town's first motion picture theater opened the year he was born; it consisted primarily of a curtain and a few cane chairs.[31] But Red Barber left no record of attending public performances, except for an announcement of his baptism at the Main Street Presbyterian Church on August 26, 1911. In her memoirs Red's sister Effie Virginia mentions less structured activities that she and Red enjoyed in Columbus and that required no admission fee: "In the summer we used to go over to the college grounds to play. One dormitory had inside fire escapes with a metal lined tube which went from the top floor to the ground in circles. We used to take off our shoes and socks and walk up the tube as far as we could, and then sit down and slide all the way to the ground."[32]

Barber seemed to be a homebody as a child. "In Columbus," he told one interviewer who pressed him about his activities at that time, "there were always things to do at home. My mother read to us a lot; there was no radio yet, but my father had an old Edison phonograph with a few records."[33] A spectacular wonder, for a child in small-town Mississippi, was available to him right in his own front yard; when World War I broke out, a military flying field was built in the nearby town of West Point: "At the sound of the first airplanes in that part of the world, I would run out of the house into the yard, and stare unblinkingly at those small, two-winged aircraft."[34]

Red also recalls one particularly memorable winter morning in Columbus. In a December 21, 1976, column he vividly evokes the Christmas of 1914, when he was nearly seven and his sister was five. The Christmas tree was glittering with *real* candles, and the two children were reaching for their presents without even asking where their mother was. "Children are like that," the sixty-eight-year-old Barber reminds his readers, "selfish and intent on themselves." Perhaps impatient with the children's single-mindedness, their father asked them if they'd like to see *his* Christmas present. "He led us to the front bedroom where mother was awake in bed. He turned back her coverings a little, and here was our brand-new brother." According to Effie Virginia, within a year or two Red would be "bundling up their brother and pulling him all over Columbus in a little red wagon."[35]

It was William Barber's "hobby," which he pursued to raise extra money to "make ends meet," that seemed to trigger some of his son's most powerful memories. Red's father raised pit bulls to sell to dog fight managers at a time when dog fights were a source of entertainment and income for gamblers throughout the country. According to Barber, his father "had thirty or forty pit bulls around the house at a time, counting puppies, and maybe three or four grown ones, on a seasonal basis. And these dogs carried us through those years in Mississippi. . . . Dad had a marvelous touch with them; he could handle them with his voice and would not let them run loose around each other."[36]

Red fondly recalls a sweet and fertile dog whom they named "Yellow Fever" because she had a yellow spot on one eye. She produced litter after litter for his father and would lie around most days in the doghouse with her puppies. Red's parents told him that on one cold winter day, shortly after he had learned to walk, his mother "could not find me after looking all over the house. My father went looking all around the neighborhood . . . and finally said, "Go look in Yellow Fever's doghouse." There she was with a litter of new pups and there I was, lying right with the puppies, all of us warm and snug and asleep."[37] Barber's niece, E. V. E. Joy, said her mother (Red's sister Effie Virginia) told her that each Barber child was given his or her own pit bull to care for and to provide protection.[38]

Barber called the final pit bull story of his Columbus years "The Family Tragedy." His father had one prolific and valuable stud whom he dearly loved. "Buck" had never lost a fight, but he succumbed to pneumonia one winter. The Barbers stayed up night after night with him until he finally died. "My father loved Buck," Barber tells us, "but that dog also was a very important economic mainstay that was just swept away on a dark night, with things getting harder and harder in Columbus."[39]

Red's only Mississippi story that is set outside his home involves a curious and frightening walk on a bridge that spanned the Tombigbee River. He tells his interviewer that he remembers some boys swimming in the river during the summer but notes that doing so was dangerous: "You would always hear about people getting drowned because it had whirlpools and cross currents; when that river was in flood stage it was a frightening thing to see." Still he walked out on the bridge anyway, although he could not have been over ten years old, and looking down, he was stunned by how "frighteningly impressive" it was to see the Tombigbee in flood, swirling with dizzying whirlpools: "You suddenly realize that nothing could live within them."[40]

Red Barber's memories of Columbus suggest a compelling contrast between the child's sense of comfort and certainty within the warm family circle and the dangerous forces outside and beyond that intimate realm. Outside of home, friendly dogs and well-mannered townspeople could turn vicious and swimming holes could transform into deadly crosscurrents beyond human control. Perhaps many young children perceive their worlds similarly, but Barber projects on his younger self an impressively poetic formulation of this unsettling contrast. In the soil of Columbus, it seems, the "Lanier" component of Barber's personality took root. His mother's voice reading to him; her patient critique and approval of his way with words; his father's storytelling, love of fine music, and empathy for others—all associated with the love the boy felt for each parent—engendered a creative spirit.

But for William Barber it was time to move on. Increasingly sporadic income from the Southern Railroad line and the loss of his stud pit bull motivated him to "take a test over in Florida to qualify for a job on the Atlantic Coast Line," where wartime demands were providing more job opportunities. He also remembered how much he had enjoyed a balmy winter in Florida during his railroad "boomer" years. His initiative, however, triggered a difficult year-long transition for his young family. In 1917, having passed the test, he packed up the house in Columbus and rented another house in Fort Myers, Florida, where he was scheduled to work. But while moving his family south to their new home, he learned that a recent government regulation prohibited railroad workers from changing jobs throughout the duration of the war. So he settled his family in Fort Myers and returned to Columbus and the Southern Railroad job he was locked into for at least another year. Red tells us how hard it was to be in Fort Myers when his father was stuck in Mississippi, not knowing when he would return. In his memoir, he tells us that the Christmas of 1917 was an especially dreary ordeal for William's wife and their three children. They had no money, their father had gotten the flu back in Columbus, and they could not be with him for the holiday: "Our first look at Florida in the winter season was not the same one that Thomas Edison and Harvey Firestone and the other rich people, who owned estates among the tall royal palms along the river at Fort Myers, had. We weren't tourists."[41]

Fortunately, William Barber followed his own expert advice and "did not let any man tell him that the job he had was the only one he could have." Not long after he recovered from the flu in Columbus, he was at work on a Southern Rail train when he discovered that one passenger was William Gibbs McAdoo, President Wilson's treasury secretary and wartime director general of railroads. By this point Red's father had been submitting waiver applications and other documents to the federal government to get himself released from his job with Southern Railroad, but with no success. As his son later remarked, "The hand of officialdom . . . lies very heavy on a person who has no influence." But William Barber, in desperation, seized the opportunity, and while the train was temporarily held up on a side track, he asked if he could speak to Mr. McAdoo. According to Red, his father explained his situation and then asked McAdoo "to get in touch with somebody" to convey the fact that William Barber was not needed in Mississippi; he had secured a job and had a family waiting for him in Florida. Red says he does not know whom McAdoo contacted, but "in no time at all" his father joined them in Fort Myers, where he continued his rail career, initially as a switch engineer. William Barber never left Florida again until after he retired. His new assignment required the family to move a few times for short stints in Sanford, in central Florida and in Tampa.[42] But after William gained several months of seniority, the family finally settled down permanently in Sanford, the setting for the next chapter of Red Barber's education in the Old South.

2

Celery Capital of the World

F or the citizens of Sanford, Florida, life during the first three decades of the twentieth century was a bruising tumble from boom to bust. By 1930 the town had suffered several devastating bank failures, triggered by a combination of corrupt management and poor planning. The Sanford banking crisis stripped Red Barber of all his savings—specifically the money that was to pay for his second year of college. Any hope of a rapid rebound from Sanford's financial bust was quashed by the oncoming ravages of the nation's Great Depression. But when the Barbers moved there in 1918, Sanford was thriving.

"Sanford—Where Things Were Set in Motion"

In his 1970 book, *Sanford as I Knew It,* Peter Schaal vividly chronicles Sanford's dramatic economic swings during the decade that Red lived there. Drawing primarily upon articles published in the *Sanford Herald* during the years of his survey, Schaal documents changes in the town's fortunes that profoundly affected Barber's own life choices.[1] When the Barber family moved to Sanford, the town was at the peak of commercial development, fueled by the real estate boom Florida had been enjoying since the turn of the century. Sanford was settled on the shore of Lake Monroe, one of the state's largest lakes and the source of navigation on the St. John's River. In 1870 Henry Shelton Sanford, former U.S. minister to Belgium, bought 12,500 acres to build what he viewed as "the Gate City of South Florida," which was incorporated as the city of Sanford in 1870. He imported laborers from Sweden to help plant and grow 140 different varieties of citrus, carved out a small portion of the land for African American communities, and began attracting investors to his city.

By 1880 construction had begun on the South Florida Railroad, which would make Sanford both a rail and steamboat terminus, attracting new residents as well as a flood of tourists. Celery proved the most prolific plant and soon made Sanford the "Celery Capital of the World and one of the premier agricultural regions of the south."[2] The vegetable also inspired Red Barber's high school baseball team to call itself "the Celery Feds" because profits from the pale green stem put food on the table. During Barber's decade in Sanford, a building boom brought new multistory structures to the city's downtown and a popular harbor and a park for its lakefront. In 1918 the city boasted a new post office—the first erected in the country after the wartime freeze was lifted on federal building-construction projects. The *Sanford Herald* chronicles the construction, during the following three years, of a new hospital, three new hotels, and a new six-story building to house the First National Bank of Sanford. The boom persisted with the opening of the Sanford Country Club, the Sanford Yacht Club, several car dealerships, and the implementation of comprehensive downtown gas street lighting. In 1923 the city boasted a new ballpark that would soon attract Major League exhibition games during spring training. The same year the first Woolworth and Piggly Wiggly opened their doors.

By 1925 boom times helped to subsidize wide-ranging cultural, entertainment, and athletic activities, including theater, moving pictures, minstrel shows, formal dances, boating competitions, a symphony and opera hall, golfing, band shell concerts by the lake, automobile shows, and baseball games.[3] Given the town's rapid development during Red Barber's high school years, it is not surprising that the president of his high school graduating class, Cloyde Russell, wrote—for his "Farewell" essay in the 1926 Sanford Senior High School yearbook, *Salmagundi*—an inspirational plea to his peers to remember always their class motto: Carpe diem. Russell, a good friend of Red's who had played with him on the school's football team, urges his classmates to be "prepared to seize the opportunity ever before us—never let one pass by unheeded. May our enthusiasm for bigger and better things help us onward to our goal."[4]

African American sections of town were also bustling with Black-owned shops, thriving restaurants, and entertainment venues.[5] But even though prospects for a developing Black middle-class population, albeit a segregated one, seemed to emerge, the Klan was still active and completely "normalized" in all aspects of life during the years that Red Barber lived in Sanford. He would have absorbed and abided by the prevailing assumptions about racial boundaries and would have been able to read daily newspaper accounts of Klan activities, including acts of violence against Blacks charged with crimes but robbed of access to adequate legal representation or a fair trial. As he later tells us, the boy who witnessed the tar and featherings of Black men in 1920s Sanford could never forget the first law of race relations: "The line that was always there was indelible."[6]

On May 24, 1918, for instance, the *Herald* reported that Sanford's mayor, Forrest Lake, had to talk a mob out of "lynching a negro who reportedly tried to accost one white citizen's daughter." A few days later it reported that a young man and woman motoring on a road outside of Sanford were "accosted by a negro." A fight allegedly ensued, the woman was bruised, and the assailant ran off. The next day a Black man seen taking a train to Orlando who "fit the description" provided by the victims was brought back to Sanford, but the couple was certain that he was not the man who had attacked them. A raging mob overlooked this compelling evidence of his innocence and attempted to hang him. Fortunately for this man, police interrupted the lynching. News then came from Orlando that another Black man, also "fitting the description" of the assailant, was approached by armed police, who assumed he was the Sanford escapee who had allegedly fled to Orlando. When he pulled out a knife to defend himself, a marshal shot him to death. No evidence was reported connecting either of the Black men to the alleged incident.

What strikes the twenty-first-century reader of many of these newspaper accounts is the matter-of-fact, nonjudgmental manner in which Klan activity was reported, as if the Klan were just one more of the town's many social clubs, business organizations, or church groups:

> On March 17, the editor of this newspaper introduced the principal hooded Klan speaker at a big rally at First and Park.

> Reverend E. D. Brownlee, at the First Presbyterian Church, preached to an overflow crowd of the Klan on April 2; many of them attended the service hooded.[7]

In 1926, the year Red Barber graduated from high school, the *Herald* columns foreshadowed Sanford's bust. Chamber of Commerce members and bank managers began objecting to ambitious City Commission proposals because they were worried about the increasing number of bank failures in other towns in the region. By August 1927 Sanford's Seminole Bank had closed, and finally, in July 1929, Sanford's First National Bank—Red's bank, where all his hard-earned paychecks were saved—also had failed. The town's longtime mayor and First National Bank's owner, Forrest Lake, was indicted for his misappropriation of funds, one of the prime causes of the bank's demise. The City Commission began the long process of "tightening its belt," closing the public golf course and the Sanford library, and suspending river boat services.[8]

"Like Looking Back over the Score Sheets"

The Barber family, fortunately, had moved into Sanford's *boom* years and with more grounds for hope than they had taken with them upon leaving Columbus. William Barber began his rail job with seniority pay, working for the Atlantic Coast Line, and with all three children enrolled in school, Selena Barber was able to renew her career as teacher at Sanford's Southside Primary School, where she soon would be promoted to principal. The family lived in a two-story home close to the school where she taught. Barber tells us in his 1968 memoir that, looking back on his life, he realized, "Sanford is where I grew up, where the things were set in motion that really shaped my life. . . . It's like looking back over the score sheets of ball games you have seen and recalling who did what in the first inning . . . and the effect of those things on what actually happened in the fifth."[9]

Barber's memories of the town's troubled racial divisions, as well as its unstable economic base, left a mark on his attitude toward the place where his life was "set in motion." His feelings about Sanford altered as the transitions in his professional journey forced him to recognize that resources and rights enjoyed by the all-white community where he had flourished were inaccessible to nearly half of the town's population. The world of his past and the world of his present collided in March 1946, when Jackie Robinson, the first Black man to play in Major League Baseball, came to his first Florida spring training. He was to train with the Brooklyn Dodgers' Triple A team, the Montreal Royals.

Brooklyn Dodgers general manager Branch Rickey had housed Robinson, for the short term, in Sanford, about forty miles south of Daytona Beach, where the Royals' spring training workouts were conducted. Another Minor League camp was operating in Sanford that spring, and Rickey believed that Robinson's debut would be easier if it took place away from Daytona Beach and the national press lining up to interview him. Rickey wanted to minimize the real threat of protests and potential violence. But on the second day of Robinson's training in Sanford, a town delegation arrived to announce that per local ordinance, Blacks and whites were not allowed to play together on the same field and requested that Robinson leave the town for good.[10] Barber later wrote that the scout who was overseeing the camp in Sanford throughout spring training informed him that "Mr. Rickey got the word on Robinson's second day to 'get these [n—rs] out of town by midnight or *we will.*'"[11] Alarmed, Rickey had Robinson transported to Daytona Beach that same night, and he never returned to training in Sanford.

Barber himself probably did not return to Sanford after July 1930, when he stopped there on his return trip to school at the University of Florida in Gainesville, after a stay in Baltimore.[12] By this time his parents and siblings had moved to Tampa, but much later in his life, after he had returned to Florida, he declined invitations to take part in events in Sanford. In 1982 he turned down an invitation from Sanford's chamber of commerce to celebrate his selection as one of the first group of inductees into the Seminole County Sports Hall of Fame.[13] Seven years later he declined a second invitation from Sanford to be guest of honor at a later Seminole County Hall of Fame induction.[14] During his years in Tallahassee, he frequently traveled to Miami and Gainesville for speeches, awards, and baseball anniversary celebrations and occasionally to New York, Cincinnati, and Los Angeles. He also accepted a 1978 invitation to deliver a sermon in his birthplace, Columbus, Mississippi. But he likely never appeared in his hometown, Sanford.

There may have been scheduling conflicts that prevented Barber's accepting invitations to return to Sanford. But occasionally in interviews during his later years, he speaks disparagingly of the town. In a protracted 1987 interview Barber was asked to describe his relationship with Jackie Robinson. In his response, he directly connected the hostility he felt toward Sanford with the treatment that Robinson suffered there: "I grew up in Sanford and they ordered the Brooklyn Dodgers to get the Robinsons out of town in twenty-four hours. And that was something serious. That was as red necked a town as you'll ever find."[15] In 1991, the year before he died, Barber was still angered enough to initiate a contentious newspaper debate with Julian Stenstrom, columnist for the *Sanford Herald*, in which he disputed with compelling evidence Stenstrom's claim that Jackie Robinson first broke the color line in Major League Baseball in Sanford in 1946, during February spring training games played there. Barber was intent upon disproving the claim and mounted easily accessible evidence that Jackie Robinson did not arrive in Sanford that spring until early March and that, because of a real threat to his safety, was hurriedly swept away from the town after his second day at the camp.[16]

After years of acclimating to big city life in the north, Barber's complex feelings for the town he still fondly recognized as having shaped his life perhaps are understandable and not uncommon for people who have moved far away from the places they once called "home." There remains a tension between the engrained part of oneself that was forged and grew comfortable there and the person one has become since leaving. But, just the same, Red Barber still holds a place in the hearts of some Sanford citizens. In 1999 the Sanford City Commission changed the name of the former Southside Park to "Walter Lanier Red Barber Park." The park is near the still standing home where the Barber family lived in Sanford; Red likely tossed a few balls there as a youngster.[17]

"Best Hair, Boy"

During his teenage years in Sanford, Red Barber grew to be a popular, self-confident young man. The seeds of "Walter" are planted; the "Lanier" side of his personality continues to sprout, while the budding performer "Red" first takes root. In his freshman high school yearbook group photo, Red stands in the last row, slightly separated from the rest of the class, and is one of only three boys not wearing a white shirt and tie; instead he sports a dark shirt with sleeves rolled up, looking a little angry. He appears to have become more of a "joiner" in his junior year class photo: he stands in the *front* row, surrounded by girls, holding up a large junior class poster and looking committed, like a young man with a purpose in life.

In the athletics section of Red's sophomore yearbook, a shot of the "Celery Feds" baseball team features Red as the proverbial "wise guy" and entertainer of the group, standing in a relaxed and cocky stance, his face lit with a broad and mischievous smile, while the rest of the team looks straight at the viewers, staunch and somber. In this book's football section, we see him in a classic posed "live action" stance: he stretches his right arm toward the camera with the palm of his hand pushing viewers away, and he caresses the football tightly in the bend of his left arm as he stares forward malignly with a macho sneer. By senior year, now captain of the baseball team, he stands as one among equals with the rest of the Celery Feds, neither threatening nor jovial, just committed. In this shot, we see only one small cluster of his massive curls—which tumble freely over his forehead in most of his yearbook photos—valiantly escaping from under his ball cap.

We get the most complete record of Red's high school achievements in his senior yearbook, where individual senior class photos are printed alphabetically, with student profiles summarized in standard dry phrases underneath, each followed by the exact high school years the student engaged in a particular activity. Red's profile appears as follows:

> Athletic Association 1–4; Treasurer Athletic Association 4; Football 2–4; Basketball Manager 4; Baseball 1–4; Captain Baseball 4; Senior Play 4; Second VP Hi-Y; Class Treasurer 2.[18]

For his senior yearbook individual photo, Red tested a new hair solution, with the massive curls still crowning the top of his head but the sides shaved. Listed on a separate page of the yearbook are the winners in the 1926 Sanford High School Track Meet, which Barber's senior class won by a large margin. Red was first in the 440-yard dash, first in the running broad jump, and second in the 100-yard dash. Most telling are the awards he won in a senior class referendum: Red Barber was voted "Best Hair, Boy."[19] He wrote later in his life that as soon as he started playing with other children and going to school, he was "called 'Red,' and that stuck. I had real red hair and it was very curly and there was a lot of it."[20] Barber also was voted "Most Studious, Boy." He tested his skills as a team manager, organizational treasurer, and even fledgling actor, playing the role of Skeet Kelly, the Clerk, in the senior class play, *And Along Came Ted*.[21] Looking back on his high school record forty-two years later, Red provides a detailed, dispassionate self-assessment supported by the facts: "I did pretty-well in high school. . . . I graduated with the highest average in the senior class and I won a cup for that. I was given another cup for the highest grade in American History. I won a twenty-dollar gold piece for the highest average of any boy in the school. I had good grades. I did good work."[22] Sanford High's 1924 yearbook noted that Red's sophomore class brought Leesburg High School's "black and white Minstrels to Sanford one evening. They were a grand success." That performance, if he attended it, may have planted a seed that grew into Red Barber's passion for a career as a minstrel show entertainer.[23]

Other news of Barber's accomplishments is sporadically reported in the columns of the *Sanford Herald*, most notably his contributions to his high school football team. An article summarizing his junior year role on the team observes the following: "Barber stepped into the front ranks by his performance this season. He has been working hard for two years on the gridiron and this year he was given his chance. He proved himself worthy for the occasion, and now is rated as one of the school's stellar halfbacks."

Barber was "sorely missed" for part of the 1925 season, according to the *Herald*, because of a broken collarbone; the team was losing a major asset without him since he was "one of the main cogs in the machine." In his first game back, Red began making up for lost time: "Sanford's flashing halfback narrowly missed a touchdown in the second quarter when he tripped on the 13-yard line after slipping through the defense and running an uninterrupted thirty-five yards. . . . His punts were fairly good and late in the fourth he knocked down Plant City's pass by a marvelous leap in the air—a pass just about to enter the arms of a waiting opponent who had open ground for a touchdown." In a game later in the season, even though neither team could score, Red's outstanding punting—several long spiral kicks for forty-five yards—accounted for much of the ground gained by his team. Finally, near the end of the season "a badly crippled and disabled Sanford team" succumbs to Kissimmee, but Red's play is universally hailed, as *Herald* sportswriter Harlan Kelley makes a historic comparison: "Barber alone gained enough yards to win an ordinary football game. He fairly emulated another Red, the famous Grange, yesterday. He carried the ball 30 times and gained 212 yards. . . . Whenever he was able to get past the line of scrimmage, he was good for a gain of from 10 to 30 yards. He borrowed some of Grange's 'stuff' and returned a kickoff 73 yards before he was downed. He also scored Sanford's only touchdown."[24]

Sanford's football team did not have a winning season during Red's years on the team; it was 3–3 with one tie his junior year and 2–5 with two ties his senior year. In Barber's later lay sermons, newspaper columns, and graduation speeches, he often mentions the spirited determination required to persevere when the odds are against us. He reminds us it is easy to win when all the players on a team are exceptional; the genuine victory is playing one's hardest against a stronger opponent. His high school football experiences may well have been the inspiration for some of these reflections.

"None of Us Could Afford a Tennis Racquet"

In several interviews and newspaper columns that he penned later in his life, Barber described the pleasures of creating his own play in Sanford, either with friends or by himself. In a 1980 column criticizing overdevelopment, both in America's small towns and in its cities, he argues that children were being deprived of places where they could play freely, "create their own entertainment . . . and discover on their own what they like to do." He recalls how unpaved streets and open spaces in Sanford enabled him to spend years kicking a ball in front of his house or playing catch with his friends.[25] He notes that he was small—5 feet 8 inches and 165 pounds in high school—but that he was the fastest runner in his crowd. His father got him an official Major League Baseball that he and his friends always used. He kept it in a "special box with threads and beeswax for repair."[26] When the heat was unbearable, Red would get under a tree and read; *Tom Swift* tales and Zane Grey's books on sports were his favorites. He and his friends would sometimes spend summer days at a Boy Scout camp five miles away on a large lake, "making fires without matches, cooking meals and sleeping under the stars. . . . None of us could afford a tennis racquet and the country club was too expensive." His parents encouraged his love of scouting, but could pay for only "one shirt when it came to a uniform."[27]

One of Barber's favorite summer activities in Sanford was sitting in the shade with other boys in the neighborhood, quizzing each other on baseball facts. All spring and summer Red and his friends would study the official baseball guides—*Spalding* for the National League and *Reach* for the American League—so that they could effectively stump one another. Barber claims: "I had never seen a big-league game, but I knew what every player hit, how he fields and the number of games a pitcher had won."[28] He marvels: "I didn't know—no way I could have suspected—that this was training for the work I have been doing for fifty years."[29]

As he approached his later teens, Red became more involved in the social and cultural life of Sanford, beyond the boundaries of home and school. In a 1975 column he recalls his excitement as a sixteen-year-old standing with his high school buddies and other eager baseball fans outside the *Herald* building, listening as a man bellowed through a cardboard megaphone. The voice delivered a rough play-by-play account of a 1924 World Series game between the Giants and the Senators, telegraphed to the newspaper building. He and his friends rooted for the Senators because they had a twenty-eight-year-old manager, Bucky Harris, whose success persuaded them that they too could make a mark on the world even as young men.[30] But for Red, two of the most compelling developments in Sanford during his ten years there, and most significant for his future career, were the completion of a new ballpark and the arrival of radio.

On September 11, 1925, Joe Tinker, of the famous double play trio long celebrated as "Tinker to Evers to Chance," was in Sanford to deliver a speech for the town's dedication of a new $35,000 baseball park that could seat a thousand in its grandstand.[31] For Red this meant he would have the chance to see players whose statistics he had memorized now that teams would come to Sanford for spring training exhibition games. He recalls the miracle that occurred in his high school when the now World Champion Washington Senators were in town for an exhibition game against the Milwaukee Brewers of the American Association. The Senators' famous pitcher—"Big Train" Walter Johnson—would be in the ballpark, as well as Bucky Harris. But the game fell early on a school day, and he and his friends would not have the chance to watch it. Incredibly, at noon the entire student body was marched into the school auditorium, where Professor G. E. McKay, the school principal, made a brief but momentous announcement: "As you know, I believe in education. This afternoon, the World Champion Washington Senators will play Milwaukee and Walter Johnson will be at the park. So will Buck Harris. I think it will be more educational for you to see this game and these men than it will be to stay here in classes. School is dismissed."[32]

In a 1975 column Barber's description of a 1927 Sanford exhibition game poignantly captures the thrilling experience of recognizing, for the first time, what Branch Rickey would later describe to him as "the pleasing skills of the professional."[33] The phrase denotes a player performing perfectly, with confidence and grace, the most difficult skills. In this case the player was Lance Richbourg. According to Red, "This man I saw that one afternoon took my eye every time a fly ball was hit to his area. He was slender, and he moved with a fluid, certain grace. It was a joy to watch him guess where a ball would come down, glide to the spot and with sure hands catch the ball." When Red played baseball in high school or on the sandlot, he always had trouble with high flies: "I used to stand out there and hope it didn't hit me." But when he saw this man start moving toward the ball as soon as it left the bat and edge "toward it easily, surely, hungrily—gather it to him as lightly as I would rub my hands together, I was struck. He showed me something."[34]

"Squealing and Spitting"

Like the new ballpark, the arrival of radio in Sanford was transformative for the young Red Barber. Early in his book *The Broadcasters*, Red vividly narrates his first encounter with radio in the home of his classmate Merrill Roberts, who, in 1921, owned one of the three radio sets in Sanford, one that he had built himself. Merrill was a studious, quiet boy who never came outdoors when Red and his other friends were kicking balls or playing hounds and hares; instead, he was inside his house building radio sets. He was an only child whose parents let him have a separate room just for working on radios. Merrill organized everything in that room: "Parts of radio sets, a table speaker, a row of batteries, headphones, all kinds of dials to be turned and tuned. The equipment was always squealing and spitting."[35]

Barber was sixteen when Merrill invited him over to listen to his radio, the medium that would make Red famous. Soon after he arrived, Red says, "I understood why [Merrill] hadn't been out in the street playing with us." It was the first time he'd ever stayed up all night, and during that night he drank in "sounds of a new world: voices speaking from Pittsburgh and New York, a banjo being plucked in Chicago and a piano keyboard being played in Kansas." Soon his father bought an Atwater Kent table radio, and though it played only static during the day, at night it got better and better the longer he stayed awake: "Dad and I used to sit up together, listening, into the night."

Fifty years later Barber would describe the effects of hearing radio for the first time that night with Merrill, comparing the experience to being knighted by King Arthur's sword. As a child Red had always admired King Arthur because "[he] tried so hard to fight for law, for reasonableness, and had concern for his fellow men." He says when first listening to the magic of radio, he now understood how "each young man felt when King Arthur took Excalibur, touched his shoulder, and made him a knight. The accolade of knighthood would send the young man out into the world to do great deeds. Deeper than I was aware, that was how I felt after hearing radio that first night in Merrill Roberts' house . . . the acolyte." Inspired by a childhood hero, Barber later believed, he sensed that night that radio was a brave and honorable force commissioning him to go out and do good in the world. This youthful idealism would deepen into conviction as his understanding of the role of mass media evolved.

"I Never Wanted to Be Anything Else but an End-Man in a Minstrel Show"

For two years after Barber graduated from high, he doggedly practiced the skills needed to become a professional minstrel show performer. Minstrel shows featuring white actors in blackface were performed in the United States from the 1840s until the 1950s. By the early part of the twentieth century, minstrel show companies had spread throughout the north and south and frequently performed in Sanford on indoor stages.[36] In his 1968 memoir, Barber tells us that in high school he "never wanted to be anything else but an end man in a minstrel show, which was an accepted art form in those days." He used to "follow the performers around" when shows came to town, attending every performance and learning all the lines until he could "sing anybody's songs and tell anybody's jokes." He took part in amateur shows in blackface and particularly enjoyed attempting "the little eccentric dances. . . . It became a passion with me." His interest in performing in minstrel shows was reinforced by his friendship with George Brockhorn, the organist at Sanford's Milane Theater. Brockhorn helped him design and rehearse his own song and dance routines.[37]

It is likely that Barber's keen interest in minstrel entertainment initially was triggered by his participation in the town's chapter of DeMolay, a nationwide fraternity for young boys aged twelve through twenty. Allied with the Masons and founded in Missouri in 1919, DeMolay touted its dedication to cultivating "community leaders and decent men." Red was a member of Sanford's Seminole chapter, which elected him master councilor in 1926. Several clippings from the *Sanford Herald* document that Barber also was a valued member of the local DeMolay chapter's minstrel troupe, which performed at local venues. According to one columnist, "DeMolay Minstrels presented a good show before a full house at Milane Theater, filled with doting admirers and performed to a degree of success rarely attained by amateurs. Humorous effects were supplied in abundance by the end men, with Red Barber taking the lead." A promotion for a subsequent DeMolay minstrel performance provides today's readers with a more unsettling sense of what passed for "an accepted art form in those days." The show featured a comedy sketch in which the humor focused upon "two scared [n—rs] to be initiated into the Lion Tamer's club. . . . The two to take part in this sketch are Red Barber and Myron Reitte."[38]

Subsequent accounts document that Barber also performed his minstrel routine outside his DeMolay chapter troupe. A December 9, 1926, column in the *Herald* describes Red in a minstrel performance at Sanford's American Legion, where "he was cast as an end man . . . and was accorded a huge round of applause." Red also crafted his own one-man act to perform in a cabaret show for Sanford's St. Agnes Guild. According to a column in the *Orlando Evening Star*, the Guild performance would feature "a very clever number . . . a blackface song and dance by 'Red' Barber, who is very talented."[39] Finally, Red performed his solo act, entitled "A Few Minutes with Red Barber," at the Hotel Forrest Lake and reprised the skit for a fashion show at the Milane Theater. An enthusiastic reviewer of these one-man shows suggested that his talents had become widely appreciated in the town; "[Red] needs no introduction to Sanford audiences. His blackface stunts and dances have long since won an enviable place here, and the fact that he appears . . . assures the public that the affair will be a success."

Barber came close to sealing his commitment to minstrelsy as a full-time profession when his musical mentor, Brockhorn, got him an audition with Hank White, who was stage manager for J. A. Coburn's Minstrel Show, one of the most popular companies on the regional minstrel circuit. He performed well at the audition and was told he had "a real chance to be black" if only he knew how to play a few good notes on a slide trombone. Undaunted, Barber assured White that this would be no problem, and he was promised a job with the Coburn company at the end of the summer of 1927 for eighteen dollars a week with all meals provided. He was told to come up to Cincinnati in September and get started with the company. Red practiced hard all summer long on the trombone until he could play "Sewanee River" and a few other pieces "pretty good" and was ready to go. His father got him a one-way railroad pass to Cincinnati, much to his mother's consternation, despite her willingness to "fix up my clothes, put buttons on my shirts and everything." However, a few days before his departure a special delivery letter arrived from Mr. White telling him not to come because the Coburn's Minstrels were no more: "The company had folded . . . and my career as an end man stopped before it began." Looking back at the age of sixty, Red claimed, "I would have been very unhappy [in a career as a minstrel show performer]: you were continually on the road, and I was never cut out to be a hobo."[40]

"Maybe I Ought to Go to College"

Red Barber also spent the two years after his high school graduation in back-breaking manual labor. He never considered going to college because he knew his father did not have enough money to pay for his tuition, room, and board. His father's job as a locomotive engineer provided a good income during the winter, when trains were running around the clock, transporting fruit and vegetables, and delivering hordes of tourists seeking Florida's mild weather. But the money he made in the winter dried up in the summer; the family lived on credit that could not be paid back until funds were available the following fall and winter. William Barber would not allow Red to work during school because he did not want his son exposed to "rough men." He told Red that if he would mow the yard and help his mother around the house, all his needs would be supplied.[41]

But shortly before graduating from high school, Red applied for a railroading job at the local train roundhouse, another possibility simmering in his subconscious mind during his Sanford years. Two years after his family first moved to Sanford, William decided that Red was old enough to ride with him while he was commanding a big freight locomotive. The young boy, who sat on the firefighter's seat in the cab of his father's locomotive, was "stunned at what life was like in the cab: heat, racket, rough ride, swirling storm cinders—I wondered how he could stand it every day, especially the side-to-side motion of the cab as the giant pistons on each side slam in opposite directions. . . . The shrieking blast of the whistle, like someone running a knife in your ears when you are up in the head-end." Red says he never told his father what a torture that first ride was: "I wanted to pay the price just to be with him and a part of his strenuous world." The experience seemed to have inspired a real longing to pursue work in that "strenuous world." He tells us that growing up, he wanted "to go to firing—the coal shoveling, back breaking work for four or five years, and then take exams for engineer."[42]

It is significant, though, that some of the most powerful recollections in Barber's later writings include images of his father's satisfaction primarily in coming home from those hard days at work: "He loved engineering but when not on a train he came home, because that is where he wanted to be. Maybe he would not get there until nearly daybreak, but he would wake himself up to see his children before they left for school. Then he'd go buy groceries, bring them home, get himself into the kitchen and start to make supper. He would not live in a house that didn't have a kitchen big enough for the stove, a big table and a rocking chair."[43]

It was his father who taught Red to cook when the family lived in Sanford.[44] He often said that these memories of his father's contentment with hearth and home haunted him during his busy broadcasting career; he was not happy about the travel required of a play-by-play sports announcer. "I do it only when I have to do it . . . I have always had a strong feeling about not being out of my home any more than was necessary to earn my living."[45] At this crucial juncture just after completing high school, two opposing scenarios of work were competing in his visions for his future—the life of a traveling performer forever on the road, touring from city to city and town to town, or a life where each day's work, even on a train, brings you back home where you belong.

However, both options fell through. Coburn's Minstrel Show died, and when he did not receive any response from his railroad application, his father informed Red he had warned the master mechanic at the roundhouse that he would quit his job if anyone there accepted his son's application. He did not want Red to suffer the hazards of that "strenuous world" of manual labor, especially in what he thought was a dying career: "I don't care what you do in this world as long as it is honest work and not railroading. The steam engine is going out—fewer crews and less work. Cars, trucks and airplanes will shrink railroads; don't go into a drying up industry."[46]

But instead of a minstrel job or a railroad job in the soon to bust Sanford of 1926, Red was forced, though he later would say "blessed," to live in that "strenuous world" for two years. Photographs of Barber in his late teens support Red's own testimony that he was physically well equipped for physical labor. He tells readers in his memoir that during his late teens, "I was strong, I was tough. I liked to give a blow and receive a blow."[47] Despite serious medical setbacks during his adult years, Red remained physically fit long after his days as halfback in high school—at least through middle age. According to Tom Villante, who began producing Dodgers broadcasts in 1950, when Barber was forty-two, he "kept in terrific shape" and had "strong working arms and always a flat stomach."[48]

After his minstrel and railroading dreams were dashed, Red found a job working with land surveyors on a civil engineering crew, digging dirt for new highways. But when the Sanford boom went bust, his generous five-dollar-a-day job "went down the drain." Then he worked at whatever odd day jobs he could find, from harvesting celery to driving trucks, putting in ten-hour days as his wages slid down to two dollars a day. His final Sanford job, in the hot summer of 1928, was "helping a fellow put on roofing with boiling pitch": "When your job is to stand over a boiling pitch pot and take two buckets of melting, steaming pitch up a ladder onto a hot roof under a broiling sun . . . and then spread it over a roof, you are more than just a little bit warm." Red recalls realizing at that point exactly what he would *not* do for the rest of his life, and then, "The thought came to me, out of nowhere, maybe I ought to go to college."[49]

Barber's two-year sabbatical from the academic life nurtured the intuitions about the world of work that been evolving since childhood, based upon his firsthand experience and from the example and advice of his father. He admired those who found work that absorbed them and in which they could test themselves. He wanted to do work that enabled a man to discover and exercise his talents. This was the source of his father's deep satisfaction in perfecting his navigation of massive, swaying freight trains. It was the source of Merrill Roberts's protracted concentration while teaching himself to build radios. He was also gleaning implications of the substantial gap between working as a laborer and being a manager. His father's income and psychic well-being depended upon where and when managers wanted their trains to be run; Merrill Roberts, focused intently on his radios, was his own boss.

Red rejected an offer to attend Rollins College, a small private liberal arts school in Winter Park, Florida, eighteen miles south of Sanford. The offer included a full-tuition athletic scholarship, as well as room and board and possible jobs in the summer. Barber was elated by what seemed a better deal than he could have imagined. But not long after the generous offer, Leonard McLucas, a friend from high school whom Red admired and who was now a senior at the University of Florida, changed Barber's mind. Leonard convinced him that Rollins was a stuffy, rich kids' school where he would not fit in. Barber was genuinely worried by the prospect of being in a realm where he might feel less than equal to his peers, and he ended up going to the big state university in Gainesville. The tuition was free for in-state students, and he was offered a vague promise of a job and perhaps a place on the football team.[50] Leaving Sanford for a new life, as far from home as he'd ever traveled without a parent, Red was bolstered by the imperative his father had imposed upon him four years earlier: "One afternoon when I was about sixteen, my father and I were out on the front yard. It was a beautiful day. 'Son,' he said, 'look just as far as your eyes will let you. It's a big world, and it's all yours. All you have to do is go out and get it.'" By moving his son deeply with this liberating challenge, Red later realized, his father gave him a resource that proved far more valuable than college tuition.[51]

3

Bumming Corner

R ed Barber's years at the University of Florida in Gainesville delivered him from poverty and joblessness to a career in which he would rise to considerable fame and fortune. Barber frequently referred to the phrase "the changes and chances of this mortal life" when, looking back, he could connect a fortunate outcome to a series of what seemed at the time arbitrary choices or actions, unrelated to the future blessing. He insists he did not take those actions or make those decisions with the conscious goal of achieving the favorable fortune to which they "led." It is as if someone else had designed a prewritten plan for him that he was unconsciously executing. For Barber the phrase "changes and chances of this mortal life" expressed his intuition that there was a "spirit"—sometimes he called it a personal God—who actively interceded in his life to fulfill what seems to have been an ordained destiny, a very blessed one. The phrase is an adaptation of a line from the *Book of Common Prayer*, which Barber loved to read and often quoted after he began attending Episcopal services in the early 1940s.

The assumption of a providence shaping his destiny also influenced the way Barber later told the story of his life as the humble small-town boy who grew up to be one of the most successful radio announcers in the country. He focused on those seemingly random events that enabled him to draw a direct line from their effects to a fortunate conclusion. After absorbing many of Barber's stories about his life, structured according to his "changes and chances" line of causation, a reader, while recognizing a genuine voice of faith, also gleans the role that the strategy plays in the view Red wanted to sustain of himself. Averse to claiming that his life had been uniquely blessed due to his own exceptional merits, he attributed his good fortune to a force that shaped his destiny—the potter who molded the clay that he was.

At the same time, Barber supplies abundant evidence that enables a reader easily to connect the good outcomes in Red's life directly to his own tireless efforts, energy, and persistence. In so many cases Barber succeeded because he so deeply *wanted* to excel and, in fact, was sickened by the memory of, or potential for, personal failure. The tape recording of Barber's account of his life up until his fifty-ninth year includes some of Red's comments regarding the sources of his "good luck," a few of which were not printed in either edition of the published memoir. These taped comments enable listeners to grasp another one of Barber's intuitions about the source of his blessings, including experiences that we address in this chapter of our biography—Barber's years at the University of Florida that led him both to radio and to marriage. After telling listeners how one arbitrary incident led to another toward a seemingly unplanned but wonderful outcome, he insists, "This is how a human being's life is being tempered and *directed.* . . . I did so little, so much *others* did—strangers, sojourners! I don't know how to account for it, these strange, occult things. Is it the world of *spirit* or is it [the working out] of the *unconscious*?"[1]

Barber frequently references Freud when attempting to explain actions he commits beyond his conscious control, such as the source of some of his memorable Barbarisms, or the reason he has surprisingly forgotten something, or when he attempts to explain the unanticipated actions of others. His reference to motivation surfacing from subconscious sources may suggest his suspicion

that it has been *personal* needs and desires or even biological proclivities and priorities that have shaped his destiny. His restless
vacillation between spiritual and subconscious explanations of his
actions and destiny is a striking feature of his memoir writing. It
is characteristic, perhaps, of a well-read and thinking man's sen-
sibility formed during a period in American culture when long-
cherished religious certainties wrestled with the implications of
modern psychology.

"That Was the End of My Football Career"

Red Barber tells us that he began his university career by hitch-
ing a ride in the rumble seat of a friend's Ford, all the way from
Sanford to Gainesville. When they arrived at the campus late in
the afternoon, his friend, an upperclassman, found him a place
in a fraternity house to spend his first night.[2] That evening, as he
strolled across the all-male campus, he recalls, "The phonograph
record I heard playing over the radio, coming from the windows
of the dormitories and the fraternity houses, was Helen Kane, of
the Boo-boop-be-doop Girls."[3]

However comfortably he slept that night, Barber was rudely
awakened the next morning to the mysteries and harsh realities
of freshman registration at a large university, particularly for a
new student lacking in funds and unaccompanied by his parents.
He was equipped with one hundred dollars to cover all expenses
until he began his anticipated job, whatever it was, that Florida
head football coach Charlie Bachman had mentioned in his verbal invitation to "come to Gainesville and play football." Red was
alarmed by the fee for course registration and the requirement
to purchase special shoes to enroll for ROTC. He also had to pay
for a month of room and board in the dormitory and a few additional fees. "By the end of the day," Red notes, "my one hundred
dollars was shot."[4]

Academic registration for college classes was also a mystery for
him. He was confused when asked which college he was entering. The question made no sense to him since he was clearly com-

ing to college at the University of Florida. Fortunately, he caught site of Leonard, the old friend from Sanford who had persuaded him to reject the more solid offer from Rollins. Leonard gave him a quick primer on the division of the university into separate colleges based upon one's chosen major, such as engineering or education. He could not enter the School of Law, for instance, because he would have to do undergraduate work first. Red knew he did not want to go into engineering or law, but he "had come to Gainesville with an open mind." He realized that there was nothing particular he wanted to study and doubted that there were any courses in minstrel performance. He told Leonard that he would choose liberal arts. Once again Leonard stepped in to keep his young friend from making what he considered a mistake and, like a watchful parent, persuaded him to be practical: "If you are going to take liberal arts, you ought to go to the School of Education. You'll get your liberal arts there . . . and when you graduate if you can't find anything else, you'll be qualified to teach school." Red welcomed what seemed sage advice—"It made sense to me," he recalls—and registered in the School of Education, just as his mother had done years before, back in Mississippi.[5]

During the first few days on campus, Red attempted to schedule a meeting with Charlie Bachman to find out where he should report for his job. He had to earn the money he would need to pay for his second month's room and board in the dormitory. But he was told that Bachman was unavailable and that he should just "go out for the freshman football squad," which he did, day after day, each one affording no access to the head coach. Finally, having played no complete football game for two years, he found himself on the field for the first inter-squad match, and it did not go well. On defense he flubbed an attempted tackle, and the player went in for the touchdown. "I looked pretty bad, sprawled there on the ground," he remarked. Worse yet, a kick to his left shin knocked a piece of bone out of place, and in his after-game shower, "The water and the sweat and the soap . . . stung like the devil." His embarrassing performance—coupled with his suspicion that the job offer from the coach was merely an empty gesture—triggered desperate measures. Red marched angrily up to the freshman coach and demanded to know, "Where's my job?" When the coach, whom Red considered "a nice man, and an innocent party," said he knew nothing about any job, Red threw down his uniform at the nice man's feet and stormed out. "That was the end of my football career."[6]

This was the first of Red's freshman trials that triggered thoughts of giving up and returning home; in this instance he forcefully resisted what he tells us would have been an intolerable humiliation. Everyone in Sanford would mock him; he was already reeling from the excruciating judgment he heard them pronounce. He thought, "I had burned all my bridges. No money, no job.... I simply could not go back there defeated after one month. I could not stand the prospect of having everyone in Sanford say, 'Well, Red's back. He didn't make it. Boy, he went up there with his tail feathers up and look at him now.'"[7]

Most painful, however, was the prospect of having to ask his father, whose judgment mattered most, to help him out. He knew his father had no extra money; his mother now was quite ill, and his younger brother and sister were still growing up.[8] Barber never told his father about "the trouble [he] ran into in Gainesville." Instead he summed up his dismal situation and attempted to fathom its implications: "Here was my beautiful four-year scholarship at Rollins—complete security for four years because ... the scholarship did not depend on my *making* the football team—all gone, irrevocably gone. Now, after only two weeks at Gainesville, I had nothing." But not exactly nothing. There were still other "fathers" to help him. Professor Talbot, the dean of men and "a very pleasant man," taught Red's introductory course in the School of Education. Talbot recalls that a faculty member, Professor Burritt from the School of Architecture, was looking for a boy to carry firewood up the stairs to the porch of his second-story apartment. Red pursued the opportunity, and Professor Burritt paid him thirty-five cents an hour for four afternoons of carting wood up an outside staircase. Red tells us, "I made a friend . . . amid the changes and chances of this mortal life . . . who later that school year kept me in college and changed my life." Red also followed up on other day jobs, including hoeing out clay tennis courts overgrown with Bermuda grass. He also had another useful source of backup funds for his freshman year. His membership in the Sanford chapter of DeMolay qualified him to apply for a $200 loan from the Masons designed to help students cover expenses in college for the 1928–29 year.[9]

Although the $200 loan and day labor did not replace the security of a stable campus job, they deferred some of Red's anxieties over making ends meet. He began to enjoy some aspects of college life, including ROTC, and also to penetrate the "facades" of other university institutions, including its sports programs. Red had fun in ROTC sessions, where he was assigned to the program's artillery division, which had just been added to the training that year. He won a university-wide ROTC award that year for being "Leader of the Best Drilled Artillery Unit."[10] In Dean Talbot's introductory education course Red discovered "the realities of college football" and how athletes were, in fact, schooled. When he returned the first exam in the course, Talbot read the names of each student and the grade he had scored on the test, but he excluded the athletes in the class. When one player asked about his score, the dean replied, "You know how it is with you football fellows. You can see me after class, and I'll give you your grades then." Red concludes, "You can add it up from there how they stayed in school. And that was the Dean of Men."[11]

Standing "On Solid Rhetorical Grounds"

Although he was lax with the athletes in his class, Dean Talbot appeared to keep a close eye on the well-being of Red, perhaps because Red so effectively jumped on his initial advice to seek out day-labor jobs. In typical rags-to-riches narratives, from *The Autobiography of Ben Franklin* to Horatio Alger's tales, some of which Barber was likely to have read, the poor but ambitious boy seeks a wealthy father figure to help him. The boy tells his hard story to a potential benefactor and lets the man know that he is eager to work hard. The poor boy's "character" is his "currency," which purchases him repeated overtures of assistance in times of need.

Accordingly, toward the middle of the semester, when day jobs are few and Red's resources again are strained and he does not have enough money to pay for the next month's room and board, he turns to the "nice man" who helped him earlier. Dean Talbot asks him if he would like to manage a small boarding house owned by an elderly woman who can no longer run the place. After confirming what "managing" means—"planning meals, ordering groceries, supervising the cook and the housekeeper, collecting room and board money and filling any vacancies"—Red learns to his delight that the reward for the work will be his own room and board. "For *room and board*? Gee, I can do that."[12] Red actually was relatively qualified for the job—his father had taught him to cook, and during his high school years in Sanford, he and his siblings cleaned the house as both of their parents had full-time jobs. "When I got home from school," he says in an interview late in his life, "I would figure out what supper would be and go to the store, buy it and cook it. . . . Work has been as natural to me as breathing."[13] Red went and talked to "the old lady" and got the job.

Now Barber had a steady job that provided him a place to sleep and eat, and he could borrow his textbooks from the library. He even had a serviceable wardrobe, especially since he wore his ROTC uniform three days a week. After midterm exams, he felt liberated enough to take his first trip home for the weekend since the semester began. His return to Sanford was not unnoticed in local newspapers, which frequently followed the pursuits of hometown boys who had gone on to college. The *Sanford Herald* reports that "he of the 'red thatch,' home from college after midterm exams, was seen hurrying down Magnolia Avenue, bareheaded, to attend a Pi Kappa Phi fraternity meeting." The *Tampa Times* informs its readers that Red was among the freshmen selected for the Bacchus Club, a dance society at the university that consisted of "talented men selected from the pledges of all other social fraternities on campus."[14]

His finances now on a firmer footing, Barber engaged himself fully in the English and history classes he took that first fall, particularly his course in rhetoric. That class was taught by a bright young instructor, Hampton Jarrell, who eventually would become Red's good friend. Since Barber was twenty when he entered college, he was not much younger than Jarrell. He believes he first made a strong impression on his rhetoric professor during a class discussion of an assigned book—an autobiography of Edward Bok, "an immigrant boy who made a fortune in the publishing business and was always being thrown up as a great example of the self-made man." All of the other students found his story "inspiring," but Red would have none of it, insisting that this rags-to-riches tale "was a bunch of rubbish. It wasn't a dad-gummed thing but a rich man with a big ego showing off."[15]

However sincere Red's critique of Bok's autobiography, he says it made Hampton Jarrell "prick up his ears. At least there was a dissenting voice in the class," a role that Red would enjoy playing throughout his career. In choosing his words to impress his teacher, Red was effectively applying the lessons he was learning from the textbook assigned for the class: *Practical Elements of Rhetoric*, by John Genung, an Amherst College professor. Red tells us that the book "was a key thing in my life" because it taught him "the difference between language that was grammatically correct and language that was *rhetorically* correct." He claimed that "knowing the difference helped me to survive and develop in the rather hurly-burly, play-by-play existence around ball parks. I can quote a ballplayer or use a piece of jargon, and even though it is incorrect grammatically, I *know* I'm on solid rhetorical grounds. If I get pushed, I can prove it. Mr. Genung . . . helped me make my living."

What was it that Red found so valuable about "rhetorical effectiveness" as described in Genung's textbook? How did it influence his work as announcer? Genung explains that rhetorical strategy is not concerned with "correctness" but with the use of language

to achieve a goal, whether it is to persuade, please, amuse, surprise, or sustain the attention of one's audience.[16]

In his chapter on "Style," Genung tells his readers that a speaker
must impart to his message "greater life than its mere factual statement would demand, in order to stimulate attention and conviction." In other words, instead of saying "This is a really close
game," the effective speaker says, "This game is as tight as a new
pair of shoes on a rainy day." And if he wants to impress his favorite young English teacher, instead of saying a book is "unremark-
able," he says it's "rubbish" because Professor Genung recommends
that "[the speaker] choose words that make a *definite* impression
on the listener, rather than a vague one."[17]

Barber also may have channeled into his future career other
advice he discovered in Genung's chapter on "Diction." To avoid
boring repetition, the professor recommends that the speaker
always have more than one expression for the same thing but
exercise caution when "coining entirely *new* formations of words
and phrases."[18] Although Red's "Oh, Doctor" after Al Gionfriddo's
breathtaking catch in Game Six of the 1947 World Series became
a celebrated response to an exceptional play, Barber insisted that
this was the only time in his broadcasting career that he ever used
it. Other announcers would sometimes echo the phrase, but Red
thought it would never again "act on" listeners as powerfully as the
first time he spoke it. As for his engaging "Barbarisms," so often
distinguished by his elegant ease with the natural, earthy facts of
humble, small-town Southern experience, Barber said he did not
consciously "invent" them. He suspects he first heard them as a
boy growing up in Columbus and Sanford; they were impressed
upon his memory and still easily accessible when he later saw an
action on the ball field that triggered the images those expressions evoked. He *saw* a ball slip out of a fielder's glove, and memory *spoke* "slicker than oiled okra."

Of course, the most specific tools for "imparting greater life"
to one's expression, "Figures of Speech," also earn a rich chapter in Genung's textbook, and Red Barber later employed them

skillfully in his broadcasts and writing. Metaphors and similes express surprising, fresh comparisons and associations between two things that heretofore have been unconnected for a wordsmith's audience; getting a bunch of hits is like "tearin' up the pea-patch"; photographers spring up around Jackie Robinson like "rain lilies after a cloudburst."[19] If Red Barber had absorbed his effective rhetorical strategies from Genung's book, he was not exaggerating when he claimed that "Mr. Genung . . . helped me make my living."

"I Don't Know What More a Man Could Do"

The college freshman had smooth sailing for the rest of his first semester and even got himself elected to the Freshman Class Executive Committee before the end of the term.[20] But after returning from a weekend in Sanford in March, his well-ordered life was abruptly shattered by the "old lady" who rented the boarding house he had been managing so diligently. She had decided to leave the place to live with her sister and instructed him to clear the boarders and himself from the building by the end of the day. Red was shocked. Again, he found himself with no place to sleep, no free meals, and not enough money to cover room and board for the rest of the semester. After purging the boarders, he threw all his belongings into a duffle bag and sat, despairingly, on the front steps to ponder his next move. He had only enough spirit to half-heartedly acknowledge Professor Burritt—for whom, in a happier time, he'd moved logs—and who now was waving to him as he drove by the house in his yellow Ford roadster. His only choice was to walk a block and a half to Bummer's Corner, where students hitchhiked out of Gainesville, and find his way home to his father's house. He was sickened by this prospect.

But that yellow Ford roadster took a ride around the block, and another kindly father figure relieved Red's misery again. Professor Burritt had a "funny feeling" when he'd driven by and came back to ask Barber if anything was wrong. After Red described his dire situation, Burritt took Red to his apartment, made him some tea, and agreed to let him stay there until he found a job and a place of his own. He bought Red a dining card that would pay for twenty-six meals at Louie's Greek Restaurant and even shared his bed with him. Perhaps in anticipation of concerns on the part of readers who might be suspicious about a man who drove around Bummer's Corner picking up good-looking freshman boys, lines were added to *Rhubarb in the Catbird Seat*, either by Red's writer, Robert Creamer; Red himself; or the publisher: "Nowadays, I suppose, eyebrows would be raised at the idea of grown men sharing a bed, though it was not an uncommon thing at that time."[21]

Gazing around the architecture professor's apartment, the college freshman was impressed. Barber later wrote that Burritt's place inspired in him an enduring aesthetic ideal. The lovely interior design reflected a uniquely pleasing and orderly life—filled with beautiful art and fine antiques skillfully arranged. He tells us that in Burritt's apartment he saw "genuine artistic taste" for the first time. He adds, "My mother had an artistic taste for language, but this man had a taste for things, things of material texture, things of quality." It was not just the things that struck him, but also the lifestyle they supported: "Here was a bachelor, a very social man, but a man who had everything in his life arranged just so, a man who didn't want anyone else in his life to disturb the pleasant pattern that he had established. And yet he took a stranger, a person he barely knew, into his home, into this fastidious, precise life. I don't know what more a man could do."[22]

Red's "Lanier" persona was struck by an image of the perfectly arranged retreat, where a man could live alone, uninterrupted by that "anyone else" who pulled one away from repose and where he was surrounded by beautiful things that remained in perfect order. Barber recreates images like this repeatedly in his writing, such as when he mentions his father returning from work and retiring to his big chair by the kitchen stove and reading his books while his wife and children sleep. His dislike of life on the road, perhaps, was not so much due to its loneliness but to the loss of the lovely and familiar haven where he was most in touch with himself, a haven far apart from the harried professional public life he led for so many years.

Fortunately, Professor Burritt did not need to share his haven with the homeless freshman for long. Burritt regularly played bridge as the fourth hand, along with Red's favorite teacher, Hampton Jarrell; his wife Judy; and their next-door neighbor, Miss Eddy, a "lovely old maid" who cared for her aging father. Not long after Burritt told them about Red's homeless plight, Jarrell offered the "dissenting voice" in his fall semester rhetoric class the extra bedroom in his home. Although Red still had most of his twenty-six meals at Louie's left to eat, Hampton and Judy often invited him to share meals with them, as did Miss Eddy. So his primary needs again were satisfied, and the bonus for Red was that he gained a surrogate family.[23]

It is at this point in his freshman year that Red, delighted by the lifestyle of college professors, determined that he should move himself into that role as well: "I liked that life so much I decided I wanted to become a college professor myself. I liked the Jarrells and Professor Burritt and all their friends. If I had become a college professor, I think I would have been completely happy."[24] There is no way to support this qualified assertion, but it's clear at this point that Red was attracted to the lifestyle he assumed professors enjoyed—stimulating discussions, faculty gatherings, getting paid for reading and talking about subjects they loved, being the "man in control" in a classroom, and being free to spend lots of time at home. After a few weeks at the Jarrells, Red's progress toward his goal was reinforced by finding a new job to help subsidize his education. Miss Eddy, who worked at the university library, told him about openings for student workers. After an interview with the head librarian, Cora Miltmore, he got the job, working a minimum of fifteen hours per week.[25]

Red also comments at some length in his memoirs about his interesting relationship with Miss Eddy during his stay with the Jarrells. The two of them apparently engaged in lively and self-disclosing conversations that awakened him to the existence of a type of woman with whom he'd never shared time before. He "loved to sit and talk with her. [They] spoke of many things." One day she happened to inform him that "she had never had sexual intercourse." It stunned him when she mentioned that this had made no difference to her: "She had never felt she had missed anything. She had no antagonism toward the idea of sex. It just seemed she was destined to grow up and live as an old maid who worked in a library and took care of her aged father. You could not imagine a more normal, pleasanter person. She looked the way you might imagine a young grandmother would look in the fullness of her life. I believe she was designed to be just what she was, a beautiful old maid."[26]

Barber was provoked by the existence of a woman who did not care about having intimate relations with men, even though she looked and acted like a "normal" woman who had had sex—like a "young grandmother" with a "fullness" to her spirit. He struggled to reach some conclusion about her constitution and ultimately declared, "I believe she was *designed* to be just the person she was—a beautiful old maid." This passage came from a fifty-eight-year-old Red Barber, who had to accept the fact that his daughter was a lesbian—and an outspoken one. It suggests that the example of Miss Eddy may have played a part in his process of understanding. Miss Eddy was not "lacking," nor did she make a choice that was to be regretted or that needed to be fixed; she was born to be just the way that she was.

"We'll Put You on Skit Nights"

Gradual improvements in his fiscal well-being encouraged Red to continue his romance with minstrel performance as a casual avocation, rather than as a serious professional goal, and his university's glee club provided just the right forum. Glee club performances also featured individual "specialty" acts in their "skit nights." He relied on one of his blackface acts for his audition, a skit in which he performed by himself *every* role featured in a typical minstrel show performance. The glee club director assured him, "We'll put you on skit nights." Sure enough, Red's acts, both individual and with a partner, became a fixture not only on skit nights, but also on the glee club's annual road tour performances in towns and campuses across the state. For the road tour, the glee club selected the top three acts from recent skit nights, including Red's.[27]

Reviews of his performances were enthusiastic. A glee club performance for Ladies' Night at the Gainesville Rotary prompted one reviewer to proclaim that Red Barber was "a one-man minstrel sensation." Barber apparently opened this skit by observing that "indications point to a boiling down of the old-time minstrel to fewer performers each year," so it was important that one man could perform all the parts. The reviewer remarks that Barber ably "executed parts which formerly were taken by as many as sixty-five men, impersonating each successfully."[28]

Barber's reengagement with minstrel performance, however, provoked an irreconcilable conflict with Miss Miltmore, the head librarian at the university library, when she refused to excuse him from work for a glee club traveling tour near the end of the semester. Red was surprised by her ultimatum, and, caught off guard, his rhetorical attempts to change her mind were uncharacteristically mediocre: "This glee club stuff is important to me. . . . it's only three or four days." His arguments failed, and Red quit the job. At the end of his first year at the university, the urge to perform, to use his own voice, was stronger in Red than a commitment to working "down in that musky morgue with all those dry old books," an experience, some might attest, that delights and motivates many a university professor.[29]

"The Prettiest Brown Eyes I Have Ever Seen"

Red attempted to shore up his resources after quitting his library job to guarantee he would have more reserves to cover sophomore year expenses than he had enjoyed as a freshman. He secured a full-time position serving meals in one of the university dining halls, to start at the beginning of fall semester, a job that provided free meals for his labor. He also found a roommate, Jerry Carter, who would share the costs of a room in a student boarding house when they came back to school in September. Soon after he returned home for summer vacation, he secured a job driving a truck supplied by the U.S. Department of Agriculture for transporting crews and equipment to combat a crop-destroying Mediterranean fruit fly infestation. He deposited every paycheck into Sanford's First National Bank and made no withdrawals. He also took time to work with Sanford's Blue Mason Lodge to complete the three degrees required to become a Master Mason because the order's philosophy "really interested" him.[30] He had some dates that summer, but, he adds, "Whenever I asked a girl out for a date, I'd say 'can I come over to your house?'"[31]

It would have been better had he put his money in a box under his bed. He was driving one of his dates around town in his father's car one July evening when he saw a "bunch of men staring at a sign posted on the door of Sanford's First National Bank." The bank had shut down, and all his savings had vanished. After driving his date home, he spent the night in his bed "cold all over." He would be returning to school in three weeks with less money than he had had his first year.[32] But by the following morning his panic gradually receded as he recalled that he had a dining hall job lined up to cover his meals and a roommate to share the expenses of lodging. His successful survival experiences of freshman year appeared to provide buoyancy for navigating future setbacks. Perhaps the wisdom he had gained as a first-year college student compelled him to serve as a peer mentor during the 1929 freshman orientation.[33]

Jerry, Red's sophomore-year boarding house roommate, also was working his way through college by driving an old Chevy truck full of bakery goods twice weekly between Jacksonville, where the goods were made, and Gainesville, where Jerry would sell them at local groceries. One Saturday during the first half of the fall semester, Jerry came back to Gainesville, his truck loaded with fresh-baked goods including cakes with lots of frosting. That night Red, Jerry, and their buddies were sharing moonshine in their boarding house room while engaging in conversations about abstract issues like marriage. Red recalls spouting, with rhetorical effectiveness, his reasons for not even *considering* marriage before the age of thirty: he needed that time to complete his schooling, teach a little, and then go back to study for his PhD and become a university professor: "I said there was no room in my plans for a woman. . . . The last thing in my future at the moment was marriage."[34]

The young men needed a pause in the conversation to go out and refill their jug; this errand involved a trip "past the country club into some pine woods," where moonshine was available at a price even poor college boys could afford. Jerry volunteered to drive his truck for the mission, and Red and three others piled into the vehicle, which had only one seat—the driver's. Along the way, a steep hill suddenly lurched from nowhere; the truck, barreling down the slope, veered off the road and turned over several times, throwing out a passenger on each roll. Miraculously, no one was dangerously injured, but since the truck struck Red's lower back after he popped out of it, he was shaken up and unable to walk. He also was covered with "dirt and sand spurs and cake dough and icing and commercial pies." The other boys carried him all the way back to the infirmary on campus.

There was only one young nurse, Lylah Scarborough, on duty that late in the evening, and she appeared weary from tending to all the injured players from that Saturday's football contest. When she saw the filthy mess that was Red Barber, "She said with utter disgust, 'take him back and lay him down.' . . . As she said it, I noticed that she had the prettiest brown eyes I had ever seen." Red stayed at the infirmary for three days; on the afternoon of his release, he returned and asked Lylah for a date; she accepted. According to Barber, on their second date, Red and Lylah agreed to go steady and to marry when they were ready; this oath was sealed just a week after Red had sworn off marriage for the next ten years. Barber notes that throughout their long marriage, his wife had a hard time criticizing him whenever he downed a few too many; had he not been drinking that Saturday night, he might never have met her. In her own memoir, Lylah recalls that the day of his release from the hospital, "He returned with a box of long-stemmed roses. I was hooked."[35]

The prospect of marriage, and the more immediate need to have some cash for dates, once again engendered money worries for Red. Always sniffing out options, Red learned from his sociology professor, Wallace Goebel, about an opening for a janitor in the University Club, a rooming house for unmarried faculty where Goebel himself lived. The establishment also served as a meeting place for faculty who belonged to the club. As janitor, Red would be expected to "make beds, sweep the place, gather up laundry and send it out." He would be compensated by a room at the club, "and it was as nice a room as any other in the house."

Red truly enjoyed his new accommodations: "I did the work—swept, made beds, took care of things," and he also swabbed toilet bowls. But, he assures us, "In every other way I lived with the bachelor professors as an equal."[36] He found their conversations illuminating, learned something of value from each of them, and became close friends with at least two of them. Red later served as groomsman at the wedding of Wallace Goebel, and Frank Gaetani, a Spanish professor, taught him about opera and was best man at Red's wedding.[37] Barber felt that all the professors "accepted [him] as one of them. . . . It was stimulating being in their company." There was always a table of bridge to join: "We lived a wonderful life. There was no doubt in my mind that someday I was going to be one of them."[38] Barber's comfort with the professors did not go unnoticed by his classmates. One of his buddies told him that "everyone is saying you are really sucking in with the professors at that University Club. . . . Is that the way you get your good grades?"[39]

During the holiday break that winter, Red and Lylah visited Barber's parents, who had recently moved from Sanford to Tampa. The railroad roundhouse in Sanford had been closed, and William Barber could not keep up on mortgage payments for their home; also, Selena Barber's health was rapidly deteriorating. His father kept his railroad job but transferred to operations in Tampa, where his wife's brother and family now lived. Lylah observed that Red's mother, "who was then an invalid, so small and frail, sat by the fire in the living room." But, however ill, Selena welcomed Lylah and assured her that Red "was like his father, who had been helpful with their three children when she was teaching and serving as principal." Barber's father, "in his warm Southern voice," playfully told her to let him know if Red gave her any trouble because "[he'd] straighten him out."[40] After Christmas, Red Barber returned to Gainesville before his winter break was over to perform his duties at the University Club and to complete a term paper for his fall history class, due the first day of spring term. His ten-year plan for his professional development was still intact—the one that he'd shared with his buddies the Saturday that ended with his vision of "the prettiest brown eyes."[41] Only now he would be sharing that journey with Lylah.

"Where She Came From and Who She Is"

Lylah Barber's formative experiences in the Deep South differed from her husband's in ways that would significantly influence the dynamics of their marriage. Barber's sixty-two-year relationship with Lylah was the most sustained intimacy of his life. His decision to marry her sealed his inclination to end his college career after two years and to commit himself to a profession in radio. For the rest of his life, he grew ever more deeply attached to his home and to his tightly bound nuclear family of three; he took care to monitor intrusions upon their privacy from the "outside world." He disliked traveling with the teams he covered because he viewed his home as a haven designed for daily renewal and the source of nourishment for his extraordinarily active public life. Lylah understood her husband's fierce ambition and encouraged him to pursue it; she also was a consistent and reliable critic of his performances and sometimes of his assumptions and values.

One of Red's favorite books was Kahlil Gibran's, *The Prophet*, popular in the 1960s and 1970s.[42] Red bought many copies of this book to give to friends who were about to marry or have a child.[43] Gibran, a Middle Eastern mystic, compiled a series of poetic essays that meditate upon the most important components of human experience. Two of Barber's favorites were "On Marriage" and "On Children." He affirms Gibran's insistence in each of these pieces that our family members, both spouses and children, are not "our own." We do not possess them, but we encourage them to follow their deepest inclinations. Gibran's image of the perfect marriage is two people walking side by side with "spaces between them" and with their eyes gazing, not obsessively at one another but ahead of themselves, each freely navigating his or her own path.[44] Red also maintained that for a marriage to last, partners needed to have some feisty arguments, particularly early in the relationship, but also from time to time thereafter. He believed that intense and animated "rhubarbs" were an essential way to absorb one another's values—the convictions that shaped a partner's character. One needed to know what one's partner would *not* accept to know who they were.[45]

There were concrete grounds for flare-ups in the early years of the Barber marriage: Lylah, two years older than Red, was college-educated and had risen to the position of director of student nurses when she married Barber. Red had become chief announcer at WRUF and was also getting accustomed to directing things. He tells us it took time for him and Lylah to figure out *who* was going to be the director of *what* in their married life.[46] These kernels of domestic wisdom seem woven into the fabric of their relationship. Red and Lylah were quite different in disposition and personality, and at various stages in their shared lives, each had to make significant sacrifices for the other, but they remained durable, forbearing, and loyal companions.

In her introduction to her 1985 memoir, *Lylah*, which she likely drafted in her early to mid-seventies, Lylah Barber explains why she published the story of her life. She wanted to thank those who had supported and challenged her and also to trace her journey through the dramatic cultural changes of the twentieth century. But she also wanted to help her daughter Sarah understand "where she came from and who she is."[47]

Lylah Scarborough was born on July 7, 1906, in Lake City, Florida, and was named after her mother, Lyla. Not long after she was born, the family moved to Jacksonville, where her father began a law practice with his brother. Lylah's brother, Mat, her only sibling, was born a year later. When Lylah was five, her father, Lyndley Murray Scarborough, died after weeks in the hospital, probably a victim of tuberculosis. Lylah most vividly recalls him smiling back at her the morning he left for the hospital in a black carriage, never to return. She says she was haunted for a long time by frightening dreams of a man being driven away from a house in a dark carriage. "[Red] must have been puzzled the first time he was awakened by my screams of terror. However, he was kindly and patient and over a number of years we worked out the reasons for my recurring nightmare." Her father's death left a vacancy, a missing piece from the whole that should have been hers.[48]

However, from these dim memories, Lylah created an idealized image of her father, with whom the actual man, had he lived longer, might never have been able to compete. Her imagined father was her standard for judging other men whom she came to know well. Lyndley Scarborough, she augured, was kind, charming, intelligent, good with children, gentle with women, well-spoken, well-mannered, and self-controlled. Her aunt told her that her father had returned home with a bouquet of roses for her mother on the day she gave birth to Lylah. This memory may explain why Lylah was "hooked" the day Red was released from the college infirmary but returned within hours to give the nurse with "the prettiest brown eyes" a bouquet of roses.[49] Later in her life, when she first met Edward R. Murrow, who hired Red to be sports director at CBS and who became a good friend, she recalled:

> [I] was amazed; he looked just like my cherished picture of my father as a young man. Like my father, he was a southerner with the charm

and courtly manners I am certain my father had. When Murrow died . . . and I came home from the church, I cried for the loss of a friend. . . . I realized also that I wept for the father whose loss I had been too young to understand. The tears for Murrow helped heal a grief that came into our cottage in 1911.[50]

Lylah repeatedly assessed the characteristic strengths and weaknesses of other men she came to know based upon the standard set by her image of her father. Although she was appalled when she observed the behavior of an inebriated Larry MacPhail, she would insist that there were "two MacPhails"—"the brawling unreasonable fighter," who frightened her, and the other MacPhail, who compensated for the bully, "the sensitive, generous man of the world," like her father. She came to know the latter MacPhail when he comforted her after learning of her first miscarriage in Cincinnati. In a private conversation, he disclosed to her the sad and touching story of his own wife's miscarriage. MacPhail's empathy with her sorrow made a difference, and, Lylah relates, "I cannot forget his caring kindness."[51] And even though, later in her husband's career, Lylah was conscious of tensions between Red and Dodgers owner Walter O'Malley, she admired what she saw of her father in O'Malley: she was touched by the loving and gentle way that O'Malley treated his wife, Kay, who suffered from a speech impairment.[52] In this sense—as a measure for her ideal of "manliness"—Lylah never lost her father.

Burdened with hospital bills after the death of her husband, Lylah's mother went to work to earn a living for her young family, maintaining a full-time job as a private secretary and a part-time job as a substitute stenographer in a large Jacksonville hotel. Her mother's "endless struggle to provide for herself and her two children left little strength for emotional ties." As a youngster, Lylah compensated for this lack of intimacy with her mother by forming close relationships with other women mentors, particularly her mother's sister, Ouida; her favorite teachers; and her two grandmothers.[53] Throughout her childhood Lylah was moved from household to household and from one private boarding school to another, all domiciles managed solely by women.[54]

Lylah's ruptured family tree and the broken core of her own nuclear family had two profound effects. First, they triggered her lifelong interest in reconstructing her own family's genealogy and domestic history through avid research. The first three chapters of her memoir are dedicated to recovering and documenting the lives of the female line in her family from four generations back. Her project to resurrect the family she never knew triggered a deep desire that the Scarborough line would continue.[55] The second effect of Lylah's being born into a "broken" family line and "passed around" to surrogate households is that she was exposed to a much wider diversity of lifestyles and values than most Southern youngsters of her time, especially children like Red Barber, who were raised in a strong nuclear family that remained intact until they were independent adults. Her youngest playmates were African American; she absorbed influences from both Episcopal and Catholic schooling; and she spent summers in Georgia, joining the humble but spirited Methodist household of her great-aunt Molly, daughter of a circuit-riding preacher. She also experienced several lonely teen years in the fashionable home of a well-heeled stepfather, whose African American chauffeur drove her to school in a shiny new car. She made him drop her off a block from the school because she was embarrassed to be driven to an academy full of students "whose families had no cars, much less chauffeurs."[56] After earning her Bachelor of Science in Nursing (BSN), she engaged in postgraduate clinical work at Cook County Hospital in Chicago, the largest and most ethnically diverse charity hospital in the country.

These exposures, at least in part, awakened Lylah's lifelong interest in learning more about the cultural "other" and the practices and beliefs of people who did not rank high on the social scale in the Deep South of her childhood. Her relative cosmopolitanism provided young Red Barber with firsthand experience of America's diverse populations at a time when her husband's career was taking him far from central Florida.

As a child spending summers with her grandmother in Lake City, Florida, Lylah played with the Black cook's children, who would come with to work with their mother. This seemed natural because her first childhood playmates had been the two children of the African American nurse who had helped her mother care for Lylah and her brother after her father died.[57] She tells her readers that she spent her formative years "in an environment where the two cultures, black and white, lived side by side."[58]

When she was eight, Lylah's mother sent her away to a girls' boarding school managed by two headmistresses who enforced an authoritarian pedagogy fueled by an oppressive and putative Protestant theology. Lylah survived by reading books and striving to score the highest grades in her class. She excelled in writing and recitation. During her adolescent years at Catholic boarding schools, she forged deep friendships with young nuns who sensed her loneliness and provided the support and encouragement she so needed. But when Lylah was fifteen, her mother married her wealthy boss, Jefferson "Buzz" Thomas, to provide a better life for her children. Lylah, her brother, and her mother moved into his house, but Lylah's experience of what finally promised to be an intact nuclear family proved dismal. Her stepfather turned out to be the opposite of the idealized father she had lost when she was five. Mr. Thomas sent her brother to military school and was morbidly possessive of his new wife and stepdaughter; he threatened to sic his Airedale on Lylah's male callers and kept her mother housebound.

Once when Lylah's stepfather was out of town on business, their "black chauffeur–yardman–heavy cleaner," Henry, who sensed the malaise in the household and "tried his best to soften" Thomas's harshness, taught Lylah's mother how to drive the family car so that she could visit friends and her own mother. Lylah knew that Henry's kindnesses, "if discovered, would certainly have cost him his job."[59] Lylah also narrates the time her stepfather attempted to seduce her into his bed when they were alone in his house: "I was young, barely nineteen. My rather sheltered upbringing, first, in matriarchal households, and then with the nuns, had not prepared me for such a situation. But I had sense enough to leave. I saw to it that I was never again alone in his company."[60] Her mother and stepfather eventually separated.

Lylah, always an outstanding student, had dismissed the dream of going away to college as an impossibility. Without her knowledge her mother had enrolled her in Jacksonville's Riverside Hospital for a nurses' training program. She had only been inside a hospital three times, and each visit had haunted her with "the odors and aura of sickness. . . . Now it was to become my life."[61] However, after months of experiential learning at Riverside, she discovered that her "hospital days" were proving interesting. She got along well with patients and also enjoyed "the drama and demand of the emergency and operating rooms." Impressed with Lylah's intelligence and curiosity, one of her professors at the hospital recommended her for Florida's first BSN program, recently launched at Florida State College for Women in Tallahassee. She now would enjoy the residential college experience she had longed for but had been "carefully taught" to believe was inaccessible.

Lylah's four years completing her BSN degree in Tallahassee seem to have been fruitful and relatively worry free, even though her finances were strained. Her only regret was not having more room in her curriculum for art and philosophy. Toward the end of her college career, Lylah enjoyed her first protracted romantic relationship—with the town newspaper's city editor: "Charles Sloan, an attractive man some fifteen years my senior. . . . We were drawn to one another." Sloan was an educated professional, as her father had been, and older than the young men her college friends were dating. "Here was a 'gentleman caller' my stepfather could not scare away with a ferocious dog." But soon after Lylah graduated as one of Florida's first three Bachelors of Science in Nursing, Sloan moved to the Midwest for a better newspaper job, and she went to Gainesville to work at the university's infirmary. There she would save some money to help fund her upcoming postgraduate clinical work at Chicago's Cook County Hospital. She chose the Chicago hospital because it was the largest charity hospital in the country and would certainly provide her with a wider range of new clinical experiences. The work she accomplished in Chicago would complete her requirements for the job—Instructress of Nurses—that she had been offered by Jacksonville's Riverside Hospital, where her professional education had begun.

"Two Strongminded, Ambitious People Learning to Live with Their Differences"

Lylah enjoyed her brief but consequential nursing stint at the University of Florida's student infirmary in Gainesville. We know of her introduction to the messy, icing-clad Red Barber, and we know she was "hooked," but she does not specifically mention their vowing on their second date to marry one another. She does, however, describe Red's sweet behavior in her account of their precious hours together: "When I was fortunate to have an evening off duty, we walked to the duck pond between the infirmary and the stadium. It was an attractive wooded area and fairly secluded. After my long twelve-hour shift, I was tired, and my feet hurt. I would take off my shoes, and Red would rub my feet and sing to me in his pleasing, tenor voice."[62] After her 1930 Christmas break visit with Red's parents in Tampa, Lylah told her mother about her plans to marry Barber after she returned from her six-month clinical assignment in Chicago. Her mother, whose father, husband, and brother had all been lawyers, took a dim view of her choice for a husband—a younger man who was still a poor college student working his way through school as a janitor. And her mother also wished that Lylah would "stop calling him by a silly nickname." But Red's fiancée had a hard time recalling his first name because everyone in Gainesville, including Barber himself, referred to him as "Red."

For the next five months in Chicago, Lylah writes, "Almost everything I saw or did was a 'first.'" Her initial placement at Cook County Hospital was in obstetrics, where, for the first time, she saw babies born with venereal diseases. Her first case, a fourteen-

year-old boy, was also the first Black patient she had ever encountered; there had been no African American patients at the private
Riverside Hospital in Jacksonville or at the all-white Florida State
College for Women in Tallahassee or at the University of Florida in
Gainesville. The boy had typhoid fever, and Lylah remained alone
and quarantined with him for two straight weeks. He seemed hostile, which frightened her. But then she realized how shocking it
must feel to his fevered body as she kept applying ice-cold sponges.
When Lylah worked in the surgical wards, she was stunned by the
number of gunshot wounds, many resulting from gang wars prev-
alent in the city. When admitting patients, Lylah was instructed
to examine all parts of their bodies and clothing for bullets, which
were turned over to the police.

When her work at Cook County Hospital was completed, Lylah
was offered her choice of two positions there: to teach on the
Nursing School staff or to be assistant supervisor of the women's
surgical unit. She was tempted because both jobs were appealing
to her, as was Cook County's outstanding reputation as both a
teaching and a charity hospital. But Lylah decided to "turn my face
south and come back home to my dear Red." She found a boarding house room in Jacksonville near Riverside Hospital, where she
was about to begin her career with "the impressive title of Instructress of Nurses." But it was hard to be separated from Red, now
an announcer at WRUF in Gainesville, so soon after their long-
awaited reunion. To seal their bond, even if they could not yet
melt the miles between them, they decided to get married in the
living room of Lylah's boarding house on Saturday, March 28, 1931.

Red's parents could not attend the wedding because his mother
was too ill to travel, but they sent a warm telegram expressing
their delight in the marriage and urging the newlyweds to come
see them soon in Tampa. Major Garland Powell, Red's boss at
WRUF, drove him and his roommate, Jimmy, up from Gainesville. Lylah's mother, still on the fence concerning her support
for her daughter's marriage, showed up for the wedding and in
time would grow quite fond of her son-in-law; shortly before

her death, her mother even told Lylah, "I love Red more than I love either one of my children." The couple left Jacksonville after their reception, drove in a borrowed car to a hotel in Savannah for their wedding night, and then traveled to Charleston, South Carolina, for a two-day visit.

Several months after their wedding, Lylah was asked to fill temporarily the job of supervisor of nurses until a permanent supervisor could be hired to assume the recently vacated position. The promotion, though temporary, required her to live in the Nurses' Home, where Red no longer could room with her when he came up from Gainesville once a week to do a sports radio show for a Jacksonville station. As the weeks went by, Red grew weary of hearing Lylah's student nurses refer to him as "'Miss Scarborough's husband,' and a part-time husband at that." Although her brief career as part of the permanent staff at Riverside Hospital would be the last full-time professional employment of her life, she tells us in her memoir, "I was relieved when the new supervisor arrived and I could go to Gainesville to live with Red and become a full-time wife." Lylah and Red finally were united under the same roof when she moved into his apartment in Gainesville in December 1931: "It was roomy and private, and we happily settled in and began planning our first married Christmas."

Lylah tells us the two-and-a-half years that Red and she lived together in Gainesville "were busy ones and on the whole happy. Two strong-minded, ambitious young people were learning how to live, peaceably most of the time, with their differences." They also had lots of fun, and lots of booze, as Lylah refers to many "Saturday night parties that must have gotten pretty noisy. . . . White lightening bootleg flowed freely." There was always a Saturday night bridge party or potluck dinners with communal food and moonshine to share with Red's college professors and former classmates and some of Lylah's college mates who had married and moved to Gainesville. "We had more energy than money," she says, "even though those Sunday mornings brought reality back with a bang."[63]

There was a sobering loss, however, during their newly wed years in Gainesville. Red's mother died on December 31, 1931, at fifty-five. When Red heard the news, he stood on his porch listening to New Year's Eve "bells and whistles at midnight, and [he] shivered." He was silent during the long drive to Tampa: "I was stunned, sick . . . unable to cry or cry out." Looking back, Red admits that some part of him knew at the time his mother was close to death; she had suffered a series of strokes during the preceding five years that had severely slurred her speech and had become so frail that she required around-the-clock care. Selena's father and brother had both died in their fifties from strokes.[64] But, Red tells us, "I had not permitted myself to accept that one day, any day, she would die." He had not allowed himself to consider, "now that her brilliant mind was dulled" and her body shattered, that this is what she may have been longing for.[65] He realizes now how unprepared he had been that night to accept death as the very condition for being alive.

In his 1971 account of that night, Red recreates for the reader vivid images of Selena's reading to him and tutoring her students in her own kitchen. She was not a loquacious storyteller like his father; her strength was quiet. She conveyed to him by her actions her belief that the core to a good life was "nurturing the quality that each of us has within us and respecting that quality in others." Once, with a few brief words, he recalls, she set her son straight when he was an adolescent confused about sex. She encouraged him to express his concerns and left him with the clear understanding that "girls have a right to quality too, and to have it respected always; that will be your responsibility." But that night on the ride to Tampa he got angry that God had let his mother suffer and then die. He got angrier still when the undertaker tried to sell him an overpriced casket and an overpriced funeral. "As I got madder at him, I got madder at God." Barber vowed not to go to church again because "[he] wanted nothing from God or his ministers. Death had become a hateful thing."[66]

In their few Gainesville years that followed, Lylah tells us, she was learning how to cook and keep house, while Red was busy learning new skills as a sports broadcaster and as a radio entertainment announcer and program producer. He spent all his vacations on the road auditioning for a radio job in a bigger city with more powerful and better-funded stations. Home alone, she might have pondered how it came about that the poor bleeding student—the janitor and would-be college professor who had been carried into the infirmary while she was covering the night shift a few years before—had turned himself so rapidly into a regional radio star.

"Certain Aspects of Bovine Obstetrics"

Red Barber told his personal "broadcaster origins" story in two of his own books and to dozens of newspaper and magazine reporters. It was perhaps his favorite personal story and captured, better than any other, the role of "accident" in the good fortune that came his way. Given the Barber family's love of language and literature, it is fitting that Barber's first broadcast was spurred by a paper to be written and climaxed with a paper that was read. The story starts in late December 1929, near the end of the first semester of his sophomore year in college.

While Red Barber liked most of his University of Florida courses and particularly those in English literature and history, he did not enjoy his English history course. Red believed that his professor was the model of incompetent teaching. He read from the textbook, rewarded sterile memorization, and tolerated no questions interrupting his lectures, which were mere readings from his outline. When the professor asked him why he was doing so poorly in his class, Barber, often willing to speak to power, told him the truth: "Well, I have never been so disappointed in a course in my life. English history should be the most stimulating course anyone could ever teach, but you make it tedious, dry, and boring."[1] At twenty-two, Red Barber had been entertaining with songs, dance, and humor for six years. He believed he knew something about working an audience.

For Barber to be free of the class, he needed only to finish his long-delayed term paper on King James I. One morning when he was working on the project, agriculture professor Ralph Fulghum interrupted Red's progress to ask him for some help. Because three of his colleagues were still on holiday, Fulghum would have to read their papers for them during WRUF's noontime "Florida Farm Hour"; he desperately needed someone to give him and his audience a break by reading the second paper (entitled "Certain Aspects of Bovine Obstetrics"), a task that would take about ten minutes. When Barber refused because he had to tie things up with King James I, Fulghum bribed the young scribe with a gift he could not refuse: free food. Since the chow house where Barber worked and ate his meals was not yet open for the new semester, he had been spending his own meager funds for meals. When Fulghum offered to buy Barber his dinner, the reluctant young voice quickly agreed to read all three papers. Fulghum said one would be enough and drove Red to the WRUF studios, housed in a compact building on the agricultural lands attached to the main campus.

Red sat down in front of a carbon microphone in a studio big enough to "get two or three people in at the same time if everybody stood up." After Fulghum finished reading his own paper in the larger studio next to Barber's, he waved at Red to get his attention and then pointed his finger at the novice broadcaster. Barber read the paper cold, as it had not occurred to him to familiarize himself with its contents while Fulghum was reading the first paper. The bovine study, according to Red, "was a thorough and frank discussion of the subject," practical but dull. Ten minutes later, Red Barber was an experienced broadcaster, looking forward only to a satisfying meal, earned with little effort.[2]

As he was leaving the building, a man approached him wanting to know if he was the fellow who had read "Bovine Obstetrics." Although the reading was unrehearsed, he liked the register of

Red's voice. Could Barber work part time at the station for thirty-five cents an hour? His first meeting with Major Garland Powell would change Red's life, but at that moment Powell was merely searching for an unknown talent to elevate WRUF's shaky status. In 1929 the new University of Florida president, John J. Tigert, brought Major Garland Powell, a genuine major, to WRUF. The station's previous manager, Bobby Griffin, who had brought little acclaim to the station, seemed more interested in hearing his own voice on the air than bringing new talent to the station or expanding its programming.[3] The station's mediocre programming and its weak, daytime-only 5,000-watt signal made its slogan, "Florida's Station," a shallow claim.

Newspapers, always threatened by radio, were especially suspicious of a state-supported radio station. The *Miami Herald* accused the station of "trading good air-time for restaurant tickets and many other items of merchandise, presumably for the sole use of the salaried operatives." It claimed the programming was limited to "second rate music, warmed over news items, and dreary features, all costing the state about $200 a day and doing nobody any good."[4] Powell worked to improve the station's programming and broaden its appeal. Sports programming, particularly Gators football, was helping, but he needed better and cheaper talent. This handsome young redhead both looked and sounded the part.

But Barber turned the major down flat. With his work at the University Club and the campus dining hall and a twenty-one-hour course load, he had no time to waste on radio for thirty-five cents an hour. The pennies he'd get for his radio work could not replace the benefits of food and shelter that came with his other positions. But Powell was persistent, enlisting Fulghum to remind Barber at regular intervals that he wanted to talk the professor's bedmaker into working for WRUF. After a couple months of pestering by Major Powell by way of Ralph Fulghum, Red went to the station to convince Powell that he could not afford to work at WRUF. When Powell asked how much Red would need to work only at the station, Barber quickly added up his monthly expenses and decided he would need fifty dollars a month. To Barber it was an exorbitant figure that would quash the matter and Red's radio career before it could start. But, instead, the major happily replied, "Okay, it's a deal!" Barber was dumbfounded. On March 4, 1930, the young man who would become the most famous employee in WRUF history started his broadcasting career.[5]

The persistent Major Powell became the first of Barber's professional "fathers" who would advance his career. In a 1974 interview, Barber credited Powell with expanding WRUF's mission to include training broadcasters: "A lot of us are very blessed because of Garland Powell."[6] Powell focused on public relations for WRUF, hobnobbing with administrators and legislators to make the station seem much more important than it was. He diligently wrote personal letters to the station's fans and its critics. Powell's diplomatic skills helped keep the state-funded station afloat during the Great Depression, when many critics considered money for a radio station a waste of taxpayer dollars. Barber concluded that "people thought that Major Powell was full of bull, but that was his assignment."[7]

The Old Orange Grove String Band

While Red Barber had no training in radio when he started at WRUF, he had been entertaining audiences successfully since high school. Although denied a career as a blackface end man comic when J. A. Coburn's minstrel company closed, Barber could tell a joke, do a dance—not of much value in radio—and even, in a pinch, sweetly croon out a song or two. But that was in front of a live audience. Radio had no audience—at least no audience he could see and whose feedback could help shape his performance. Other than a few part-timers and chief announcer Ralph Nimmons, WRUF had no experienced voices. The station filled much of its airtime with the reading of agricultural reports and news items from local papers and, especially, by playing 78 rpm recordings.

Most of Red's initial work was as a "disc jockey," long before the term was coined. The needles on the turntables required changing so frequently that Barber developed a callus on his thumb from turning the screw that held the needle in place.[8] To expand the programming mix, Barber repurposed his minstrel show material for WRUF. While there was no money for an actual variety show, Barber could offer his own "play every part" material; WRUF added his "One Man Minstrel" to the schedule.

Conditions were rough at WRUF. There was no air conditioning as a respite from the brutal Florida summer heat and only a portable electric heater for winter cold snaps, when the announcers wore overcoats until the station gradually warmed up. The morning staff would tidy up the station, emptying the wastebaskets and dusting the desks.[9] WRUF also had no money for talent, but fortunately for the station, some local performers would work for no money. The station, however, acquired a large new facility in 1928. It housed two (and later three) studios, one of which was large enough for a small band and a small audience.

Local and visiting musical performers would ask for airtime to promote an upcoming concert. Many of these groups were quite good, some including African American musicians and singers. While WRUF and the University of Florida were strictly segregated, the station welcomed African American musicians and entertainers to perform over its airways, especially if they worked for free. For example, in 1930 the quartet of the Florida Normal and Industrial Institute for Negroes offered comics, jubilees, and plantation melodies to WRUF's audience.[10] Later in his life, Barber remembered "any number of traveling bands that were comprised of black musicians" and recalled that Ralph Nimmons brought the African American Bethune Cookman College Choir to the station. Red stood "in the studio listening to them; they were marvelous voices."[11] The station, he said, "didn't identify them as Negro" over the air. A generation later, when he made his historic call of Jackie Robinson's first game in the Major Leagues, Barber again refrained from calling attention to race, perhaps channeling his experience at WRUF.[12]

The station, however, could not rely completely upon visiting acts. Sometimes both their reliability and their talent were poor, providing little to promote and nothing upon which to build a steady audience. Local groups with some talent would be a better solution. They could appear each week or several times a week and become part of the station's image. In 1929 one such group walked through the WRUF doors: a "hillbilly" band led by Mack Criswell, a fiddle-playing army sergeant assigned to the university's ROTC. The group had another fiddle player, Ray Pierce; a female banjo player, Mrs. Al Duke; and a Hawaiian guitarist, Joey Williams. Lloyd Parks worked the mouth organ and guitar. Others would occasionally join the group, which "played strictly by ear." Red thought the "little band was unlettered, untrained, and fairly untalented" but did not lack "enthusiasm."[13] The players were all working folks who had no time for rehearsals, but the more they played, the better they got.

When Red joined the show, the group had no name and no vocalist. Barber supplied both, calling it "the Old Orange Grove String Band" and designating himself its singer. Red was not cut out to be a soloist, but it did not matter. He just added a voice and the lyrics to familiar tunes like "Coming around the Mountain" and "Casey Jones." But significant for his future broadcasting career, Red learned how to adjust his speaking style to his audience and the message, dropping his poor imitations of the formal announcers he'd heard on WLW and other stations. Instead, Red adopted a more casual "folksy, cracker sort of thing of just kind of leaning over the back fence visiting."[14] With his participation, Red's newly named band began receiving some good press and lots of fan mail: "Red Barber has certainly brought out the Orange Grove String Band, appearing twice each week over Station WRUF. Red makes the program interesting, and we never thought we would wait for a program from a 'barnyard' orchestra, but we do."[15] Over four decades later Barber would write that at WRUF, he "was better known for announcing the Old Orange Grove String Band than I was for calling the first downs, fumbles, and touchdowns."[16]

"The Worst Broadcast Ever Perpetrated on an Innocent Radio Audience"

Sportscasters remember their first broadcast of a game, likely recalling their errors more vividly than their hits, and Red Barber's first grid game broadcast was no exception. The host and occasional singer on the popular Old Orange Grove String Band program was a listeners' favorite, inflating the ego of the young announcer. He seemed to broadcast everything with ease—classical music, news, sports analysis, children's shows, and his admired "One Man Minstrel." With success came confidence. So when WRUF's talented sports announcer Jack Thompson was called home by his father to take his intended place in the elder's successful law firm, Barber nominated himself to replace him. Major Powell, who realized that Barber was now his best broadcaster, quickly agreed.

On September 27, 1930, Barber broadcast his first football game, and his first sports event, at Fleming Field in Gainesville, a contest between the Florida Southern Moccasins from Lakeland and the University of Florida Gators. He was unprepared to describe the "organized chaos" that was about to unfold. Barber "didn't have enough sense or knowledge to get a program and some pencils, let alone do any preparation," assuming "you just sat down by a microphone and talked about a football game."[17] Barber struggled to identify the players and often could not tell his listeners who was carrying the ball or making the tackles. According to the charitable reporter for the student newspaper, "Red was doing pretty well for the way he had to do it. Trying to catch the plays, the players, naming the substitutions, estimating the yardage, keeping track of the downs, calling off the penalties and reeling off a line of patter at the same time."[18] But Barber's boss, Major Powell, was unimpressed with Red's maiden sportscast. After the debacle, Powell told Barber, "I think we'll let Ralph Nimmons do the next game." Barber agreed: "I messed up the broadcast. I suffered, and a lot of other people suffered." Red Barber was "burning with embarrassment" over what he called "the worst broadcast ever perpetrated on an innocent radio audience."[19]

Major Powell made good on his promise, and chief announcer Nimmons called the next game against North Carolina State, but Powell was not satisfied with his effort. Next up was Red's close friend, Jimmy Butsch, who covered the game against Auburn. Again, Powell was unimpressed. So he gave the nod to a local movie theater owner and sometime entertainer, Claude Lee, who had been a Florida player. Lee was part of the "Bud and Easy" program on WRUF, the station's own version of "Amos 'n Andy," but he had always wanted a chance to call a game.[20] The *Florida Alligator* sports reporter panned Lee's call of the next game against Furman University for interjecting his "Bud and Easy" act during the height of the game action: "I could hear the crowds yelling and the bands playing, and I know something good was being pulled and I wanted to hear about it."[21]

Having run through his staff and one amateur, a desperate Powell next looked inward for a solution. He decided that he personally would announce the team's fifth game at the University of Chicago from wire reports. The major, an excellent judge of radio talent and a politically savvy administrator, was not a confident announcer; he was plagued by a fear that his false teeth would slip in his mouth during a broadcast. But motivated by his initial failure, Barber had been studying the Florida football team, learning not just the players' names, but also their backgrounds and performance tendencies. He enlisted the help of assistant coach Nash Higgins, who provided scouting reports on Florida's opponents. Powell, eager to avoid taking the mic, was easy to convince. He assured Red, "If Nash Higgins thinks you should get another shot at announcing the Gators, that settles it."[22]

Red's response to his poor performance in his first football broadcast triggered a lifelong commitment to intense preparation for each sports event he covered. In *The Broadcasters*, Barber made preparation the first of his "six serving-men" that every sportscaster must rely upon. He often said that 75 percent of the work in a broadcast is preparation for a game.[23] For the Chicago game, Barber's advance football research and conversations with Nash Higgins fueled a dramatic improvement. But the young red-head also enjoyed a much easier production environment. Since the game information came from a Western Union summary, the broadcast took place in the studio where there would be no game-day noise or distraction. Barber could concentrate, use written notes, and have all the basic information fed to him by the tele-graph summary. He could play to his strengths—a vivid imagi-nation, strong memory, quick wit, and brilliant verbal skills—to enhance the bare-bones telegraph information. According to one newspaper, Red's improvement was dramatic: "By unanimous vote of football fans Red Barber, one of the WRUF announcers, breaks in the Hall of Fame. Everybody agrees he is the best ever with that Scotch-Irish wit of his; he was half the show in the Gator triumph against Chicago yesterday."[24]

According to Barber, WRUF received two hundred congratula-tory telegrams after the game, including one from the governor's mansion.[25] Earning the praise of those in prominent places, Bar-ber's re-creation also cemented his place as the station's sports-caster. Major Powell's false teeth would not be slipping before a WRUF microphone, at least not during Gators football games. But Barber, who still had not successfully called a live game from his home field, still had kinks to work out. In the next Gators home game against a powerhouse Alabama team, Barber would learn, painfully, a crucial lesson that he would remember for the rest of his sport broadcasting career.

"Eleven of the Biggest Men I Ever Saw"

The Alabama game was played at the newly opened Florida Field in Gainesville. For the first time Barber had a dedicated spotter and a spotting chart of his own design. He knew the Bama team members by name and performance but could not visually iden-tify the players, who did not wear numbers on their uniforms. Bar-ber appealed to Alabama coach Wallace Wade, who, after some jawboning, offered an injured third-string guard to spot for the Gators' announcer. Barber updated the spotting chart he had created after the Florida Southern fiasco. He penciled in the Florida players' names, and his spotter added the Crimson Tide tags. College football had limited substitution in those days; players removed from a game remained on the bench until the next quarter, making it easier for an announcer to keep up with player changes.

Once the game began, all seemed well. The spotter pointed to Alabama players' names as they became part of the action. Thoroughly prepared, Barber could handle the Gators' eleven with ease, even as the game began by turning into an unexpectedly close contest. Florida was holding its own against an Alabama team that was a four-touchdown favorite, advancing early within the shadow of the visitors' goal line. Barber remembered telling his audience, "Folks, it looks like a great upset in the making here. The Gators are pushing the vaunted Crimson Tide all over the field."[26]

But the Gators' surge was short-lived. After a timeout, Red was stunned when "eleven of the biggest men I ever saw" entered the game for Alabama. Barber's spotter had not noticed that Coach Wade had started his *second* team, keeping his dominating regulars on the bench. When Red saw the new Alabama eleven entering the game, he looked at his spotter, who had "turned a rather pale shade of green." The spotter quickly admitted his error, and Red humbly confessed to his listeners, "Friends, the Alabama first team is just coming into the game now. Everything I've said about them earlier this afternoon, please forget I said it." Alabama's starters cruised to a 20–0 victory. Despite his improvements, Barber's preparation still had been incomplete. He would never again depend solely on spotters to identify even the visiting players. The spotter would help with speedier identifications, but Barber would know the players as well. Red also concluded that he had not seen the spotter's mistake earlier because he wanted his Gators to "push the vaunted Crimson Tide all over the field." His emotions had affected his perceptions. While preparation was the first of Barber's six serving-men, on that day he would add impartiality to the list.

Chastened and motivated by his grave error, Red received excellent reviews of his work for the rest of the 1930 season. According to the *Tampa Bay Times*, "The Sanford lad certainly did himself proud and we hope that the sorrel-topped youngster will be used in other sports broadcasts from the Gainesville station. Red's quaint southern dialect, and the scores of humorous exclamations kept our radio matinee from becoming just another football broadcast."[27] Another paper opined that Barber's "descriptions of Florida's football games this fall have attracted unusual attention and there are many folks who are ready to put 'Red' Barber on the boards as the All-American Announcer of 1930."[28] His football game reports were so popular that Major Powell assigned him to do that year's Notre Dame–Army game from wire reports, a harbinger of things to come. Barber would cover Notre Dame in person for the first time in 1935 and broadcast every Irish game in 1936. Red's football broadcasts continued to impress his listeners throughout the 1931 season.

As fall 1932 approached, Barber and his listeners eagerly anticipated a new season of Gators football broadcasts. But the Southern Conference leadership had other ideas. Attendance at conference games had declined, likely because of the deepening economic depression, but the conference blamed radio coverage for suppressing attendance. Although it could not control the Great Depression, the conference could eliminate live game broadcasts, and it did. The university's student newspaper was aghast that Barber would no longer broadcast live games. It saw an immediate threat to WRUF's state funding during difficult economic times. "With Red Barber's sports announcing the finest and most distinctive single asset of the state-owned station, it is evident WRUF will be hit as hard by the Conference ruling as any other of the many stations affected."[29]

Barber shifted his focus to a weekly forecast and analysis program. To increase his audience, he worked a deal with WJAX, a much more powerful station in a much larger market, that would bring Red to Jacksonville once a week for a "Football Talk" on Wednesday evenings from 10:15 to 10:30. Barber's pay was bus fare there and back, but his motive was personal, not financial. The gig enabled him to visit weekly with Lylah, now director of student nurses at Riverside Hospital in Jacksonville. Despite the Southern Conference ban, interest in Gators football was high, and Red's informed football commentary received much broader exposure.

WRUF covered what sports it could, including Florida's football practices, re-creations of football road games, college boxing, and the most important U.S. sports event of the year: the World Series. Barber would do his first live broadcast of the fall classic in 1935, but his first World Series experience would be his re-creation of the 1931 clash between the Philadelphia Athletics and St. Louis Cardinals. Barber broadcast the third game of the series, and "the telegraphic report the station received was only thirty seconds behind radio reports broadcast directly from the scene of the action."[30] When coverage of Gators games returned, WJAX in Jacksonville took WRUF's feed.[31]

Since the radio boycott affected only Southern Conference games, Barber still could broadcast live from Florida Field the Gators' match against a non-conference opponent, UCLA, in the next-to-last game of the season. One reporter noted that Barber "did so well that those who will not be able to attend the contests next year should anticipate with a great deal of pleasure the lifting of the radio ban."[32]

With the depression at its depths, WRUF's costs to the state were under scrutiny. In early 1933 Russell Kay, secretary of the Florida Press Association, wrote that it looked like "Florida was about to lose her 'Voice,' but a state Senate committee decided that instead of hittin' WRUF over the head with an axe, maybe if we just operate on her tonsils and nurse her along a little, it might be a better idea." Kay saw the station as "a first-class pain in the neck to the average radio listener," with too little power to reach enough of Florida to serve the state or even the region. But football broadcasts may have saved the day. "The only time WRUF was really popular with a lot of people was when they were broadcastin' the foot-ball games with Red Barber at the mike. Give that boy a mike with some power behind it and he'll popularize that station."[33]

More Than Football

While Gators football brought the most attention, Barber broadcast many sports during his University of Florida days, including semipro, college, and American Legion baseball; college boxing; college and high school football; and high school basketball. Basketball was his toughest assignment by far. The game itself was no problem, but Barber's task was not to cover single games but the entire Florida state high school basketball tournament. This job meant broadcasting ten games over two days with breaks only for lunch and dinner.[34] Although young and certainly full of energy, Barber described the basketball marathon as "the most grueling broadcasting job I have ever had. I used to be physically sick by the time the tournament was over. . . . I have never liked the game since."[35] He executed this form of announcing hell in 1931, 1932, and 1933. When Barber left WRUF in March 1934, he was relieved that he would never have to cover the tournament again.

While he never covered Major or Minor League baseball over WRUF, Barber, as noted, broadcast semipro, college, and American Legion games. In 1933 he broadcast a full season of the Gainesville team in the semipro Northeast Florida Baseball League, which played on Tuesdays and Sundays. Barber's partner was Earl Blue, a sportswriter and former business manager of the league's St. Augustine team. Red did the play-by-play, and Blue added the color. Blue also scored the game for the two broadcasters. The duo developed a weekly WRUF program focused on the league called the "Red and Blue Hook-Up," a reference to both their names and the two NBC networks, the Red and the Blue.[36]

Game broadcasts were usually from Gainesville, but Barber did a live Fourth of July broadcast from Jacksonville in an era where road broadcasts were rare even for Major League teams.[37]

Another road game came from St. Augustine, with the production costs covered by the Gainesville Chamber of Commerce and local businesses.[38] Red's baseball broadcasts made a lasting impression; his papers at the University of Florida include a fan letter written fifty years after the fact. The widow of Gainesville catcher P. S. McEachern wrote to Red in 1982 to tell him that her late husband mentioned Barber's name "with almost reverence" and "surely thought an awful lot" of him. She wanted to let him know about "one more star in [his] crown."[39]

"Something about Your Case . . . 'Isn't Right'"

In his first three years at WRUF, Barber became the station's most valuable announcer, handling each new program format with relative ease. He could shift his style from the formal announcements needed for classical music to the "cracker" homespun patter that made the Old Orange Grove String Band the station's most popular program. He quickly moved from part-time announcer to the station's featured sportscaster. In early 1931, when WRUF's chief announcer, Ralph Nimmons, left the station to take a job at WBIG in Greensboro, North Carolina, Major Powell offered the position, with its salary of $150 a month, to his most popular and versatile announcer. It was enough money for him to quit school and marry Lylah Scarborough. But Red Barber's rise to the top of WRUF's staff, and perhaps even his marriage to Lylah, almost never happened. As he hitchhiked to Gainesville from Sanford in the summer of 1930, just a few months after starting at WRUF, he experienced an excruciating pain that felt like "someone had gotten his fingers in the socket and had grabbed [his] eye and was very slowly and diabolically pulling it out by the roots."[40]

Barber dropped to the roadside, laying in agony as cars sped by. Blessed with excellent health, this pain was like nothing he had ever experienced: "It went down my right cheekbone, past my right ear, into my right temple," and it did not subside until after an hour of torture.[41] When he got to Gainesville, Barber went to the university infirmary, and the staff referred him to a local ear, nose, and throat specialist. The doctor treated Barber by shrinking his sinus tissue, but the pain, just as intense as during the first attack, recurred every couple of days. Red became anxious, obsessively anticipating his next attack. He sought privacy, so he stayed in his room, except for visits to the doctor.

Barber's doctor was perplexed and recommended that Red see a neurologist in Jacksonville.[42] Barber had no car, but Major Powell generously drove him to his appointment. The physician's examination convinced him that Red was suffering from tic douloureux, a condition that caused twitching and "as severe a pain as medical science knew."[43] He concluded Red had to go to Johns Hopkins University Hospital in Baltimore to see a highly regarded surgeon, Dr. Walter Danby, who had developed a surgical procedure to end the pain by removing the nerve that was producing it. Red's neurologist procured an appointment for him to see Danby, Red's father arranged for complementary rail transportation to Baltimore, and Barber made his first trip north. Red had not yet informed Lylah of his condition, but while she was interning at Cook County Hospital in Chicago, he mailed her a description of his ailment. When she consulted with her hospital's resident specialists, they provided a much more detailed and frightening picture of what Dr. Dandy's nerve surgery would mean, a prognosis that she passed onto Red.

The surgery would end the pain, but removal of the nerve would dramatically alter Red's appearance and likely his professional future. Removal of the nerve would reduce muscular control on the right side of Red's face. His face would wilt; his mouth would slump; and his speech, the source of his radio talents, would be labored. His radio career would be over. In time he would likely lose his right eye from infections that he could no longer sense. The handsome, curly-haired young man who had won Lylah's heart would be disfigured and disabled for life.

When Barber got to Baltimore, he was in "complete despair." The expected side effects of the surgery were severe, but the pain was unbearable. Red decided that if it did not stop, he did not intend to live: "I could not continue to live with that pain." When Red finally saw Dr. Danby, he experienced another attack during the examination. The results seemed to confirm the Jacksonville neurologist's diagnosis, tic douloureux, but Dr. Danby ordered more tests to be sure. Although Barber's symptoms showed a classic case of the condition, there was one oddity: the affliction had never been diagnosed in anyone under forty. Red was twenty-two.

While Red was waiting for his surgery, a young woman who worked for the hospital's library service brought the deeply depressed Barber a copy of *Fortitude*, a formulaic but inspirational novel by Hugh Walpole. The book's central message was just what Red needed to hear. Walpole argued that "it isn't life itself that matters so much as the courage we bring to it." We exhibit true courage when we fully understand the risk and potential pain that may come from actions we feel obligated to take, but we boldly take them, nevertheless. Barber saw a parallel to Hamlet's call "to take arms against a sea of trouble and by opposing end them." If he had the courage to resist his despair, even though facing a life-changing setback, he could at least master his emotional pain.

Just a few days before Red's scheduled surgery, Dr. Briggs, a junior resident and Dr. Danby's surgical assistant, came by to see Barber. Briggs was deeply worried because he believed there was something about Red's case that wasn't right. He offered Red some off-the-record advice that would cost him his residency if word of it ever got back to Danby. After impressing upon Barber that the surgery was a "maiming operation," Briggs told him there were strong reasons for doubting that Red had tic douloureux, particularly because there had been no recurrence of his attacks in two weeks. He advised the patient to leave the hospital quietly and return to Florida; he could come back if he suffered another attack. Barber followed his advice, and the insufferable pain on the right side of his face never returned.

Two years later Red was drinking a glass of ice water and felt a pain in his front teeth nearly as intense as his earlier facial agony. X-rays revealed two large abscesses above his upper front teeth on the right side of his face. Barber's dentist removed the teeth along with the abscesses that had been developing for some time. Despite extensive testing by his doctors in Jacksonville and at Johns Hopkins, none had ordered X-rays of his teeth. The pain attacks likely stopped when the abscesses had eaten through the nerve that was causing his suffering. His happy fortune was that the abscesses numbed the nerve just before the surgeon's knife made its permanent cut. Rotten teeth were the "something" that Briggs had felt wasn't right.

"The Broadcasting Friend of Yours from Down South"

Working at WRUF gradually transformed Red Barber from reluctant employee to local radio star. But early on he recognized the station's limitations. Funding from the state would always be as inadequate as the station's 5,000 watts of power and daytime-only status. After a day's work at WRUF, Red and his colleague and friend Jimmy Butsch spent many evenings listening to high-powered stations. They were especially fond of WLW in Cincinnati, a regional powerhouse that did much of its own programming live and had the resources of a major network: orchestras, singers, performers, writers, and directors. Barber was fond of their announcers, including Robert Brown and Milton Cross. When he first started at WRUF, the insecure young broadcaster would imitate, rather poorly, his more formal announcing idols. The entertaining young man known to his friends as "Red" would tell his audience, "This is Walter Barber announcing." Major Powell took him aside one day and offered him some career-saving advice: "You're not a very good somebody else. . . . Stop saying 'This is Walter Barber announcing.' You stop being Robert Brown and Milton Cross. Just go in there and be Red Barber." Barber believed Powell's "be yourself" was the best broadcasting advice he'd ever received. Later in his life, it would be the first directive he offered aspiring broadcasting students.[44]

Having become head announcer at twenty-three, Barber realized he had reached the top at WRUF. He started searching for better career opportunities after he married Lylah in 1931. It was the nadir of the Great Depression; announcing positions were rare, and most stations were laying off personnel. Nevertheless, Barber made the rounds to Atlanta, Charlotte, Louisville, Cincinnati, and Chicago. Ralph Nimmons, the chief announcer whom Barber had replaced at WRUF, had moved to WBIG in Greensboro, North Carolina, then to WHAS in Louisville, and had finally landed in the announcers' mecca, WLW in Cincinnati. Nimmons's success convinced Barber that the right announcer could move up, and after finding his voice at WRUF, Red was eager to succeed in a more competitive arena. To save the cost of a hotel, Red would ride the bus all night, stop by a barber shop to get cleaned up—a bath, shave, and shoeshine were available at many shops—and audition at as many stations as would see him. The stations usually gave him an audition but told him there was no opening. Still, after each trip, he would send follow-up letters that included humorous stories, using his considerable writing skills to keep his name fresh in the station manager's mind.

Red struggled most with his auditions in Chicago. He arrived ill-suited for the weather, and the people crush of the nation's second largest city stymied him. As Barber later recalled, "I wasn't used to a big, vigorous, driving place like Chicago. . . . I had linen clothes on that were alright for Florida, but in Chicago my teeth actually rattled, I was so cold."[45] The Windy City, however, was hardly as cold as the receptionists at the major radio stations. The gatekeeper at WGN told Red that, as the station had no positions, it would not bother to audition him, nor could he even meet with anyone. His reception was not much better at WBBM, the CBS station. He got to talk with a staff member who told him the station had just let an announcer go and that it was too late for an audition that day. Next, Barber walked across the bridge over the Chicago River to the Merchandise Mart, at the time the world's largest building by volume. He wanted to audition for the NBC station, WMAQ. The NBC receptionist greeted him coolly, a reaction that, by now, he expected in Chicago. She would call no one to see him, wouldn't take his name, and directed him to return to the elevator he'd just left. Red entered the elevator, but instead of going "down and out," he pushed the "up" button that took him to the next floor of NBC's offices. He needed a strategy that would guarantee a more effective entry into the National Broadcasting Company. Ascending, he thought of one: just lie.

This time Barber asked the receptionist if he could see an old friend of his, Robert Brown, the announcer he had tried, unsuccessfully, to imitate at WRUF. Just before Brown had migrated to NBC in Chicago, Barber heard his final program on WLW announcing his move. Red figured that he must be somewhere in the building. The receptionist smiled and summoned Mr. Brown. Barber introduced himself to the announcer as "the broadcasting friend of yours from down South. Let's get out of here for a minute and talk." Once Barber confessed his deception, Brown laughed, offered him a cup of coffee, and then invited him to meet the program head, Clarence Menzer, who told Barber the familiar story. The station had laid off many others, had no openings, and expected none soon. But if Red would come back after lunch, he would give him the full NBC audition. The audition was thorough and demanding, but when it was over, Menzer told him, "Your audition was fine. I don't know where you're going to end up. I know that you're ambitious and impatient and burning to get someplace. . . . You go back to Florida and keep working at that station, keep job-hunting, and don't let anybody discourage you. You are not only going to be an announcer. You *are* an announcer."[46] Barber felt he had earned the seal of approval from the greatest power in radio, the National Broadcasting Company. He returned to Florida more confident. Chicago had roughed him up but had not broken him.

Red was so encouraged that once he got back to Gainesville, he bought himself a new wardrobe, all on credit. Though lacking funds for a stylish wardrobe in his youth, throughout his adult life Red was a meticulous dresser, conscious of always appearing well put together from head to toe; later in Barber's career, his

Dodgers broadcast producer, Tom Villante, observed that Red "was always a terrific dresser . . . he wore clothes very, very well— had beautiful ties."[47] For his Gainesville shopping spree after his encouraging NBC audition in Chicago, Red bought a new linen suit, brown and white shoes, shirts, ties, and new underwear. He would look his very best at his next audition. And that performance would be at the station he still most idolized, despite two previously unsuccessful appearances: WLW in Cincinnati.

PART 2

CINCINNATI

Big Break

5

Pay Cut

Young though not inexperienced, Barber arrived in Cincinnati as a talented but little-known broadcaster. He left it as a regional celebrity with a solid national reputation and a touch of arrogance. The Queen City years were filled with long days and diverse assignments at the nation's first true superstation. In May 1934, a few months after Barber's arrival, industrialist Powell Crosley convinced the Federal Radio Commission to allow WLW to boost its power to 500,000 watts, ten times the strength of any other radio station in the country. Its signal could reach most of the continental United States, making WLW, at least in coverage, a national network. Crosley also owned WSAI, WLW's lower-powered sister station in Cincinnati. During his years in Cincinnati, Barber would split his work between the two stations: baseball broadcasts on WSAI and football broadcasts on WLW.

Many years later, after reading a profile of Barber, Chet Thomas, who had hired him, un-hired him, and then rehired him to Crosley Broadcasting, wrote Barber to explain the station's past mixed messaging. When Thomas, a year younger than Barber, first heard Red broadcast a game on a super sensitive receiver provided by Crosley to help him scout for announcing talent, he recognized the play-by-play announcer as the young man in the "white linen suit" who had auditioned earlier at WLW. Thomas was impressed and wrote Barber that if he ever came to Cincinnati, he should audition again at WLW. When Barber arrived only ten days later, Thomas's receptionist told him there was a young man waiting for him dressed in a panama hat, a light-weight suit, two-tone shoes, and without an overcoat. The temperature that day in Cincinnati was near zero with ice and snow everywhere. Perhaps wondering if this young fellow was just too naïve for WLW, the secretary asked Thomas if he still wanted to see him. He did, and during the audition he was struck by Barber's sports knowledge and the "interesting way in which [he] expressed [himself]." But Red's "rather broad southern accent" concerned him. Barber reminded Thomas of Bill Munday, an announcer with a strong deep Southern drawl who had faded fast after his popularity peaked. Thomas believed it was because "his accent made it rather difficult to understand what he was saying."[1] In fact Munday's fall was from alcohol abuse. When Barber began producing the *College Football Roundup* in the late 1940s and early 1950s, he would hire Munday and help resurrect his career.

Red auditioned three times for WLW, traveling to Cincinnati at his own expense. The auditions were for a general announcer's position, not for a sportscaster. Crosley Broadcasting had no plans to broadcast live sports. The standard audition included reading the names of places and people, some challenging to pronounce, and voicing several commercials previously used on WLW. Usually the auditions were private, but Barber's last one at WLW was a true cattle call: the station tested thirty announcers, each requested to read a couple of commercials.[2] Like Barber, most of these men were experienced announcers; still Barber stood out. After the contest Barber got the response he had been pursuing for three years through many auditions: big-time radio wanted to give him a chance. Chet Thomas wanted him to start immediately, but Red believed Major Powell and WRUF deserved the customary two-week notice before he left his radio cradle. During those two weeks, WLW changed its mind.

Chet Thomas wanted to wait those two weeks for Barber, but management above him wanted the announcer slot filled immediately. Lylah Barber woke her husband from an early afternoon nap to give him the telegram. Instead of confirming his hire, it read, "REGRET DUE TO CHANGE IN CONDITIONS JOB NO LONGER OPEN, CHET THOMAS."[3] The frustration of three auditions, leading only to a revoked job offer, enraged Red. He proceeded to do what a novice with no leverage should ever do: he wrote Thomas a nasty letter. Barber remembers ending the letter as follows: "Chet, you lied to me. I am glad, painful though it is, to find out the type of person you are and the type of organization you represent and to learn that I don't want to work for either one of you. Yours truly, Red Barber."[4] When Chet Thomas read Barber's letter, he was flooded not with anger but with guilt. A more experienced man might have buried Barber's application and possibly Red's career on the spot. But Thomas knew what the WLW job meant to a college radio announcer. He had reneged on an offer to a talented, motivated, and clearly worthy young broadcaster. Barber later learned from Thomas's secretary that he vowed to give Red the next available announcer slot.[5] Red was about to ask Major Powell to ignore his resignation, when, on March 4, 1934, he unexpectedly heard from Thomas again.

By this point, Larry MacPhail had convinced the Crosley management to promote the company's recently acquired Major League team on the radio, a change requiring a play-by-play announcer. Barber had experience broadcasting baseball games but no Major or Minor League experience. Despite this deficiency, in its 1933 edition, Who's Who in Major League Baseball published a brief biography of the young man it called "The Red-Headed Announcer" in its catalog of baseball broadcasters.[6] His inclusion in this Who's Who was prescient. The Cincinnati Reds needed a baseball announcer, and Chet Thomas needed to purge his guilt. When Barber read Thomas's second wire—"WILL YOU DO CINCINNATI REDS GAMES TWENTY FIVE DOLLARS A WEEK,

CHET THOMAS"—he had no second thoughts. He wired back, "YES, WIRE INSTRUCTIONS, RED BARBER."[7]

Barber proudly reported his big break to his father, but William Barber was shocked to learn that the "good" news meant his son's salary would drop from $50 to $25 a week. The elder Barber had worked all his life to increase his income and responsibility, starting as a locomotive fireman and becoming an engineer with a small but secure pension. He admonished his oldest son: "I am aghast. You have no sense. Have I raised a son who is going to an uncertain job in a strange part of the country, an expensive part of the country, and leaving his wife home alone *for twenty-five dollars a week*? . . . Can you tell me *why*?"[8] Red offered a five-word explanation: "Because I want the chance." William Barber wanted home and security; his twenty-six-year-old son wanted a profession. The young man preferred his father's earlier, more inspiring advice: "It's a big world and it is all yours. All you have to do is go out and get it."[9]

Barber was told to go to the Reds' spring training camp in Tampa and ask for Scotty Ruston, who would get him started. When he asked for Scotty *Ruston*, he was told that he was really looking for Scotty *Reston*. Reston was a successful amateur golfer from Ohio whom Larry MacPhail had brought to his new team to serve as road secretary. Reston and Barber became friends, and in Red's early Cincinnati days, Lylah would often cook dinner for the three of them at the Barbers' apartment. After buying the Reds, Powell Crosley changed the name of Redland Field to Crosley Field and put a replica of a Crosley Shelvador refrigerator at the top of its scoreboard. Reston thought both changes were bad ideas and said so publicly. Annoyed by opinionated young Reston's criticism, Crosley pressured MacPhail to sack him. MacPhail instead protected him, telling Crosley, "If he goes, I go with him."[10] Scotty Reston soon left Crosley for a job with the Associated Press in New York. He would gain fame as the *New York Times* columnist James Reston, who helped negotiate the end of the Cuban missile crisis, pulling the world back from the brink of nuclear war. Barber and Reston would maintain a life-long professional friendship.

Red spent only a week getting to know the Reds manager and players in spring training, departing before they played any games. He arrived in Cincinnati in early March 1934, weeks before the season started. His visit to the Reds' spring training camp and arrival at WSAI was noted in *Radio Dial*, which reported that his Gainesville "football, baseball, polo, boxing and motor-boat racing broadcasts ... won for him the title of 'the south's most popular sports announcer.'"[11] Barber's hiring also brought him his first photo and notice in *The Sporting News*.[12] Red's first residence was a room at the local YMCA, and his chow houses were among Cincinnati's cheapest. He hated his dreary quarters, where, he tells us, he was really alone and lonely for the first time. But on twenty-five dollars a week, he could not afford to bring Lylah to Cincinnati, where they could begin furnishing their own private nest. He soon felt compelled to ask for a modest five dollar per week increase. The raise was granted, and it was just enough. Shortly before the start of the baseball season, Lylah arrived, and his spartan YMCA days were over. By the end of his first year, Red's salary returned to the fifty dollars per week he had been earning when he left WRUF. While not yet a radio star, he at least had broken even financially on his bold career move.

When Lylah was riding the train to join Red in Cincinnati, it occurred to her that "the rituals of [their] life soon would be shaken and changed." The first major change was Red's choice of "a small, one-room efficiency." Lylah was more intrigued than dismayed because one set of double doors opened "into a pullman kitchen, and the other hid a pull-down double bed, neither of which [she] had ever seen before." She loved "the residential, tree-shaded section of Cincinnati," where the apartment was located, within walking distance of the radio station. Units in the brand-new building were "attractively furnished with spacious baths and the place was filled with young people, many from the radio station ... rather like a superior dormitory with no restrictions." It would serve their needs until Red's next raise afforded "more spacious quarters."[13]

Opening Day for the Reds came shortly after Lylah's arrival, and she sensed the citywide excitement. That day she stayed at the apartment by the radio so that she could critique her husband's first performance in Cincinnati, a role she played consistently throughout his career. During their first summer in Cincinnati, Lylah had a pass "to sit in the row of seats on the mezzanine where Red did his broadcasting—a five-cent streetcar ride and [her] pass got [her] into the game. The price was right." She attended many home games that first season, sitting in the press box, close enough to hear Red's announcing: "The games became my entertainment and my escape from the confinement of the one-room apartment."[14]

Though hired to broadcast baseball, Red's job entailed much more mundane tasks. His twenty-five dollars a week was for being a staff announcer; his baseball announcing was seasonal work. Most days he did routine announcements during the station breaks in network programs. Barber read, "This is WSAI, the Crosley Broadcasting Corporation, in Cincinnati" and then waited fifteen minutes for his next "big" announcement.[15] But the dull routine gave Barber plenty of time for his favorite activity: reading. The station provided Red with newspapers from every National League city, all of which he read. Though a Major League novice, Barber knew all the players and developed a solid background on every team by Opening Day of 1934.

Once the season started, Barber's duties expanded to include a fifteen-minute summary of the Reds' game of the day, along with other baseball news, that aired at 6:35, Monday to Saturday. By season's end, McCann-Erickson Advertising, which represented the program's sponsor, told WSAI that "these sports resumes have been well received by listeners in Cincinnati. We have also been told that Red Barber's work has been very well done."[16]

"The Biggest Game I Ever Broadcast"

Red called it his biggest game because it was his *first* game and his toughest test. It was not just the *first Major League game* he had ever broadcast but the *first professional regular season game he had ever seen*! While he had learned the National League teams for his first time at a Major League mic, Red had neglected to learn how to score and still needed help. In time Barber would become an expert scorer and even publish an article, "How to Score," for a baseball collection credited to Joe DiMaggio.[17] He also included a brief chapter on scoring in his book *The Broadcasters*. In Cincinnati, Barber did not work the game in a comfortable broadcast booth—the Reds had none—but from a box seat on the upper deck of the newly renamed Crosley Field.

On Opening Day, Tuesday, April 17, 1934, Barber felt anxious:— "Beads of sweat [were] in the palms of my hands as big as chinaberries." But he still felt well prepared for his first contest between the previous season's last-place Reds and third-place Chicago Cubs.[18] His bosses at Crosley, however, were not as certain. Barber was hired to do baseball only because long-time sports commentator Colonel Bob Newhall did not want to call games, preferring to work from a script. Red was a pup, an unknown, so the station sent its top announcer, Peter Grant, to sit behind him, prepared to take over as "relief announcer" if the young redhead lost his verbal fastball. Barber knew he must pass inspection, but once the broadcast began, he focused on the action and quickly forgot his overseer. By the fifth inning Barber's scorer, Elton Parks, told him, "Peter is going back to the station."[19] Red knew he had passed his field test.

The game itself protracted the pattern of good fortune that Barber enjoyed during his early career. While an Opening Day game broadcast on a station new to baseball certainly aroused interest, the contest provided the rookie announcer with an even more powerful attention sustainer: a near no-hitter. Cubs starter Lon Warneke kept the Reds hitless for eight innings. Likely unaware of the unwritten rule that discouraged announcers from calling attention to a developing "no-no," Barber fully exploited the suspense of the building drama by pointing it out. In the ninth, Reds left fielder Adam Comorosky singled and the drama ended, but wsai's first and future most famous baseball announcer had taken his audience on a great ride. Warneke completed his one-hit, two-walk performance, and the Cubs took the Reds, 6–0, on the opening day of Red Barber's Major League career.

Feedback on his inaugural effort was immediate and positive. While praise was sometimes a rare commodity in the competitive environment of Depression-era radio, Barber reported that Bill Stoess, musical director and key player at Crosley Broadcasting, told him, "That was a great job. That was a ball game." Others at the station "went out of their way to say nice things." Show business bible *Variety* also reviewed the game, reporting that Barber was "a rapid-fire spieler and displays familiarity with the pastime. Always saying something, he hands out descriptive and statistical dope between pitches and plays." *Variety* applauded Red for his grammar but also critiqued his "constant chatter and want for change of tone that wears down [listeners]."[20] Barber called Opening Day 1934 "the most joyous day of my life, next to my wedding day." He rushed home to share his triumph with Lylah, like "the hunter come home from the hill, and this hunter was loaded with meat."[21]

While the first game was a grand success, Barber's second new assignment of the day started with a tussle and ended with Barber's undying gratitude to Cubs manager Charlie Grimm. "Jolly Cholly" Grimm was an entertaining baseball lifer who moved between the Cubs manager's office and radio booth at various times in his career. Barber was fortunate to land him for his first interview because Grimm was always a great gabber and because the young redhead, in his Opening Day ignorance, broke a hallowed clubhouse rule.

For 1934 MacPhail's radio plan was to offer very limited home coverage, full coverage of road games through re-creations based on Western Union "Paragraph One" summaries, and "live from Crosley Field" interviews during all home contests—a strategy designed to bring some additional customers through the turnstiles. On Opening Day Barber learned he was scheduled to conduct a live interview that noon before his game broadcast. With little time to prepare, he went for the obvious. Reds players, coaches, and the manager would be available all season, so the best choice was to interview visiting Cubs manager Charlie Grimm. But how to get a grip on Grimm? Well, just go to the visiting clubhouse door at 11:30—a half hour before airtime—and lay a fist to it.

But Manager Grimm was fully engaged in an Opening Day meeting with his players, a ritual that reporters were not welcomed to join. Cubs trainer Andy Lotshaw—"a sloppy, loudmouthed fellow, belligerent and bellicose by nature, who satisfied his ego by hollering at people"—came to the door and told Barber that Grimm could not be interrupted.[22] As the clock moved toward high noon, Barber contemplated a first interview filled with dead air. He desperately pushed his case while Lotshaw hurled profanities, defending the sanctity of his clubhouse. As the confrontation heated, Grimm left his players' chat to check out the rumpus and ultimately agreed to meet Barber for an interview, barely five minutes before airtime. Barber had his interview, and Grimm had Barber's lasting gratitude for saving him from an Opening Day disaster. According to Barber, despite no preparation, Grimm "gave me a wonderful interview . . . without much help from me. . . . It was good because he made it good."[23]

After his Opening Day triumph and interview success, Barber returned to a typical rookie announcer's routine: regular re-creations, home game interviews, and a few actual game broadcasts. Covering the 1930s Reds was challenging but fruitful training. Winning teams are easy to cover. The players are talented, and listeners can find heroes most days. But the Reds were a bad baseball team with a limited chance of winning. In Barber's first four years in Cincinnati (1934–37), the Reds won an average of sixty-one games and finished last, sixth, fifth, and last. They were on Crosley Broadcasting's 5,000-watt WSAI, not its 500,000-watt WLW, for a good reason. Looking back on his career in 1968, Barber realized that his dedication to rigorous research and preparation took root in the Reds' failings: "I had to learn right from the beginning what that hard core of work was. I had to find out things and do things and broadcast things that were over and above the straight reporting of cheer-inducing victories."[24]

In his first season, Barber was not the best known nor the most popular baseball voice in the Queen City. Since 1930 Harry Hartman had been calling Cincinnati Reds games over WFBE (later WCPO) while simultaneously handling the public address announcements from the stands behind home plate. To do the public address announcements, Hartman switched the radio mic off and turned the PA mic on and then reversed the process to broadcast the game. Harry was short (about 5 feet 6 inches), stout (about three hundred pounds), and . . . well, hairy. On the frequent blazing hot Cincinnati summer afternoons, despite the very public setting, the rotund Hartman often removed his shirt, revealing massive amounts of dark chest hair. He was hot, and there was a simple solution. In Barber's words, "Harry was a beautifully simple man."[25] Hartman was also beloved in Cincinnati for his childlike expressions ending in the letter "o"— "socko," "whammo," and "bammo." Baseball Hall of Fame historian Lee Allen remembered Hartman from his younger days in Cincinnati: "Harry was sort of rough around the edges, it's true, and his dictionary was not thick, but he was earthy and people liked him."[26]

By the time Red arrived from Gainesville, Harry already had been recognized by *The Sporting News* as the nation's best baseball broadcaster. In 1936 it would be Harry and not his radio competitor, Red, who would win the recognition again. Barber would get his first *Sporting News* award in 1939, after he moved to New York. Harry may also have taught Red a few things. In 1990 Jack Davis, who worked at Harry's station WCPO in the 1940s, wrote Barber that "a large, jolly, jovial fellow sportscaster—bigger'n John Madden—told me that he taught YOU how to re-create a game, play-by-play, by taking it off the wire."[27] While Barber had done re-creations of both football and baseball in Gainesville, he may well have picked up a few pointers from Hartman.

Barber wrote that he cost Hartman his baseball broadcast job. "If ever an announcer had cold reasons for hating the guts of another announcer . . . it was Hartman for Barber."[28] But in fact Hartman continued doing Cincinnati Reds games for two years after Barber left for Gotham, so Barber probably cost Harry some of his popularity but not his ballcasts. While Barber believed Hartman had every reason to regard him as a young interloper on his established baseball turf, he tells us that Harry never did: "*If* Harry Hartman ever said a bitter thing, a mean thing, a snide thing, a small thing, a critical thing about me . . . I never heard about it." And given the love of gossip in the insular world of Cincinnati radio, Red would have heard.[29] In 1988 Hartman's son Gary, a pediatric oncologist, wrote Red that he "was pleased to read your kind words about [Harry]" in *The Broadcasters* and that he still possessed letters that Red "wrote on behalf of [Gary's] father many years ago."[30]

Hired to be an announcer, not just a baseball announcer, Barber on a typical game day put in two to three hours of studio announcing before he went to the ballpark. In his first two winters, he was a full-time studio announcer, six days a week, signing on the station at 6 a.m. His only break from the routine was when he covered football on Friday or Saturday. By his third year, sick of dull studio announcing, Red requested and received the opportunity to work in program production. Drawing from his work with the Old Orange Grove String Band, his announcing of classical music at WRUF, and his love of opera, Red had enough musical background to rehearse musicians and time them. After consulting with a program's music director, he would select the pieces, determine the rotation, and balance the instrumentation. Then he was on to dress rehearsals, directing the performers and giving time cues.

In October 1934 station manager John Clark programmed a new ninety-minute weekly variety show, *The Crosley Follies*, offering singing, music, drama, five-minute news segments, and style hints for women. The show featured "five individual orchestras, two dramatic sets, and a mixed chorus of 16 voices in addition to individual artists."[31] A ninety-minute live variety program this complex was, in the words of *Variety*, "a tall undertaking."[32] Clark wanted Barber to emcee it and also add a baseball segment. He wanted a new voice—a *Southern* voice. At the first airing, Barber spoke in his natural accent, only slightly Southern, prompting Clark's intervention; the Floridian who earlier had been too Southern for a job at WLW now was not nearly Southern enough for the new show. Barber quickly adjusted, but *The Crosley Follies* would last only a year. *Variety* found it a "hodge-podge routine."[33]

A Dressen Down

Two-thirds of the way through Barber's first Reds season, the team was 30-60, and Larry MacPhail had seen enough. Since he couldn't fire the team, he fired the manager, Bob O'Farrell, replacing him with Charlie (Chuck) Dressen, manager of the Nashville Vols. MacPhail knew that firing the manager wouldn't change anything immediately, and he was correct. The Reds were 21-39 under Dressen for the rest of that season. They were an old team with few stars and fewer prospects; building a farm system would take time. Barber had cultivated a good relationship with O'Farrell, starting in spring training in Tampa. When the team flew from Tampa to Cincinnati to start the season—the first time a Major League team flew—Barber's live airplane interview with the affable Reds skipper was a public relations coup.

With his friend O'Farrell gone, Barber wanted to lay the foundation for an equally good relationship with Dressen. Eventually Barber would build that rapport with Dressen during his time with the Reds and later the Dodgers. Barber insisted that "Charlie taught [him] more about baseball than any other man."[34] When Dressen died in 1966, just before Barber's firing by the Yankees, Red offered an earnest radio eulogy for his friend Charlie, recounting Dressen's remarkable up and down career and marveling at his strength of spirit and ability to bounce back from disappointments.[35] But in 1934, at the start of their relationship, an incident pitted Barber against Dressen's domestic loyalty.

Barber was re-creating a Pittsburgh road game in which Dressen pinch-hit for his regular second baseman, Alex Kampouris, and replaced him with rookie Frank McCormick. In the bottom of the ninth a single passed by the second baseman, scoring two Pirates runs, and the Reds lost, 7–6. Barber embellished the sparse telegraph information on the deciding play, telling his listeners that "McCormick had made a great effort for the ball" but to no avail—a familiar ending to a Reds' game. However, when the Reds came home, Dressen ordered writers and broadcasters barred from the dugout. When the baseball writers complained to Dressen, he told them the reason for the ban; the next day's headline in the *Cincinnati Enquirer* read "Radio Announcer Harmful Influence." Dressen believed a certain radio broadcaster "had been picking up tidbits of personal information and putting them on the air to the embarrassment of the players."[36] The article did not name Barber, but he was a likely suspect. Red went to his boss, station manager John Clark, to assure him he was not the "harmful influence." Clark talked to owner Powell Crosley, and Crosley talked to Larry MacPhail, who ordered Dressen to open the dugouts to the press and radio. Then Barber tackled Dressen. What was his beef?

Dressen said friends told him that Red had criticized the team's skipper for inserting McCormick late in the game, telling his listeners that regular second sacker Kampouris would have converted the Pirates' grounder into a routine double play and saved the game. Barber denied this emphatically. Barber was young and Dressen more experienced, but the redhead was hot. He decided he would never again be accused of criticizing Dressen. He would simply never mention his name on the air. For the next few months, the manager of the Cincinnati Reds, in name or in office, disappeared from WSAI coverage of the games. When relief pitchers were summoned, listeners had to infer who brought them. Barber also banned himself from the Reds' dugout, maintaining his Dressen boycott for the rest of the season. Only after

Larry MacPhail insisted did Barber attempt to make peace with Dressen just before the start of the next season. Neither man backed down from his position on the Pittsburgh substitution, but both agreed to a fresh start.[37] In his 1966 radio eulogy for Dressen, Barber credited him with forgetting completely the rift between them: "It's easy to say, 'I forgive,' but real forgiveness is complete forgetting-ness and Charlie Dressen forgot that half year of bitterness between us, and from his forgetting, I forgot it."[38]

The Dressen conflict reveals that even early in his career, Red Barber would confront experienced authority when he believed he was wronged and exert stubborn, even arrogant, resistance. But first he carefully guarded his position with his own bosses, and after some time had passed and at their insistence, he would consider changing his position. Barber was a man of principle but not a principled fool. After Red's radio eulogy for Dressen, Barber learned why Charlie had been so convinced that Red had criticized his player substitution. Dressen's sister, after hearing Barber recount the rift with her brother, told him that the "friends" who had reported Red's transgression actually was Dressen's wife, who had never warmed up to Barber. Charlie had to choose between sticking with his spouse or believing what outsiders told him. He remained loyal to his home team.

Biggest Break

Barber's stock rose quickly with Crosley Broadcasting, and the greatest break of what would be a long career came in October of only his second year as a Major League broadcaster. This blessing resulted from "changes and chances" far outside of his control. The biggest sports event in the 1930s was the World Series. Starting in 1921, local stations and later all national radio networks broadcast the Series, coverage that helped sell receivers and build interest in the major networks (CBS, NBC Red, NBC Blue).[39] Until 1934 the World Series was unsponsored; CBS and NBC regarded their Series broadcasts as a public service and valuable promotion for radio. By 1935 a fourth network, the Mutual Broadcasting System (MBS), wanted a share of the action. Three powerful stations—WOR-New York, WGN-Chicago, and WXYZ-Detroit—formed MBS. This fledgling web actively courted a fourth powerhouse station, WLW-Cincinnati. For the 1935 Series between the Detroit Tigers and Chicago Cubs, MBS wanted permission from the baseball commissioner, Judge Kenesaw Mountain Landis, to join CBS, NBC Red, and NBC Blue in covering the games. Landis agreed but only if MBS strengthened its station lineup. Getting WLW to drop NBC-Blue (NBC's weaker network) and become part of MBS was essential. MBS persuaded WLW's owner, Powell Crosley, and station manager, John Clark, to join its network after it agreed to one necessary condition: MBS would use the station's top sportscaster, the twenty-seven-year-old Red Barber, for part of the Series play-by-play.

Barber's MBS team included Bob Elson and Quin Ryan of WGN in Chicago, both experienced play-by-play men. Ryan would do the pregame and sign off; Elson and Barber were to split the play-by-play. Initially, Red was to do the middle three innings, and the more experienced Elson, the first and last three. But after Game One John Clark intervened with MBS and Series sponsor Ford to give Barber equal play-by-play time. The MBS trio was among a dozen broadcasters and executives who met with Judge Landis the morning before the Series commenced to hear his lecture on just how radio should cover the Series. For Barber, a slight figure in the back of the commissioner's suite at the Statler Hotel in Detroit, the judge's lesson would be life-changing.

Landis first reminded the radio men of who was not in room. Ted Husing, who had been CBS's principal play-by-play broadcaster on the preceding (1934) Series, had been banned by Landis. Husing had questioned some umpires' calls during that Series, and Landis wanted to make sure no such transgression would be repeated. The substance of Landis's address to the group was etched in Barber's mind, evolving into the core value that fueled his approach to baseball coverage: "Gentlemen, you report. Report everything you can see. Report each move each manager makes, but just report it. He knows more about what he is doing than you can know. . . . Report what the umpire calls the pitch—not what you think he should have called. In fact, you are in the stands. . . . He is right behind the plate. Don't voice your opinions. Don't editorialize. Report." To further emphasize his point, Landis offered a hypothetical. If a player walks up to the commissioner and unloads a spray of tobacco juice right in his high honor's face, "Report each step the player makes. Report how much spit hits me in the face. . . . Report my reaction, if any. . . . Report but don't feel disturbed about the Commissioner. Your job is simply to report the event."[40] "Just report" became Red Barber's mantra. He repeated Landis's proclamation many times over the years, recalling the speech in great detail in his books *The Broadcasters* and *1947* and in several magazine and newspaper pieces.[41]

Barber's coverage of the 1935 Series was first rate, but given that four different networks covered the game, it hardly stood out. However, his boss, John Clark, complemented him on his performance and asked him if he was happy that they had increased his innings from three to four and half after the first game. Grinning, Barber responded, "Yes, sir!"[42] Quin Ryan's work was another matter. Ryan was one of the earliest play-by-play men and a radio generalist, but he had become more of a WGN executive than an announcer. Barber was shocked at Ryan's lack of planning for the first Series game. "He had done no preparation. He went on the air and bumbled along for fifteen minutes." Barber thought, "Holy mackerel, is this the way they do the World Series?"[43] After Ryan's second weak effort, he was deep sixed from the Series; the rookie Barber added the pregame and signoff to his own assignment.

The next season, when Barber went to Florida for spring training, a friend told him how proud he was to hear his old buddy on the World Series, congratulating him on the big bonus he must have received to cover sport's greatest event. Barber could not bear to tell him he got nothing more than his regular Crosley salary and expenses. Although World Series pay would become a significant issue for Barber later in his career, Red was now a nationally heard, if not yet recognized, sports broadcaster. The 1935 World Series had been his biggest break.

Meeting "The Mahatma" and Purchasing the Catbird Seat

While Larry MacPhail and Powell Crosley influenced Barber during his Cincinnati years, he would be touched in a more profound way by arguably baseball's most celebrated, most innovative, and shrewdest executive for the first half of the twentieth century, Wesley Branch Rickey. Some thought he was the most frugal baseball boss as well. When Barber first encountered the man writers would later call "The Mahatma" in the winter of 1934–35, Rickey was already a dominant figure in the national pastime. He was general manager of the 1934 World Champion St. Louis Cardinals, the legendary "Gashouse Gang," of Dizzy and Daffy Dean, Pepper Martin, Joe Medwick, Ripper Collins, and player/manager, Frankie Frisch. Rickey transformed the Cardinals by developing Major League Baseball's first farm system.

Barber first saw Rickey at a "hot stove" dinner at Cincinnati's Gibson Hotel, where, according to Red, "They [served] rubbery chicken and even more rubbery peas." Dinner started late, service was slow, and speakers said the obvious in a room filled with too much tobacco smoke. Red was new to Cincinnati, and it would be a while before he would gain a seat at the head table or rise to the speaker's podium, but baseball dinners had already become a "heavy chore." They put him at the mercy of men leading "empty lives" who "step on your toes and blow their breath in your face . . . and ask innumerable questions and argue with you over your answers."[44] Expecting little from such an evening, Red Barber instead heard an enthralling voice that would change his life.

In both his memoir, *Rhubarb in the Catbird Seat,* and his book of inspirational essays, *Walk in the Spirit,* Barber devoted chapters to Branch Rickey. He would reference him in dozens of newspaper and magazine articles over the next five decades. Barber would credit Rickey with ushering him from his path of self-centered careerism to a higher plane of public service. When Jackie Robinson came up in an interview, Barber, while always acknowledging Robinson's courage, skill, restraint, and determination, made clear his conviction that there could not have been a Jackie Robinson without a Branch Rickey.

From the moment Rickey began his hot stove talk that winter evening, Barber was captivated. He later affirmed, "There was a strength. There was a magnetism. There was a depth. There was great art. Above all, there was purpose." Barber sensed that "This man, when he had made up his mind, would walk through a twelve-foot brick wall to get to where he wanted to go."[45] That evening Red got his "first practical valuable lesson in how to give an after-dinner talk."[46] On that smoke-filled night, just after his first season as baseball announcer, Red Barber met the man who would become his most revered employer and, spiritually, his second father.

In the mid-1940s Branch Rickey would play a central role in Red Barber's movement away from a heritage steeped in racial prejudice. In the mid-1930s Lylah Barber had been awakened for the first time in her life to the cost of racial bigotry that was born by the bigot. Red and Lylah's first visit to the Cincinnati Symphony exemplifies the "shaking up and changing" that Lylah anticipated in their move to Cincinnati. Red had planted the seed for Lylah's love of symphonic music during their courting days in Gainesville through records at the radio station. The official organist at the university, a close friend, had taken them to a performance of the Minneapolis Symphony when it was in town. Now in Cincinnati they could afford to take the five-cent streetcar ride to a Sunday symphony performance, when balcony seats cost only twenty-five cents. Climbing to their balcony row, they spotted a Black couple sitting next to their seats. Lylah and Red said nothing to each other, but both deliberately headed higher up the stairs to the vacant rows above. Lylah tells us that sitting in that higher seat, she missed the symphony entirely because she spent the two hours castigating herself for being so blind. She could see that the Black couple below them were truly enjoying the symphony; she and Red could be sitting there beside them sharing the same pleasure: "I realized my reaction had only hurt me. I never felt quite the same again. Absurdity had cracked the wall of prejudice. This child of the south had taken her first step to becoming a citizen of the world. Looking back, I see that this was a preparation for Red."[47]

In Red's after hours from work, he and Lylah continued card playing with friends, a hobby they truly enjoyed. One night when they were playing with neighbors in their apartment building, suffering an embarrassing loss, Red "purchased" a phrase for which he became famous. Barber tells us that unable to win a single pot, he decided to "force the issue" during a round of seven-card stud: "I raised on the first bet, and I raised again on every card. At the end when the showdown came, it was between Frank Koch and me. Frank turned over his hold cards, showed a pair of aces, and won the pot. He said, 'Thank you, Red, I had those aces from the start. I was sitting in the catbird seat.'" Red says he did not know of the original coining of the phrase "sitting in the catbird seat" to mean "in a privileged position," but he understood its meaning; "I had paid for it. It was mine."[48] In a 1972 column Barber reported that the expression derived from the catbird's habit of perching high up in a tree, securing an excellent view in every direction. When a smaller bird located a worm or an insect, the catbird would dive and snatch the other bird's meal.[49] In 1988 a *Cincinnati Enquirer* columnist, John Kiesewetter, interviewed the man from whom Red had "purchased" the phrase, Frank Koch. Koch, then eighty-seven, said that he thought it important for readers to know the phrase did not come from the "Deep South": he first heard it spoken in Georgetown, Ohio, by his father-in-law, an avid poker player. But from Red's perspective in 1935, he now owned a phrase that captured the privileged position he would occupy above the baseball diamond for over three decades, and it became his best known "Barberism."[50]

"Kid You've Got It"

If Barber's inclusion in the 1935 World Series lineup seemed last minute, his insertion into the 1936 Series was chaotic. He actually missed the first game between the New York Giants and Yankees, the first subway series since 1923. And he had to switch networks to announce the rest of the Series contests. Don Becker replaced John Clark, who had moved to New York. Becker wanted a new WLW World Series partner: NBC, the supreme force in network radio. Negotiations dragged on for so long that Barber assumed he would not cover the fall classic. He was in South Bend doing research for the upcoming Notre Dame football opener against Carnegie Tech when a call from WLW came through: get to New York and be ready for Game Two on Friday, October 2. Barber arrived in Gotham in time for a morning meeting with John Royal, NBC program director, at his office in the RCA building. Also attending were Red's fellow NBC announcers, Tom Manning, who covered the Cleveland Indians, and Ty Tyson of the Detroit Tigers. Tyson would do the first three innings, Barber the middle three, and Manning would finish up. Barber's first 1936 Series game was hardly a tense contest. Smarting from a 6–1 loss on Wednesday, the Yankees crushed the Giants, 18–4. By the time Barber got the mic, the Yankees were already ahead, 9–1. But despite calling a suspenseless game, Barber that day earned praise that would come to mean as much to him as any other he received during his thirty-three-year career as a baseball announcer.[51]

After the NBC meeting, Red met Graham McNamee, the announcer he most admired. McNamee, the first sportscaster superstar, had taken over the mic in the third game of the 1923 World Series from newspaperman W. O. McGeehan, and his presence dominated radio throughout the next decade. McNamee became synonymous with NBC's popular coverage of the Series. But McNamee covered many other sports and national events, including the 1924 national political party conventions. Even though he never broadcast regular-season baseball games on a daily basis, he won the Hall of Fame's Ford C. Frick Award in 2016 for baseball broadcasting excellence. Barber always thought that baseball had overlooked McNamee's contributions and actively politicked for him to win the Frick Award when he became part of its selection committee. McNamee had a minor role in NBC's coverage of the 1935 Series, but by 1936 he was off the Series completely. Although only forty-seven, his superstar shine had faded; he would finish his career as an announcer and straight man for comedian Ed Wynn before he died of an embolism in 1942 at fifty-three.

When Manning, Barber, and McNamee left John Royal's office at the RCA building, they entered McNamee's beautiful black Cadillac, parked conveniently in front of the building. Barber's idol would chauffeur them to the Polo Grounds for Game Two. McNamee's star may have been falling at NBC, but he was still a major New York celebrity who ignored traffic lights at will, waving to cops along the way. Sitting between Manning and McNamee in the front seat of the Caddy, Red felt he had really arrived: "I had never been to New York before, and here I was riding to the World Series with Graham McNamee."[52] In Barber's mind, his bond with McNamee had been cemented five years earlier. When Red and Lylah married in 1931, a *Gainesville Sun* headline read, "WRUF's Graham McNamee Gets Married."

But at the 1936 World Series, McNamee was a spectator; Barber was the player. At the Polo Grounds the announcers worked from box seats above the press box, a wood plank and a single microphone serving as their broadcast booth. After the game started, Barber completed his scorecard and carefully noted what Tyson had said during the first three innings. Just before the top of the fourth, Barber slid past the chain that separated the other box seats from the broadcast area and took possession of the national pastime's crown jewel. Unnoticed was the man sitting beside him, Graham McNamee. Barber, working solo, as announcers did in those days, was fully engaged. After a couple of innings, there was a brief station break, and Red checked his scorebook for a moment. As he did, a firm hand grasped his elbow and turned him left. The rich baritone voice, the voice that had thrilled the young redhead with the best boy's hair at Sanford High School, said simply, but warmly, "Kid, you've got it."[53] It was Barber's first and only time basking in McNamee's glow.

In his first years in Cincinnati, Red Barber grew from minor staff announcer to star sports reporter. He established a strong local following as a baseball announcer and got national exposure with his work on the World Series. Red made his first trip to his future home, New York, and was heartened to meet and receive acclaim from his boyhood idol, Graham McNamee. He also learned he could lock horns with grizzled baseball veterans—Charlie Grimm and Charlie Dressen—and stand his ground. He learned that his bosses—Chet Thomas, John Clark, Larry MacPhail and Powell Crosley—would look out for him. Finally, at a smoky mid-winter hot stove dinner, his spirit was awakened by a powerful speaker whose voice would encourage him to pursue goals more profound than professional renown.

6

Rising Expectations

Barber came to Cincinnati with limited experience as a baseball announcer but with a strong regional reputation as a football announcer. His live coverage of the University of Florida games, starting in 1930, won listeners for WRUF and acclaim for himself. He began broadcasting football for Crosley in 1934, covering games at Xavier University and a few grid matches at Ohio State University (OSU). In 1935 he jumped to the big time, covering as the play-by-play man for the full schedule of the OSU Buckeyes on WLW. A newspaper ad for the OSU games, purchased by sponsor Linco Gasoline and Motor Oil, reminded listeners they could hear "the vivid running account of the games by Red Barber, former football star and noted sports announcer."[1] This was likely the only time in his broadcasting career that anyone called Barber a "football star." The next year he hit the college football jackpot, covering the nation's best-known football team, the Notre Dame Fighting Irish.

Barber found football "more difficult to cover than baseball." While the long baseball season was "the real test" of a sports announcer, football's "organized confusion" made an individual football contest more daunting.[2] After learning the players on his team and in his league, a baseball announcer could use that information for the full season. The college football announcer had to learn the players and tendencies of a new opponent each week. Studying prior game films and working with competent spotters could help, but the game challenged the announcer to identify players quickly and keep up with intense action taking place all over the field during each play. Barber developed a solid local reputation as one of the radio voices of the Reds, but it was his excellent work in college football that brought national recognition.

Red always celebrated the November 2, 1935, Notre Dame–OSU game played in Columbus, as the greatest college game he ever broadcast. Coming into the contest, Notre Dame and OSU were undefeated and evenly matched. This game featured the best of the big ten versus the legendary "Fighting Irish." WLW had exclusive rights to the game, but the national interest was intense, and after considerable discussion, WLW agreed to let MBS carry its broadcast nationally.

By halftime the Buckeyes had built a 13–0 lead but also had booted two additional scoring opportunities. Notre Dame finally scored a touchdown in the fourth quarter, and another six points came with only fifty-five seconds to go. The extra point would salvage a tie. But the Irish missed it. They kicked off, and the Buckeyes ran the ball back to their own 30-yard line. If they ran out the clock, the game was theirs, but they fumbled, and the Irish recovered. Notre Dame would have a chance. With the game on the line, the Irish quarterback, Bill Shakespeare—a weighty name if ever there was one—passed toward two receivers, Marty Peters and Wayne Millner. One of them caught the pass in the end zone, and the Irish won, 18–13. Barber couldn't tell which receiver had caught the ball, and his Notre Dame spotter was nowhere to be seen. Barber guessed the receiver was Marty Peters and signed off with Peters as that day's football hero. It was a fifty-fifty chance, but Barber was 100 percent wrong. Wayne Millner had saved the Irish's day.

Despite his mistake, Barber expertly broadcast a sensational contest, still considered one of the games of the century. Although he was the OSU announcer, the presidents of the Notre Dame senior, junior, and sophomore classes recognized Barber in a November 1935 letter. The three class presidents wrote the managing director of MBS: "During the first half, when our hope was all but gone, [Barber] gave us something to cling to by telling the radio public that though the team was outplayed, it was not outfought. In the second half, he accurately pointed out that the tide of the game was being turned by our line and prepared us for the last-minute rally that brought victory."[3] Listening to the game in New York was Bill McCaffrey of the NBC Artist Bureau; he would become Barber's long-time agent and one of his closest friends. In 1936 Barber switched from the OSU to the Notre Dame side, broadcasting all the Irish games. His excellent work continued, prompting a thank-you letter from another, higher-ranking president, John F. O'Hara, head of the university: "Just want to add a word of thanks for your broadcasts this fall. They seem to have met with universal favor, as I hear about them wherever I go."[4]

Barber's skill as a football announcer brought him to the attention of NBC. In late November 1935 NBC asked Barber at the last minute to substitute for an ill sportscaster in the network's coverage of the Army-Navy game, one of the biggest contests of the year. Lylah was pregnant and bedridden from pernicious nausea, but she encouraged Red to grab the opportunity to perform on a national stage. Though he had little time to prepare, Barber's broadcast seemed to go well. Even better was the surprising news he received shortly after the game. John Royal, NBC's head of programming, wanted Red to fly directly to New York for a one-day interview, which he was to conceal from his Crosley bosses. Bumping along on his flight, Barber thought, "Now this is serious."[5]

Years later Barber recalled John Royal sitting behind his desk, "shaking that massive head of his; he was in command; he *was* command, and he knew it." Royal told Barber, "I want you to come in here and go to work." When Barber asked, "What do you want me to do?" Royal responded, "Whatever sports on this network

I want you to do." Red had to think for a moment. Lylah and he were established happily in Cincinnati and trying to start a family. He knew the NBC job would mean abandoning regular-season baseball broadcasts since the network covered only the World Series and the All-Star Game. Although for some time a jump to New York had been one of his career goals, he did not want to pursue too eagerly a position in Gotham. Perhaps this was the right moment. Leaning toward accepting Royal's offer, Barber asked innocently, "What are you going to pay me?" Expecting a specific figure, Barber was stunned when Royal replied, "I'll pay you what you're worth. You come in here and go to work." Red processed Royal's reply as an instance of NBC's arrogance and retorted that he had a fine job in Cincinnati, enjoyed doing daily baseball games, and would not come to New York until Royal clarified some duties "and what you are going to pay me." The twenty-seven-year-old's bluntness unnerved Royal, who told him, "I'm not going to do either one. You can go back to Cincinnati and sit there by Fountain Square till you die."[6]

Despite a shaky first pass, NBC and Barber continued their dialog. In July 1936 Alfred H. Morton, NBC's program manager, wrote Royal that he saw Barber as an "ambitious young man" determined to be "the outstanding sports announcer in the country." In September Barber wrote to Morton that he still was interested in the network but saw himself "as a specialist in sports," not a general staff announcer.[7] However, John Royal, the man in command of NBC programming, likely still annoyed by Barber's earlier rebuff, wrote Morton that Barber was "a little too much of a prima donna for us" and "just a trifle conceited."[8] In later years Barber and Royal would have a good chuckle reminiscing about their bumpy first encounter.

Old Redhead Meets the Roaring Redhead

Don Warfield's 1987 biography of Leland Stanford "Larry" MacPhail is most appropriately subtitled *Baseball's Great Innovator*. Its title, *The Roaring Redhead*, is also spot-on. MacPhail introduced to baseball season ticket sales, night games, air travel, full-season radio broadcasts in the game's largest market, and live road broadcasts, among his many innovations. He cleaned and painted his aging ballparks, put their ushers in new uniforms, and refurbished their restrooms, making the parks hospitable for women. Then he brought them through the turnstiles with "Ladies' Day" promotions. His daily baseball broadcasts and interviews educated women and children about the national pastime and turned gruff, profane ballplayers into appealing personalities. Throughout his career as a broadcaster and writer, Red Barber applauded MacPhail for his vision and passion for change, often pitting him against the Luddites of the grand old game. Still, for Barber, Larry MacPhail was an innovative Doctor Jekyll who could easily transform into a crazed "roaring redhead."

MacPhail's short fuse, explosive rage, and fist fighting were legendary, as were his quick reversals—proclivities he would exercise throughout his career. He "fired" Leo Durocher over a perceived snub after the Dodgers won the 1941 pennant and then rehired him the next morning. He once had a physical fight with reporter Red Patterson of the *New York Herald Tribune*. Patterson decked MacPhail, but Larry did not hold a grudge and later hired him to handle publicity for the Yankees. Barber wrote that MacPhail "could be as thoughtful, generous, and forgiving as any man who ever lived. He certainly had a creative genius. Then he could suddenly go into a rage fearsome to be around." The more drinks MacPhail downed, the more likely a blowup would follow. Once, while MacPhail and Barber were enjoying cocktails, the Roaring Redhead laid into Barber after he spoke favorably of Dixie Walker, with whom MacPhail was feuding over a contract. After that episode Barber developed a plan to avoid future furies: "Never again did I stay around him one minute after I saw him take the first drink—from then on I was already late for an appointment. Very late."[9] Since Red worked for Crosley Broadcasting and not for the Cincinnati Reds, requests for Red's services came indirectly, from MacPhail to his Crosley bosses and then to Barber. But Red regularly saw and talked to MacPhail at the ballpark, and MacPhail made his needs known, as exemplified by his insistence that Red bury the hatchet with Charlie Dressen. But in Cincinnati the MacPhails rarely partied with the Barbers, who had not yet scaled the peak of the city's social hierarchy. Barber was labor; MacPhail was management.

Lylah Barber recalls one unforgettable social affair subsidized by MacPhail. She was delighted when, near the end of the 1935 season, she and Red received a handwritten invitation from MacPhail to a fish fry for "a small group of friends," to be held at the new and "very elegant" Netherland Plaza Hotel.[10] The guests would listen to a radio broadcast of the Max Baer–Joe Louis fight after dining. Red and Lylah arrived when the cocktail hour was in full swing; they discovered that the "small group" was over thirty people, including the press, all top officials of the ball club and their wives. Professional musicians played at a bar that "offered fancy drinks with names [the Barbers had] never heard of. . . . Nothing in Gainesville had prepared [them] for such splendor." When a pair of folding doors opened, they saw a beautiful table decorated with ice sculptures and flower arrangements, the likes of which they'd never seen. The "fish fry" turned out to be just one of several courses for dinner. She and Red "drank it all in," including the memorable "planter's punches decorated with Japanese parasols." After floating through the after-dinner boxing broadcast, Red and Lylah took their five-cent streetcar ride home to their modest apartment.

The next day Lylah could not wait to share details of her splendid evening with her next-door neighbor. After absorbing Lylah's account, the woman asked gently if she had read the morning paper. Lylah discovered that MacPhail had continued to party into the wee hours of the morning. Then, on his elevator ride to the basement, where he'd parked his car, he got into a heated argument and then a fist fight with two hotel detectives who "thoroughly roughed him up and left him with a black eye as a souvenir of the occasion." Powell Crosley, who did not welcome controversy in the press, confronted MacPhail about the newspaper stories covering the elevator altercation. MacPhail, apparently believing the adage that there was no such thing as bad press, told Powell, "Boy, isn't that great publicity?"[11]

The volatile MacPhail's tenure with the Reds was successful but brief. It was a pattern he repeated throughout his Major League career: Cincinnati Reds, 1934–36; Brooklyn Dodgers, 1938–42; and New York Yankees, 1945–47. With the Reds, he laid the foundation of a team that would win the 1939 National League (NL) pennant and the 1940 World Series. MacPhail could turn around a team but could not control his temper or his intemperance. After the 1936 season Powell accepted MacPhail's resignation, thanking him "for what he [had] done for baseball in Cincinnati," especially the improvements at Crosley Field and the introduction of night baseball.[12] But Red Barber's association with Larry MacPhail was just beginning.

Under the Lights

While the Cincinnati Reds were usually losers during Barber's tenure as the voice of the Reds, he would revisit three specific Cincinnati games throughout his life, two of which he called. The game played on May 24, 1935, was another MacPhail "first" and his most important: the first night game in the history of Major League Baseball. Despite Minor League success in using night games to reverse declining attendance during the Great Depression, Major League owners and their aging commissioner, Kenesaw Mountain Landis, were united in their disdain for artificially illuminated baseball. But MacPhail, who had witnessed the attendance boost from night baseball when he had installed lights for his Columbus Red Birds team in the early 1930s, prepared a forty-page argument for night baseball to present at the NL owners' meeting in 1935. During a conversation with Landis prior to the NL meeting, MacPhail told the commissioner about his night baseball proposal. Landis bellowed, "Young man, you can write this down. Not in my lifetime or yours will you ever see a baseball game played at night in the majors."[13] Before the NL meeting New York Giants owner Charles Stoneham also warned MacPhail that he would never vote to approve night baseball. After a three-hour discussion of MacPhail's night baseball brief, Stoneham proved good to his word. When the National League took the vote on limited night baseball, Stoneham abstained, but the other seven owners approved. MacPhail's first-year plan called for only seven Reds night games, one against each NL club.

Landis's "my lifetime or yours" turned into a few months. On Friday, May 24, 1935, the Reds played the Philadelphia Phillies in the first Major League night game under the lights. MacPhail offered the fans more than just a night game; he treated them to a drum and bugle corps and an enormous fireworks display. To convince skeptics that the lights would provide enough illumination for top-quality play, the game began in darkness. Both league presidents, Ford Frick of the NL and Will Harridge of the American League (AL), attended. In a publicity coup for the ages, MacPhail persuaded President Franklin Roosevelt to turn on the game lights by pressing a special key on his desk at the White House. The event was an attendance bonanza; 20,422 paid to see MLB's first night game. Attendance the next day, Saturday, was down nearly 90 percent.

Red's call of the game was nothing out of the ordinary except for the late hour of its start. He worked all nine innings alone. But the breadth of the game's audience was a fresh experience. It was the first sports event carried by the newly organized MBS. In only his second year as baseball broadcaster, Red Barber scored his first national network sports broadcast. Barber recalled, "There was no criticism of the effectiveness of the lights. The fans loved the game under the lights, and the brilliantly lit park against the background of dark night." He notes that fans also relished relaxing in the ballpark after a day at work and the chance to see a game without suffering the intense heat and humidity of Cincinnati's summer afternoons.[14]

The Most Memorable Diamond Event

Red Barber's other two choices for most exciting Cincinnati games were validated in 1976, when they were voted the most memorable diamond events in Queen City baseball history. One game without the other would have been only mildly memorable, but, together, Johnny Vander Meer's consecutive no-hitters on June 11 and 15, 1938, became baseball legend. In the first no-no, before a modest crowd of 5,814, Vander Meer dominated Casey Stengel's Boston Bees, 3–0, striking out four and allowing three walks. Barber wrote that the game was nothing "earth-shaking until the last couple of innings," but "there was, of course, considerable excitement when Vandy got his first no-hitter."[15] Later in his career Barber would insist on pointing out that a no-hitter was in progress. But for this game "[he insinuated] the fact in every way possible except coming right out and naming it."[16] For Vander Meer's second gem, Barber would not need to fret over this baseball taboo.

Larry MacPhail brought his passion for night baseball to Brooklyn in 1938, fueling a game on June 15 that Red Barber did not cover but "re-created" for decades. It was also a game that taught him a lesson about the perils of popularity. Vander Meer's second no-hitter was played under the lights in Brooklyn. The first night game in franchise history drew a capacity crowd to a newly illuminated Ebbets Field on a Wednesday night. Vander Meer was much wilder that evening, walking eight Dodgers while striking out seven, but the Bums could produce no hits and no runs in their 6–0 loss to the Reds. Barber, however, would be shut out of the contest altogether. The Dodgers were in the last year of a five-year agreement with the Yankees and Giants that banned all radio broadcasts, even re-creations by visiting teams. So Barber, back in Cincinnati, had the night off. But it was not a relaxing one.

Back when he was still emerging as a public figure, Red had listed his number in the Cincinnati phone book as Walter Red Barber. He occasionally got unwanted calls from strangers intent upon settling a bar bet but "felt that was part of the job [and] put up with it." When the wire report of Vander Meer's second no-hitter was read over the radio, "It set that staid old town right on its ear. . . . Those Germans in their beer gardens . . . jumped up and down." After a few more brews, they began calling their favorite baseball announcer to get his take on a game that he did not broadcast. The phone rang until 4 a.m. Red complained, "It was a very long night. Every time I'd get my head back on the pillow, *ring*, there went the phone again."[17] From then on, although Barber's number remained in the phone book, it was under Lylah's name. Friends and family would know to look for it there; barroom betters could write Red a letter, care of the team, after they sobered up. Amazingly, Barber received compliments from "listeners" who had "heard" his broadcast that night. For a while Barber corrected the fans but soon just offered thanks and let them enjoy their memory of listening to him call a game that he did not cover.

For his first two years with Crosley Broadcasting, Red Barber worked the few Reds' games by himself. But in 1936 Larry MacPhail authorized a full schedule of broadcasts. All home games were broadcast live. Road games were re-created in Cincinnati except for the contests against the Giants and Dodgers that were blacked out by those teams.[18] The recent move of wsai's transmitter into Cincinnati proper enhanced the reach of the fuller schedule. One paper predicted that with "the attendant increase in the station's listening audience, Red Barber [would] come into his own."[19] A season press pass, signed by Powell Crosley Jr. and preserved in Barber's 1936 clippings book, confirms that he was now a member of the "working press." whio now carried Reds games in Dayton, and "the town [was] baseball crazy."[20]

Now listeners were expecting to hear every home game from Crosley Field. So when Barber took a "holiday" from the booth for the July 19 Sunday doubleheader against the New York Giants, controversy ensued. One paper reported that his sponsor, Socony-Vacuum Oil, believed Red had "earned a vacation." But when he attended the games as a spectator and then covered them in his

Baseball Resume program that evening, Barber's "holiday" was exposed as "a cheap and miserly trick." According to one newspaper, "It was conceived and promoted by MacPhail . . . in an effort to bolster up the attendance at Crosley Field that has been sagging for weeks because of the inferior showing of the Reds." Harry Hartman's broadcast on WCPO was also missing in action. The paper quizzed, "If last Sunday was to be a holiday for Barber and Harry Hartman . . . what in the h— were they doing at the ball yard? One would think that after broadcasting the games for the past two weeks they would welcome an afternoon off."[21] Whatever the ethics, MacPhail's radio holiday apparently worked; attendance on July 19 was eighteen thousand, a fourteen thousand increase over the most recent Sunday home doubleheader on July 12. While Larry MacPhail's commitment to radio was growing, he still saw it as a threat to attendance on Sundays, traditionally the day with the largest crowds. In 1937 the Reds would ban broadcasts of all their Sabbath games.

Although fans may have been angry about Barber's "holiday," his sports schedule was a full one. To provide some help, Crosley Broadcasting hired Al Helfer, a former sports announcer at WWSW in Pittsburgh, to serve as Barber's assistant. Helfer was only twenty-five, and like his twenty-eight-year-old boss, he was the son of a railroad engineer. Like Barber, Helfer had played football; but Red was a small, fast high school halfback, while Helfer's 242 pounds supported him as an end for the Washington and Jefferson College team. He also had experience calling a range of sports, including football, basketball, baseball, hockey, and boxing.[22] Helfer's job was to fill in for Barber when needed. He would move on in 1938 to join CBS, but he reunited with Barber in Brooklyn as the Old Redhead's first Dodgers associate broadcaster. He also served as the announcer on Barber's *We Want a Touchdown* football quiz program on MBS. Helfer's WSAI replacement was Dick Bray, a fine sportscaster in his own right, who would call the 1938 All-Star Game in Cincinnati for MBS, while Barber manned the mic for NBC.

A Rising Star

As the Reds' broadcasts began airing on more and more regional stations, Barber's press grew overwhelmingly positive, and he appeared more frequently in station promotions and sponsor ads. At first, however, some columnists had trouble spelling his name, using the old French variant, "Barbour." Crosley's publicity director, Bill Bailey, facetiously wrote *Cincinnati Times-Star* columnist Nixson Denton, "Despite the fact that he was born in Mississippi and that his kinfolk a couple of generations back started a newspaper there, Red has not been a bit snooty. He spells his name 'Barber.'"[23] In his personal scrapbooks, Barber included a few articles in which persnickety listeners documented his occasional errors. Two listeners won theater tickets for reporting Red's "boner" when he doubled up on shortstops in one game, applauding "a nice play from shortstop Myers to shortstop McQuinn."[24] On Red's *Baseball Resume* program, he told listeners that "the Reds by winning today broke the Boston Bee losing streak."[25] But some papers believed it was unfair to nitpick errors in spontaneous speech sustained for two hours: "Red Barber's descriptions have never been counted as boners—and the same will apply to fall football games on any station."[26]

Most sports page readers applauded what they considered Red's great plays. They began to identify the habits and skills that would, in time, forge Barber's legacy as the announcer whose example helped most to professionalize the craft of baseball announcing. One reader wrote, "I'm now convinced that Red Barber's the 'goods,'" commending the quality of his reporting.[27] Another fan more specifically insisted that "the redheaded gentleman in Cincinnati [was] absolute 'tops' in baseball. Loyal to his sponsor, broadcasting in his own inimitable style, his intelligent descriptive powers make it a pleasure to listen to him."[28]

On the whole, sportswriters echoed what Red's listeners were saying. In August 1937 a *Cincinnati Enquirer* profile of Barber noted that "it didn't take baseball followers long to learn that when they listened to him, they were getting every detail of the game and an accurate description of every play."[29] Another newspaper found Barber "a veritable walking dictionary of baseball information [who] maintains one of the most complete statistical sheets of the major leagues possible, [which he uses] to give up-to-the-minute data on clubs and players."[30] From far away in Flatbush, a letter writer to the *Brooklyn Eagle* proclaimed Barber "the best individual announcer" in the 1936 World Series. Barber "added ninety percent of the dramatic force of the event" when he described Mel Ott's home run in the fifth inning of game six. His detailed account enabled his listeners to see that the left-handed batting Ott's homer "was opposite field and against a shift."[31]

Station advertising and promotions featured the rising star. A 1935 ad featured a photo of a smiling, curly-haired Red swimming in a Cincinnati pool with two lovely singers from *The Crosley Follies*. The caption read, "One Way Stars Keep Cool during the Warm Weather." In the photo his appealing WLW colleagues are about to dunk Barber.[32] An ad for WSAI alerted potential advertisers the station had "Red Barber at the Mike," listing the sponsors for his play-by-play, pregame interviews, fifteen minutes of sports oddities, and *Baseball Resume* programs. Another ad urged listeners to "Hear the Ballgames as Red Barber Sees Them," compliments of Felsenbrau Beer.[33] Strategies for promoting Red were not limited to earth-bound publications. A photo in Barber's scrapbook from the Cincinnati years shows an airplane towing a banner announcing "Red Barber on WSAI."

Barber profited from the technological resources of Crosley Broadcasting, particularly WLW's 500,000 transmission wattage. But Crosley also had a strong engineering department that guided the installation of lights in Crosley Field, enabling Barber's historic first night-game broadcast. Even more significant for Barber, WLW engineer Bob Booth developed a portable short-wave radio transmitter strapped on an engineer's back, allowing Red to interview players from the dugout. A 1937 photo shows him interviewing Reds manager Charlie Dressen, with Booth packing the WSAI portable transmitter.[34] By 1938 Red's partner, Dick Bray, was using the portable transmitter strapped to Booth's back to interview fans prior to home games for a ten-minute program, "Fans in the Stands."[35] Barber followed Bray with his ten minute "Dope from the Dugouts," using the portable transmitter to broadcast interviews of players and managers, including Dizzy Dean, Tony Lazzeri, Ernie Lombardi, Charlie Grimm, and Bill McKechnie.[36] The portable short-wave transmitter and the long baseball off-season gave Barber the opportunity to exercise his mobile interviewing skills all over the Cincinnati area. A program called "Man in the Neighborhood" debuted on October 25, 1937. At 1:00 p.m. on every day but Sunday, Barber visited "various residential sections of the city and interviewed housewives in their own home," discussing a potpourri of topics, including "the Spanish situation, football, the Sino-Japanese war, women's clothing styles . . . and any other question that [popped] into his head."[37]

Problematic Parenthood

Red and Lylah postponed starting a family until their finances were in order. Shortly before the beginning of 1935 spring training in Tampa, Lylah was pregnant. But early in her pregnancy, her morning sickness grew increasingly intense; when she was with Red in Tampa, she grew so ill that she left their hotel to stay with her favorite aunt, Ouida, who had an apartment nearby and offered to serve as Lylah's caretaker. Red returned to Cincinnati, and just after his Opening Day broadcast, he learned that his wife's condition had grown so serious that Ouida had taken her to Riverside Hospital in Jacksonville, where Lylah knew all the doctors. She was diagnosed with pernicious nausea, a condition that had so weakened her that her life was at risk; her pregnancy had to be terminated. In her memoir Lylah tells us, "I lost the baby," and recalling Red's painful absence at the time, she adds candidly, "and I began to learn that my husband's professional career came first."[38]

In his 1971 book *Show Me the Way to Go Home*, Red tells his readers that "the second Opening Day I broadcast in Cincinnati was the day we lost our first attempt to have a baby." Reflecting the views of a sixty-year-old soon-to-be member of Planned Parenthood's Board of Advocates, he adds, "Had we been bound by the inflexible rules imposed by a group of celibate men, I would have had no wife or child, or the child we did have in 1937." He grieves because he was unaware at the time that Lylah's condition was so dire; "Weeks later when she got off the train from Cincinnati, she was painfully thin and weak."[39] But like an athlete who is challenged rather than crushed by defeat, "Lylah," Red says, "had guts" and was ready to try again to get pregnant in the fall. His admiration may have been influenced by what he'd learned about his mother after her death: "Days before I was born she was very ill from her kidneys and I should have been her first and last child." She had two more children, he says, "because she wanted them both; she wouldn't have thought of saying anything about such a risk; she just took it."[40]

Lylah regained her health. Shortly before the time Red had to leave for spring training in 1936, she was pregnant again, and her mother had been summoned from Florida to look after her while her husband was away. But just before he left, Lylah went into labor, less than six months pregnant, and failed in her second attempt to have a child, whom Red identified this time as a son. Still, he tells us, Lylah "would not give in." When she got pregnant for the third time, the pernicious nausea returned; she was in and out of the hospital under constant surveillance for the next seven months. Toward the end of the 1937 baseball season, Lylah went into labor, and they rushed to Christ Hospital in Cincinnati. Later that evening, however, their doctor told Red, "She's quit, nothing is happening. We will have to make a decision soon." Finally, the doctor was compelled to induce labor. Red had been allowed to stay close to Lylah, hold her hand, and talk with her. "She seemed almost defeated. . . . She had come so far. . . . She wanted a child so much . . . for herself . . . and for me."

When she was taken away for the induced birth, Red plopped on a stretcher outside the delivery room, exhausted and unshaved, "with a dark-red beard, like Judas." His clothes were dirty with dust and smelled like the ballpark. He knew that the labor pains had stopped and wondered, "What about the baby?" Then he did what he had not done for seven years: he prayed. He explains: "I didn't pray in specific words. . . . I just reached for help. . . . I showed God a broken, troubled heart. Not contrite, just broken." And then at 2:17 on the morning of September 17, 1937, someone opened the delivery room door, and Red Barber heard his daughter, Sarah Lanier Barber, crying. He thanked the doctor and nurses, but "didn't even think to say, 'Thank you, Lord.'"[41]

Barber once observed that "ball players don't say 'thank you.' . . . They expect to receive, not give." But he did receive an unexpected gift from a player after Sarah's birth that he still recalled poignantly fifty years later. Several days after she was born, a Cincinnati player, "a very rough, uneducated, real country bumpkin . . . came in the dugout and he had a box, wasn't even wrapped, and his dirty finger marks were all over the box as he was holding it and he said, 'This is for your baby,' and walked off. And it was a beautiful little blanket."[42]

Two days after Lylah returned home from the hospital with Sarah, Red had to leave Cincinnati to cover the first Notre Dame football game of the fall. From there he would go to New York to cover the World Series, which stretched to five games. During his ten-day absence, a hired nurse assisted Lylah with her new baby until Lylah realized in horror that the nurse had been giving Sarah paregoric, constantly, to keep her quiet. After firing the nurse, Lylah was left with a sick baby who would not eat, drink, or stop screaming. When she called the pediatrician, he told her to relax, adding that "graduate nurses always make nervous mothers." During a blur of days and nights, neither Sarah nor Lylah got much sleep. When Red returned one night at 2:00 a.m., the first thing he heard was an anguished voice imploring, "Baby, for God's sake, please stop crying!" Ever quick to shift gears, Red was on the phone at 7:00 a.m., and by 9:00, the family of three was at the hospital. Sarah was X-rayed and diagnosed as suffering from a pyloric spasm rather than from the mothering of an anxious graduate nurse. With the necessary medication and some food in her tummy she soon became "a happy baby with relaxed parents."[43]

Sarah Barber's birth "Scrapbook" is stacked with postcards, telegrams, and letters of congratulation from the Barbers' friends, relatives, neighbors, former mentors and teachers, and current and former co-workers.[44] There are also many carefully clipped newspaper announcements of her birth in a section with the handwritten caption "Sarah's First Notices in the Society Columns."[45] Letters from family and close friends suggest the writers' relief, enveloped with genuine joy, now that the couple's strenuous efforts had finally been rewarded with a healthy baby.

"You're Under a Contract to Us"

His reputation as a broadcaster spreading across the region, Barber tapped his performance skills, cultivated in Sanford and Gainesville, for speaking engagements throughout southern Ohio. In November Barber was featured in an "evening of entertainment" for University of Dayton alumni as part of their homecoming celebration. He recounted highlights of the exhilarating Ohio State–Notre Dame game.[46] The next week Barber spoke in Cincinnati at the Notre Dame Club.[47] In early 1936 he joined Charlie Dressen and other Reds officials in presenting civic leaders in Covington, Kentucky, with news about the upcoming baseball season.[48]

During the final days of the Barbers' Cincinnati years, Red was invited by Cincinnati's Shubert Theater to perform a vivid re-creation of the crucial last inning of Johnny Vander Meer's record-breaking second consecutive no-hitter. Each night of his week-long gig, Red's act directly followed the theater's featured vaudeville show—the popular Blackstone the Magician. Red first introduced his Vander Meer no-hitter re-creation in Cincinnati but continued to hone and perform it and other re-creations of breathtaking final innings for audiences almost until his death. These performances would stun even a twenty-first-century listener who has no idea who Vander Meer was. Recordings reveal that Red mesmerized his listeners by making them see every detail on the field and each movement of key players as they performed remarkable feats in a game he was not even watching except in his mind's eye. His low-key voice, speaking at a lively pace, accentuated the tension of the scene, second by second, and then it rose ever so slowly and deliberately to a roaring crescendo, almost like a piece of opera. Reviews of his performance at the Shubert were quite positive, one critic quoting Red as saying that "he [was] thinking now of perhaps making a few stage appearances in New York, after he [got] his radio act in the groove up that way."[49]

By 1938 Barber was one of the most widely admired sportscasters in the country. Despite his lack of a national network job, he placed fourth among sports announcers in the *New York World-Telegram* poll of 253 radio editors, behind Ted Husing (CBS), Bill Stern (NBC), and Clem McCarthy (NBC).[50] The radio press speculated that he would leave WLW for either NBC or CBS. His popularity in the Ohio Valley continued to soar. An ad in *Variety* reported that a WSAI promotion for a gasoline distributer sponsoring Barber's *Sports Resume* resulted in dealers giving away twenty thousand Red Barber stickers during a two-week offer.[51] In August Red received fan mail that included nine testimonials telling him that "in the opinion of its authors, he [was] the swellest baseball reporter on the job," signed by 653 fans. Another letter came from 216 fans in Piqua, while a letter from Aberdeen added 70 more signatures.[52] As part of a "Valley Day" promotion at Crosley Field on September 7, 1938, local grocers and delicatessens put large rolls of paper in their establishments, gathering names and endorsements for Barber and his Reds broadcast sponsor, Wheaties. The testimonials were "pasted together into one huge roll which [would] be ceremoniously presented to the sports announcer."[53] When Red missed some games while recovering from a cold and laryngitis, he received 500 letters from well-wishers, along with eighteen suggested cold remedies and a few bottles of medicine.[54] His mail was becoming too vast for him to answer personally, as he had always done in the past. So Barber and Dick Bray "hit upon a novel idea": a Monday, Wednesday, Friday *Sports Question Box* program on WSAI, where they would answer as many queries as they could. On Tuesday and Thursday the two performers flipped roles with the listeners, asking them the questions on a program called *Sports Quizzer*.[55]

Barber's popularity, however, had a price. As he rose to the top of the talent heap at Crosley, his new boss, Bob Dunville (John Clark's replacement) wanted Red on more programs. He was already doing games, either live or by re-creation, and his *Sports Resume* show at 5:45, while also contributing to *Sports Question Box*. In addition, Crosley's long-time sports reporter, Bob Newhall, had retired, and Red and his sportswriter friend Nixson Denton now filled his 6:30 sports news and commentary spot. Barber had a pressure-filled day on the air and also chose to write his own material. When Barber finished his exhausting day at Crosley, he went home, ate dinner, and fell into bed. But Dunville still wanted more from his sports radio star.

In the middle of the 1938 season, Crosley sold the idea for a new show, sponsored by Bavarian Beer, offering highlights of the afternoon game: a shortened re-creation. The fifteen-minute, five-days-a-week *Baseball Nightcap* would air at 9:00 p.m., when Barber was usually anticipating his trip to dreamland. The *Cincinnati Enquirer* and many other regional newspapers reported that the idea for the program had originated in a petition from several hundred listeners to provide a Reds game re-cap for those who could not listen to that afternoon's live contest.[56] The improving on-field fortunes of the Reds—they would finish fourth in 1938—also generated more interest in an evening replay. While the demand for the broadcast was clear and the station had signed a sponsor, the assignment did not have to be Barber's; Dick Bray could easily have done it. But Dunville wanted Barber. When his boss informed Red of his extra assignment, Barber was aghast: "You want me to come back and write another show and rouse myself to the pitch of doing a dramatic presentation in full voice? It's too much to ask. I won't do it." But Dunville insisted: "You will do it. You're under a contract to us. When we get a chance to sell a show and make money on you, we're going to do it."[57]

Red knew his choices were limited. He could break his contract and leave a position that had brought fame and some fortune, endangering his radio career, or he could do the show. For the first time, Barber fully realized the limitations of being a salaried employee with no union protection. When he moved to New York in 1939, he immediately joined the American Federation of Radio Artists (AFRA). In his confrontation with Dunville, Barber accepted defeat but not quietly. He informed his boss, "All right, but I'll tell you this. When my contract expires, I don't care whether there are no other jobs left on the face of the earth. I won't be back to work for you next year."[58] Barber's knowledge that a New York baseball job might well be in his future likely emboldened his bravado. Before making pronouncements to power, Red usually had "Plan B" in his hip pocket.

Red recognized that Larry MacPhail wanted the Dodgers to broadcast games in 1939 now that the five-year New York radio blackout agreement would finally expire. He also knew that General Mills, the nation's leading sponsor of baseball, would want to enter the largest market in the country. General Mills' signature product in baseball sponsorship was Wheaties, "the Breakfast of Champions." Barber's Reds were one of the many teams General Mills used to sell Wheaties to children and their mothers on daytime baseball broadcasts. A poem in the *Cincinnati Times-Star* even poked fun at Barber's Wheaties huckstering:

> Red Barber has charm and he shows it.
> And over the air he sure throws it—
> But with all his entreaties
> To munch those damned Wheaties
> He eats ham and eggs and he knows it![59]

By the end of the 1938 baseball season, Barber had already attended several General Mills conferences where the company trained broadcasters in the subtleties of selling cereal while also promoting ballpark attendance on behalf of team owners.[60] Through his contacts in the company, Red knew two New York positions would likely be available: one broadcasting the Brooklyn live home games and road re-creations and another broadcasting most of the home games of both Giants and Yankees, which were rarely scheduled on the same day. General Mills contacts told Red he was a strong candidate but made sure he knew they were considering thirty or more others for the two Gotham jobs. What Red did not know—and what his General Mills contacts made sure that he did not know—was that the score and ten candidates had dwindled quickly to one: Walter Lanier Barber. Larry MacPhail insisted on three things before signing with General Mills to sponsor Dodgers games: $75,000 for the broadcast rights, a 50,000-watt maximum power station to carry the games, and Red Barber to broadcast them. General Mills agreed to MacPhail's demands but also asked him to remain mum on his demand for Barber, at least until the Old Redhead was under contract. General Mills offered Barber $8,000 a year to leave the security and heavy demands of Crosley Broadcasting. It did not publicly commit to what team's games Barber would cover, but Red was certain it would be the Brooklyn Dodgers.

Red's run-in with Bob Dunville did not sour him entirely on Crosley Broadcasting. He still deeply respected Powell Crosley, who wanted to keep him in Cincinnati. He offered Barber both more money—$16,000—and more control over his assignments: "I'll make you our sports executive, answerable only to the general manager. You'll be free to select and broadcast any sporting event you want." The offer was magnanimous, particularly from an owner who was not by nature a generous employer. According to Barber, "The standard joke in Cincinnati was that WLW stood for World's Lowest Wages." But Barber wanted another career boost, like the one he'd earned by moving to Crosley from WRUF, a boost he could secure now only by moving to New York. When Crosley asked him why he was turning down his generous offer, Barber told him, "I want to go to New York for the same reason that you went broke six times before you came up with WLW." Red was reminding his boss that the greatest successes required taking risks and delaying rewards. Powell Crosley smiled, came from behind his desk, and shook Barber's hand: "I completely understand. Good Luck!"[61] With that goodwill from the owner of Crosley Broadcasting, Red Barber bet on himself once again, believing that his talent, drive, and luck would yield success in America's most commercially lucrative and competitive metropolis.

PART 3

BROOKLYN

The Barber of Flatbush

7

Making of a Legend

Red Barber was red hot. While he always tried to control his anger in public, he often shared his private fury with Lylah. The April 27, 1939, issue of *Time* magazine had just hit the newsstands with a feature on baseball broadcasts coming to the Big Apple. The five-year boycott of radio by the Yankees, Giants, and Dodgers was finally over. The teams in the nation's largest city and arguably the Major League Baseball epicenter had at last agreed to permit daily live broadcasts of home games and re-creations of road contests. In its radio section *Time* offered lavish praise for and a photograph of Arch McDonald, the new voice of the Yankees and Giants. *Time* told its readers about McDonald's colorful figures of speech and his special approach to the game. It recounted a rousing story about the time he challenged abusive listeners to a fight. *Time* even reported that the vice president of the United States thought Arch was the nation's best baseball announcer.[1]

As Barber reviewed the nation's most important news weekly, he noted two obvious omissions: *Time* did not mention the Brooklyn Dodgers, the team that broke the New York boycott, or their new announcer, Walter Lanier "Red" Barber. Perhaps Barber could have excused the slight if he were just the new kid on the block and McDonald the veteran voice. But Barber was an experienced baseball broadcaster, having logged five years as the voice of a Major League team. Although McDonald had done re-creations for many years, the Washington Senators, his former Major League team, only allowed live broadcasts starting in 1938.[2] Despite his relative youth, Barber was not only the more experienced broadcaster of live regular-season Major League games, but he had also broadcast every World Series since 1935. McDonald had broadcast none. In 1968 Barber recalled his anger: "I don't know when I have ever been as mad. . . . As far as I was concerned, *Time* had given me the ultimate insult. It had ignored me."[3] As with other slights during his career, both perceived and real, Red Barber used his rage as psychic rocket fuel to power his professional ambitions.

Now the chip was lodged firmly on Barber's shoulder. The chip on Brooklyn's shoulder had been there for years. In 1898 New York City annexed Brooklyn, at the time the nation's fourth-largest city. The borough became a second-class citizen in the nation's largest city, and resentment mounted over the decades. While many in the borough worked in Manhattan, they never identified with it; they were the outsiders and so was their baseball team, the frequently hapless Brooklyn Dodgers. When Red arrived in 1939, the Dodgers had exactly one pennant and no World Series win to their credit. In the eighteen years following their lone pennant in 1920, they finished sixth or seventh twelve times, including seventh in 1938. During this stretch of Dodgers doldrums, their Gotham rivals dominated: the Yankees had won ten pennants and seven World Series, while the Giants had won seven pennants and three World Series. The press called the Dodgers the "Bums" for a reason. But in 1938 Larry MacPhail became general manager and transformed his team, as he had done in Cincinnati. In 1937, 480,000 had moved through the Ebbets Field turnstiles, a figure that grew to 660,000 after MacPhail's first year. But to grow attendance even more, MacPhail needed something else: a winning team and radio coverage to build daily interest in his "new and improved" product. The radio part was easier.

In late 1938 MacPhail announced the Dodgers would break the New York radio broadcast ban. They would offer both live home games and road game re-creations on the 50,000-watt station, WOR, and General Mills and Socony-Vacuum Oil (Mobil) would sponsor the broadcasts.[4] By late January 1939 the Yankees and Giants had followed suit, allowing home games, excluding Sundays, on WABC with Procter & Gamble joining the Dodgers' two sponsors.[5] General Mills assigned Red Barber, MacPhail's choice, to the Brooklyn broadcasts on WOR and WHN. Barber claimed his right to select his associate broadcaster. Already in New York, Al Helfer, Red's first partner in Cincinnati, joined the broadcast team. "Brother Al" teamed with Barber during his first three years in Brooklyn.

To improve the team, MacPhail began working his baseball magic through astute trades and purchases. In short order he created a stellar lineup, featuring Dolph Camilli, Pete Reiser, Mickey Owen, Dixie Walker, and Billy Herman. MacPhail gave Leo Durocher—a brilliant baseball mind equipped with a personality almost as volatile as his own—his first chance to manage a big league team. The seventh-place Dodgers of 1938 improved to third in 1939. The 1940 club advanced to second with an 88-65 record. The next year brought the team its first pennant in two decades and the first of many heartbreaking World Series losses to its Bronx rivals, the Yankees. While Barber had learned his craft calling the games of a last-place club in Cincinnati, he became the voice of the Dodgers' great renewal in Brooklyn. But his unveiling was a disaster.

A Defeated Broadcaster

MacPhail told Barber that when he had announced his intention to put the Dodgers on the radio in 1939, the Yankees threatened to blast him out of the water with a more powerful station and a better-quality broadcast. Their station, WABC, and the Dodgers' principal carrier, WOR, both broadcast at 50,000 watts.[6] So station power was even. In Barber, MacPhail believed he had the better broadcaster. But MacPhail also wanted to beat his New York rivals to the radio punch. He wanted some Dodgers spring training games re-created by Barber at the WOR studio in New York. Red would cover the last few contests as the team barnstormed up the Atlantic Coast from its Clearwater, Florida, spring training site.

Just as Barber had settled into re-creating the first of these games, played in South Carolina, he encountered serious obstacles. The small-town telegraph operator, who had no experience transmitting baseball information, failed to provide Barber with the batting order. From the time the transmission began, he was not being told how far the runners had advanced on a hit. At one point he realized that the transmitted "hit to short" meant only that the ball was hit in the *direction* of the shortstop. The play had really resulted in an out, but Barber had no idea how the out had been made. After struggling with this garbled transmission, Barber, for the only time in his career, was "defeated" on a broadcast. He told his new and eager WOR audience, "Folks, I'm very sorry, but we are unable to get the Western Union report on this game," and he walked out of the studio.[7]

When he left, there were three men on base with no outs, but the telegraph operator had the wrong team at bat. Barber and everyone else, including WOR; General Mills, the game's sponsor; Knox Reeves, their ad agency; and Western Union in New York were "wild." But none of them were as "wild" as Red. Fortunately, Barber remembered that *New York Times* reporter Roscoe McGowen, who had some experience as a telegraph operator, was traveling with the team. Barber convinced him to take over transmitting the dots and dashes for the rest of the spring training games.[8] With an experienced baseball writer providing accurate information, Barber righted the re-creation ship, and New Yorkers got their first taste of the Old Redhead's work before the Yankees and Giants even made it to the airwaves.

Red's perennial "luck" continued during his broadcast of the Dodgers' Opening Day. While photographers in the radio booth documented Barber's first live Dodgers game, a flashbulb dropped to the floor and exploded, sending fragments of glass into the mouth of the new "Voice of the Dodgers," a dangerous send-off for any new launch. Barber froze and Al Helfer stepped in to cover the game. But after delicately extracting the sharp fragments and finding no cuts, Barber continued his first broadcast from Ebbets Field.[9]

Learning Brooklyn

The year 1939 was not the worst for a Southerner to arrive in Brooklyn, one of America's most un-Southern towns. As the threat of war in Europe loomed, Americans increasingly realized that the "united" in "United States" might soon be tested. Meanwhile, the glories of the Old South were being touted in the year's best picture, *Gone with the Wind*, which in 2014 was named the highest-grossing film of all time.[10] Brilliantly staged in color, the film's glorification of a defeated South and a slave-holding plutocracy glossed over the brutal realities of the Jim Crow era of Red Barber's youth, realities still potent in 1939. For three hours and fifty-eight minutes of fictional re-creation, the screen projected the beauties of antebellum mansions, genteel Southern traditions, and affectionate relationships between masters and slaves. Nearly three quarters of a century after the Civil War, white America was embracing this romanticized version of the Old South. Barber's timing was perfect.

Always eager to learn, Red came to Brooklyn knowing what he did not know, which was pretty much everything about the borough. In his early off-days in Brooklyn, with Lylah and toddler Sarah in tow, Red took scouting drives along its streets, learning their names, buildings, and special character. On game days he rode the subway to the Franklin Avenue stop and then walked the five blocks south to Montgomery Street and Ebbets Field. Along the way he talked with store owners standing outside their shops and sometimes grabbed a sandwich and a soda at a local deli. A twenty-something Howard Cosell once saw Barber, whom he had heard on shortwave radio when Red called Cincinnati games, standing at the corner of Franklin Avenue and President Street. He wanted to ask his favorite announcer for his autograph but never did.[11] As a white Protestant Southern stranger in a strange, religiously diverse, multiethnic land, Red wanted to mix with Dodgers fans as much as possible to learn what fired their loyalty to the often awful Bums. Barber understood and practiced one of the first steps in successful communication in any new situation: analyze your audience.

What Barber learned was that Brooklynites, like Red himself, were "outsiders." They resented the tall towers and skyscraper pretensions of Manhattan. Brooklynites were angry that most Americans thought the entire city was on an island between the Hudson and East Rivers. They showered both love and disgust on their Dodgers, fiercely critical of the team's shortcomings but just as fiercely protective when other New Yorkers belittled the borough's club. They were interested in their team, but most fans were men, and most of them could visit Ebbets Field only on weekends. Attendance was growing but still limited compared to the crowds that showed up for the Yankees and Giants. MacPhail saw radio as the tool to keep workers talking about the team, some of whom could listen while they worked. He also knew that the right announcer could interest and educate women about baseball, providing General Mills with a market of mothers who would buy cereal. In addition, some of those women would bring their families to Ebbets Field, and several would become Dodgers "superfans."

Barber's success in bringing women to baseball was a product of the times and his own keen talents. Night baseball games would not become common until after World War II. During Barber's formative years, teams played during the day, and the most available weekday radio audiences were comprised of women and, after the school day ended, children. Companies selling male-targeted products, like automotive essentials, beer, and cigarettes, were major game sponsors, but cereal makers General Mills and Kellogg and soap sellers Procter & Gamble and Lever Brothers were even more aggressive in pushing reluctant baseball owners to broadcast their games.[12]

Red Barber appealed to women. His slight but solid build; handsome face; snappy dress; and curly red, strawberry blond, lemon, taffy colored—depending on the reporter—hair were key components of the charm. His amazing verbal skills and soft Southern accent were appealing to women weary of loud-mouthed barkers. He also respected and valued women. His mother, Selena, had been a college-educated teacher and school administrator who had instilled in him a love for and precision with the English language. He viewed his wife as his intellectual equal. Although he never finished college, he was proud that Lylah was one of the first three women in Florida to earn a Bachelor of Science degree in nursing. In his later writings he expressed his admiration for the advice and perspective that Branch Rickey received from his wife Jane and the strength of character that Rachel Robinson displayed during Jackie Robinson's battle to end segregation in Major League Baseball.

Barber also listened to women. Half of his mail came from women, and he read the letters they sent. Barber told the *New York Times*, "Mail is my barometer. . . . Only 1 percent of the mail is critical of me." For instance, a listener might encourage him to mention the score more often or correct Red's rare mispronunciation of a word. The letters could also be personal: "Housewives write to tell how they have rearranged their household routine. Vacuum cleaning becomes a chore to be done before or after the game. Darning and shelling peas can be taken along to the ball game by radio."[13] Tom Villante, producer of Barber's broadcasts starting in 1950, believed that "without a doubt, the women in the New York area were Dodger fans because of Red." Barber could explain something as complex as the infield fly rule "in such a way that he didn't offend the male listeners but that women also could understand."[14] Barber had gained considerable experience talking to women on the air when he interviewed Cincinnati homemakers on the events of the day in his "Man in the Neighborhood" program on WSAI.

Journalists were noting Red's appeal to women. According to writer Maxwell Hamilton of *Cue* magazine, before Barber broadcast the Dodgers, "The number of females in the metropolitan area who knew a blessed thing about baseball could be counted on the buttons of your vest," and ladies' days didn't draw enough women "to start a bridge game." Barber told Hamilton he was "especially proud of his campaign to educate [new fans]," believing "the future of baseball rests on the laps of women and children."[15] By the middle of the 1939 season, Barber's broadcasts helped attract a record ladies' day attendance at a game with the Giants that "almost crowded out cash customers."[16] Still, while Barber brought women to the games and helped their children become Dodgers fans, it was his *Time* magazine slight that most forcibly drove his passion to succeed.

Old Redhead versus Old McDonald

While *Time* magazine may have ignored Red Barber and the Dodgers' entry into the New York radio scene, the Gotham press was invested deeply in both of the city's new baseball broadcasters. Reviews of Barber's arrival were mixed, with some columnists preferring Arch McDonald. Even though McDonald's live baseball broadcasting experience was limited, his re-creations of Senators' games had been a major attraction in the nation's capital since 1934. They were so popular that a Peoples Drug Store three blocks from the White House created a second-floor studio equipped with bleachers so that an audience could watch his dramatic re-creations—and buy a few things in the store.[17] Initially, Ben Gross of the *New York City News* seemed to prefer McDonald, writing that "Red Barber squinted his eyes and exercised his larynx" while "Arch McDonald mixed Broadway chatter with ball jargon to amusing effect."[18] Other newspapers criticized both broadcasters. The *World-Telegram* complained that Barber and McDonald rarely told listeners if the pitcher had thrown a fastball, curve, or slow one.[19]

Some commentators saw Red Barber as an outsider forced upon them. Before he even "verced" his first Brooklyn home game, one scribe complained that Barber, following Larry MacPhail, was the latest person "from the land of knockwurst and sauerbraten" to join the Dodgers. He "was chosen after the powers-that-bees scanned a list of applicants which included everybody and his cousin. That is, everybody but a Flatbusher."[20] But Robert Windt of the *Boro Park Herald* congratulated "Laughing" Larry MacPhail for outwitting both the Giants and Yankees by landing "one of the mid-west's premier sports announcers [with] a soft Southern manner and those honeysuckle expressions that seem to slide off the redhead's tongue."[21]

Only a month into the season, the *Brooklyn Eagle* opined that Barber's colorful expressions "enriched the play-by-play descriptions immeasurably." This was perhaps the earliest Gotham report on what would become known as "Barberisms." Among the earliest reported by the *Eagle* were some of Barber's most famous— for example, "tearing up the pea patch," meaning the Dodgers were "going to town" on their opponent for the day. Also new to Brooklyn ears were "the catbird seat," as well as Red's simile for a challenging ball to hang onto—"slick as okra," the particularly slippery vegetable. Where a more pedestrian announcer would say a lopsided game was "in the bag," Barber had the contest "tied up in a croaker sack." Pitchers with a big breaking ball threw "a jug-handle curve." Batters trying to kill the ball were "swinging from Terre Haute." The hopeful slugger too often "hit one off the thumb"—that is, failed to hit the ball squarely and instead produced a weak pop up.[22]

The fierce rivalry between the Dodgers and the Giants may well have resulted in one of the more memorable "Barbarisms" that Red popularized while in the broadcast booth: his use of "rhubarb" to mean "argument," "fight," or other form of lively disagreement. Barber said he first heard the word used with that meaning by Garry Schumacher, a New York sportswriter, and started saying "rhubarb" himself whenever "the fur began to fly" on the field.

Schumacher told Red he had picked up this usage of "rhubarb" from another New York sportswriter, Tom Meany, before Barber arrived in New York. Meany first heard "rhubarb," in the sense of a fight, from a bartender in Brooklyn "[the day after a] Giants fan ragged a Brooklyn fan so unmercifully that the Brooklyn fan left the bar, came back with a gun, and shot the Giants fan in the stomach," a tragedy widely reported in local papers. When Meany went to the tavern the next day, the bartender told him, "We had quite a rhubarb here last night, Mr. Meany."[23]

By late June 1939 the New York honeymoon seemed to be over for Arch McDonald. In a short but blistering review, *Variety* described the "colorless and academic" McDonald as "the original cliché kid," offering "irritating repetitions [of] ducks are on the pond" for the bases are loaded and "right down Broadway" for a strike in the middle of the plate. McDonald's relentless promotion of Wheaties also annoyed *Variety*. Every Major Leaguer making a decent play has "a plug for Wheaties . . . tacked onto him in a farfetched manner." The show biz publication speculated that McDonald "must chase plenty of fans over to Red Barber on WOR."[24] Although less critical, *Billboard* also sided with Barber over McDonald. Red "seems to be faster on the draw and punchier," while Arch was "a bit less handy with the verbiage."[25]

Indeed the Dodgers were doing better than the Yankees in drawing listeners to baseball. In May 1939 *Variety* reported that baseball drew in about a third of the New York daytime audience. Barber's call of the Dodgers' games got 18.5 percent, and McDonald's Yankees, 12.2 percent. The audience size picked up later in the games. *Variety* speculated that the final innings gave homemakers "just enough of the game to make conversation around the dinner table."[26]

Throughout his competition with McDonald, Barber's stamina behind the mic was also gaining attention. Robert Windt reported that among "radio men" Barber was the "Lou Gehrig of the air lanes" because he had missed only one series of broadcasts in nine years behind the mic.[27] Barber's stamina, however, received its widest acclaim when the Dodgers waged a nineteen-inning draw of attrition against the Cubs on May 17, 1939. The game ended in a 9–9 tie when it became too dark to play at the unlit Wrigley Field. Barber's 1939 scrapbook contains nineteen clippings of the AP's Eddie Brietz's "Sports Round-Up" column and eighteen more from a second article picked up by Florida newspapers and published under variations of the headline "Florida Announcer Makes Good." Brietz called Red "the demon announcer," noting he had been on the air from 3:55 to 8:47 p.m. (EST). Since it was a road game played in Chicago, Barber's marathon was a re-creation; nearly five hours of watching and instantly voicing the telegraph reports of the game left Barber exhausted and "hoarse at the finish."[28] The *World-Telegram* reported that Barber's voice held out during the marathon, but his legs gave way after standing for so many hours. The paper then recalled Barber's arduous twelve-hour days broadcasting the Florida high school basketball tournaments in the early 1930s.[29] Despite the publicity, the nineteen-inning affair was only a warm-up for Barber's longest game as a broadcaster.

Just over five weeks later, on June 27, 1939, Barber re-created all twenty-three innings of the Dodgers' 2–2 tie with the Boston Bees. The game lasted five hours and fifteen minutes before darkness arrested the contest. Barber stood for the entire game, calling it one of "his roughest days." When it ended, it was the longest game ever played, measured in time rather than the number of innings. At the end of the season, Barber wryly informed *The Sporting News*, "I can still feel the pain in my legs."[30]

Barber also designed an alternative way to do re-creations that strengthened his position in his rivalry with McDonald. The eleven games the Dodgers played with the Giants at the Polo grounds brought McDonald's live broadcast into direct competition with Barber's re-creation of the same game. New York area listeners could choose their broadcaster. Barber knew his re-creation could not match McDonald's live broadcast for speed. Arch could call the action as it happened, while Red had to wait for the Western

Union report. Determined to shorten the delay, Barber instructed the telegraph operator at the Polo Grounds to send "a simplified version of the standard Paragraph One report." He clarifies: "Instead of using pilot words, we used letters, and we didn't wait for details. He'd send 'S' and immediately I'd say, 'Strike' and then as I saw a second 'S,' I'd add, 'Swinging,' and so on." Barber claimed that the new shorthand meant his call was only briefly delayed. Listeners could hear McDonald's call on WABC, and by the time they tuned their radio to WOR, Barber was giving his re-created version.[31] Red was re-inventing the re-creation.

Barber's competition with McDonald would continue through the 1939 season, which ended in yet another Yankees World Series victory, a four-game sweep of Red's former team, the Cincinnati Reds. But it was Barber and not McDonald who would do the Series with Bob Elson. At season's end McDonald returned to Washington, where he would resume duties as the beloved voice of the Senators until 1956. Barber felt no hostility toward McDonald, whom he saw only as a professional rival. But in his 1968 memoir, Barber still celebrated his rival's retreat: "I must admit, in all candor and despite my personal regard for him, that I felt a great deal of satisfaction when Arch McDonald left New York and went back to Washington after that season. I had shown them, I had shown *Time* magazine. Most of all, I had shown New York."[32]

Television: Flying Blind

A historic highlight of Barber's first Brooklyn year was the first telecast of a Major League game on August 26, 1939: one game of a doubleheader at Ebbets Field between the Dodgers and the Reds. To showcase the new medium, NBC launched an aggressive promotional campaign called "Television's First Year," which included extensive remote broadcasts of New York area events.[33] But 1939 was far from television's first year. Experimentation with television transmission had started in 1923, and a live drama was broadcast in the United States in 1928. In 1931 Japanese engineers even televised a baseball game using a low-resolution mechanical television system, the forerunner of the electronic system used by NBC.[34]

NBC's first telecast of the national pastime had aired on May 17, 1939. It was a college contest between Columbia and Princeton at Baker Field in New York. The effort was perhaps acceptable for a first attempt, but the handful of viewers in the New York area learned much more about the game from the audio commentary than from the low-quality images on their small screens. NBC used only one camera, positioned on a twelve-foot platform on the third base line. The camera operator panned to follow the flight of a hit ball and the progress of the runners around the bases. Foul balls were especially problematic since their unpredictable voyage meant the operator often had to search for them in flight. The camera operator lost the image of the baseball, and the dizzying movement annoyed the viewers. The television coverage gained some national publicity for NBC; *Life* magazine reported the story with pictures of the action taken from a television screen, concluding, "The reception that day was rather fuzzy."[35]

But for NBC's experimental station, W2XBS, the first televised baseball game in the United States was just the start of a learning curve. Bill Stern, NBC's ace sportscaster, voiced the affair without benefit of a video monitor. He simply called the game as if it were on radio and let the camera find what it could. Although not modest by nature, Stern knew the telecast was, at best, a rough draft for future efforts: "God, we were dunces. Whoever said one camera could cover a baseball game? In that one game, we learned a complete lesson about how not to televise a sports event."[36]

Through the summer of 1939 NBC televised some other outdoor events and now wanted to crown the summer with a contest from the nation's most popular sport, Major League baseball. Red Barber's previous connections with NBC and his familiarity with Larry MacPhail's psychology made it happen. Barber knew NBC vice president in charge of television Alfred H. "Doc" Morton from his unsuccessful interview with John Royal in 1935 and maintained a cordial relationship with him. In the summer of 1939 Morton asked Barber if he thought NBC could interest MacPhail in telecasting a Dodgers game on W2XBS. Morton told him, "The Giants and Yankees do not like broadcasting, and I'm sure they would turn me down. But from what I hear, MacPhail might go for it."[37]

Barber was interested in the new technology, anticipating that a televised game would be a publicity coup for the Dodgers and himself. He also knew that MacPhail took pride in being a baseball innovator. If he could pitch the NBC request as a chance for MacPhail to add another baseball first to his legacy, Larry would go for it. Red surprised him with a visit to the Dodgers' offices at 215 Montague Street, where Barber had never met with MacPhail before. When Red asked if he would like to be the first man ever— ever in history—to put on a television broadcast of a Major League baseball game, MacPhail answered in one word: yes. Barber wrote and was interviewed about the broadcast throughout his career; for the game's thirty-fifth anniversary, he published his vivid recollection of the event, "We Were Making History," in TV Guide.

By August 26, when Barber took the mic for the first Major League televised game, NBC had made significant improvements in its baseball coverage. Now there were two lower-resolution iconoscope cameras, each equipped with a telephoto lens. NBC positioned one, the home plate camera, on the second deck behind the catcher, providing a view of the entire field. It placed the second camera near the visitors' dugout, left of home plate.[38] While the ball was often hard to see, the home plate camera covered the entire field, and the visitors' dugout camera could follow the pitch to home, the swing of the bat, and the movement of runners.

Once the game began, Barber's work was challenging. NBC gave him a communication link with director Burke Crotty, but he had no monitor to see what the viewers saw. During the game he looked at both cameras to see which had its red tally light on and guessed what the camera might be showing. Soon he lost his communication link with Crotty and had to proceed with no help from the telecast's director. Red summarized the situation succinctly in his *TV Guide* remembrance: "We were making video history—and all of us were flying blind."[39]

Although commercially licensed television would not begin until July 1, 1941, Barber did three commercials on camera during the game, one each for Wheaties, Ivory Soap, and Socony-Vacuum (Mobil Oil). These pitches were part of NBC's ongoing experimentation with "semi-commercials": television ads presented by NBC at no charge to assist the network in developing video ads and interesting future clients in the commercial possibilities of the new medium.[40] For Wheaties, Red poured cream and sugar into a bowl full of "the Breakfast of Champions" and added some banana slices. For Ivory soap, he displayed the trademark and "waved a wad of stage money to illustrate the first prize in a contest" sponsored by Ivory's producer, Procter & Gamble. For Mobil, Barber put on a gas station attendant's cap and held up some of the company's products.[41]

The telecast received favorable reviews, especially compared to NBC's first effort in May. Florida papers were beaming with pride over Barber, their "Cracker Boy," who broadcast the historic first TV game from a table in a lower box seat.[42] Doc Morton wrote Red to thank him for his contribution to "a very successful and interesting experiment we conducted Saturday last," praising Barber's work as "just about perfect." Morton enjoyed Red's handling of the commercials and his "sympathetic manner with different ball players [which] brought out their little idiosyncrasies."[43] NBC sent Red a more tangible recognition of his historic broadcast: a silver cigarette box with the inscription "To Red Barber Pioneer Television Sports Announcer in grateful appreciation, National Broadcasting Company August 26, 1939." NBC also sent Barber a bill for thirty-five dollars to cover the cost of his silver souvenir, a gesture that became, for Red, a favorite exemplum of corporate stinginess.[44]

An Exclusive World Series

Barber's call of the first televised Major League game was perhaps his most historically significant moment, but it was not his only signature game during the 1939 season. For the fifth straight year, Barber broadcast the World Series, this time between the Yankees and his old club, the Cincinnati Reds. It was only the Cincinnati club's second appearance in a World Series and its first since 1919. What made that broadcast historic was the new contract signed among the Gillette Safety Razor Company; MBS; and Commissioner Landis, who was representing Major League Baseball. For a fee of $100,000, the contract gave Gillette and MBS exclusive rights to the 1939 World Series, with an option for the 1940 Series. Gillette's total bill for the Series would be $225,000 when line charges were added to the costs.[45] MBS put its full weight behind its shining moment on the national sports stage, even changing its microphone for the contests. The chief engineer of WOR, one of the MBS flagship stations for the Series, made a special baseball themed microphone: the base of the microphone stand was shaped like home plate, its shaft like a baseball bat, and the mic at the top of the stand was enclosed in a replica of a baseball.[46]

Unlike previous Series, where as many as four networks and a cacophony of voices called the games, Barber and his fellow broadcaster, Bob Elson, were the lone play-by-play reporters for baseball's fall classic, and they received the full attention of MBS's advertising and promotional efforts for the Series. Elson had a wealth of World Series experience, calling his first Series in 1929. During the regular season he covered Cubs and White Sox games for WGN, MBS's Chicago outlet. According to profiles of the two sportscasters that appeared in newspapers across the country, Barber was "a human box score [who had been] talking, eating, sleeping baseball for almost all of his thirty-one years."[47] While Barber and Elson did the play-by-play, four noted sports and news authorities provided color commentary during the Series: Grantland Rice, Edwin C. Hill, Lowell Thomas, and Gabriel Heatter. Sportscaster Stan Lomax handled Gillette's commercial announcements.

Barber was proud of his selection for this first exclusive coverage and dedicated a separate fifty-plus-page scrapbook to the 1939 World Series clippings. The Series was far from dramatic; the

Yankees swept the Reds by scores of 2–1, 4–0, 7–3, and 7–4. But Barber's reviews were positive and nationally circulated by two of the nation's best-known commentators. Barber and Elson got a brief favorable mention in Walter Winchell's influential nationally syndicated column: "Orchids to the safety razor sponsor of the Series games and Bob Elson and Red Barber, whose reporting is big league stuff."[48] The announcing pair also got kudos on national radio from Lowell Thomas, the most famous newscaster of the day. Thomas did a fifteen-minute commentary before Game Two of the Series and then listened to Barber and Elson's calls. On October 5, 1939, he told his vast NBC audience: "I myself have had some experience in this art of talking into a microphone, and I could appreciate the skill and adeptness of my colleagues Elson and Barber. They clicked it off with practiced precision, always something to say, and they said it in a way that kept moving comment right on the nose of every play."[49]

Barber ended his 1939 World Series scrapbook with a letter and a telegram. Gillette's advertising manager, A. Craig Smith, with whom Barber would feud in later years over his World Series pay, wrote, "We very much appreciate the swell job you did for us on the World Series broadcast" and "[The] best way of expressing our thanks for your excellent services is the fact we are electing to double your compensation."[50] Barber surely prized the recognition and the additional money, but his greatest kudo for the Series was pasted in the scrapbook page just before Smith's letter. It is a brief telegram from his primary role model: "HEARD YOUR BROADCAST TODAY FROM ELKS CLUB SARASOTA CAME IN GOOD AND I AM PROUD OF YOU." Signed, "DAD."[51]

In a year of baseball firsts, Barber's crowning achievement was receiving *The Sporting News* trophy as the Outstanding Baseball Broadcaster of 1939. Edger G. Brands, TSN editor, presented the award to Barber at ceremonies broadcast on the MBS network.[52] Ever the aspiring teacher and not one to oversimplify, Barber used the occasion of an interview in *The Sporting News* at the time of the award to offer fourteen (!) rules for successful baseball announcing.[53] Barber's protracted list of baseball broadcasting do's and don'ts summarized some of his most valued professional traits. Broadcasters must focus on preparation by studying baseball, their listeners and location, and improving the language skills they will rely upon to describe the game. They must take initiative and be self-directed, compiling their own statistics, reviewing their own mail, and staying sober and physically fit. Their honesty and fairness should be clear to all; to maintain objectivity, they should never play favorites. Finally, it makes excellent sense to know with whom one is talking and to cultivate friendships in the right circles. Barber successfully courted the press in his first years in Brooklyn. No better example was his telling *The Sporting News* editor who was interviewing him that broadcasters should carefully read each issue of *TSN*, the "baseball bible." He also knew most of his fellow baseball broadcasters were likely to read the interview. So Barber accepted the award "in all humility, and with the feeling that baseball broadcasters as a group are doing a marvelous job all over the country."[54]

Out of the Catbird Seat

In a 1965 interview with Barber, Howard Cosell speculated that Red's start in Gotham must have come with considerable insecurity because he needed "to make good in the big city in a big way." Barber jumped on Cosell's assumption, informing him that Crosley had offered him twice the Dodgers' salary to keep him in Cincinnati, and he also knew how much Larry MacPhail wanted him in Brooklyn: "I didn't come from a sense of insecurity; I came from a sense of really wanting to get my hands on this job up here and do it."[55] And do it he did. Barber's move to New York was a professional triumph. But there were occasional hiccups and, despite his success, some uncertainty about his continuing as the voice of the Dodgers.

The trigger for Barber's first hiccup was his own popularity and his favorite medium, radio. By the late 1930s portable, battery-powered radios were becoming more common. As the popularity of Barber's broadcasts grew, fans brought their receivers to Ebbets Field so they could hear Barber's call of the game that was right before their eyes. Barber soon found that radios were pounding out his voice right in front of his open broadcast booth at Ebbets Field. Because of the transmission time needed, he would hear over the radios what he had said only a split second earlier, just as he was trying to articulate what was happening next on the field. For Red the delayed feedback was a dreadful distraction. When a frustrated Barber told his listeners, "I'll have to do something about this," his own words returned from the stands to mock him.[56] Barber complained to Larry MacPhail, and the aroused and Roaring Redhead promptly banned all radios from the ballpark, confiscating fifty-two of them at a Dodgers-Giants night game. A few weeks after the radio confiscations, perhaps wanting to appease some angry radio fans, MacPhail scheduled a "Radio Appreciation Day," honoring Red Barber and "Brother Al" Helfer.[57]

Barber's second potential hiccup was more dangerous. When Larry MacPhail found out that wor radio would carry a speech by former President Herbert Hoover rather than the start of the first game of a Memorial Day doubleheader with the Giants, he snapped into one of his patented rages. wor's contract with the Dodgers allowed the station to preempt game broadcasts if they conflicted with other scheduled programs. The first game of the doubleheader often overlapped with some of wor's daily soap operas, so the station, as it had before, planned to pick up game one in progress. But then the station decided to preempt one of its fifteen-minute soaps for a Memorial Day address by Hoover. That set off MacPhail. Regularly scheduled programming preemptions were part of the routine. The Hoover speech was not. MacPhail demanded that wor broadcast both games in their entirety or not at all.[58] wor went with the former president.

Barber was sitting in the broadcast booth preparing to pick up the first game as soon as Hoover's speech ended when MacPhail suddenly called him to the pressroom and told him there would be no broadcast that day. Larry was forbidding Red to go on the air. Barber knew MacPhail had no right to stop his broadcast under the terms of the Dodgers' contract with WOR. He also reminded MacPhail that Red worked for General Mills, not the Dodgers. He planned to broadcast unless his sponsor or WOR told him otherwise. MacPhail was livid. After Barber returned to the booth, MacPhail sent the Ebbets Field electrician and his assistant to tell Red they would physically eject him from the booth if he tried to go on the air.

Although Red understood the workers were only following orders, he made it clear he was not leaving. As visions of the voice of the Dodgers being hauled kicking and screaming from his catbird seat surfaced in everyone's heads, Red's WOR audio engineer called the station to report the situation. WOR scrapped the broadcast of the first game of the doubleheader. On orders from the station, the WOR engineer never gave Red the start cue. That first game was a contest Barber always missed calling. Giants ace Carl Hubbell, Red's favorite big game pitcher, tossed perhaps his greatest game, a nearly perfect one. A single by second baseman Johnny Hudson produced the Dodgers' only base runner, and the Giants quickly erased him on a double play. King Carl faced only twenty-seven Dodgers. It was the closest Barber ever came to broadcasting a perfect game.

Eventually, WOR's general manager was pulled from his holiday golf match and told to call MacPhail to settle the dispute. By this time MacPhail had cooled, and the WOR executive politely asked him for permission to broadcast the second game—a permission that he knew the station did not need. But the request gave MacPhail the attention he craved, and he quickly agreed. At the time, Barber and MacPhail did not discuss the incident. With MacPhail water moved under the bridge rapidly. But decades later, at a Key Biscayne cocktail party, a laughing MacPhail told the story: "Do you know what this man [Red] did to me once? He almost made me throw him out of the broadcasting booth. . . . I really hadn't noticed him very much until then. But all of a sudden, he bowed his neck at me."[59] The Old Redhead, only thirty-two, won the Roaring Redhead's respect.

A third hiccup nearly ended Barber's stay in Brooklyn's catbird seat. Red ended 1940 as a rising local star, receiving the Brooklyn Young Men's Chamber of Commerce award as "[the man] who has made the largest civic contribution for the betterment of Brooklyn." He received the award during the broadcast of his WOR show, "Battle of the Boroughs," a popular local quiz show that pitted representatives of Gotham's five boroughs against each other.[60] Despite his award, however, Red's future in the borough was uncertain. Larry MacPhail shocked the audience at Red's testimonial dinner, speculating that the award winner might not come back "because of other commitments." Competition from other sponsors was driving up the Dodgers' rights fee, and General Mills, who had Barber under contract for 1941, might drop its Dodgers sponsorship, moving Red to cover another team's games.[61] Both *The Sporting News* and *Broadcasting* reported that Barber would shift from WOR to Philadelphia's WPEN and broadcast the 1941 Phillies games.[62] But their reporting failed to take Brooklyn's reaction into account.

MacPhail's comments provoked borough president John Cashmore to survey local business leaders about the possibility of assuming sponsorship of Dodgers broadcasts to promote Brooklyn-made products and to keep Red Barber at Ebbets Field.[63] The business leaders certainly were interested, but since they had already committed their advertising budgets for 1941, no local businesses would pledge their sponsorship. While they could not lend their support for 1941, they clearly wanted their favorite announcer to stay in Brooklyn. Fortunately for Barber fans, General Mills decided to continue its sponsorship of Dodgers games.[64] Yankees and Giants fans were not as fortunate. Camel cigarettes, their 1940 sponsor, dropped its sponsorship, and no other sponsors offered to snap it up. For the historic 1941 season—the season of Joe DiMaggio's fifty-six-game hitting streak, Ted Williams's .406 batting average, the Dodgers' first pennant in two decades, and the Bums' dramatic World Series with the Yankees—Red Barber's soft-flowing Southern drawl was the voice of all New York baseball.

"Symphony in D"

In July 1941 Barber served as "soloist" for Russell Bennett's "Symphony in D for the Dodgers," presented by the New York Philharmonic Symphony Orchestra at the City College of New York's Lewisohn Stadium. Not to be confused with what Barber called the "Sym-Phoney," a rag-tag group of comic musical performers at Ebbets Field, the "Symphony in D" was a serious musical composition with a four-movement plot: The Dodgers Win, The Dodgers Lose, MacPhail Looks for a Pitcher, and The Giants Come to Town. The symphony was first presented on Bennett's wor *Notebook* radio program. Red's singular performance was showcased in the fourth movement, when Barber narrated the Dodgers fan's happiest fantasy: a ninth-inning winning rally against the loathed Giants.[65] While its climax certainly pleased Brooklyn fans, the *Louisville Courier-Journal* panned the radio presentation of "Symphony in D for the Dodgers" as "one of the most ridiculous musical extravaganzas it has been our baffled amazement to have heard. . . . We don't know how long it took Mr. Bennett to write this opus, but we wish he never had thought it up."[66] In his column Bob Considine summarized other critical responses: "Thoughtful music critics, their ears cupped for the tell-tale wheeze of a weak woodwind, are inclined to believe that the symphony succeeded only in putting the Dodgers a little deeper into second place, and that its chances of replacing 'Take Me Out to the Ball Game' are remote."[67] While the "Symphony in D" might not have been a grand critical success, the Dodgers played better after its performance, winning their first pennant in two decades and advancing to the World Series to face the standard for Major League success, the New York Yankees.

At the end of the 1941 season, Barber received his second outstanding play-by-play announcer trophy from *The Sporting News*, during MBS's World Series preview radio special.[68] Commenting on recent World Series broadcasts, TSN saw Bob Elson, Red's partner for the last three Series and the 1940 *TSN* award winner, "as a straight ball caster," while Barber was "an inside-stuff stylist," always learning more about the game. He has grown "an extensive and picturesque vocabulary. . . . Baseball slang, colloquialisms, vivid phraseology, all pour, one might say 'spray,' from Barber's lips."[69]

Red's commitment to the spoken and written word was reflected in his favorite free-time activity: perusing New York for books and building an extensive personal sports library he would later contribute to the University of Florida. Red hunted for books in department stores, publishing houses, and "ratty little second-hand stores on 6th avenue." His collection included all the yearly *Spalding's Official Baseball Guide*(s) since 1899 and books on football, horses, fighters, baseball players, anglers, and automobile daredevils.[70]

WOR recognized Barber's professional commitment and the impact that his long days at work had on his family. The station acknowledged Lylah's contribution to Red's success with a seemingly ironic gift, a fitted traveling case, to compensate her "for the many hours Red has spent on the air and away from home," and it also offered thanks "for [her] co-operation and efforts, which have spurred him on to greater achievements."[71] The tension between Red's professional ambitions and the role he believed he should play in the life of his family would trouble him throughout his career as a sports announcer.

Full Football Schedule

Barber's Brooklyn legacy is rooted in baseball; his 1941 season, free of any local broadcast competition, cemented that legacy. But Barber was much more than just a baseball announcer. When he came to New York, he was more recognized nationally for his broadcasts of Ohio State, Notre Dame, and Army-Navy football than for his coverage of the Cincinnati Reds. His New York football footprint covered both games and a quiz show.

In 1939 WOR produced *We Want a Touchdown*, a weekly football game show with Red as host. In the MBS network show, two teams of former players from colleges scheduled to meet on the gridiron the upcoming Saturday tested their football knowledge. The team members answered football questions; correct answers moved their team down field, scoring touchdowns and extra points. Barber started hosting the show during the end of the 1939 baseball season. The November 17, 1939, panelists included Fordham University alumnus Vince Lombardi, at the time an assistant football coach at St. Cecilia Catholic High School in Englewood, New Jersey. No information is available to document how well the legendary coach, whose name graces the Super Bowl trophy, handled Barber's football queries.[72] Red published a guide for listeners who wanted to develop a home version of *We Want a Touchdown*, complete with sixteen sample questions and a plug: "Believe me, fans, there's plenty of suspense and excitement in a football quiz, if you've got a crowd at the house who really know their football . . . or think they do!"[73]

At the end of the 1939 season, Barber, Dick Fishell, and Harry Wismer broadcast the NFL championship game in Milwaukee between the New York Giants and Green Bay Packers, sponsored by General Mills over a nine-station ad hoc network.[74] *Variety* found Barber and his crew's labor "a good workmanlike job" and "above average in accuracy" when the broadcast was compared to newspaper accounts the next day. But *Variety* made fun of General Mills' insistence upon overplugging Wheaties on the broadcast, lamenting that it was "too bad the boys had to perform in this swell manner while handicapped with a mouth full of Wheaties."[75]

On New Year's Day 1940, Barber broadcast his first major bowl game, the Sugar Bowl, featuring Texas A&M and Tulane, on NBC Blue and sponsored by Gillette. This was the only time he handled the New Orleans classic. Reviews for his performance were stellar, particularly compared to those for the Rose and Orange Bowl announcers. The AP's Eddie Brietz commented that "Red Barber set a wicked pace for the other spielers."[76]

Barber's greatest 1940 football highlight produced one of his most treasured memories. Gillette was pleased with the response to the 1939 World Series broadcast on MBS. It also wanted a second opportunity to bring listeners another major sports exclusive. While the NFL championship game was not serious competition to the World Series, it mattered to devoted football fans. Gillette and MBS got the rights to the 1940 contest, the first NFL title game ever broadcast coast to coast. The contest featured two seemingly evenly matched teams: the Washington Redskins, the home team with a 9-2 record, and the visiting Chicago Bears, 8-3 during the 1940 season. The Redskins had beaten the Bears in a tight 7–3 match a few weeks earlier at Griffith Stadium. Following the successful introduction of a baseball-themed microphone for the World Series, MBS constructed a "football mic" for the occasion; remarkably, it featured a microphone encased in a regulation football suspended between two miniature goal posts mounted on a small gridiron.[77] On Sunday, December 8, 1940, the football mic delivered acceptable sound quality and a little additional publicity for MBS. The Chicago Bears delivered the most lopsided victory in the history of the NFL.

George Halas's Bears scored 21 points in the first quarter, spurring them to a comfortable 28–0 halftime lead. Then they kicked into high gear, scoring 26 more points in the third quarter and 19 in the fourth. Washington scored nil. The 73–0 final score became part of NFL lore. Bears assistant coach Carl Brumbaugh told Barber the night before the game that "[Red] had better be ready for an explosion the next afternoon." Dismissing the prediction as pregame hype, Barber wrote in 1972, "I wasn't [ready]—but neither were the Redskins."[78]

With the Bears' points mounting rapidly, Barber feared that the incredible disparity he was announcing would compromise his credibility as a sportscaster. The thirty-six thousand fans at Griffith Stadium saw the slaughter unfolding, but the radio listeners could not. They relied on Red, who envisioned that some of his listeners, who were just tuning in and hadn't heard the game develop "[were] going to hear this score 50/60 to nothing and [were] going to say the broadcaster [was] drunk or full of dope or crazy."[79] To confirm his account, Barber called in the troops. Sitting behind him were two World War I army officers whom Barber recognized as "well known football men": Biff Jones of Nebraska, a future College Football Hall of Fame coach, and Everett Yon of Florida, who had served as the school's athletic director. In the fourth quarter Barber asked them one at a time to confirm the score. Barber's credibility, but not Washington's pride, was restored.[80]

The 1941 football schedule triggered a conflict between Barber and Dan Topping, owner of the Brooklyn Dodgers NFL football team and his future boss with the Yankees. Barber always viewed Topping as a socially distant member of the privileged class who enjoyed "nightclubs, yachts, Café Society, private airplanes."[81] Their relationship was shaky from the start. In a 1987 interview, Barber revealed his disdain, reinforced by his working-class roots: "Topping inherited his money. He never earned a nickel. And I have learned to beware of any man born rich because they don't understand fellows that earn a living."[82] Topping expected WOR to use Barber for the 1941 NFL season of the Dodgers' football team. Barber could do the games with one exception, a Sunday contest with the Packers in Milwaukee. Red had already contracted with Atlantic Richfield to do the Saturday Princeton University games. He could not make it to Milwaukee in time for the Dodgers-Packers football game the next day, a fact he made clear to his WOR boss. The message, however, apparently did not get to Gene Thomas, the station's sales manager, who had promised Dan Topping that Red Barber, New York's most popular sportscaster, would call all the games.

When Topping found out that Barber would miss the Green Bay game, he angrily and quickly "moved on." The Monday after the Green Bay game Topping phoned Barber to let him know, "You're off the broadcast and Bill Slater's going to do it," and he promptly hung up.[83] Barber demanded a meeting with Thomas and Topping to clear up the misunderstanding. Thomas admitted that Barber had never agreed to do the Green Bay game, but Topping just shrugged his shoulders and said, "Too late—Slater does the games."[84] Barber also moved on, signing with sponsor Old Gold Cigarettes to broadcast the New York Giants' NFL games from 1942 to 1946 with Connie Desmond. For those five years Red was the voice of both Giants football and Dodgers baseball.

Since Red was no longer doing 1941 Dodgers football radio games, he was free for another Sunday assignment, and NBC came calling. During the previous football season, Barber had announced a televised football game for NBC's experimental station W2XBS on November 10, 1940, at Ebbets Field, when the Dodgers defeated Washington, 16–14. *New York PM* called Barber "the big star" of the game; his "microphone quarterbacking was unerring," and "[he] let you in on lots of inside stuff." Barber and television were "a big threat to football turnstiles." Viewers "got a lot more out of the game just sitting at home, taking the broadcaster's version of it." But the *World-Telegram* still thought TV was "no substitute for a seat in the stands," complaining that late in the game, when the daylight was waning, the picture "fades out of the screen almost entirely."[85]

NBC now wanted Red to do the televised home games of Dodgers football for the 1941 season on its commercially licensed station WNBT. Barber recalls doing the Dodgers' home games on NBC's WNBT using a specially built football television booth in front of the right-field fence at Ebbets Field.[86] MBS also wanted Barber back with Bob Elson for its exclusive national broadcast of the 1941 NFL championship game. One team in the contest would be the New York Giants, who would play their last game of the regular season at the Polo Grounds against the Brooklyn Dodgers football club. Barber, having fulfilled his television commitment to broadcast Dodgers home games, was free to scout the Giants as part of his preparation for the championship contest. Since the Giants had already won their conference, the game was of little importance to them; the Dodgers won easily, 21–7. But the date of the "meaningless" game would "live in infamy."

On December 7, 1941, Barber took his seat on a freezing day at the Polo Grounds in the section reserved for special guests, mostly the wives of players and writers. He wrapped himself in blankets and sat on the end of the row. As the game progressed in the first half, he heard the public address announcer twice request a General Donovan to call his office. Red thought nothing of it. Then at halftime Arthur Daley of the *New York Times* walked down from the press box and spoke to fans some rows in front of Barber. As Daley walked by Red on his way back to the press box, he leaned over and said, "Red, the Japanese have bombed Pearl Harbor." Stunned, Red sat for a minute until "the realization, the winds, suddenly swept over me." He got up, folded his blankets, walked to his car, and snapped on the radio. His scouting of the Giants had come to a shocking halt: "I don't know when I have ever thought as hard about anything as I thought about the United States, the world, my wife, daughter, myself."[87]

Barber still planned to broadcast the championship game scheduled the following Sunday. But the NFL had to delay the game, not because of Pearl Harbor, but because the Packers and Bears needed a playoff game to decide the Western Division title. The Bears won the playoff game, 33–14. On Sunday, December 21, 1941, Barber and Bob Elson broadcast the championship game nationally for the second time on MBS, this time from Chicago. Although the first half was close, the Bears easily beat the Giants, 37–9. But Red's strongest memory of the game was his first encounter with wartime censorship.

Barber and Elson were told not to provide listeners any information about the weather. Enemy forces intent upon a submarine or air attack on the U.S. mainland could use weather reports to formulate their plans. Since the game was being played only two weeks after Pearl Harbor—a devastating air strike supported by submarines—attacks on either coast remained a genuine possibility. The broadcasters followed instructions and ignored the weather, but Barber's passion for detailed description unwittingly produced a breach in the weather blackout. A few minutes into the game, he reported that the Bears' center was wiping mud off the football before putting it back in play—an innocent comment under ordinary circumstances but a violation in wartime. If the ball was muddy, the field must be wet, and if the field was wet, there must be rain. Weather deduced is weather reported. In discussing the breach with Robert Creamer twenty-five years later, Barber made light of his transgression: "They cut the broadcast. You can't talk about mud on the field; all those Japanese submarine commanders and all those German pilots . . . by a process of reduction they can figure out the whole weather pattern and therefore they got the United States right in front of their sights."[88] But Red had received the message. When he returned to the air, he never mentioned the condition of the ball again.

Red Barber's first brush with wartime censorship brought home the earthshaking events that would forever alter the lives of his audiences. It also brought to a close his very fruitful first years in Brooklyn. According to one of Barber's producers, "You could walk through Brooklyn during a day game, and any neighborhood you walked in, all you heard was Red Barber's voice doing the play-by-play."[89] His legion of borough fans included future media legends Larry King and Howard Cosell. With his professional reputation well established, a comfortable income, and considerable acclaim, the Barber of Flatbush would shift his focus from careerist ambitions to the greater good, deepening his reach into the soul of Brooklyn.

8

"Blood" on the Radio

I n his fourth season as announcer for the Brooklyn Dodgers, Red Barber was interviewed and profiled in two national publications; the two articles provide an informative measure of Barber's reputation as an uncommonly gifted professional and an early forecast of restlessness with the acclaim he was garnering. "The Barber of Brooklyn," Richard Hubler's protracted piece in the March 21, 1942, issue of the *Saturday Evening Post*, appears to have been written to guarantee that all of America would appreciate the inimitable Voice of the Dodgers. After documenting the virtues that New York papers had ascribed to the "Old Redhead," Hubler provides his own colorful account of how Barber's performance had transformed the borough of Brooklyn and much further beyond. From a psychological perspective, Red's Southern-soft staccato is not only the outlet for thousands of suppressed souls in Brooklyn; it is also "the release catch for inhibitions all over the world.... His canny descriptions make the Dodgers ... live, move and glow, complete with halos, in the mind's eye of every Brooklyn fan. Geographical limitations mean nothing to Dodger dervishes. They dwell in latitudes ranging from Saskatchewan to Suez."[1]

Hubler's extravagant claim regarding Barber's worldwide impacts was not unique among the press. The argument that Red was making waves around the globe later was graphically displayed on the cover of the October 7, 1943, issue of *The Sporting News*. The bottom third of the cover page featured a large sketch of Red Barber, from chest up, speaking into his mic as he called one of the 1943 World Series games. Sparks representing sound waves are flying from his mic to locations far and wide, depicted in four large clouds floating through the upper two-thirds of the cover page. Each of the four clouds contains a sketch of a group of servicemen huddled outdoors around a radio: in a frigid zone where a polar bear is edging his way into the group to catch the score; on a Pacific island near a smoking volcano; in a ship's forecastle; and in a desert somewhere. Word bubbles in each setting contain snippets of Barber's play-by-play and the faraway servicemen's responses—responses that link exciting play of the game back in the United States to their own distant wartime locations. For instance, after a third strike, one of the men on the volcanic island says the pitcher sure has "got smoke," and an attempt to steal home provokes a sailor at sea to say, "Yeah, but it's a long way home."[2]

Like *The Sporting News* artist's sketch, Hubler's attempt in his *Saturday Evening Post* profile to capture a sense of Red's global reach actually echoed what for years would characterize commentary on Barber's Brooklyn broadcasts: Barber had the gift that distinguishes all great story tellers and artists; he was able to take the local and make it universal. He could transform Brooklyn into everyone's hometown and Ebbets Field into everyone's own backyard.[3]

Hubler attempts to support his claim empirically. He mounts persuasive numbers, not only the twenty million fans worldwide who tuned in for the 1941 Barber-Elson World Series broadcasts, but also the dramatic spikes in attendance at Ebbets Field since Red's arrival. And even more significant, he apprises readers of the increasing fortunes that sponsors are paying for advertising on Dodgers broadcasts. Throughout his account, however, Hubler takes pains to persuade readers that Barber is not merely a successful performer who knows how to hook a crowd with his vivid homespun expressions. Red is the consummate professional who long has been obsessed with accuracy, objectivity, tireless preparation, and mastery of the disciplined techniques that enable him to channel all that he sees on the ball field into captivating word pictures for his listeners. All these skills have earned him a slew of broadcasting awards, significant salary increases, and hundreds of fan letters every week.

"A Man's Reach Should Exceed His Grasp"

Several months later in the 1942 Dodgers' baseball season, another lengthy article profiling Barber appeared in *The Witness* magazine, a widely read publication of the American Episcopal Church known for its progressive "peace and justice" orientation. In his profile of Barber, Rev. Harry Price, the rector of Scarsdale's Episcopal Church, wants to know more about how Red had advanced so quickly in his career. Barber says he just kept working and working until he "got hold of something which I could put my teeth into. As I see it the important thing is to work for something, some *goal*." When Rev. Price queries Red about what he could possibly do next, now that he has already reached the top of the broadcasting profession, Barber's response is surprising:

> I feel as if I know less about baseball today than I used to. I don't feel as if I've achieved much. There's lots more to do. I'd like to get into the editorial side of sports. In play-by-play, the announcer tries to give you exactly what you would see if you were in the ballpark. But in commentary, the editorial field, you get *something of yourself* into the game and analyze it. I'd like to do that. In the earlier years the objective was just to get the job.[4]

Barber implies that while he is fully committed to his job and to professional reportorial objectivity as a play-by-play announcer, he now has other work—a higher goal, at least in his distant sites. He wants to *evaluate* the game, to critique it, and to comment upon its meaning and value from his own unique perspective. A year after this interview, Red pinch-hit for New York sportswriter

Tom Meany by agreeing to write a piece for his column on one of Meany's vacation days, just as Barber occasionally invited his sportswriter pals to pinch-hit for him for an inning in the radio booth at Ebbets Field. In Barber's article, entitled "The 'Verce' of Brooklyn," Red tells readers that "the best memories in my broadcast career are the people around me" and that his richest experience is "the daily association with writers. Events on the diamond spur more conversation afterward with writers."[5] According to Red, this is where one uncovers the best stories.

At the end of *The Witness* profile, Rev. Price's interview with the Voice of Brooklyn is interrupted because Barber must hurry off from his home in Scarsdale to announce a Dodgers game. Price had just admired Red's beautiful pine-paneled library, but Red tells him that "This is where economic determinism catches up with me," referring to a "twenty-year mortgage."[6] Higher goals must simmer on the back burner because the celebrated baseball announcer, for the present, must do his job serving as the eyes of his Dodgers broadcast listeners. However, to keep feeding his nascent ambitions to move beyond play-by-play announcing, Red continued to publish occasional analytical articles in a range of newspapers.

Within a few years of *The Witness* profile, Red had published two articles in the *New York Times*. A 1942 piece, entitled "Prescription for Baseball Players," outlines for promising young baseball prospects both the physical and dispositional qualities that scouts are seeking.[7] The second, published in 1943, discusses how "The Fans Make Baseball." Here Red classifies fans based on their behavioral tendencies and pays tribute to those patriotic fans who have been supporting the game during the war; baseball broadcasts have bolstered the spirits of servicemen abroad.[8] He also published an interesting 1943 piece, upon request, for *Victor Record Review*. The editors asked him to discuss his favorite Victor recordings; his top choices were classical symphonies and "negro spirituals."[9] In 1945 he wrote a long piece for *Redbook*, also upon request, when the editors asked for the story of how he got started in radio and how he prepares for each game.[10]

Barber's ability to produce articles of significant scope during his action-packed weekly schedule throughout the mid-1940s suggests a desire to deepen his messages and widen his audiences. His perseverance is not surprising if we recall one of the moral teachings his father impressed upon him when Red was still a boy: the need always to recognize the difference between *pride* and *self-respect*. At sixty Red explains how significantly that distinction has impacted his conduct in life. Pride, he tells us, is feeling that "I am *better* than you," an assessment based upon any convenient criteria—for example, "better because my skin is a different color" or "better because you are poor and have to live in overalls and in a cheap shack." By 1943, he might have added proudly that he was better because of his distinguished broadcasting awards. But self-respect, Red explains, is "seeing yourself as you are *compared to what you ought to be*." Red notes that he has always done fine work, work that met his own rigorous standards; his recognition of this "fact" is not triggered by pride but by honest self-respect.[11]

But the challenge of this kind of self-respect is that a person cannot really enjoy it for long based on *achieved* excellence. Barber tells us that as early as 1935, he realized Cincinnati fans had accepted him as an accomplished announcer, rewarding him with accolades and applause. Soon, however, the accolades faded because his level of excellence was what they now *expected* of him: "The acceptance sets in. It is ordered and normal, but it is a silence." He castigates himself for having missed the applause, but the reaction is coupled with a new "restlessness." Missing applause became a *symptom* of dwindling self-respect because it signaled that he could be successful in a more demanding arena than Crosley Field, and that was what he *ought to be* doing. Accepting the offer to move to New York was an effort to bolster self-respect.[12] As he confessed to Rev. Price, "No matter what excuses I might have given for staying in Cincinnati, I would have known within myself that I was afraid to take a chance in New York. . . . I guess I live by Browning, 'A man's reach should exceed his grasp.'"[13]

Red Barber made another significant and challenging move in the fall of 1942 when he decided to attend church, ten years after his mother's death had triggered his powerful "anger at God." He wrote in 1970 that by this point his anger had actually subsided somewhat because during that decade, he primarily thought only of himself: "My health was good; I kept making more and more money. The broadcast assignments kept getting bigger. . . . Whatever heights I had set out to reach as a sports announcer, I had reached. We built a two-story house. . . . I had money in the bank. I had a Lincoln automobile." Barber tells us he started going to church that fall not long after Lylah asked him if he thought Sarah, now five, should attend Sunday school. He answered, "without any thought," by saying, "Of course." Recalling that Lylah, at one time at least, had been an Episcopalian, he recommended that she take Sarah to St. James the Less, the Episcopal church in Scarsdale. He spends several following Sunday mornings sitting on his front porch reading the *New York Times* and watching his "two girls" trotting off to church in their Sunday best. He tells us that driving back and forth to Brooklyn for several weeks, he would try to plan what he would he say if some Sunday morning Sarah asked, "Why isn't Daddy going with us?" He cannot construct any honest answer. Lylah, he tells us, nearly "choked on her morning coffee when I told her 'I'm going to church with you today.'"[14]

During those autumn Sundays, Red "fell in love with *The Book of Common Prayer*" because "of the beauty and conciseness of the English language, the fact that everything the Episcopal Church stood for was right there between the two covers, and the inclusion of the entire *Book of Psalms*." But in addition to his love of the conciseness and poetry of Episcopalian worship, Barber also acknowledges, "I was an instant convert. I had been in a spiritual desert for a dry decade. I was thirsty for the waters of the spirit. . . . I had not known I was so dry, so thirsty, so lonely." He became a member of the church in April 1943. To accommodate Red's busy broadcast schedule, the rector arranged a private confirmation, attended only by Red, Lylah, and the "venerable Negro sexton." By

1942 Barber was prepared to fall under the tutelage of a new mentor who would briskly shove him along the path to "higher goals."

Sportswriters Assess the Voice

Before climbing to higher ground, however, Barber had to negotiate an already crowded schedule in the early 1940s: regular-season live and recreated Dodgers baseball games; New York Giants football broadcasts, both home and away games (1942–46); Princeton football broadcasts; periodic World Series, All-Star, and college bowl games; and daily or weekly sports roundup shows. He also continued to perform as host for entertainment gigs and quiz shows and to make other regular radio appearances that came his way from Dodgers sponsors or that he and his agent, Bill McCaffrey, sought out to supplement his income and to subsidize his family's life in Scarsdale. Red had been on McCaffrey's radar since he first heard Barber broadcast the celebrated 1935 Ohio State–Notre Dame game. When Barber moved to New York, he and McCaffrey struck up a warm acquaintance; in 1944 McCaffery formally became Red's agent, a rich association and a deep friendship that endured for a quarter century. Barber had an associate to help in the broadcast booth from the time he arrived in Brooklyn. When "Brother Al" Helfer was called to military duty in 1942, Alan Hale, a former FBI agent who had been announcing in Chicago, joined Red in Brooklyn, but family demands forced Hale to move west a year later. Red then procured Connie Desmond from the Yankees to replace Hale.[15]

Throughout the 1940s Red Barber's sports announcing and commentary continued to receive positive critical notice in New York City's sports columns. Writers respected Barber's facility with the English language; they were impressed because he could spontaneously speak with the felicitous rhythms, evocative phrasing, and verbal precision that they labored for hours to produce at their typewriters. In April 1942 the *New York World-Telegram* published a column critiquing sports roundup shows that must have delighted Red Barber. The writer, assessing the effectiveness of those play-by-play announcers who also appeared on sports commentary programming, complains that "with one exception, radio announcers are 'weak on commentary.'" They report merely the "obvious"; even when they attempt to "dig into form and background, they generally sink into the commonplace." But "Red Barber is the exception—he is an intense worker and always comes up with meaty anecdotes and personal items about the players. He is a close student of every sport he covers, and his opinions and prophecies are worth attention; he supports them with enough factual background to make it clear these are no mere conjectures or hunches—this is the hard way of doing the job, but neither sports nor wars can be covered from a comfortably tilted swivel chair."[16]

In a July 1942 WOR press release, Barber himself commented on the pressure he felt in compiling copy for the pieces on his evening *Baseball Roundup* program: "They're just like a sports column. I have to have one good feature story, taking about eight minutes to tell, for each program. This requires every minute of time I have available from the end of the ballgame that day until I go on the air at 9:15 p.m. Then, of course, the facts on every story must be correct, and this means checking with sports authorities . . . not always easy to find." Red also added, "Now I understand why many reporters turn down offers to write columns."[17]

When the Yankees and Giants returned to radio broadcasting in the 1942 season, sports columnist Tom Meany expressed sympathy for Red's disadvantage in having to do a telegraph re-creation of the opening series pitting the Dodgers against the Giants, while Mel Allen would broadcast the games live from his booth in the Polo Grounds.[18] But a column by Alton Cook several weeks later, based on an interview with Barber, suggests that Meany's sympathy with Red's "disadvantage" in the re-created game against the Giants was unwarranted. As we know, Barber had already worked with telegraph operators to speed up their delivery of the game's calls. But now he is insisting that it takes no *extra* time for him to supply descriptive details lacking in the telegraph's bare data. Moreover, he estimates that the details he supplies "are accurate ninety percent of the time." Cook, in support of Barber's claim, explains that as soon as the telegraph says, "Camilli Called Out," Red tells his audience, "Camilli just looked at a big curve in there and it's another strike out." Barber can do this because he knows the pitcher Melton "*always* throws a big curve to Camilli in this situation." And a high curve is the *only* strike Camilli ever takes except for a high fastball inside. "But Melton would not have thrown him that as things stood there."[19]

The New York press also paid significant attention in the 1940s to the *effects*—from the material to the spiritual—of Barber's broadcasting. Old Gold Cigarettes reported in *Advertising Age* that its 1942 sales significantly increased, in part because of its broader reach and its high ranking in a *Reader's Digest* recent "Smoking Quality" report. But the "remarkable" increase in sales was "substantially due to the popularity of Red Barber and his Brooklyn Dodgers broadcasts," sponsored by Old Gold.[20] A July 1942 article in *The Tobacco Leaf*, a publication of the United States Tobacco Trade, documents a far less tangible but still powerful effect. The piece describes an afternoon luncheon at New York City's Astor Hotel, hosted by the Tobacco Table, a local social club, a gathering arranged "to pay homage to the famous baseball announcer and sports commentator," Red Barber. The president of the Tobacco Table, who introduces the guest of honor, describes how he had missed the intimacy of small-town baseball when he moved thirty-five years ago from the upstate village of his youth to New York City, where big league baseball seemed like "just a racket." But two years prior to this luncheon, "There came into his life via the radio this strange and remarkable wizardry of Mr. Red Barber"; almost instantly the baseball cynic's resistance to the game melted away. He is convinced that Barber has "liberated thousands of Americans from the confines of their chimney corners, either by giving them the great national game vividly by radio, or more importantly, giving them a renewed interest in life that brought them out to the ballparks, fresh air and sunlight to enjoy the sport first-hand."[21]

Sportswriters also reported unique impacts of Barber's live broadcasts upon specific listeners. Around the seventh inning of the second game in a doubleheader against Chicago in July 1942, Barber began to worry in the broadcast booth about feeding his cat back home in Scarsdale. His wife and daughter were out of town, the chore was left to him, and he knew that the cat would be getting quite hungry this late into the evening. When the game went into extra innings, he began voicing his concerns about his cat to his radio audience, "adding little coloratura touches here and there." Soon people started phoning into WHN, some anxious about the cat's well-being, some offering advice regarding cat feeding, and some playing with a little satire. There were twenty-five calls during the game, over one hundred the next day, and even a telegram asking, "When do we eat? Signed KITTY."[22] A more poignant piece in the *New York World-Telegram* profiled an enthusiastic Dodgers fan, a blind woman, who said she had never seen her beloved team play until she heard Red Barber's broadcasts: "I listen on my little radio. . . . Red Barber describes it so well I can *visualize* all the plays, just as though I were right back of first base."[23] New York's mayor, Fiorello LaGuardia, claimed that Red Barber was "the only man who [could] outdraw me on the air"; the mayor was glad that Dodgers games began at 1:00 p.m. so that he did not need to compete with Red's voice during his own Sunday broadcasts.[24]

Red's popularity as a sport broadcaster had spread widely enough for him to appear in a "Chart of Celebrities' Favorite Drinks," published in *Sir*, a mildly titillating "gentlemen's magazine" catering to male interests and pleasures. Barber appeared with nine other celebrities, including William Saroyan; Orson Welles; Robert Benchley, Red's neighbor in Scarsdale; and, with clever satirical justification, Adolf Hitler. A cocktail recipe was provided for each celebrity's favorite drink, with an accompanying photo of the famous person. Red's recipe for a mint julep was, characteristically, the most detailed and directive of the ten.[25]

Barber's play-by-play work clearly impressed Gillette, sponsor of the World Series since 1939. After the 1943 Series was over, Gillette contracted to sponsor 1944 Yankees and Giants home games. Craig Smith, advertising manager for the company, invited Barber to meet with him at the Ritz Hotel; he wanted Red to break his contract with the Dodgers and begin announcing in 1944 for the other two New York teams. Barber dismissed the proposition, in part because he thought it was unethical, but also because he had no desire to give up his Brooklyn job.[26]

Big Bands and Jazz for the "Hep-Cat"

Red Barber's performances as host or guest in entertainment broadcasts also were reported and critiqued in the press, documenting his participation in New York City's arts and cultural communities. In January 1943 Red assumed the emcee role on the popular swing band leader Sammy Kaye's *Old Gold Show*, a CBS weekly variety program that aired on affiliated stations nationwide. The show's original format included numbers by the band, choral singing, popular soloists, comedians, and surprise guest stars. During the war years Sammy and Red both took part in a segment called "Good Turn." They would interview a young serviceman in town on furlough, encouraging him to share with the studio and broadcast audiences his wartime experiences. These episodes always ended with "surprise" and moving reunions of the men with close family members who had been contacted before the show and transported from their hometowns to the New York studio.[27]

In its review of early episodes of the *Old Gold Show*, *Radio Daily* particularly praised Barber's low-key delivery and the "soft spoken, southern-drawl handling of commercials." His laid-back endorsements make for easier listening than the "nerve jarring jargon that some of the gents give out with."[28] The *Old Gold Show* incorporated new elements as the months went by; in one guest appearance celebrated jazz musician Woody Herman formally dedicated his cover of the classic piece "Red Top" to the program's host, Red Barber.[29] The show also began to feature short comic skits in which Red would play a part, providing him the opportunity to exercise the on-stage theatrics that he had been cultivating since his Gainesville days in minstrelsy. *The Sporting News* reported that in one skit, he played the "the jazz-crazed husband" of an opera singer and bandied the "peculiar language and style of a juvenile hep-cat." The reviewer found the performance a truly "odd" one for Red Barber, the baseball announcer, but conceded it was an "in-the-character-cast hit."[30] Two Gainesville women who used to listen to Red on WRUF and who were visiting New York City in 1943 enjoyed a refreshing manifestation of Barber's characteristic courtesy toward strangers who sought him out. The women noticed his name on the marquee of the CBS studio where the *Old Gold Show* was usually broadcast and went through the door to ask for Red Barber. Although he was in rehearsal, he came down to meet them, conducted them up to the studio, and invited them to watch the show when it aired.[31]

A survey of New York City radio station program listings for all of 1945 documents that beyond his steady gig emceeing the studio variety show, Red also appeared several times most weeks as a guest on other shows, including the quiz show *Information Please* and *Stage Door Canteen*, along with other celebrated guests, such as Lena Horne and Edward G. Robinson. Barber also showed up as a guest speaker on special episodes of regularly scheduled talk or interview programs. For instance, he appeared on John Daly's *Report to the Nation* as part of a tribute to radio, on *The Red Cross Program* to talk about his work in the charity's wartime blood drive, and on *The Faith That Fits* to explain "the need for the application of Christian principles in the post-war world."[32]

The Voice Cracks

Few of Barber's radio fans realized that his voice was nearly silenced after the final game of the 1942 World Series. Barber cracked his vocal codes when he announced Whitey Kurowski's home run that won the game and clinched the series for the Cardinals. Red later wrote that he could feel his voice "flying away from him, along with the ball, into the stands."[33] He had been having trouble with his voice in the weeks leading up to the Series because he had been speaking too much and too loudly during an unusually busy schedule—broadcasting a pennant race and a World Series, appearing on radio shows, and emceeing public rallies promoting the sale of war bonds. After that home run call, whenever he tried to speak, "Nothing but awful sounds came out." He was afraid that his radio career might be over. He found a throat specialist recommended to him by the general manager of the Metropolitan Opera. After examining him, the physician told him his voice would come back, "but it would take time." His cracked vocal cords were now flooded with blood, and the doctor told him he had to say *nothing* for an entire week.

Barber acknowledges that this was a difficult prescription to follow, but horrified by the vulnerability of his vocal cords, he followed the doctor's orders to the letter. He took some medication and received several localized heat treatments, but the crucial prescription, Barber claims, was behavioral modification—"Silence, rest, and a quiet mind." He trained himself never to raise his voice in any situation, and, when talking on air, to maintain "a natural range, well under full strength." Although Barber was recognized for silencing himself after a home team home run so that his listeners could hear and fully savor the cheers of the fans at the park, his motive for implementing the practice was to save his voice by never attempting to shout over the roar of the crowd.

One criticism of Barber's play-by-play announcing that occasionally showed up in newspaper commentary focused upon the low volume of his voice. Red's producer Tom Villante thinks that Barber's only limitation as a broadcaster was that "he had a very, very weak voice. No timber to it, no carry."[34] His listeners may not have known that Red's carefully modulated volume of speech was prescribed by his doctor, "the best medicine I ever got."[35]

Barber's disciplined efforts to preserve his voice throughout his career may have reinforced both his lifelong efforts to secure his privacy and a perception among some of his peers that he was "standoffish." Throughout his career some colleagues associated with Red Barber referred to him as a "private" person, surprisingly shy when away from a mic, stage, or pulpit—a man of few words, reserved, formal, even detached. According to Villante, on radio, "Red was like an actor playing a role of the Old Catbird, the Old Redhead. When he wasn't playing that role, he was just a very quiet, very shy guy. Once he got on the air, suddenly he became the Old Redhead; he was acting. Mel Allen was Mel Allen, Scully was Scully, but on air, Red was a completely different guy." There are grounds for the impression that Barber was standoffish. He did not, as a rule, allow visitors in his broadcast booth: According to Villante Red felt, "This is my office, and we are going to keep it private." Some of Barber's deepest friendships appear to have developed more intimately by letter writing than physical meetings. Still, Red describes in his own writing many engaging focused conversations he shared with people he deeply admired, often people whom he interviewed, but he was always impatient with "small talk," as if it would be "wasting" his voice.[36] He wanted conversations to go somewhere and, like many gifted storytellers, was most comfortable when he was controlling them. Even after Bob Edwards had worked from a distance with Red for years on NPR, he still sensed in a visit to the Barber home that, however warm the conversation, he should be prepared to leave at a "reasonably early hour."[37]

When Barber began announcing for the Dodgers, he resisted the requirement imposed by a representative of General Mills, sponsor for the Dodgers, Giants, and Yankees. The representative wanted all the announcers and the advertising agency men to check in with him at his office in downtown Manhattan for a meeting every game day, both before and after their games, to talk with him "about how things [were] going." Realizing that there was no specific purpose for the meetings, Red protested: "If you have something important to tell me about the broadcasting job, I'll come into the office at three-thirty in the morning. . . . But if it's this thing . . . where I come in for no reason in the morning and again for no reason in the afternoon, then you have the wrong boy. Because I'm not going to do it."[38]

Still, we know that however "standoffish" he seemed or how-ever much he resisted unnecessary and uninvited intrusions upon his privacy, Barber could yield completely—forgetting himself—once he had truly warmed up to another person. In his taped con-versations with Robert Creamer, Red laments the hesitancy in Anglo-Saxon cultures for physical expressions of affection:

> I've had the opportunity to travel in a lot of Latin countries and, gee, those are pretty rugged masculine men. But they hug each other when they meet, and they touch each other on the shoulder and pound each other on the back. I'm not talking about kissing cheeks. There is something about the warmth of body-to-body contact of the Latin man. I don't know how we got this restraint over here. . . . But some men that I really like, I like to throw my arm around [their] shoul-der[s] for five or ten seconds. It says a great deal more than words.[39]

"You Have a Potential for Civic Value"

After that evening in the smoke-filled Cincinnati banquet hall where Red first heard Branch Rickey speak, he realized he had been "in an unconscious quest for the things that [Rickey] could express. He was perhaps thirty years older than I was, but some-thing flowed from him to me, and it never stopped flowing."[40] Barber was willing to walk in the footsteps of a man whose spo-ken words could so move his audience to open themselves up to the persuasions of his powerful spirit. Red tells us he had enjoyed brief interactions with Rickey over the following years but knew him only slightly by the time of the 1942 World Series between Rickey's Cardinals and the Yankees. Leaving Yankee Stadium after his broadcast of the first game of that contest, he "happened to fall in step" with Rickey and his wife Jane. Red tells us he was "dumbfounded" when Rickey paused and introduced him to Jane as "Walter Barber, who is not only as fine a man as I know, but by far the greatest baseball broadcaster we have ever had." Red was stunned as much by Rickey's choice to identify him by his birth name, which only his father still used when speaking to him, as by

Rickey's magnanimous appraisal of his work: "I didn't realize that Mr. Rickey had any idea what my first name was. . . . [He] put his arm around my shoulder as he spoke and gave me a bear squeeze. It was precisely the sort of gesture my father often used; just put his arm around my shoulder, squeeze, and then turn me loose."[41]

Barber would soon learn what it was that had been "flowing from Rickey" into him since the rubber chicken banquet in Cincinnati. Just months after the Cardinals won the 1942 World Series, Branch Rickey accepted the invitation to become general manager of the Dodgers to replace Larry MacPhail, who had left the team to enter the army. Rickey and his wife first rented a house in Westchester County, not far from where the Barbers lived. Shortly after settling in, they invited Red and Lylah to visit for a Sunday luncheon. Red recalls the warm conversation he and Lylah shared with the Rickeys: "They were genuine human beings, people of sensitivity, gentle people, and wise."[42] He was convinced that Rickey had invited them because he wanted a more personal knowledge of the Dodgers' broadcaster. But he thought Rickey especially wanted to learn more about Lylah.

According to Barber, Rickey made no serious decisions without consulting his own wife, and he genuinely believed that one could ascertain the most important aspects of a man's character and behavior by getting to know the woman he had married and surmising how she influenced him. Red also suspected that Rickey understood the depth of affection that Brooklyn fans felt for their club's announcer and wanted to make best use of that bond: "He wanted to begin his own motivation of me in his own way. . . . He motivated people by finding out who they were and what they thought and what they wanted and what troubled them. I didn't know that then, but it doesn't bother me thinking about it because his motivation was a blessing."

Just before Red and Lylah left the Rickey home that day, the new Dodgers general manager said to his club's announcer, somewhat mysteriously, "You think I don't know much about you. But there is more I know than you have any idea. You have a potential for civic value that has not been touched. . . . And I am going to do something about it." Barber tells us that until this moment in his life, no one had ever asked him to get involved in civic work: "I never even thought about it." He claims not to know exactly what Rickey *did* to launch his disciple's extraordinary program of civic engagement for the next several years, "but before long things began to jump and I was right in the middle."[43] Barber misleads his readers, however, when he claims never to have engaged in civic activity before Rickey ushered him into heading the Red Cross fund-raising campaign for the Borough of Brooklyn in 1944 and then, in 1945, overseeing the entire citywide campaign including all five boroughs. As soon as the country entered the war, Barber began to share his free time and room in his Dodgers broadcasts to help sell war bonds and to promote blood donations. Like other well-known voices in American society, Barber assumed that it was his role as a public figure to contribute his talents to the war effort.

There is no complete record of all Red Barber's activities from 1942 through 1945 supporting the sale of war bonds, soliciting blood donations to the Red Cross, and fund-raising for the Red Cross War Fund. However, a survey of war-related events during these years reported by the New York City press demonstrates Barber's unceasing activity and leadership for all three causes. He began his efforts in January 1942, when he agreed to speak at a rally of 2,800 Abraham and Strauss employees in the grand hall of the company's flagship department store in Brooklyn, urging support for the Red Cross War Fund.[44] During the 1942 Dodgers' baseball season, Red promoted war bond sales on a grand scale during his play-by-play broadcasts. He and his WHN colleagues devised a meticulous program for each war bond broadcast; it involved scores of telephone and telegraph operators at the station processing pledges in response to Barber's calls for contributions. Dodgers players served as ushers, passing out pledge cards row by row at Ebbets Field. One article reports that according to pledges received, Barber sold well over $100,000 in war bonds at the first war bond baseball broadcast: "Barber is doing a whale of a bond selling job. He cagily inserts war bond plugs throughout the broadcasts, reaching his telephone sales peak when a bell rang at *fifty thousand dollars per hour*. After he read his first war bond appeal, the next two hours developed into five hundred calls at one time, getting the busy signal at the station's huge switchboards." Although not every pledge resulted in a completed sale, this article notes that the sales totals included "wire orders from 18 states and calls from members of the Army and Navy far outside the metropolitan region."[45]

Red employed several strategies to squeeze war bond pledges out of his listeners. An August 1942 piece in *Advertising Age* informs readers that when Barber offered to air names of listeners calling the station to buy war bonds, sales began to soar. This piece optimistically asserts that "90% of the WHN listeners who pledged to buy bonds have consummated their promises by check or money orders." Red also introduced an extra incentive when he promised an autographed photo of the Dodgers to every purchaser; those who pledged within the next five minutes would also be rewarded with autographed baseballs.[46] In response to Barber's success, the U.S. Treasury Department asked him to write an article describing his strategy for selling war bonds on radio. At the end of the 1942 baseball season, the Treasury Department sent Barber's article to all radio station managers in the country, informing them that "Red Barber at WHN had generated $476,000 in War Bond sales" during his four Dodgers war bond broadcasts. He urged them to consider implementing Red's strategy at their stations during the upcoming football season.[47]

Barber repeated the same war bond procedure at Dodgers games during the 1943 season. Once the bond campaigns got under way, Red regularly emceed war bond rallies at locations throughout Brooklyn: Borough Hall, Brooklyn College, various neighborhood high schools, Bush Terminal, and the Hotel St. George. In 1943, along with Mel Allen, Red joined Brooklyn's mayor at the Waldorf Astoria to "auction off" star players from all three of New

York's Major League teams as the first phase of the clever "Base-ball Bond League" competition. Launched by the New York and Brooklyn Baseball Writers Associations, the fund-raising contest enabled fans from the entire city to "play ball" to advance the sale of war bonds. A Bond League participant could purchase players with dollars that bought bonds. Teams were formed, and every time auctioned players scored hits in actual play, their "owners" pledged, with varying incentives, to contribute a specified amount of additional money toward war bonds.[48]

"Hell, There's a War On!"

Red insisted in his memoirs and other writings that the wartime service from which he received the most gratification was not his fund-raising efforts but his radio appeals urging listeners to donate their blood to the Red Cross. Supplies were needed to send to the front lines for wounded soldiers abroad and to hospitals treating them back home. On Opening Day of the Dodgers' 1942 season, a Red Cross volunteer asked Barber if he would announce on air the location of the blood donation center in Brooklyn. Red had to tell him that, unfortunately, the word "blood" was not allowed on radio according to "unwritten law." The reason for this de facto prohibition was not clear, but Barber suspected it was deemed too indelicate to inject the word into the private domestic spheres that radio now penetrated. Still, he was convinced that the prohi-bition itself was inappropriate when soldiers could die because of inadequate blood supply. He promptly presented the volunteer's request to general manager MacPhail, also reminding him of the blood taboo. MacPhail responded with characteristic directness: "Hell, there's a war on!"[49]

This was all Red needed to hear; that same day "blood" was on the radio. Listeners responded by "jamming the switchboards at the Red Cross trying to make appointments to give blood." From that day until the end of the war Red urged his radio listeners, during every Dodgers game he broadcast, to donate blood, pro-viding the phone number and address for the Brooklyn and Manhattan donation centers. As with the war bond campaign, Barber expanded his appeal to the stadium audience as well. On "Blood Donor Nights," he would emcee pregame ceremonies at Ebbets Field where all the Dodgers' players, executives, and staff would line up before the stands and pledge to give blood for the war.[50]

Once again, Red carried his mission beyond the ballpark, building upon his initial success in moving radio listeners to give their blood. He appeared at public demonstrations where volunteers would donate their blood as Red provided a running "play-by-play" commentary on each step of the process over a loudspeaker. He wanted to persuade the audience that the process was painless. Often in these public demonstrations, the donor would be a war hero, such as a forty-seven-year-old World War I veteran giving his twelfth donation.[51] Red would also recruit Dodgers players to go with him to industrial plants, department stores, and military bases to appeal for blood donors.[52] On one occasion near the end of the war, he was photographed at a donation center giving his own blood; with reporters conveniently on the scene, Red apprised their readers of the alarming drop in blood donations in recent days. Perhaps, he suggested, people had been distracted by their preparations for the upcoming Easter and Passover holidays and by the lovely weather they'd been enjoying recently. He reminded them that there could be no better way to honor these sacred holidays than by giving blood for those who were dying to keep the world free.[53]

Serving as a leading figure for wartime blood donations was an experience that seemed to cement the profound bond that Red had been forging with the people of Brooklyn, a tie that he cherished for the rest of his life. Looking back on those Red Cross appeals, he recalled them as his baptism by blood into the soul of Brooklyn: "Brooklyn people responded with a steady supply. I kept seeing the veins that said, 'put your needles here—take out what you need.' The blood of Brooklyn, in this broadcast booth, washed over me whenever I sat down."[54] He believed that the blood broadcasts would be remembered "long after no one cared who played or who won those games."[55] Radio's support of the blood drive also symbolized for him an ideal of what mass media could do to unite citizens in civic endeavors that promoted the well-being of their communities and the nation. Barber wrote that his blood donor effort "was participation in life itself. This was what mass communication was intended to be. This was selling life, not baseball, not tickets, not cigarettes."[56]

Red *Cross* Barber

In December 1943 Barber was named chair of the 1944 Brooklyn Red Cross War Fund campaign, validating the truism that if one performs well in one leadership role, one will be asked to take on a tougher task. The fund was crucial during the wars years to cover the demands for equipment, facilities, and staffing to care for injured servicemen overseas and to meet all the needs of veterans returning home. The *Brooklyn Eagle* reports that the Red Cross chose Barber for this role because of his "inspiring leadership in the Blood Drive." He was considered a powerful resource because his name was one with the Brooklyn Dodgers; through his broadcasts he had entered the homes, apartments, and subways of the borough. "People respond to his sincerity and appeals. Now he will be 'Red *Cross* Barber.'"[57] His first official announcement in his new role was a proclamation that the 1944 goal would be $3,333,100, a figure that doubled the goal of the 1943 campaign.[58]

From January through March 1944 Red spoke at gatherings to recruit canvassers who would go door to door in every neighborhood of Brooklyn seeking contributions. He parlayed his baseball credibility by insisting that if all volunteers on the team were as inspired as the Dodgers had been when they won the 1941 pennant, they would succeed in lifting our men in battle to victory as well. He would be accompanied by wounded soldiers who had given their best or an outstanding war hero, like the pilot who had completed 130 missions in the Pacific and had won two distinguished medals. He appointed Branch Rickey, the mentor who had fueled his civic consciousness, to be his communications director. Rickey came through for him, employing his own talents as an energetic and persuasive speaker.

Rickey and Red spoke at mass rallies featuring celebrity guests, including Frank Sinatra, Janet Gaynor, Bonita Granville, and scores of opera stars and Broadway favorites. When Sinatra was scheduled to participate, promotions for the rally excluded mention of his name to avoid attracting unruly "mobs" of young women admirers that his appearances generally inspired. In his speeches Barber particularly enjoyed showcasing the donations of schoolchildren, such as the members of the Brooklyn Boys and Girls Club who collected and sold paper and scrap metal until they accumulated ten dollars to give to the Red Cross War Fund, "hoping that they might help to save the life of a soldier in war." He also loved singling out and telling the stories of seniors living on meager pensions and of wounded veterans who had sent their checks to the Red Cross War Fund with notes of apology for not being able to contribute more.[59]

The 1944 Brooklyn Red Cross War Fund exceeded its challenging goal, and in December 1944 Barber was asked to serve as chairman of the entire citywide Red Cross War Fund campaign for 1945, coordinating the efforts of all five boroughs. The press hailed his willingness to take on the daunting task, considering it magnanimous for a man who was not even a New Yorker by birth to work so hard for the entire city.[60] Barber added one new money-raising event to kick off the 1945 campaign, likely enabled by his status as citywide campaign chair: a three-game, preseason baseball "round robin" series among the Dodgers, Yankees, and Giants. The teams agreed to take part in the series, in which each would play two games—one against each of the other two; the Red Cross War Fund would receive the proceeds of all three games.[61]

Once again, under Barber's leadership, the Red Cross War Fund campaign exceeded its challenging goal for 1945, a feat often enabled by generous "surprise" contributions at the last minute from "donors who wish[ed] to remain anonymous," pushing the campaign over the finish line. The Brooklyn Eagle printed a gracious "Thank you, Red Barber" column for his leadership both citywide and in Brooklyn: "He deserves thanks from the whole city for the job he has done." The piece ascribes Barber's success to his fortunate combination of "executive talent and a flair for dramatic public presentation."[62]

9

On the Home Front

Lylah Barber supported Red's efforts to recruit blood donors, sell war bonds, and raise funds for the Red Cross, even though the demands of the work consumed all his spare time. Her brother Mat, a thirty-year-old bachelor, was drafted into the Army Air Corps, and Red's brother Billy, married but childless, volunteered at age twenty-seven but failed the physical due to an abdominal hernia. Irrepressible and determined to serve, Billy paid to have reparative surgery, got himself accepted into the army, and saw extensive action in Europe. Red had not enlisted; as a married man in his mid-thirties with a child, he would not have been called until later in the war. Barber said he could have accepted one of the wartime temporary officer commissions that "sources" had told him would be "available to him in several areas." He thought the option of going into uniform and becoming an officer seemed "rather attractive, for *me*, and interesting things might have followed." But he felt it would be selfish to run off suddenly with an officer's rank, abandoning his wife and child. Barber decided to wait until he was drafted and to do "everything he could" as a civilian. He added, "I'm sure that's partly why I got so heavily involved in the blood drive and the Red Cross War Fund campaigns."[1] Red was reclassified as 1-A in spring 1944, shortly before General Lewis Hershey, head of the draft, issued a directive that no more fathers or men of Barber's age, thirty-six at the time, were to be inducted. Red had cleared both hurdles.[2]

"There Was Not a Neighbor in Sight"

When Red and Lylah first moved to New York with two-year-old Sarah and some suitcases, they had not yet secured a place to stay. "With the supreme confidence of youth," the thirty-one-year-old broadcaster pulled into a drugstore parking lot and phoned a sales manager for WOR whom he had met on an earlier visit. When Barber asked him where he could find a two-bed, two-bath apartment, the helpful manager directed him to the Beaux Arts building two blocks from Grand Central, where "they will have everything you need . . . including a balcony with a view of boat traffic on the East River." By nightfall Lylah records, "We were at home in New York City."[3]

Red began broadcasting re-creations of 1939 spring training games shortly after he arrived in the city, so Lylah assumed the immediate task of "finding a house in the suburbs for the family." With the aid of an agency contact man for Ivory Soap, one of the Dodgers' broadcast sponsors, she soon found a small house to rent only two blocks from the commuting station in Scarsdale. The Barbers would live there until January 1942, when they would finance a much larger house in Scarsdale. What Lylah remembers most vividly among those first New York weeks at the Beaux Arts was discovering, with her husband, the beauty, culture, and diversity of the city. They ate snails for the first time at what became their favorite French restaurant and were overwhelmed by the decor, exuberance, and huge menu at Mama Leone's, where "so many people came in from the world of the theater and sports." The Barbers had the agreeable opportunity to chat with the owner, Gene Leone. They were surprised and delighted to discover that Leone knew Red's best man at their wedding, Frank DeGaetani. Raised in New York, DeGaetani was the resident professor at the University Club in Gainesville whom Barber had befriended when he worked as a janitor there and who had introduced him to the subtleties of opera. "I knew him well," Leone exclaimed; "we grew up on the same block in Little Italy." During those first three weeks Red and Lylah took in several Broadway shows and a performance of the New York Philharmonic. "Everything was new and wonderful," Lylah wrote in her memoir. She adds that when the rental house was "finally ready for us to move into, I left the Beaux Arts with a twinge of regret."

During the war years, life for the Barber family, as for all Americans, was punctuated with unique challenges that tested the stamina of the country and assumptions about the country's national character and values. Lylah describes particular family displacements resulting from moving from their rental property to their new home in Scarsdale just as the country was adapting to the exigencies of wartime: "I recall vividly my sense of personal isolation. . . . [The house] sat on the top of a hill with its own heavily wooded two acres. There was not a neighbor in sight. Our small daughter had no companions within walking distance."[4] Because gasoline was so limited, the Barbers tried to avoid using their automobile. The new home was two miles from the train that took them to the city, instead of the walkable two blocks to the train from their rental house. Lylah knew she was fortunate to have her husband with her, but between his broadcast and Red Cross commitments, he was usually gone from mornings until he arrived home for a late dinner.

Lylah's challenge was to make the most of visits, sometimes extended, from family and friends and to forge surrogate families as she had always done growing up in central Florida. Because their home was situated in the northeast near the ports of embarkation and return for troops, Lylah explains, their house "became a way-station for relatives and friends in the service." Her brother Mat spent all his free days at the Barbers' during the weeks when he was stationed at a fighter plane factory on Long Island before he was sent to England. She and Mat spent more time together those weeks than they had during the previous twenty years. Lylah's now divorced mother, who had been living with her son in Florida before the war, moved in with the Barbers when Mat enlisted in the army. Red's brother Billy also stayed with them before reporting for his port of embarkation in Boston. Lylah was surprised when her friendly, uninhibited brother-in-law arrived with his captain and the captain's wife, but the new house had room for everyone, including Red's sister Effie Virginia, who also arrived to see Billy off: "Sarah slept with her grandmother, and Virginia curled up in Sarah's little bed. The captain and his wife moved the day bed into the library, and Billy, who was quite tall, did his best on the living room couch." The night before Billy's departure, Red, Lylah, Billy, and Virginia stayed up late talking but never "voicing . . . fears that this might be the last time [they] would all be together."

Lylah also mentions the pleasure she took, during the war years, when she and Sarah attended Dodgers games on Sundays. They were always invited to sit with the Rickey family in their stadium box. During those wartime Sundays at the ballpark, she grew close to Jane Rickey and her children and grandchildren. She recalls Mrs. Rickey advising her about how to navigate the inevitable frustrations of being the wife of a man unflinchingly committed to a successful career. Among Lylah's favorite wartime memories were the evenings she went to the city to be with Red "at work." When Barber was emcee and commercial announcer on Sammy Kaye's radio show, he had to work both the 8:00 p.m. and 11:00 p.m. live broadcast for the West Coast. Lylah would take a train in for the first show. Then she would enjoy dinner at a restaurant near the studio with Red, his producers, staff, and often the guest stars—Woody Herman, George Jessel, Jackie Gleason— who had appeared that evening on Sammy's show. "I loved those dinners," Lylah tells us; "they were a welcome break from lonely evenings in the country."

Although the Barbers saved a rich cache of family photos and some home movies taken during their Scarsdale years, we have only one opportunity to hear a live family conversation. In a charming audiotape, likely recorded at a downtown studio, we hear Red sharing some intimate moments with seven-year-old Sarah over the Christmas holiday in 1944. In the recording, which is to be a Christmas gift for Lylah, Barber performs the role of emcee as he introduces several short piano pieces—"Spanish Fiesta" and "Wee March"—that Sarah then plays on the piano and several Christmas carols—"Silent Night" and "Away in a Manger"—that he asks her to sing for Lylah. Sarah sings sweetly on key and plays the piano competently. After each piece Red comments on his daughter's performance and then, falling naturally into the role of curious "interviewer," asks her if she is satisfied with her performance and if it was an easy or difficult piece to learn. Sarah's responses are brief but certain, and she appears to be enjoying the session.

In another playful segment of the tape, as if his daughter were a guest on one of his radio gigs, Red conducts a protracted interview with Sarah about her finances, beginning with the question, "What do you do about money; do you have any money of your own? Do you get money day by day or week by week now?" Undaunted by the barrage of questions, Sarah says she has two and a half dollars. She receives a weekly allowance, and on Sundays she gets "some church money and some bank money and some money to spend." Then, after a little prodding, she explains she can also earn up to four more pennies each day: one for "setting the table," one for "practicing," one for "being good," and one for "picking up [her] shoes and socks." In a rapid-fire follow-up, her father asks her how many times she has earned all *four* cents. She giggles and says, "Only once." The session ends when Red asks her what they have planned to do next that day. She replies, "Go to Grand Central" and then go home and "look at a Boy Scout book, or maybe Christmas cards." It is easy to see some of Red's own fixation with preparation, practice, and cultivating good habits manifested in the Barbers' child-rearing strategy.[5]

The Barbers enjoyed the stimulating wartime opportunity to welcome two American-born teenage daughters of Japanese immigrants into their home during the last months of the war. Lylah explains: "People were realizing that a grave injustice had been done to many Japanese immigrants and . . . that there should be some efforts to make amends."[6] Through the efforts of a Methodist Church agency attempting to relocate Japanese residents from West Coast internment camps to East Coast locations where they could find jobs, eighteen-year-old Kimi and sixteen-year-old Michi, daughters of the owner of a small chain of West Coast "Japanese-type inns," joined the Barber family nominally as "housekeepers." They had spent three years in an internment camp and now, with the approval of their parents, would find "a safe and kind home" with the Barbers until the war ended. Their parents had been placed in a post-internment setting in Brooklyn that they did not consider appropriate for their daughters. Sarah was delighted with her new "big sisters"; Lylah's mother was "interested and kind"; and in a few days, Lylah concludes, "We were all friends." Lylah taught Kimi how to cook simple meals for the household that now included six, and Kimi taught Lylah how to brew tea and cook rice the proper way.

Some of Red and Lylah's Scarsdale neighbors were unnerved by the Barbers' opening their home up to "those girls" because "the Japs are not to be trusted." A father of one of Sarah's friends told the Barbers his daughter could not come over to play with Sarah unless Red or Lylah monitored all her interactions with the Japanese girls. One evening, when the sisters were leaving a movie theater in nearby White Plains, they were verbally accosted with ethnic "slurs and profanities" shouted by a group of teenage boys. The girls were distressed when they returned home; they wanted to go back to the city to stay with their parents. Lylah and Red tried their best to calm them and urged them to sleep on their decision to leave their Scarsdale family. Just as she and Red were about to turn out their bedroom light that evening, they heard footsteps in the hallway, and soon the girls burst into their room to hug Lylah and tell her, "Mrs. Barber, we stay with you." The Barbers' months with Kimi and Michi were "a learning experience for the whole family." Sarah grew up, Lylah believes, more accepting of other people for "who they are inside." The Barbers would enjoy learning more about Michi's and Kimi's culture during their travels in the Far East later in their lives.

"I'm Going to Quit"

During one of the most intense half-years of Barber's dense life—the first six months of 1945—three powerful experiences significantly altered his views about three issues that troubled him: social inequities, his fear of death, and the conditions for gratification in his broadcast career.

In March 1945 Branch Rickey and Barber had just sat down for lunch at Joe's Restaurant in Brooklyn when Rickey shared a painful story about a young Black player on his baseball team back when he was a student coach at Ohio Wesleyan. Lee Lowenfish, Branch Rickey's biographer, identifies the player as Charles "Tommy" Thomas, the only Black player on the team. When Rickey took the team to play at Notre Dame, the manager at the hotel in South Bend refused to register the Black player. Branch was incensed but resolved the problem by allowing the young man to share his room. When Rickey and Thomas arrived at the room, Thomas began to cry and to pull at his skin "as if he wanted to forcibly remove the stain of its color."[7]

In Barber's version of the story, the young man then looked at Rickey and said, "It's my skin. If I could just tear it off, I'd be like everyone else."[8] According to Barber, Rickey confided that "I have never been able to shake the picture of that fine young man tearing at his hands. . . . And I have made up my mind that before I pass on, I am going to do something about it." He informed the stunned Red Barber that he had already set up a Negro League team called the Brooklyn Brown Dodgers, so his scouts would assume that they were screening Black players for the Black team. He added: "I am telling you there is a Negro player coming to the *Dodgers*, not the Brooklyn Brown Dodgers. . . . I don't know who he is. . . . But he is coming."

Barber records that he said nothing during Rickey's entire narration. He expressed "no support" for his plan because he had been "shaken to his heels" and was literally speechless. He surmises that Rickey told him about his secret plan because he wanted Barber to remain with the team but suspected that Red's Southern background would prevent him from welcoming a Black player on the Dodgers.[9] He wanted Red to have time to wrestle with his prejudice and to reason his way through it. Lowenfish also suspects that Rickey took Barber into his confidence because "he understood that Barber's broadcast voice would be a vital asset in the successful acceptance of a black ballplayer in the Major Leagues." Even though Red was raised in the Deep South, Rickey knew him well enough to believe that his reason and deep sense of fairness would persuade him to accept the integration of baseball.[10]

If these were his actual reasons, then Branch Rickey's confidence that Barber eventually would support a change that could make America's Pastime more fair was vindicated, but not without protracted soul searching on Red's part and some vivid firsthand observations. It would be the experience of *watching* Jackie Robinson play on the ball field under tremendous pressure while also enduring episodes of blistering ridicule that weakened Barber's psychic resistance to a Black man in the Major Leagues. It was also getting to know Robinson personally over time as a man, a husband, and a father that would begin to melt the obdurate, mind-forged line between the Black and white races he'd never considered crossing. Barber notes in his memoir that when he went home after the conversation at Joe's Restaurant, he told Lylah, "I'm going to quit." At this point, Red asks his readers to understand that he was "southern": "I had been carefully taught by Negroes and whites alike: the line that was always there was indelible. . . . I was raised by wonderful, tolerant people who taught me never to speak unkindly to anyone or to take advantage of anyone. But there was a line drawn that was always there." Barber also describes a physical discomfort he feared he might experience with a Black man on the team: "I would still be broadcasting baseball, with all its closeness and intimate friendships and back-and-forth and give-and-take, but now a Negro player would be part of all that. . . . The complexion . . . in the dugout and the clubhouse was going to be drastically and permanently changed."[11]

When Red told Lylah about Rickey's plan, she was surprised by the intensity of her husband's response: "My reaction was low-key and different." She, too, "was southern" and had been "carefully taught," but she had learned some different lessons. Her earliest playmates had been Black children; a kindly Black chauffeur had helped to shield her and her mother from an abusive stepfather; and she had spent two weeks in quarantine with a feverish Black youngster, soothing his body with ice cold sponges. In a Cincinnati Symphony Hall, appalled by the ramifications of her own prejudice, she had "taken a first step toward becoming a citizen of the world." Lylah listened to Red as he expressed his resistance to the changes that he thought a Black player on the Dodgers' team would trigger. She knew exactly how he had been taught. She reminded him that he did not have to quit his job that evening, proposing instead that they both have a martini and then go to bed. Lylah trusted that in time, Red's "innate sense of fairness and intelligence" would persuade him to change his mind.[12]

In his memoir, other writings, and interviews, Red frequently described the "self-examination" he conducted during the weeks after he learned of Rickey's plan to integrate Major League Baseball. He was eager to get at the source of his resistance to Rickey's decision and to overcome it. But the thought processes he describes himself conducting took place on decidedly different levels. On a practical level, he was not eager to quit a job that paid well in a community where he had been so warmly embraced; he had to convince himself that he could still perform his job well with a Black man on the team. He resolved that dilemma quickly. During the days following his conversation with Lylah, Red recalled Bill Klem's claim that *his* job as umpire required of him simply to "umpire the ball." His own job, then, would be to simply continue "broadcasting the ball," regardless of who was hitting or catching it. This conviction that he could navigate the threatening challenge he faced just by being the impartial and accurate announcer he had always been quelled Barber's anticipatory anxiety in 1945.[13]

The harder work was recognizing and then challenging his assumptions about race, a process that may well have continued to the day he died. He began the process shortly after his conversation with Lylah by forcing himself to recognize that no one could control the color of his or her skin, so no one had grounds for claiming to be superior to Blacks simply because he or she had been born white. But during that spring of 1945, Barber made the most valuable progress toward a more profound grasp of his problem "coincidentally," through the process of writing a speech he was scheduled to deliver not long after his unsettling lunch with Rickey. He was asked by the rector of his church to deliver a radio talk that addressed recent tensions in Scarsdale between Jews and non-Jews; the rector wanted Barber to tie his remarks to St. Paul's claim that "all men are brothers." Barber reveals that his personal struggle at the time—to reconcile his attitude toward Blacks up to this point in his life with the arbitrary facts of his own birth as a white man—propelled his thinking throughout his composition of the speech. As it turned out, he tells us, the speech was rooted less in the current tensions upsetting the "wealthy community of Scarsdale" than in the "relationship between one white southern broadcaster and one unknown Negro ballplayer who was coming. . . . That talk—working it out, preparing it, giving it . . . helped me a great deal."[14]

A copy of the speech does not survive, but we can document Red's references to and reflections upon St. Paul's dictum of "Men and Brothers," the title of his radio talk. He reads St. Paul as teaching us the power of "*agape*," a Greek term often translated to mean "love," in the sense of "opening up to" and "having concern for." *Agape* is the foundation of the crucial commandment that we love one another, even when we cannot bring ourselves to like *each* "other" whom we meet. Barber interprets *agape* to mean that "if he's hurting, you're to help him; if he falls, you pick him up; if he is hungry, you feed him," just as Red's father had always instructed his mother to leave out some food for the homeless men who came to their door, because "you can't let a man grow hungry." In the parable of "The Good Samaritan," Barber recalls, it was not the rich man or the priest but a man of a different color and religion who bandaged, fed, and lodged the victim who had been beaten and robbed. "That is concern, that is love," Barber tells us. "It is a great thing to have."[15] Looking back on those months after his lunch with Rickey, Barber gratefully acknowledged the patience of Rickey and Lylah, "who gave me time to think."[16]

"That Will Have to Be Enough for Me Now"

On June 28, 1945, William Barber died at his sister's home in Lilesville, North Carolina. The *Brooklyn Eagle* reported on June 29, "The Voice of Brooklyn was checked and silent yesterday. Red Barber's father has died." Barber wrote about his father's death in 1971, describing it as the event that enabled him to overcome his own fear of death, which had plagued him since he was a child. He connects that fear to two childhood experiences, each of which exposed him to a corpse horribly disfigured by a gruesome death. In Columbus some older boys once took the seven-year-old Walter into an undertaker's workroom, where Red's first view of death was the "bloated, bloody body" of a man who had drowned in the Tombigbee River and had been floating there for days.[17] The undertaker at work on the body "was just as bloody. The nightmares lasted for years." Later, when he was a Boy Scout in Sanford, one of Red's friends was accidentally killed by "a shotgun blast at close range to his face." Barber, forced to stand by the boy's open casket as an attendant, gazed into his friend's face, "covered with shot wounds that I can see now."

When he learned his father had died, Barber was not shocked because he had been sitting in a chair beside him just three days before, observing, step by step, his father's peaceful acceptance of his oncoming death, a series of images that buffered Red's future encounters with human mortality. Barber had been visiting his ailing father periodically throughout the year before he died, "taking a Sunday-night sleeper," staying with his father on Monday, and returning to Brooklyn on Tuesday before noon. William Barber refused to rest in bed because he believed he would die if he laid his head down. At one point, William told his oldest son for the first time that he loved him, which, says Red, he always had known.

When his father saw the bold newspaper headline announcing V-E Day, he sighed in relief: "Billy is all right." Although his father had not been a churchgoer, he surprised his family by asking for a preacher. They summoned a local clergyman, and after his prayer, William Barber said to the young minister, "All my life I have loved God Almighty. That will have to be enough for me now." Red said he believed that his father's terse statement was the most complete confession of faith he had ever heard. That very afternoon, the last day Red saw his father alive, William Barber gave his son the watch that had monitored his life's work at the railroad and told him to "go back to [his] job." Barber did as his father asked. When he and Lylah returned several days later for William's funeral, Red learned from his Aunt Virginia that not long after he and Lylah had last left the house to return to New York, his father "[had] asked to be put into his bed. He was completely calm, peaceful, unafraid," silently teaching his children another life lesson. Barber's deepest regret was that his brother Billy, still overseas with his unit in Rouen, France, could not be with the family for his father's funeral.[18]

Yankees Come Calling

A few weeks after Barber and Lylah had returned from his father's funeral, Larry MacPhail, now general manager of the Yankees, offered Red the Yankees' announcing job for a three-year, $100,000 dollar contract to begin with the 1946 baseball season. Although Barber was deeply satisfied with his position in Brooklyn, this lucrative offer seemed too good to be true for three reasons. First, the salary would be record-breaking for a broadcaster. Second,

Red would have the chance to broadcast live at both home and away games because MacPhail had decided to broadcast out-of-town Yankees games live—another Major League "first" for the innovator who had already accumulated so many. Starting in 1946, there would be no more wire reports of Yankees games.[19] And third, Red would be hired by the Yankees instead of by the club's sponsors, another change that MacPhail believed was essential for attracting the best radio and television talent. Barber had been frustrated by his recent negotiations with Old Gold because the company had refused to consider any salary hike for his upcoming contract: "I felt I was still on my way up. I didn't want to level off. If you are not going up, you start going down."[20]

Red and Lylah discussed MacPhail's generous offer. They agreed that the only downside was leaving "Mr. Rickey . . . and, of course, Brooklyn itself." In Barber's various accounts of his difficult decision-making process, he provides a host of factors he had to weigh, some with his heart and some concerning his budget. After his first conversation with Rickey about MacPhail's offer, Rickey expressed his disappointment but complete understanding of Red's inclination to move to the Yankees. His only request—a strategic one—was that Barber wait three days before sealing the deal with MacPhail. Those three days made a big difference. In Barber's account they were spent recalling all he owed MacPhail, on the one hand, and on the other, his vivid recollections of the support that the Brooklyn fans had given him, particularly when he had appealed for their blood. He considered the friendliness he encountered everywhere he went in the stadium and the borough: "the clubhouse, the dugout, through the stands, and then along the streets to the subway station, guys hollering 'hello' from trucks. With Brooklyn the radio booth was mine, completely mine, and I hadn't realized it before."[21]

When Rickey and Red met after three days, the man who had thrust Barber into the interminable labor of fund-raising and into the sometimes painful conflict between "men and brothers" would keep his loyal servant on board for a few more years, until Rickey himself jumped ship. He offered Barber all that it took to persuade him to stay. Rickey had decided that, like MacPhail's Yankees, the Dodgers would also begin hiring their own announcers, and he exceeded MacPhail's salary offer by $5,000. Just the same, Barber admits he sometimes wondered what would have happened had he accepted MacPhail's offer. His typical proclivity was to accept new workplace opportunities and challenges even when they did not offer more money. "Perhaps I would have become known as the Voice of the Yankees."[22]

"Because You Have To"

Before 1945 ended, Barber found himself engaged in another fund-raising project, to which he would remain committed throughout the rest of the decade. Looking back, Lylah was certain that Red's fourth major fund-raising effort in the 1940s, coming just after he had spent so much of his time and energy on the war bond, blood donation, and Red Cross War Fund campaigns, was the source of the stomach ulcer that would trigger the hemorrhage that nearly killed him in July 1948. The Episcopal Diocese of New York ran St. Barnabas House, built in 1864 to provide temporary shelter and care for homeless and otherwise troubled children, as well as for pregnant unwed women in need of support. Located at Bleecker and Mulberry Streets near the Bowery, St. Barnabas House consisted of three brick buildings that were falling apart and that had been declared a fire hazard, too dangerous for those who lived and worked there. Just as Barber was entering the busiest month of the 1945 Red Cross War Fund campaign, board members of the Mission Society asked him to head a fund-raising campaign to tear down the current building and construct a modern St. Barnabas House on the same site.

This fund-raising project is unique in Barber's long resume of charitable endeavors because it sorely tested his faith in the diocese's commitment to its social mission. Barber at first declined the board members' invitation to head the project because he was already overwhelmed with his work for the War Fund. But they nailed him with an argument he could not refute: "This is the problem with the Episcopal Church," they told him. "All its members who would be capable and willing to help us have filled their schedules volunteering for other causes" instead of committing themselves to the needs of their own church. Feeling duly chastised, Red agreed to begin leading the St. Barnabas campaign at the end of March, when his work with the Red Cross War Fund would be winding down. Because of the elegant appointments of the Episcopal churches that he had attended and his familiarity with some of their well-heeled members, Barber assumed that it was a wealthy denomination with plenty of money for worthy causes. But he was forced to conclude early in the fund-raising project that many Episcopal Church members and their leaders in the New York diocese "could not care less about what went on at Bleecker and Mulberry Streets," a neighborhood they rarely frequented. He was warned that many of the diocesan churches were unwilling to support projects that served not their own members but "blacks, Puerto Ricans, Italians and other immigrants who were not Episcopalians."[23] Those prejudices had sabotaged two previous campaigns to rebuild St. Barnabas.

The previous campaign attempts had raised enough to pay for an architect's plans, and Barber proceeded to request $25,000 from each of the four wealthiest churches in the diocese to jumpstart the new effort and persuade other churches to pledge what they could afford. One of the four churches agreed to give that amount, but the rector of the wealthiest of the four refused to meet with Red once he realized why he was calling. The third rector referred the matter to his vestry, a group of church trustees that voted to decline Red's request. When the rector informed Barber of their decision, he at least offered Red a tour of the church's "beautiful marble and rich tapestry." The gesture inspired Red, whose spirit was sinking, to coolly inform the rector: "All I see here is a lot of cold slabs of marble that cost a lot. I want you to tell your vestry that I believe their hearts are as cold as this marble." Red tells us that he lost his composure altogether when the fourth rector reported his vestry's decision to decline the request for a donation. He demanded that the rector ask them again for the money "because you *have* to." The rector agreed and subsequently informed Red that on second thought, the vestry decided to approve the donation. When Red asked what made them change their minds, the rector replied, "I told them they *have* to." Apparently that was all it took when the men in charge made the effort.

But Red still needed to squeeze out $50,000 more. Summer was approaching, a season when many wealthy New York Episcopalians left town to vacation in their summer "cottages." Desperate, he sent telegrams to what he was told were the wealthiest hundred members of the diocese, explaining, in brief, the urgency to save St. Barnabas and requesting their donations. He received but one reply from a church member who affirmed that he would never contribute to a cause that wasted so much money on telegrams.

Red finally raised the money that got the campaign rolling and that ultimately rebuilt St. Barnabas House. The bishop of the diocese connected Barber to a wealthy Jewish philanthropist who, after some recent soul searching, had decided that he should be giving ecumenically instead of funding only Jewish organizations. After talking with Barber, the broad-minded man then scheduled a meeting with twenty of his contacts in the philanthropic community, eighteen of whom were also Jewish, and invited Barber to come and make his appeal to the group. During his presentation Red noticed that the oldest man sitting across from him at the table kept checking his watch, and he was convinced he had lost his audience. But when he finished defending his cause, the old man stood up and said, "I'm busy and I have got to get out of here. . . . I'll write my check for $5,000 right now. Then I am going to go around this table and ask each one of you men what size check you will write." Red reports that "every man in that room wrote out a check," adding that the two Christians' checks were the "most modest."

Barber remained a board member of the Episcopal Mission Society for years, and he continued to raise funds required to complete the new St. Barnabas building well after the campaign had been successfully launched. Finally, in October 1949, Red spoke at the dedication of the new St. Barnabas House on Mulberry Street, "the only building in the United States designed specifically as a temporary shelter for women and children of all races and creeds." Barber told his audience that in his twenty years of broadcasting he had announced many "resounding victories," but he was convinced that this one would be "the finest victory and the most lasting."[24] In 2015 the "new" St. Barnabas building was torn down by residential developers of the increasingly upscale neighborhood.

10

"Oh, Doctor!"

His father's death robbed Red Barber of his most significant mentor, but by 1945 William Barber's role in his son's life had passed on to others. Larry MacPhail taught Red the power of innovation and aggressive action and the self-destructive potential of anger and alcohol. Branch Rickey offered lessons in shrewd negotiation, the importance of spousal advice, and the need to embrace service to others. Rickey's single-minded efforts to integrate Major League Baseball made Barber question his racist legacy and demonstrated the power one individual could have in shaping history. With Rickey's urging, Barber developed his own administrative chops, organizing the Red Cross War Fund campaigns in Brooklyn and greater New York. When an opportunity to apply that administrative acumen arose in 1946, Barber was ready to seize it with the endorsement of a new mentor, Edward R. Murrow.

cbs: Labor and Management

In early 1946 Murrow returned from London, where, as director of cbs's European operations, he had developed a legendary staff of news professionals, "Murrow's Boys," including Eric Sevareid, Charles Collingwood, Howard K. Smith, and William

L. Shirer, among others. For many Americans, Murrow had been the voice of the war before the United States entered the international conflict. He won wide acclaim for his vivid reporting of the London Blitz. "This is London," his introductory phrase to his broadcasts, became one of the most memorable in radio history. Barber hailed Murrow as a "genuine big shot," "a first-rate fellow," and a "center ring man."[1] In late 1945 William S. Paley, head of CBS, convinced a reluctant Murrow to become vice president of the network and head of CBS News. Ted Husing, the voice of CBS Sports since 1927, also headed CBS Sports, now one of Murrow's new responsibilities. Perhaps weary of the demands of sports reporting and game broadcasts, Husing accepted a lucrative contract in early 1946 from WHN in New York to host his own daily disc jockey show. Barber's agent, Bill McCaffery, alerted him he might be in line for Husing's spot with the network. Always committed to proper workplace protocol, Barber contacted Husing to confirm his departure from CBS before pursuing the opportunity. Husing gave his blessing.

When Red interviewed with Murrow for the director of sports position, Murrow was so new that carpenters still were building the shelves and a stand-up reading desk for his office. He saw in Barber a mature broadcaster—born like himself in 1908—who shared his own commitment to accurate reporting and who also knew how to make precise and imaginative use of the English language. Red Barber was someone he could trust to run the sports division with integrity and little supervision, freeing Murrow to build the CBS news division that would be his legacy. Red recalled bonding easily with Murrow at their first meeting: "We came to a complete agreement and in a hurry. . . . We were both willing."[2] Barber was eager to work for a celebrated and respected boss, one who had the ear of the most powerful man at CBS, William S. Paley. Paley was Barber's final interview hurdle and the most intimidating one for any new CBS hire. From 1926 until his death in 1990, Paley controlled the fortunes of CBS, the network that made his fortune several times over.

When Barber met with Paley in July 1946 at his 485 Madison Avenue office, he was concerned about Paley's professed affection for two of Barber's football broadcast rivals. "I listen to Bill Stern and Harry Wismer do football games," Paley announced, "and they make even a two-yard gain exciting." Barber felt the ground shifting. Murrow liked him, but Paley seemed to be questioning his report-first approach. Unable to dissemble, Barber told one of the most powerful men in American broadcasting, "No sir—I can't announce that way." Paley smiled and told Barber, "Good, I wouldn't want you to."[3] Flush with profits from wartime advertising, Paley wanted to build a network of the highest quality. Despite a full schedule of Major League baseball and countless public appearances, Red Barber found the time to take his place in what would become known as the "Tiffany Network." Regrettably for Barber, his time with Ed Murrow as his boss was brief. After two years, Murrow went back to daily news reporting, moving away from day-to-day administration. Barber understood. He told Robert Creamer, in words he might later have applied to himself, "The desk and the interoffice gut-fighting were for smaller men. He [Murrow] went back to where the talent and action were, the microphone and the camera."[4] But Red never lost his esteem for Murrow. When Murrow died of cancer in 1965, Red grieved: "His funeral nearly broke my heart."[5]

Barber hired two new associates, John Derr and Judson Bailey. Both would have lengthy careers at CBS. A native of North Carolina, Derr came to CBS looking for a job as the network's golf specialist, a position that did not exist. But CBS hired him as a writer, editing Barber's weekday sports broadcast. By April 1947 Derr had become an assistant director for sports.[6] In late 1951 he would replace Barber as CBS director of sports when Barber downsized his role to counselor for sports. Later, Derr realized his dream: he covered the Masters Tournament on CBS television from 1956 to 1982.[7] Judson Bailey, the more experienced of the recent hires, joined Barber's team in October 1947. Bailey had covered the 1932 Los Angeles Summer Olympics for a West Virginia newspaper syndicate before joining the Associated Press in Pittsburgh in 1936 as a sportswriter. Two years later he became an AP baseball writer in New York.[8]

Barber credited Murrow with teaching him to think of his staff as colleagues rather than as employees or assistants. Barber loved the term "colleague": "It's a wonderful word for your associates, it gives them a certain dignity, it lifts them. . . . It takes everyone into a partnership."[9] Barber as boss also seemed to captivate at least one lower-level staff member. In September 1948 the *Brooklyn Eagle* profiled Red's secretary, Luba Terpak. She described Barber as a boss with "the most beautiful descriptive vocabulary I've ever known." According to Terpak, he also "has a phenomenal memory, can dictate for hours—phone-call interruptions can never throw him—and never loses his temper." Terpak was qualified to comment on Barber's language skills. She knew eight languages, worked as a Russian interpreter, and translated a Ukrainian opera.[10] While Barber aimed for a collegial office atmosphere, he also exerted his authority. There was never any doubt who was in charge of CBS Sports or of the Brooklyn Dodgers' broadcast booth.

Barber's first duty at CBS Sports was writing, producing, and hosting a variety of sports-related programs, initially on radio and then television. Among the first was the CBS *Radio Baseball Clinic*, introduced in August 1947. The program featured one-on-one interviews with some of the most important figures in Major League Baseball. Red's first interview was with baseball's grand old man, Connie Mack, and the second, with its most famous player, Babe Ruth. Mack explained how he built a batting order: lead-off hitters should take walks, cleanup hitters should be sluggers, and the second-best hitter, in the fifth slot, should protect the cleanup hitter. Mack also shared his philosophy of managing, especially the importance of having great coaches.[11] Babe Ruth, his voice raspy from his throat cancer surgery, focused not on hitting home runs but playing the outfield, an underappreciated part of his game. Ruth discussed judging the speed of a base runner, positioning for different batters, adapting to changing weather, and playing the sun field.[12]

Barber's CBS programs also included *Red Barber's Club House*, a children's quiz show on sports, produced by Barber, Derr, and Bailey. Two teams of young athletes fielded sports questions from Barber and, in another segment, offered solutions for "a hypothetical critical situation in a sports event to test their powers of strategy." The winning team took home sports equipment as prizes, and each week the show celebrated an American town "demonstrating unusual leadership in promoting local sports."[13] Red's efforts to enrich the network's programming were making a difference. By early 1948 Audience Research's Enthusiasm Quotient measure of popularity found Barber and his CBS colleague Edward R. Murrow among the top three radio commentators.[14]

Rounding Up College Football

Barber's ten years at CBS extended his reach as a national media personality and positioned him for several lucrative spokesperson assignments in the next decade, including contracts with General Electric, Gulf Oil, and State Farm Insurance. Barber, however, was most proud of his creation and launch of CBS's *College Football Roundup*, a novel concept for covering the diversity of college football. Until *College Football Roundup*, national networks covered only a single game each week. Although NBC, CBS, and MBS often had access to the biggest contests each week, the quality of the game was still unpredictable. A great match-up could produce a boring, lopsided contest. A national audience, with no particular loyalty to either team, would quickly flee to another network or a local station's game. Some weeks there was no clear-cut "biggest" game of the week. College football was essentially a regional sport. How does a national network keep different regions interested in one game, especially if it's a dog? Barber's solution evolved during the 1946 and 1947 seasons.

On the last weekend of the 1946 season, the 1946 Big Ten Championship and its Rose Bowl representative would be decided.

Michigan would face Ohio State in Columbus, and Illinois would vie with Northwestern in Evanston. If Illinois won, it would go to the Rose Bowl; if Illinois lost or tied and Michigan won, Michigan would represent the Big Ten at the "granddaddy" of all college bowls. Barber didn't know which game to cover. He sought counsel with Murrow, who asked him which game Barber preferred. Red responded honestly, "I'd like to do them both." Murrow told Barber, "Do it."[15] Red covered the Michigan-Ohio State game, and Gene Shumate, the Illinois-Northwestern contest. Using a private phone line, the two announcers coordinated their reporting.[16] On November 23, 1946, Michigan crushed Ohio State, 58–6, but Illinois also won, 20–0, over Northwestern. The Fighting Illini capped their season with a 45–14 victory over UCLA in the Rose Bowl.

In 1947 CBS broadcast two more dual match-ups, but the essential question remained: How do you cover a weekly regional sport nationally? After broadcasting a blowout lost by Florida to Georgia Tech early in the 1948 season, Barber implemented a bold new plan: the CBS *College Football Roundup*. He scheduled announcers for six different college football games each week. From the CBS studio in New York, Barber decided which game's play-by-play to feature at any moment. Throughout the broadcast, audiences enjoyed updated summary reports from each of the six games.[17] As the concept developed in 1949, Barber integrated additional wire service and phone reports from designated stringers at additional games. During the three-hour broadcast, Barber and his location announcers reported on up to thirty games each Saturday. On-the-spot reports from the games were 2–4 minutes long. Barber's Dodgers broadcast colleagues, Connie Desmond and Ernie Harwell, were regular contributors, and his Dodgers statistician, Bob Pasotti, was his studio assistant.[18] At the urging of his agent, Bill McCaffery, Barber put aside his reservations and hired the now-recovering alcoholic Bill Munday, one of Barber's sportscaster role models, for on-the-spot reports. In 1949 Red hired another redhead, twenty-one-year-old Vin Scully, to cover a Boston College game from a freezing perch at Fenway Park.

College Football Roundup put Barber in the position he loved most: complete control. He "edited" each college football weekend as it unfolded. The broadcast was as exhilarating as it was exhausting. In weeks when one game was clearly of greatest national significance, Barber would focus on that contest. But most weeks were a round robin. Some critics disliked the fragmented approach, preferring a traditional broadcast of one game. But most applauded the innovation. At the point when television coverage of college football was siphoning listeners, *Football Roundup*'s strategy maximized the flexibility of radio, covering multiple games when television could barely cover one. The program also foregrounded Barber's talents in selecting the best moments, adding imaginative ad-lib commentary, writing excellent copy quickly, and training and maintaining a talented staff. Citing his innovative expansion of the *Football Roundup, The Sporting News* recognized Barber as the outstanding football announcer in 1949.[19]

While executing administrative duties with CBS, Barber was still the principal on-air sports talent, and the network featured him at a variety of events. One of his first assignments was the first postwar National Air Races from Cleveland.[20] Barber also provided color commentary for the Hambletonian Stakes harness race in 1947, the only time he ventured into the equestrian arts.[21] When CBS Radio covered a sports event, if Red was available, it was his to broadcast. His showcase CBS events, however, were New Year's Day football bowl games. After influencing the CBS decision to buy the rights, Barber broadcast the 1950 and 1951 Rose Bowl games. But his history with the Orange Bowl was the most extensive; Barber called the 1947–49, 1952, and 1955–56 New Year's Day games in Miami.[22] Along with spring training, the Orange Bowl brought him back regularly to his home state, where he developed long-term friendships during his assignments.

Thirteen Rooms and Five Baths

The demands of Red's job as CBS director of sports lengthened his workday, triggering the Barbers' decision to move from Scarsdale to an apartment in the city. Martha McCaffery, the wife of Red's agent, gave them a lead on a large, rent-controlled apartment directly across Fifth Avenue from the Metropolitan Museum of Art. On the fourteenth floor with a view of Central Park from 59th to 110th Streets, it was available because the elderly tenant had recently died. The apartment, with "thirteen rooms and five baths [including] a servant's wing with three small bedrooms and a sitting room," had more space than their home in Scarsdale for the price of only $400 a month. Lylah admits that the space was a luxury, but with "a three-generation family, a live-in maid, and always a cat or two, it was wonderfully comfortable."[23]

For Lylah, the family's four and a half years at 1035 Fifth Avenue were "the richest of my life." Her husband's career was "expanding in interesting ways . . . and the city itself was a constant delight." She loved the accessible museums, shops, galleries, opera, and Broadway musicals, stimulating for herself but also providing valuable resources for educating Sarah, now approaching adolescence. Because of her "inherited reticence," Lylah was too embarrassed to answer the questions that her daughter asked her about the physical differences between boys and girls. Instead, Lylah writes, "I took her for an afternoon visit to the Metropolitan Museum, where I saw to it that Sarah spent considerable time in the Greek wing, with the naked life-size beautiful marble statues."

One highlight of those years was the party celebrating Ethel Barrymore's seventieth birthday, hosted by *New York Post* theater columnist Leonard Lyons. An avid baseball fan, Barrymore specifically requested that the guest list include Joe DiMaggio and Red Barber. Guests were seated by fours at card tables; Barrymore had insisted that Barber and DiMaggio sit at her table. Lylah was pleased to be seated at a table with William Saroyan and John Steinbeck, who "exchanged ideas and episodes" for upcoming stories. Red and Lylah, "dazzled by the occasion," stayed until well after midnight, when the room was still crowded: "They kept coming, the well-known of the entertainment world, to pay homage to Ethel Barrymore."[24]

Sarah, who sang well and performed in school musicals, also had a memorable brush with fame when her mother took her to a matinee performance of *South Pacific*. Bill McCaffrey, who also represented Mary Martin, mentioned to Martin that Red Barber's wife and daughter would be at the show, and she kindly invited them to her dressing room after the performance. When Martin asked Sarah what she wanted to be when she grew up, Red's daughter replied, "To be an actress like you, but I get a stomachache when I have to sing solo." Martin perceptively admitted, "I do too," but explained "That's because we are artists." A few weeks later, Sarah "sang well, very well" the soprano role in her school's production of *Pirates of Penzance*, even with a cast on her arm, which she had fractured a few days before the performance.

Red and Lylah's initiation into life on Fifth Avenue also provided new insights into pedigree and privilege among Manhattan's wealthy upper class. Sarah had some initial difficulties transitioning from the "casual, freer lifestyle" of children in Westchester to the more "formal, ritualized environment" in which Upper East Side youngsters filled their days in transport from private schools to dance classes and then to music lessons.[25] Lylah was uncertain which private school to select for Sarah: the most academically challenging, the one ranking highest on the social register, or the one she finally selected, the Spence School, which Lylah believed was academically rigorous but not "blue-stocking." Sarah's new "best school friend," Whitney, attended dance class on Friday afternoons, along with other private school girls, and when Sarah asked her mother if she could join them, Lylah discovered just how much "pedigree" really mattered. Whitney's mother told her there would be no opening for Sarah at this studio, which children had to be "born into." Sarah got into the class only because the rector of the Upper East Side Episcopal Church was friends with the Barbers' former church rector in Scarsdale, who must have put in a kind word for her.

When Lylah urged Red to get tickets for the opening night of *South Pacific*, he tried his best to tap connections he had in "high places." He was driven finally to appeal for tickets from the pension and labor negotiator at CBS, which had bought a piece of the show. The negotiator finally came up with two seats in the next-to-last row on the ground floor. When Red and Lylah reached the theater for the opening, they spotted William Paley's "big black Cadillac limousine parked at the curb." Lylah observed that at intermission, Paley and his wife entertained guests for drinks in the limo. "The Barbers were not invited."

The Barbers' years in their New York City apartment also included gratifying travel experiences connected to Dodgers spring training locations. Lylah's memories of those trips suggest her evolving left-leaning political persuasions, which would culminate years later in her decision to serve as co-chairman for Tallahassee's chapter of Citizens for George McGovern in 1972 under the name "Mrs. Red Barber."[26] In 1946 the Barbers took a long car ride to Daytona Beach via Columbus, Mississippi, and New Orleans. They designed the itinerary to connect Sarah to some of her Southern roots and to satisfy Lylah's desire to try Oysters Rockefeller, which Red had raved about when he returned from his broadcast of the Sugar Bowl in 1940. Red wanted Sarah to see Mississippi State University for Women, where his mother had matriculated when she was only sixteen. Lylah loved the oysters in New Orleans and the colorful French Quarter Mardi Gras parade. Red got three of the coveted seats in the viewing stand from "one of his radio connections."[27] The parade was delayed for hours, however, because all the young Black torch carriers had gone on strike for higher pay. Lylah was gratified when she learned later that they won and that "unions have finally made it to New Orleans!"

The Dodgers held spring training in Cuba in 1947 because Branch Rickey feared Jackie Robinson's appearance on the team in Florida would trigger racist reactions, sabotaging his pursuit of a smooth launch to integrate Major League Baseball. Red rented a car so that he, Lylah, and Sarah could explore the countryside, where tourists rarely ventured. They observed the poor villages whose residents worked nearby in the huge sugar plantations owned by U.S. corporations. According to Lylah, the destitute people lived in "primitive conditions . . . the poverty, unbelievable. Naked children with bellies swollen from malnutrition stood on the road watching us pass; they seemed to lack energy even for play." The experience enabled Lylah to understand six years later why the revolution to overthrow the Batista dictatorship was successful: "In a country where everyone is very rich or very poor, what did the poor have to lose?"

Spring training at Vero Beach, Florida, in 1949 provided an opportunity for the Barbers to grow more familiar with Jackie and Rachel Robinson and their three-year-old son, Jackie Jr. The Rickeys brought their granddaughter, the same age as Jackie Jr., to the camp, and, with the color-blind freedom of innocence, the two toddlers "became constant companions."[28] But Red and Lylah witnessed a discouraging scene in the fallen adult world at a spring training game played in West Palm Beach. A white police officer refused to let Rachel Robinson "take little Jackie to a restroom in the stands." Instead, he said, "You go out in the woods behind the fence." Red says Rachel Robinson never told her husband about that incident or other indignities that she suffered.[29] Lylah later wrote, "I felt ashamed. I was indignant for her. How did she stand it?"[30]

Lylah tells us that Sarah was old enough in 1949 to grasp the significance of the Robinsons' struggle; her firsthand witnessing of their ordeal, Lylah believes, influenced her later social activism and her decision to begin her career teaching children in Harlem.[31] The effect of their experiences with the Robinsons was more immediate for Red and Lylah. When a couple who had been the Barbers' close friends in Gainesville visited New York, Red invited them for dinner. During what began as a pleasant reunion, Red asked them to be his guest for some Dodgers games. The husband, a practicing lawyer from an "old Gainesville family," abruptly exploded: "No, I'll never set foot in Ebbets Field as long as that [n—r] is playing there!" Lylah tells us that "Red didn't hesitate.

He softly replied, 'We won't miss you.' The evening was over. We never saw them again."[32]

Perhaps the most unsettling drama during the Barbers' time in their New York City apartment was the painful argument that resulted in Red's insistence that Lylah's mother return to Jacksonville to live once again with her son Mat, now home from the war. During a stretch when Sarah was having difficulty adjusting to her upscale private schooling, she was plagued with panic attacks and bouts of tears, begging to stay home. The Barbers sought professional counseling and were instructed to insist on Sarah's going to school, "no matter how hard it [was] to get her there." Lylah's mother, who had formed a strong bond with her granddaughter, upbraided Lylah about her "cruel treatment of Sarah, making her ill and forcing her to go to school." When Red overheard one of these intense arguments, he made an abrupt and unyielding decision to send his mother-in-law, who had grown fond of him, back to Jacksonville. He believed the four of them could no longer live together.[33] Barber habitually sought and adhered to professional medical advice, even when it resulted in painful consequences. He may have felt compelled to assert control in a messy situation that threatened the peace of his cherished time at home. He also was likely moved to defend Lylah.

Sadly, on December 16, 1950, only a few years after Lylah's mother returned to Florida, a hit-and-run driver in Jacksonville struck her. She fell into a coma from which she never recovered, dying in the hospital two months later. The vehicle eventually was traced to a police officer whose brother was the uninsured nineteen-year-old driver who had fled the scene. Barber attempted, unsuccessfully, to force an investigation of the accident and prosecution of the perpetrator, an investigation that he believed his mother-in-law deserved. In one of his syndicated columns several weeks after the event, Walter Winchell included an appeal imploring any Jacksonville citizen who had witnessed the deadly accident to step forward.[34] Criminal charges against the driver, however, were summarily dismissed because of "lack of prosecution." Barber long suspected that he was fighting against entrenched powers in Jacksonville who were vested in protecting the driver. Local lawyers refused to take the case because "you can't get blood from a turnip . . . and [in Jacksonville] you can't prosecute the police." Barber later asserted, "Whenever I think of poor people without money, without friends, without influ-ence involved with law and politics and the police—I spit."[35] In a civil suit, though, Lylah's brother Mat was awarded $3,500 in damages.[36] In 1953, motivated by his mother-in-law's death, Bar-ber narrated *Dead Stop*, a harrowing, widely circulated documen-tary on the tragedies caused by reckless driving. He would insist that it was the most heart-rending use of his voice throughout his broadcast career.[37]

Robinson Arrives

Jackie Robinson's arrival has been documented in his own auto-biographies and in many other books, magazines, newspaper arti-cles, and at least two feature films—*The Jackie Robinson Story* and, most recently, *42*. His breaking the color line in the Major Leagues has been identified as the most significant baseball event of the twentieth century.[38] On April 15, 1947, Red Barber could have told his Brooklyn Dodgers audience that history was in the making: the first African American player in the Major Leagues since the 1880s had taken the field. But Barber did not.

Since his March 1945 meeting at Joe's Restaurant with Branch Rickey, Barber had two years to adjust to the coming of a Black player. In his own mind, he had done so. He realized that his privileged position as a white American had been an accident of birth, not an endowment of worth. He fully trusted Branch Rickey to select the right man to integrate baseball, but as the day to cover that event approached, Barber still was uncertain how to announce it. Should he highlight the historic nature of the day and comment on the progress it represented? Should he describe Robinson's skin color along with the other physical features he would report for any player? Should he comment on rumors that other teams might walk out, refusing to play with a Black man? Should he speculate on the race baiting that Robinson was likely to face? What did the other Dodgers have to say about their new teammate? All these issues might be voiced in a twenty-first-century baseball broadcast. But this was 1947, and baseball announcers rarely dealt in social controversy. Barber also felt he just needed "to report."

In his personal account of the 1947 season, Barber wrote, "I heard the voice . . . of that white-haired, slender man with the sharp features . . . saying 'You are not to manage . . . you are not to play . . . you are not to umpire . . . you are to report.'" Judge Landis had given Barber this mantra. Red continued: "I heard that word, 'Report,' and peace came. I knew who I was and what I was to do and how I was to do it." Barber also knew that listeners to his "Southern voice" would be waiting to hear "what [he] said as well as what [he] didn't say." Accordingly, Barber just "reported what Robinson did as a ballplayer. That was all there was to it. That was all the public wanted, all Rickey wanted, and all Robinson wanted." Tom Villante, Barber's broadcast producer, confirmed Barber's assessment of his approach: "When Jackie Robinson came aboard, [Barber] faced a dilemma. 'How do I handle it? I'm going to handle it like I handle any other ballplayer; I don't say he's an Italian, I don't say he's a Greek, I don't say he's Polish, and I'm not going to say Jackie's a Negro.' Red referred to him as a person."[39] Barber reviewed this disciplined approach to covering Robinson with Connie Desmond, who followed suit, as would Ernie Harwell and Vin Scully when they joined the broadcast team.

Landis's instruction "to report" offered Barber a way out of his situation that was consistent with his goal of "objective" journalism. He knew that when calling a game, he was not a sociologist or a civil rights reformer. He was a baseball announcer whose job was to provide an accurate and entertaining description of a game. In the broadcast booth, Barber decided, he would avoid *any* discussion of Robinson's race. He would be color blind. Besides, everyone already knew that Robinson was Black. He did not need to say it.

Although the motion picture 42 depicts Barber referring to Robinson as a "brunette," there is little evidence that Barber referred to race at all on Opening Day 1947.[40] It is important to note that in this respect, he was in step with the practice of sportswriters who covered that historic game. Barber's friends Roscoe McGowen of the *New York Times* and Bill Roeder of the *New York World-Telegram* mentioned only Robinson's play, while Michael Gavan of the *New York Journal-American* did not specifically mention Robinson, who made no exceptional plays that day, in his summary of the game. Dick Young sidestepped Robinson's race, calling him "the majors' most-discussed rookie." A few reporters, merely in passing, referred to Robinson's race—"first Negro," "muscular Negro," "Negro first baseman," and even "dark and anxious young man," and "first colored boy."[41] Baseball historian Lyle Spatz argues that the New York press's understated treatment of Robinson's Opening Day likely was not a product of racism but of the reporters' belief that "their sole duty was to report what took place on the field."[42]

Still, despite his dogged commitment as *broadcaster* to just reporting, Barber could not always completely conceal his personal concern for Robinson's plight. In a 1950 interview with Sam Lacy, the first African American in the Baseball Writers' Association of America, Barber repeated his standard account of how he had reported on Robinson. But when pressed by Lacy, Barber admitted: "I was guilty, though, of letting my feelings influence me once or twice where Robinson was concerned. I remember once last year, when Jackie was kicking up on umpires. He had come through so much and had proved himself such a gentleman, I hated to see him doing it and before I realized it, [I said,] 'I wish Robinson wouldn't do that. I wish he wouldn't.' . . . Then I remembered I was simply a reporter."[43] Barber claimed that he received considerable support for his treatment of Robinson and no backlash about his on-air coverage: "I broadcast what Jackie

Robinson did. . . . Jack has told me he appreciates what I did for him."[44] Barber's oft quoted acknowledgement, "I thank Jackie Robinson. He did far more for me than I did for him," was also, in part, a declaration of his reportorial ethics;[45] he did little for Robinson in the broadcast booth beyond what he considered his job as a play-by-play announcer.

But when Barber left the Dodgers' booth in 1953, African American columnist Joe Bostic of the *New York Amsterdam News* describes a powerful impact of Red's reporting on Robinson that Barber himself could not have perceived. In an open letter to "Dear Red," Bostic movingly articulates the powerful effects of Barber's approach upon the population for whom it mattered the most in mid-century America:

> Robinson and the other Negro players who followed him carried so much of the hopes of so many of us. No use saying they were just other ballplayers; they weren't. They were a state of mind. And you know what, Red? Without any breast beating or declarations of social crusading, you seemed to be a solid champion campaigning like mad to ensure that Robinson *et al.* be considered as ball players, nothing more. . . . We all figuratively put our arms around Jackie and guided him through the entanglements of hatred and jealousy through the instrument of your word. You were our contact with our idol. It was you who humanized him.[46]

In his tribute to Red, Bostic recalls the time when Enos "Country" Slaughter went hard into Robinson at second, "spikes flashing high" to break up a double play. It was a moment pregnant with potential for racial conflict. Bostic remembers Barber cautioning listeners: "'Slaughter plays that way and it makes no difference who happens to be playing second, Robinson or anybody else.' That was that. Nobody got a chance to get riled up because this was nothing out of the ordinary." Barber "reported" what he saw, including the context, "Slaughter plays that way," which made the scene tough baseball, not a racial incident. Although some listeners might have heard a white announcer covering up for a white ballplayer, to Bostic, Barber was easing tensions by treating Robinson like any other man roughed up on the field in a close play.

"All Hell Broke Loose"

The 1947 season was the pinnacle of Red Barber's work in the medium he loved the best, radio. After that historic season, he gradually and reluctantly assumed more time broadcasting on television, Red's great nemesis. In 1982, the twenty-fifth anniversary of Jackie Robinson's first season, Barber published his last book: *1947: When All Hell Broke Loose in Baseball*. While the title might suggest a focus on Robinson's breaking the color line, only a modest portion of the book covers Robinson's arrival and the tensions it triggered. Barber's account of that year in his book covers Rickey's recruitment of Robinson, the alleged Dodgers' team members' petition against his playing, the race baiting by Philadelphia Phillies manager Ben Chapman, the support Robinson ultimately received from his teammates, and other tales from Robinson's arduous first year. But most of the book focuses on the suspension of Leo Durocher by Commissioner Happy Chandler and the feud between Barber's two mentors, Larry MacPhail and Branch Rickey, that resulted from Chandler's action. Barber also covers the hiring of Burt Shotton to replace Durocher; the dramatic 1947 National and American League pennant races; a stunning World Series between MacPhail's Yankees and Rickey's Dodgers; and MacPhail's biggest blowup after the Series, triggering the sale of his interest in the Yankees and his departure from baseball. Robinson's arrival was far from the "all" in the "All Hell" that broke loose.

Barber devotes his longest chapter to "The Most Exciting World Series—1947," offering a game-by-game analysis. The Yankees' victories in Games One, Two, Five, and Seven thrilled Bronx Bomber fans, while the Dodgers' 9–8 win in Game Three got the Bums back in the Series and elated Brooklyn. But it was Barber's call of the Dodgers' wins in Games Four and Six that sealed his place in

World Series history. Mel Allen was Barber's Series partner, each man broadcasting half of the innings. Fortune shined on Barber when, after a coin flip, he drew the assignment for the first half of Game One. The two broadcasters rotated their assignment throughout the rest of the Series. This meant that Barber covered the last half of Games Four and Six, producing two of the signature calls of his thirty-three-year career as a big league broadcaster. For this World Series, Red Barber, in full command of his craft, was in the veritable catbird seat.

Game Four provided slow-building drama and a climax for the ages. When Barber took over the broadcast, Yankee pitcher Bill Bevens was working on a no-hitter. Mel Allen had just given the totals, taking "a big long pause when he should have said how many Dodger hits there were."[47] Following the popular tradition of not revealing that a no-hitter was in progress from the fifth inning onward, Allen did not tell his listeners that Bevens had not yet allowed a hit. Barber, who by this point in his career ridiculed the taboo as the "fifth inning no-hit hoodoo," made Bevens's progress toward a "no-no" the story of the game. As he wrote in 1947, "What maturity as a broadcaster I achieved came in 1947 over the long season when I was the announcer for the first black man in the big leagues. It was completed in the last half of the fourth game of the World Series. I remained a reporter, not a dealer in superstition."[48]

When Barber gave the complete totals, including Brooklyn's lack of a hit, Allen emitted sudden "choking sounds like he was trying to swallow chinaberry seeds."[49] Barber continued to report that Bevens was denying the Dodgers any hits, even as his walk total reached eight by the bottom of the ninth. Bevens retired the first batter, Bruce Edwards, on a fly ball, then issued Carl Furillo the ninth walk of the game. Spider Jorgensen hit a foul ball that was caught. Burt Shotton put Al Gionfriddo in to run for Furillo and Pete Reiser to pinch-hit for Dodgers reliever Hugh Casey. Gionfriddo then stole second, prompting Yankees manager Bucky Harris to walk Reiser, the tenth free pass of the game, putting the potential winning run on first base. Eddie Miksis ran for Reiser. Shotton then had Cookie Lavagetto swing for Eddie Stanky, setting the stage for Barber's first call for the ages:

> Stanky is being called back from the plate and Lavagetto goes up to hit. The Yankees are ahead, 2–1. Gionfriddo, the pinch runner, is at second—the tying run; Miksis, the winning run, at first base, both of them on from walks; both are pinch runners. No hits off Bevens. Eight and two-thirds innings, two out, last of the ninth, the pitch to Lavagetto swung on and missed. A fast ball that was in there, strike one. Gionfriddo walks off second; Miksis, off first; they're both ready to go on anything. Two men out, last of the ninth. The pitch, swung on. There's a drive hit out toward the right field corner. Henrich is going back; he can't get it; it's off the wall for a base hit; here comes the tying run and here comes the winning run. [Sixteen seconds of loud cheering.] Fans, they're killing Lavagetto. His own teammates! They're beating him to pieces. And it's taking a police escort to get Lavagetto away from the Dodgers.[50]

Barber's efficient fullness is manifest. He provides the key information: who is up, who is on base, how the base runners got there, what their presence means to the outcome, what action is taking place on the field, and the monumental result: "Here comes the tying run and here comes the winning run." Then Barber takes a lengthy pause to let the crowd roar, releasing the emotions of the moment. Finally, just a touch of hyperbole: "they're beating him to pieces. And it's taking a police escort to get Lavagetto away from the Dodgers."

Barber recalls that the local sports media criticized his call of this game for breaking the unwritten no-hitter rule. Yankees fans apparently called newspapers and radio stations to complain that he had "jinxed" the Yankees' pitcher. But according to Red, neither Yankees manager Bucky Harris nor the near no-hit Bill Bevens blamed the Old Redhead for jinxing the no-hitter. The next day Harris told him, "If you can control what the ball does by what you say about it, I'll pay you a lot more money than radio does to sit by me on the bench." Bevens assured Barber, "Red, you had nothing to do with it. . . . It was those bases on balls that did it."[51] Barber also received praise from the broadcaster he most respected. Before turning the broadcast back to Mel Allen for his summation and sign-off, Red finished with one of his most celebrated Barberisms: "I'll be a suck-egg mule." Ed Murrow, "a stickler for straight reporting, precise grammar, and due care with adjectives," told Barber later that the idiom "had ended [Red's] account perfectly."[52]

Barber's second 1947 World Series "call for the ages" also centered on Dodgers bencher Al Gionfriddo. Manager Shotton said that Gionfriddo's steal of second was the key to the Bums' ninth inning comeback in Game Four. In Game Six, the Dodgers took an early 4–0 lead, but the Yankees tied it in the bottom of the third and took a one-run lead in the bottom of the fourth. The Dodgers jumped back in the lead with a four-run sixth off the Yankees' ace reliever Joe Page. In the bottom of the sixth, Dodgers reliever Joe Hatten retired pinch hitter Allie Clark on a liner to Pee Wee Reese. Snuffy Stirnweiss walked. Tommy Henrich hit a long one that had home run length but was foul. Then he fouled out. Yogi Berra singled to left. The Yankees were down three runs with two outs, but they had the Yankee Clipper, Joe DiMaggio, coming up. The man widely deemed "the greatest living ballplayer" after he retired in 1951, was now the Yankees' "Casey at the Bat." Barber's call offers all that's needed and two everlasting phrases:

> The Dodgers are ahead, 8–5, and the crowd well knows that with one swing of his bat this fellow is capable of making it a brand-new game again. Joe leans in. Outfield deep and around toward left, the infield overshifted. Here's the pitch—swung on, belted. It's a long one, deep into left center. Back goes Gionfriddo, *back, back, back, back, back, back*, he makes a one-handed catch against the bullpen. *Oh, doctor!* [Six seconds of loud cheering.] He went exactly against the railing in front of the bullpen and reached up with one hand and took a home run away from DiMaggio.[53]

Barber claimed that he never used the phrase "Oh, doctor" again but happily gave it to his protégé, Vin Scully. He was also pleased that one of his favorite former players and later football announcer, Pat Summerall, often used the phrase. Barber's six-pack of "backs"—*back, back, back, back, back, back*—inspired the home run call of longtime ESPN *SportsCenter* anchor Chris Berman.

Olympic Adventure

The pace of Barber's professional life seemed to accelerate as fast as a skier on a downhill run. After his long baseball season capped by the World Series, Barber continued his regular CBS productions and started 1948 with his second Orange Bowl. He then labored to become CBS's expert on Winter Olympics sports—quite a challenge for a sports reporter from the Deep South who never saw his first snow until he moved to Cincinnati. The 1948 Winter Olympics in St. Moritz, Switzerland, were a minor event in the United States. The country had won few medals, and none for skiing, at the previous Winter Olympics. CBS sent Barber, the only radio reporter from the United States, to cover the games. Red's job was to write and voice a daily report at 1:00 p.m. local time that CBS aired live via shortwave radio. In what was his first of many trips to Europe, Red also worked with the Armed Forces Radio Service and the USO to schedule visits with American servicemen stationed in Germany.

As the time approached to cover the winter events, Barber, in his words, was "scared silly." His knowledge of winter sports was thin, and CBS sent no expert commentator to assist him. At his last USO stop in Garmisch, Germany, fair fortune struck. The Old Redhead met Ed Link, an army officer with an extensive background in skiing and a lifelong passion for winter sports. Link was sorely disappointed that he hadn't been able to get the tickets he wanted to the games, while Barber very much needed an expert to edit his reports before he broadcast them to America. In no time, Link accepted an up-close press pass to the events, and Barber had secured his expert. Ed Murrow would later marvel that a son of the South could become a winter sports expert so quickly. Barber just told him, "A working sports announcer is supposed to know about such things."[54]

Barber's most lasting memory of the 1948 Winter Olympics was the stellar feat of Gretchen Fraser, a twenty-eight-year-old U.S. skier. Fraser finished only eleventh in the first half of the downhill combination event, but then she became the first American ever to win a medal in skiing, finishing second in the slalom half of the combined event. Barber interviewed her after her silver medal performance, promising to watch her in the slalom-only competition. On slalom day, Barber was the only reporter to trudge up to the top of Mount Piznair for the event.[55] Fraser's two golden-haired, red-ribbon-bound pigtails flying straight back, she blistered down the sun-brightened, white-covered slope, besting her nearest competition by five-tenths of a second.[56] Barber called Fraser's gold medal run one of the top ten sporting events he had ever broadcast.[57]

While the Winter Olympics received limited coverage in the United States, the London summer games were a different beast. CBS Radio planned to send Barber, John Derr, and Judson Bailey to join CBS London correspondent Stephen Laird in July 1948. The plan was for Barber and Laird to do the broadcasting, Derr to supervise production, and Bailey to do a London production of *Red Barber's Clubhouse*.[58] Barber even wrote an article about CBS's plans for the upcoming London Olympics for *Sport* magazine's August 1948 issue. The title was "I Cover the Olympics."[59] But as the Yiddish proverb goes, "Man plans, and God laughs."

"I Knew I Was at the Brink"

By July 1948 Barber was "as busy as a one-armed paperhanger in a big wind," working out detailed arrangements for his Olympics coverage. He also was about to take his first road trip with the Dodgers, which included games in Cincinnati, Chicago, and Pittsburgh. When he arrived in Pittsburgh early on July 23, Barber went with Connie Desmond, sportswriter Roscoe McGowen, and Dodgers road secretary Harold Parrott to play golf at the Pittsburgh Field Club before the ball game. It was a round he could barely finish on a day that would powerfully influence the rest of his life.[60]

The day was hot and, no matter how much water Red drank, he kept getting thirstier. He felt himself losing strength as the hours went by until he could no longer hit the golf ball even halfway to the next hole. Red wanted the game to be over so that he could shower and lie down. He made it through the shower, but as soon as he got dressed, he realized his mouth was full of blood, and he was unbearably nauseous. Red vomited violently into his panama hat, which proved too small a bucket to contain the bloody fluid he was spewing. The shiny white tiles of the golf club shower room floor now were drenched in red. On his knees by the toilet bowl, he thought, "I am dying . . . dying alone in a men's room."[61] But the bleeding subsided long enough for Parrott to drive him, barely alive, to Pittsburgh's Methodist Hospital.

Barber was in an exhausted, numb, semiconscious state at the hospital while the doctors were attempting a diagnosis, but he still could hear them talking to one another as if they believed he was asleep. What they were saying was dismal: Red had lost over half of his blood, and any movement of his body could trigger another hemorrhage. They could do nothing for him unless his internal bleeding stopped. During the interminable night, Red knew that his assistant at CBS, Judson Bailey—with whom he was to do a morning show from Pittsburgh the next day—had stood by his bed, crying. He knew that Desmond and Harold Parrott had come into the room and realized the night game must be over: "Connie tried to say something about Dixie Walker breaking up the game, then he broke down and left." Even later, Lylah arrived from New York, held his hand, and just stood staring at him: "Her face was stricken, she knew something."

After Lylah left, Barber later recalled, "I knew I was at the brink. I was about to go over . . . and I didn't care. I was too weak." He wanted to "slide over the edge. . . . It was so close." Then he felt "a presence in the room . . . not a person and not something [he] could see or hear," and he knew he was no longer alone. Red described it as "so real I was flooded with a feeling of complete comfort." Whatever it was, it assured him he need not be afraid; it made no difference at all if he passed over or just stayed here on earth. That realization comforted him, as if "there were soft, tender hands beneath me holding me." When he woke up the next morning, the doctors told him a "silent" gastric ulcer had developed until, with no warning, it had exploded.

Barber was moved to New York Hospital, where he stayed for several days, and then he was prescribed several weeks of complete bed rest, milk, and bland food.[62] He even took a rare August vacation in Martha's Vineyard, falling into the rhythm of "lazy summer days."[63] For the first time in his life, he was not eager to go back to work; he was obsessed with the fear that he would have another hemorrhage and would start spouting blood: "[I was] drifting, just drifting, but down deep, I was afraid."

After Labor Day, Rickey called and told him to come back to work; Red's doctor had informed him he thought Barber was doing well. Barber grudgingly returned to announcing but fell into what he describes as a protracted bout of self-pity. He had to give up smoking and alcohol; all he could drink was milk and water; he tired easily. He was not the eager, energetic man he used to be. When he started doing football that fall, he was so afraid of having another hemorrhage that he made CBS pay for a nurse, Lylah, and a backup announcer to travel with him in case he got sick again. One afternoon in his office at CBS he felt so oppressed by his fatigue, his boring diet, and his fear of mouthfuls of blood that he "shut the door and cried for an hour," although he had never been "much of a fellow to cry."

Barber describes two experiences late that fall that lifted his sinking spirit and got him back into action. He was forced to

announce the annual Alabama high school football championship game for CBS—a Thanksgiving Day charity game that it
was his turn to cover. He tried but failed to get out of the gig and
went down to Birmingham with chips on both his shoulders. It
was Zipp Newman, a veteran local sports editor and chief fund-
raiser for the Crippled Children's Clinic, who unwittingly shook
Red out of his depression. Newman had originated the idea for
the Alabama championship game, all the proceeds of which would
go toward a new state-of-the-art building for the clinic. Red was
annoyed that Newman had planned a protracted itinerary, dragging him around from Tuesday to Thursday. He was taken to the
current clinic building, where he "had to pay a visit to each little patient and listen to each nurse and doctor." Red had to go to
the plot of ground where the new building would stand. He complains: "All I heard for two days was Crippled Children's Clinic."
He even had to attend a special pregame Thanksgiving Episcopal Church service. But when Newman was driving him to the
church, Red looked over at him, and he later wrote, "Some of the
scales dropped from my eyes. . . . I realized how hard and how long
he had worked for the crippled children whose parents couldn't
pay for them to get help. I understood suddenly that here was a
man who was fulfilling the second great commandment; he had
an active concern for his fellow man." When Barber asked Newman why, for years, he had been working harder for this clinic
than for his newspaper job, his Birmingham guide "answered very
simply, 'Red, you have to give back.'"

A few weeks later, at the Orange Bowl between Texas and
Georgia, Red was in a hotel room with Blair Cherry, the Long-
horn coach, and several other men, including Cherry's brother.
One of them picked up the phone to order drinks—beer, scotch
and soda, bourbon—but Red could only have milk, explaining
with disgust, "I had a hemorrhage from an ulcer." When Cherry's brother asked about the experience, Red told a long story
about "the terrible time [he] had in Pittsburgh and the terrible
time [he] was still having." When he was finished, the room was

quiet until Cherry's brother said gently, "I know what you mean, Red, I've had eight hemorrhages, and three perforations." Red felt ashamed: "Coach Cherry didn't have a running back in the game against Georgia who moved as rapidly as I did in getting out of that room." Barber tells us that since the end of 1948, whenever he lingered in the slough of self-pity, he thought of "Zipp Newman in Birmingham and Blair Cherry's brother in the room at Miami Beach."

Magazine and newspaper profiles of Barber after 1948 identify his near-death episode as a turning point in his life. In a 1950 *Look Magazine* profile, Barber said, "The ulcer did it." It compelled him to take an "inventory of his life," one that forced him to realize how his peripatetic work schedule and his unstinting professional ambition had robbed him of meaningful control over his life.[64] A 1953 profile in *Cosmopolitan* informs readers that "Barber's life has taken on more meaning since July 23, 1948." His experience as a sports announcer had made him keenly aware of the "power of the spoken word," particularly to move people to action, as his voice had done during the wartime blood drives. But now, although he was still deeply committed to his work as a broadcaster, he was "delighted to use his talents for a more important purpose than recounting how young men play games."[65] In a 1954 *Reader's Digest* profile, Barber affirmed that on the day his life was spared, he knew that the time had come for him "to discharge a part of his debt."[66]

New Medium, New Colleague

The 1948 baseball season brought change to Barber's professional world. CBS planned to televise the Dodgers on its New York station. While the audience was still small—less than 1 percent of the country's homes owned receivers—baseball embraced the new medium much more rapidly than it had welcomed radio.[67] In 1947 ten of MLB's sixteen teams had televised at least some of their games, and the World Series was telecast.[68] New York was the nation's television epicenter, and taverns found in televised baseball a fresh way to bring customers to the bar. For 1948 CBS assigned Barber to do two innings of the Dodgers' home televised games; it would be his first sustained experience with the new medium. It was becoming clear that with more telecasts, Barber and Connie Desmond might need more help in the Dodgers' broadcast booth. Barber's sudden near-death experience in Pittsburgh forced the issue. To fill in for him and give the Dodgers' booth the third voice it would need in the television age, Branch Rickey swung one of his better deals; he traded catcher Cliff Dapper to the Atlanta Crackers for Ernie Harwell.

Harwell was new to the Major Leagues but hardly new to big-time baseball. His hometown Atlanta Crackers were in one of the largest Minor League markets. He started covering them in 1943, returning to the team in 1948 after four years in the Marine Corps. Harwell's jump to Brooklyn brought a second Southern voice to the borough. He respected Barber, but Red did not mentor him as fully as he would mentor Vin Scully when he joined the broadcast team in 1950. Unlike Barber, who believed friendships with players might compromise his objectivity, Harwell liked to socialize with them. On train trips, he played cards and had meals with Robinson, Pee Wee Reese, and Gil Hodges. Barber stated his opinion on the matter of player fraternization but never forced his view on Harwell.

Ernie found Barber to be a tough boss and sometimes overly demanding. He remembered Barber throwing pencils at his statistician, Bob Pasotti, because the young man had given the wrong numbered pencil to Red before a broadcast.[69] But Red taught Harwell about the value of talking with the players, managers, and umpires before the game rather than trusting secondhand information. He reinforced Harwell's inclination to report what was happening on the field rather than burdening the listeners with his opinions. When the Giants inquired about Harwell's availability for the 1949 season, Ernie decided it would be unfair to leave the Brooklyn broadcast team after only one season.[70]

Red always praised Harwell and wrote a column congratulating him on his winning the Ford C. Frick Award in 1981.[71] Barber claimed that Harwell's expertise intimidated Connie Desmond and that Connie felt relieved when Ernie left after the 1949 season, moving to the number-two slot on the Giants' broadcasting team. From Harwell's perspective, the move was a step up. He was no longer third on a broadcasting team where the top two had a long-standing, tight working relationship. The three ballcasters's 1949 yearly salaries reflected their relative status in the eyes of Branch Rickey and the Dodgers. Barber made $38,500, nearly double Desmond's $20,000. Harwell finish third with $15,000.[72]

Barber's other challenge in 1948 was the Dodgers' decision to begin live broadcasts of their road games. The Yankees began doing all of their road games live in 1946, and the pressure had been building on the Dodgers to follow suit. As much as some older fans romanticize radio re-creations in the folklore of baseball, most listeners preferred hearing an announcer who was viewing the game action with his own eyes. By 1948 even Red Barber—who wanted to follow his father's example of coming home after work and who loved nothing more than curling up with a good book with his wife and daughter nearby—had to accept that traveling to broadcast road games was the new reality of baseball in the nation's largest market. In future years he would typically make three out of every four road trips, although his contract often required fewer.

"If You Had Not Written Those Columns We Wouldn't Be Here"

Throughout the late 1940s Red continued to write and publish occasional articles in newspapers and magazines, persisting in his intention to cultivate skills in the "editorial aspect" of sports commentary. He wrote about the most memorable moments from his first ten years with the Dodgers; how Yankees and Dodgers managers won their respective 1947 pennants; the complexities of baseball explained to the primarily female readers of *Redbook*; and his favorite college football player, Jay Berwanger.[73] His 1948 near-death experience in the emergency room in Pittsburgh spurred Red to think more seriously about a second act in his career. Writing seemed the best medium for exploring broader issues with his audiences.[74] In 1950 the *New York Journal-American* offered Red the opportunity to substitute for sports columnist Bill Corum for several months while Corum oversaw preparations for that year's Kentucky Derby. The gig involved Red's penning five or six columns per week from March 15 through May 18 while still performing all his duties for the Dodgers during spring training and the early months of the 1950 baseball season. He was initially uncertain about accepting the offer because he still was a broadcaster, not a writer, but decided it was necessary to test himself as a pinch hitter for Corum.[75]

A survey of Red's fifty *Journal-American* articles supports the impression that Barber *was* trying to explore deeper issues embedded in the world of sports and to move readers to travel with him. Drawing upon live interviews he conducted during spring training, current issues in baseball and golf, and his own encyclopedic knowledge, he wrote pieces about the ethical dimensions of baseball, such as bonus and other recruiting regulations, the need for better safety and health protection for players, the demands of the long baseball season and their effect upon the family life of players, and the effects of different managerial styles. He profiled sports figures whose character and courage he admired: Branch Rickey, Burt Shotton, Edward Barrow, and Ed Furgol, the professional golfer who played with a withered arm. Red always sought to uncover, in his analysis of their actions, sources of the courage and composure with which these men navigated uncommon challenges and obstacles. A substantial number of articles examined the "second acts" of sports figures who, having peaked in their careers or who had been forced to retire because of injuries, now faced the question of what to do with their lives outside the limelight. The series suggests that Barber was writing partly to channel his own uncertainties about his professional future in broadcasting. Some of the figures he mentioned—George Sisler, Bob Zuppke, and Bobby Jones—provided positive role models by finding meaningful, stimulating employment in new arenas or less visible positions within the sport to which they remained committed.

Among these *Journal-American* pieces the most psychologically frustrating nut for Red to crack was Fred Merkle (of the infamous "Merkle's Boner"), whom he interviewed at Merkle's home in south Florida. He discovered that Merkle was still suffering bitterly over the career-defining error he allegedly made in the ninth inning of a late-season game in 1908 by failing to touch second base after the potential winning run of the game had already scored, ending any chance for the Giants to clinch the pennant that day. Red insisted that Merkle must "move on" after all this time and continued prodding him until Merkle cried out, "Past sins should be forgotten, I have been paying for 40 years!" Red had no immediate therapy to cure him, but he was frustrated that Merkle had cut himself off from all connections to professional sports. Barber lamented that Merkle refused to attend a Dodgers' reunion that Branch Rickey subsidized in Brooklyn, where Merkle played after his time with the Giants. He wanted to get Merkle back in the game.[76]

Undaunted, Red carried the case to respected retired umpire Bill Klem, who also lived in a nearby south Florida community and who also had been haunted since 1908 by what he knew had been an unfair call in Merkle's case. However, Klem had heretofore honored the traditional "no comment" response to questions about a fellow umpire's decisions. Finally cracking under Barber's relentless questioning, Klem revealed, in a protracted and compelling analysis, the grounds supporting his conviction that Merkel had suffered "a bad rap" for forty years. Red believed the expert's persuasive analysis, if published to the world, would set Merkel free. So with the veteran ump's approval, Red penned a passionate follow-up column for all to read, titled "As Klem Would Have Called It" and subtitled "An Umpire's Mistake Cost Giants Pennant and Heaped Lasting Shame on Merkle." The piece laid out Klem's argument and, in a curious experiment in "journalism as public therapy," urged Merkle to return to the Polo Grounds, the source of his pain, confirming for all time that the "boner" was too feeble a myth to keep him down. Barber received no response from Merkle on the piece.[77]

Still, there was a pleasing epilogue to the story that may have ultimately reinforced Barber's suspicion that the newspaper columnist could make a deeper impression on people than even the most popular play-by-play announcer. Several months after Red's columns on Merkle were published, Fred Merkle and his daughter made a surprise visit to Red's office at CBS in Manhattan, Fred "wearing a brand-new suit and grinning broadly." Merkle would return to the Polo Grounds, the very site of his shame. His daughter explained to Red that her father wanted to show up for the Old Timers' Day game. "If you had not written those columns," she told him, "we wouldn't be here."[78]

In his last column of the series, Barber expresses his keen satisfaction in sitting in for Bill Corum. Of particular interest was his unexpected discovery that writers absorbed in composition lose themselves in their subject yet unconsciously end up revealing sides of themselves they never intended to disclose. Red concludes: "But there it is, and something of yourself has come into view, almost as a personal confession. . . . It is a fine experience to learn something more of yourself, which is not what I had bargained for."[79]

Barber entered midcentury at his professional pinnacle. *Billboard* estimated his annual income from the Dodgers, CBS, his writing, and all other sources was $125,000—over $1.3 million in 2020 dollars.[80] Joe DiMaggio, the game's highest-paid player, had a salary of $100,000, while the average Major Leaguer played for slightly over thirteen grand a season.[81] The Old Redhead even had his own baseball board game—*Red Barber's Big League Baseball Game*—with endorsements from Stan Musial, Casey Stengel, Burt Shotton, Pee Wee Reese, Roy Campanella, and other baseball stars.[82] But more significant, Barber called the games of a successful team that he loved. He had a family he cherished, a boss who was like a second father, and he had recovered his health. Vin Scully, whom he would hire as an apprentice announcer for the 1950 baseball season, would become the student that Barber the teacher had always wanted. But the problem with reaching professional pinnacles is that they inevitably precede a downward ride.

1. Red's mother, Selena Barber, read him the classics, imprinting upon his memory
the rhythms and cadencies of engaging speech. Her early death turned him from God.
Photo courtesy of the George A. Smathers Libraries, University of Florida.

2. (*opposite top*) William Barber, Red's father, was his first hero. He passed on a gift for storytelling, a commitment to excellence in one's chosen profession, and a belief in one's self worth. Photo courtesy of the George A. Smathers Libraries, University of Florida.

3. (*opposite bottom*) Red's parents once found their toddler curled up with pit bull puppies in the doghouse. William Barber raised the fighting dogs to help make ends meet during hard times in Mississippi. Photo courtesy of the George A. Smathers Libraries, University of Florida, ca. 1909.

4. (*above*) Red always remembered his parents' Christmas 1914 surprise: his baby brother, Billy, pictured here with Red on the right and sister Effie Virginia on the left. Photo courtesy of the George A. Smathers Libraries, University of Florida.

5. Red was a promising high school halfback, but college ball was too big a stretch. Photo courtesy of the George A. Smathers Libraries, University of Florida.

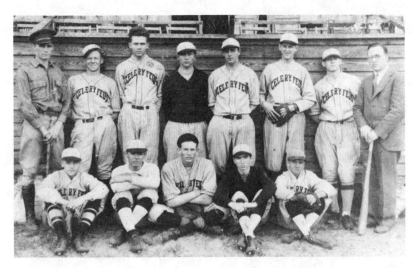

6. Second from the left, top row, is cocky Red Barber, a member of the Celery Feds, the Sanford baseball club named after the town's cash crop. Photo courtesy of the Sanford Museum.

WALTER BARBER

"A man convinced against his will,
Is of the same opinion still."

A. A., 1, 2, 3, 4; Treasurer A. A., 4; L. S., 1, 2; Football, 2, 3, 4; Basketball Manager, 4; Baseball, 1, 2, 3, 4; Captain Baseball, 4; Senior Play, 4; 2nd Vice-Pres. Hi-Y, 4; Class Treasurer, 2.

7. The boy with the "best hair" and his activities as listed in the 1926 Sanford High School yearbook. The Dale Carnegie quotation under his name suggests his belief in the power of persuasion. Photo courtesy of the Sanford Museum.

8. Hard work under the brutal Florida summer sun in rugged conditions convinced Red (*left*) that he should go to college. Photo courtesy of the George A. Smathers Libraries, University of Florida.

9. At the University of Florida infirmary, Red first gazed upon "the prettiest brown eyes I've ever seen." On their second date, Lylah and he agreed to marry one day. Photo courtesy of the George A. Smathers Libraries, University of Florida.

5000 WATTS

WRUF
"THE VOICE OF FLORIDA"

STATE AND UNIVERSITY STATION

UNIVERSITY OF FLORIDA
GAINESVILLE

February 11th, 1931

BULLETIN.

To Members of the Staff:

        This is to formally advise you that Mr. Walter Barber has been made Acting Chief Announcer of Station WRUF. He takes the place of Mr. Ralph Nimmons, who has resigned. Mr. Barber is in charge of all studio activities.

Garland Powell,
Director.

GP/jhw

10. Red's first radio promotion, to acting chief announcer. The letter is signed by Major Garland Powell, his radio mentor. WRUF was branded "the Voice of Florida," but its weak signal made that claim specious. Photo by J. Walker; document courtesy of the George A. Smathers Libraries, University of Florida.

11. The Orange Grove String Band gave Red (*far right*) his first hit program and the chance to create a new on-air persona. Photo by Bone, courtesy of the George A. Smathers Libraries, University of Florida.

12. The staff at WLW remembered Red, the man in the white linen suit, braving the Cincinnati winter. Photo courtesy of the George A. Smathers Libraries, University of Florida.

13. After Lylah's terminated pregnancy and subsequent miscarriage, Red couldn't restrain his joy over his new daughter, Sarah Lanier Barber. Photo courtesy of E. V. E. Joy.

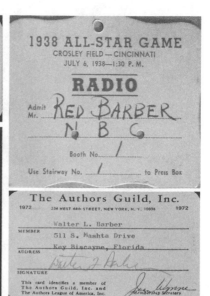

14. (*opposite top*) Red saved some of his most cherished identification cards. *Clockwise from the top left:* first-year (1934) press pass for the Cincinnati Reds, NBC pass to the 1938 All-Star Game, 1972 Authors Guild membership, and 1935 Navin Field (Detroit) World Series press pass. Photo by J. Walker; documents courtesy of the George A. Smathers Libraries, University of Florida.

15. (*opposite bottom*) To broadcast Dodgers games, Larry MacPhail wanted $75,000, a 50,000-watt station, and Red Barber. Red's bond with Brooklyn began on WOR in 1939. National Baseball Hall of Fame Library, Cooperstown NY.

16. (*above*) Red always said, "Jackie Robinson did more for me than I ever did for him." CBS Photo Archive/Getty Images.

17. Vin Scully, Red's great protégé and the son he never had, was a baseball play-by-play broadcaster for sixty-seven years, more than double Red's thirty-three years behind the mic. In the rear is Barber and Scully's colleague Connie Desmond. National Baseball Hall of Fame Library, Cooperstown NY.

18. Red is smiling in front of a WPIX camera here, but he claimed that television usurped his control of a game's story. He used a signal board to recapture some of his power over the telecast. National Baseball Hall of Fame Library, Cooperstown NY.

19. Red's obsession with preparation, perfectionism, and hard work triggered physical and emotional strains. Here during a break in studio television production he reveals his stress. Photo by George Zimbel; *Look* magazine Photograph Collection, Library of Congress, Prints & Photographs Division.

20. Red's near-death experience moved him in new directions. He became a lay reader in the Episcopal Church. Photo by George Zimbel; *Look* magazine Photograph Collection, Library of Congress, Prints & Photographs Division.

21. Red, gazing over Phil Rizzuto's shoulder, wanted Phil to be the second coming of Vin Scully, but the Scooter had his own style. Photo by George Zimbel; *Look* magazine Photograph Collection, Library of Congress, Prints & Photographs Division.

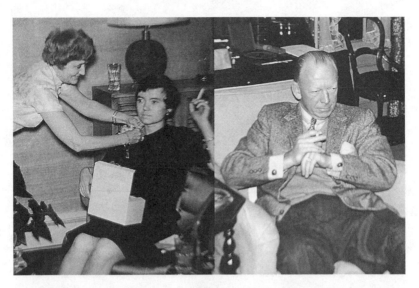

22. *Left:* Lylah and Sarah had some difficult times. Sarah felt her mother never accepted her lifestyle, but their familial bond remained unsevered. *Right*: Red at home, where he loved to unwind with a cigarette and highball, his rewards for a long day at work. Photos courtesy of the George A. Smathers Libraries, University of Florida.

23. By 1965 Mel Allen, the Voice of the Yankees, was silenced. Red, far right, struggled with Joe Garagiola, second from left, for control of the mic. Jerry Coleman, far left, became the second of Red's protégés to win the Ford C. Frick Award. Ralph Houk, general manager of the Yankees, is second from right. MEYER LIEBOWITZ/The New York Times/Redux.

24. Red's forced "retirement" from the Yankees opened up enlarging worlds of travel and writing. He came to see his sacking by the Yankees as a blessing. Pictured here are he and Lylah on vacation in the Rocky Mountains. Photo courtesy of the George A. Smathers Libraries, University of Florida.

25. Red's visit to Vietnam changed his view of the war. He urged his senator to specify a date for ending America's involvement in the conflict. Here he is pictured on a helicopter (*left*) and a gun boat (*right*). Photos courtesy of the George A. Smathers Libraries, University of Florida.

26. Red receiving the Ford C. Frick Award from Ralph Kiner. In 1978 Barber and Yankees colleague Mel Allen were the first honorees. National Baseball Hall of Fame Library, Cooperstown NY.

27. Red shows Ronald Reagan, former baseball announcer and now president of the United States, his book *The Broadcasters*. The two men had very different approaches to radio re-creations of the game; Barber was the reporter; Reagan, the fabricator. Official White House photo courtesy of the George A. Smathers Libraries, University of Florida.

28. Red loved his berets and his daughter. Sarah would inherit many of her father's gifts. Like the Old Redhead, she used her voice to educate others and to address compelling issues of public concern. Here they are pictured in the White Mountains. Photo courtesy of the George A. Smathers Libraries, University of Florida.

11

Losing Control, Gaining a Purpose

I n 1950 Red Barber entered the second half of the twentieth century and the second half of his life as the most critically acclaimed baseball announcer in the nation's largest media market. He also was recognized by fans and celebrated by sports writers for his *College Football Roundup* and his calls of New Year's Day bowl games. Barber was developing his skills as a writer, voicing commentary beyond the circumscribed range of the play-by-play announcer. He had survived a near-death experience, emerging with a greater appreciation of the fragility of human life and a newly awakened ambition to leave a lasting contribution to humanity. But just as his sense of control over his own mortality was shaken by illness, he also was facing threats to his professional self-determination from two imposing forces: the emergence of television as the dominant electronic medium and Walter O'Malley, the new leader of the Brooklyn Dodgers.

"You Have Lost Control of the Work You Are Doing"

Red Barber belonged to the radio generation. When he was a boy, the medium had magically transported him from Sanford, Florida, to the nation's major cities. Radio was the perfect platform for his strongest talents: verbal skills, soothing Southern speech, incredible memory, and fast thinking. Once the game began and he leaned into the mic, he was in complete control of his broadcast. In his days with the Dodgers, he rarely worked for long stretches with color announcers; his associate broadcasters handled their innings, and he handled his. In football broadcasts, spotters helped identify players, but he painted all the word pictures. In the slow moments of a ball game, radio gave him the freedom to roam. He was a radio master, but television increasingly made him feel like a servant.

Barber's initial reaction to television was optimistic. He did not believe it would hurt attendance at the ballpark by giving away the product; radio had discredited that argument. In the first games he called for television, he did not even have a monitor; the announcer was not expected to synchronize his reporting with the television picture. Barber wrote in 1950, "I came to the then comfortable conclusion there would be little change in technique necessary for the radio play-by-play man in moving over to television." But the addition of a monitor made all the difference. Instead of the television director's following the announcer's commentary, the announcer needed to keep one eye on the monitor to match his words with what the director was showing viewers. According to Red, "It has now become a demanded technique that the television commentator confine his remarks of the game basically to what is on the television screen. You can no longer talk about a centerfielder if the picture that is being televised is [of] the pitcher." As the number of cameras increased and directors became more expert in following the action, the demand upon the announcer to follow the action on the monitor intensified. The need to follow the action on the field and in the monitor simultaneously meant, Red explained, that "you are bound to make mistakes on television that you would not make in radio for the simple reason that the television commentator has too many things to observe at the same time."[1] Barber saw the TV play-by-play announcer as closer to the newsreel announcer's "voicing" of a film than to the radio announcer's calling of a game. For Barber, television was harder, something that never discouraged him very much, but it was also diminishing, something that bothered him a great deal. Barber, the cleanup batter on radio, was a seventh-place hitter in television.

Red believed that stripping the announcer of his control weakened the telecast. His most moving example of TV's sabotaging the story came at the conclusion of the 1948 World Series telecast. The Cleveland Indians had just won Game Six by a score of 4–3 at Boston's Braves Field, wrapping up the Series, four games to two. Naturally, the cameras focused on the ecstatic Cleveland teammates as they celebrated and departed the field through the third base dugout. But Barber thought the moment should be enriched by another poignant and deeply humanizing image, one upon which his experienced eye focused. Indians owner Bill Veeck walking alone on a wooden leg—he had lost part of his leg during action as a Marine in World War II—was moving slowly across the infield from his first-base-side box seat. Barber wrote in the *New York Times*, "No one was close to him as he slowly hobbled along on that game leg, on his way to the clubhouse. Here was the guy who'd made the team, reawakened fires of baseball enthusiasm in Cleveland, walking alone in this great moment. And to add to the drama of the picture, walking with a decided limp. But nobody saw that picture on television. Despite frantic appeals from the booth, the cameras stayed on the mob outside the dugout."[2]

Barber's experience of losing control of the narrative at the conclusion of the 1948 World Series, like many of the roadblocks in his life, pushed him to action. He would try to control the new technology of television with a newer technology: the signal panel. The signal panel was a box approximately two feet square and six inches deep. On the surface was a diagram of a baseball diamond with twenty-five toggle switches strategically placed on the diagram. By each switch was a small round light. In the control room at Ebbets Field, an identical signal panel sat near the television director. When Barber pulled a switch down, its companion light turned on, as did the same light on the control room signal panel. With this relatively simple device, Barber would signal silently to the director where he wanted a camera to focus. The options included both outfield foul lines, all nine on-field positions, first and third base coaches, dugouts, bullpens, field umpires, and all the men at home plate. The signal box, combined with Barber's own stature as the Voice of the Dodgers, transferred some control over the telecast back to the Old Redhead. Tom Villante, who produced the Dodgers' telecasts at the time, pointed out that Barber "was still controlling his part of the broadcast. I always thought that was ingenious." Barber continued to use the signal box until he left the Dodgers.[3]

However ingenious, the signal panel had drawbacks. First, Barber already felt television made it harder to concentrate on the game. He had to keep checking a monitor, the action on the field, and the position of his mic; he had to mark his scorebook and keep track of the commercial copy. He also had to monitor an assistant who served as his liaison with the control room. The signal panel added another layer of complexity for a broadcaster compared to the much simpler radio broadcast. A second problem was the speed at which television moved. The director focused on instantaneously calling the shots from multiple cameras. Interruptions from the announcer's booth were a major distraction; the director could not always respond promptly, and the moment was lost. Red lamented denying his viewers compelling scenes that the broadcaster's eye caught but the camera could not.

But for Barber, losing control of the image was less significant than losing control of his commentary. In a *New York Times* television tell-all, he vents his frustration with the medium: "You want to speak of this play and the cameras go elsewhere. You wish to tell a little story about a player and the picture comes up in the opposite dugout. You have to speak in a short sentence, then wait for the next picture. You have no idea of the sequence of pictures. You must wait for them to flash. You have lost control of the work you are doing."[4] For the rest of his career as a baseball announcer,

Barber would split his on-air time between television and radio. He adapted to the needs of the new medium but always pined for his radio days. As the decades rolled on, he became a passionate critic of television, arguing that it had commercialized sports beyond recognition. Clearly television had diminished the role of the radio artist who was Walter Lanier Barber.

"The Most Devious Man I Ever Met"

The second significant challenge Barber faced at midcentury was the loss of his second "father," Branch Rickey. In 1950 Rickey's contract as the Dodgers' president expired, and O'Malley, who now owned 50 percent of the club, offered a new contract that would dramatically reduce Rickey's power. Rickey sold his interest in the Dodgers and in short order became executive vice president and general manager of the Pittsburgh Pirates. Up to this point as a Major League broadcaster, Barber had dealt primarily with only two club executives, Larry MacPhail and Branch Rickey. He was spoiled. Unlike many employees, he had fruitful working relationships with his bosses, but now O'Malley's control of the Dodgers ruptured Red's protective bubble.

Barber never openly feuded with O'Malley. The Old Redhead could handle open conflict, although he hated getting angry, but O'Malley, trained as a lawyer and with a family history in New York politics, was rarely confrontational.[5] His more circumspect approach differed from the more forthright temperaments of MacPhail and Rickey. Like many lawyers and successful business executives, O'Malley made sure he got things in writing and reviewed all of his options. Barber was still somewhat a country boy in the big city in his personal business dealings. He assessed an individual's character, and once he made his judgment, he either trusted the person or did not. He believed that protracted legal contracts were of little value if one could not trust the other party. Barber told Robert Creamer, "If they are honorable people, you'll have no problem; everything that comes up you'll work out, without either side running to the contract. . . . If they're dishonorable people, you can get sixteen of the best lawyers you can find, and they can't save you because if they're dishonorable, they'll find that weasel word some place."[6] O'Malley believed in contracts and rarely showed all his cards in any negotiations. What Barber saw as the actions of "the most devious man I ever met," other New Yorkers likely would consider business as usual.[7]

Barber and his new boss seemed to have gotten off to a smooth start. In a letter to O'Malley in late September 1948, while Rickey was still president of the club, Barber copiously thanked O'Malley for his concern over Red's recovery from his recent hemorrhage: "These few words may seem by the calendar to be quite belated but the sentiment they convey has been in my heart ever since late July, when in a rough spot you sent me your kindness, solid good offices of any needed help, and your prayers. Your thoughtfulness in calling, in wiring, and in writing will always be deeply and warmly remembered."[8]

Once when O'Malley did him a favor, Red wrote him a letter steeped in baseball metaphor and almost embarrassing in its effusive gratitude: "With each day that passes, I am more and more impressed with your generous treatment of me. You have given me a tremendous vote of confidence, and I cannot help but send you in writing this word of my deepest appreciation. In other words, you really went to bat for me and delivered a grand slam home run, and I want you to know I am happy to be in your bullpen."[9] Although the letter does not specify details of O'Malley's "generous treatment," the favor might have been an advance on Red's salary that O'Malley extended to him. Barber desperately needed the advance to deal with financial losses he had recently suffered in building a new house on the Hudson.

The friendly rapport continued even after Rickey left and O'Malley assumed control of the club. In early November 1950 Red wrote his new boss: "Whenever you are ready, I am completely at your service and will be most happy to come to you at any time. . . . My warmest and fullest congratulations and complete confidence for great success."[10] But despite appearances, the Dodgers' new leadership likely concerned Red at a time when he was growing weary of the baseball season grind. Only a month after Barber wrote O'Malley his "warmest congratulations," an article in *Billboard* titled "Red's Blues" reported Barber might quit play-by-play broadcasting after his contract ended at the conclusion of the 1951 baseball season. Perhaps still processing his 1948 health crisis, Red complained that "the job has more than taken its toll" on him physically.[11] More stories about Barber leaving the Dodgers would emerge before the 1953 season. Despite his initial letters to O'Malley, the Old Redhead seemed set on a new start.

Gone but Not Forgotten

Branch Rickey's departure from the Brooklyn Dodgers did not diminish Barber's fondness for "the Mahatma." The connection between them was deep and personal. During the long night in the Pittsburgh hospital as Barber struggled for his life, Branch Rickey, who at the time was being prepped for back surgery, called Lylah every hour to learn when he could come and see Red. Three days after Red's hemorrhage, Rickey flew to Pittsburgh to comfort his "employee" in his time of need. Red never forgot that kindness.[12]

Rickey's letters preserved at the Library of Congress reveal the sustained richness and evolution of their friendship. They begin in November 1942, when Barber writes on his WHN stationary to congratulate Rickey on coming to the Dodgers and to express "how happy I am for Brooklyn and its fortunes that the reins are placed in your most capable hands."[13] After William Barber died, Red thanked Rickey for the beautiful wreath he and the Dodgers sent and Rickey's "kind" and "thoughtful" telegram.[14] Future letters offered thanks for Christmas gifts, including the gift of a Dodgers-themed radio. Red jokes that the gift might lead to rumors of his demise: "Suppose the press learned of this? Wouldn't it be a natural supposition for the writers to suggest . . . that the subtle Branch Rickey had given Barber the gentle hint that the old country boy should take his radio from the receiving end rather than the sending?"[15]

In a November 1, 1950, letter written after Rickey's departure from Brooklyn, Barber provides his most vivid statement of his affection: "I do not want to write this letter. I had hoped you would not leave Brooklyn. . . . The sole purpose of this letter is to tell you how much I think of you, how much you have meant to me, and how much you always will be an enrichment of my life. You have given me very much of baseball insight, technique, vocabulary, philosophy, point of view, and these gifts have been increasingly and lastingly helpful." Barber then confides: "I have had a closeness and confidence and a warmth for you personally which, as I told you some years ago in Brooklyn, approached very much the relationship I had with my father. More than that, I still cannot say today." But he does say more. Barber tells Rickey when he declined the Yankees' offer for the 1946 season, it was "you as a person and not your offer of dollars that changed my decision." In closing, he movingly acknowledges, "I am losing something very vital in your departure from Brooklyn, but then again I feel overjoyed at the riches gained by the years we were together."[16] After his move to Pittsburgh, Rickey continued to play a role in Barber's personal life. In early May 1951, on CBS letterhead, Barber offered Rickey best wishes for the "farm-estate" that he had purchased outside of Pittsburgh, telling him that the Barbers had moved into their new home in Scarborough, New York. Red affectionately added, "It can never be completely home to us until you and Mrs. Rickey have crossed our doorstep."[17]

A letter from Barber written at the end of the 1951 season reveals he was still seeking Rickey's guidance. Barber tells Rickey, "It was wonderful to have been with you and Mrs. Rickey at Pittsburgh" and "I think your house and farm are perfect." Then on a more personal note, he acknowledges the assistance he had just received from his most trusted adviser: "I enjoyed talking with you on the telephone from Chicago, and your talk, as all our talks have ever been, was most helpful." Barber appears to be undergoing some soul searching: "I spent most of my off-time on the last road trip getting a little better acquainted with myself. I am glad to write that I made some progress and am more content to go along not forcing any issues but taking the future in stride one day at a time."[18] While he never identifies the issues he is not "forcing," it is likely that O'Malley's leadership of the Dodgers was part of the problem.

While Barber revered Rickey, Rickey also believed Barber's achievements should be acknowledged. Starting in the fall of 1952, Rickey used his influence with the board at his alma mater, Ohio Wesleyan University, to push for an honorary degree for Red Barber. He wrote Barber, requesting his resume: "a complete breakdown on who you are, where you have been, what you have done, etc., etc., and don't be modest about it." Rickey tells Barber he has "a reason for it" that he does not reveal. Rickey followed up with board member C. B. Mills in April 1953, highlighting Red's role as director of the Red Cross drive in Greater New York. He also acknowledged that Barber had "no degree from any college but he really has a classical mind and in anyone's definition of education he has it. It [sports broadcasting] is perhaps a very unusual field to find a candidate for an honorary degree." Mills was quite supportive of Rickey's request but indicated that he did not know "whether someone without a college degree is eligible or not. I assume he is. If there is no such barrier in our way, let's consider ourselves on third base."[19] Third base, however, was not home plate; Barber did not receive the honorary degree. The school did invite him in mid-May to give a lecture at the Ohio Wesleyan University chapel. Rickey was told that Barber "mowed them down and left them in the aisles in the greatest chapel speech we have ever heard."[20]

Barber would maintain his close relationship with Branch Rickey until Rickey's death in 1965. He hosted Rickey for several television interviews in the mid-1950s. In early 1956 there were rumors that the two would create a sports program with Barber interviewing Rickey.[21] When it was time for Sarah Barber to apply for college, Rickey wrote her a letter of support to Rollins College. Barber acknowledged Rickey's milestones by sending his congratulations to Branch and Jane Rickey on the occasion of their fiftieth wedding anniversary and to Branch on the publication of his book *American Diamond*.[22]

"Our Dream House on the Hudson"

In the spring of 1950 the Barbers learned that their apartment building in Manhattan soon would be converted into a co-op and broken up into smaller units; none of the current leases would be renewed. Red, who enjoyed gardening whenever he had access to a yard, wanted to move back to Westchester County. Lylah observes that "[Red] never really cared for big city apartment dwelling," so her "idyllic years as a New Yorker were over."[23] They had remained members of the Sleepy Hollow Country Club in Scarborough, which they had joined when they lived in Scarsdale; in their search for the perfect site to build their dream house, they discovered two acres for sale on top of a hill overlooking both the country club and the Hudson. They worked with a prestige New York architectural firm to design a "contemporary house that took advantage of the majestic view." Red was so busy professionally—both at CBS and with broadcasting both home and away Dodgers games—that he paid the firm extra to take over all the business arrangements with whatever builder the firm selected. The firm would simply "tell Red whom, when and how much to pay."

The dream, unfortunately, soon descended into dread. Things seemed fine in the early summer; ground was broken for the home, and the Barbers were comfortably settled in the third story of the Sleepy Hollow Country Club's "Main House" mansion, which they would rent for the months it would take the builders to complete the job—ideally by late fall. But by late fall, the work had slowed down. The builder, the architects explained, was experiencing a minor problem paying contractors some of their bills, so necessary deliveries were on hold. The builder advised Red to advance the money to him; all contractors would be paid, and all would be well. Nothing went well. By February, although Red had advanced the full amount of the contract to the builder, the work still was far from completed. At the Dodgers' spring training in 1951, Red got the painful news that the builder "went broke, left the country, and sub-contractors were howling for blood."

Red was forced to become "legal contractor and builder," a role, Lylah notes, "for which he certainly had no training." Lylah mentions that Red had to "put up his life insurance for collateral and borrow money from his bank to finish the job."[24] According to Barber, Walter O'Malley agreed to give him a sizable advance on his salary to complete the building of the house.[25] A good friend of the Barbers who was president of a construction company contracted to send in a work supervisor and a crew to finish the house to the point where the family could live in it. Inadequate structural supports had to be reinforced and part of the plumbing redone. Lylah recalls that she and Red were "years getting all the bad workmanship straightened out."[26]

In one of his letters to Branch Rickey, Barber recounts the "Shakespearian" struggles that Lylah and he were encountering in completing their new home: "We have been doing as Hamlet was loath to do, taking arms against a sea of troubles. On the heels of the ten-weeks' unconsciousness and death of Lylah's mother came the rather crushing blow that the builder of our house went broke before the job was done. It is hard to have desired such a house, to have strained for it to the uttermost of your resources, and then to have such a series of events dissipate its final attainment." As painful as the process was, the "final attainment" was rewarding. Photos reveal that their new home on the hilltop was indeed beautifully situated, with expansive and stunning views overlooking the Hudson. Red also seized the opportunity for unusual transport to work when the Dodgers played the Giants on the road. According to Tom Villante, Barber grew obsessed with his boat and would motor it "from his home in Scarborough down the Hudson, docking it right by the Polo Grounds," wearing a captain's hat all the time.[27]

During the fourteen years that the Barbers lived in the house, Lylah was often home alone. Red made the now longer commute

to the city most workdays and frequently was out of town to cover
road games. After their first year in Scarborough, Sarah attended
the Masters School, a residential girls' prep school in Dobbs Ferry.
Lylah discovered early on that she was not interested in becoming "a suburban housewife," which in the community at that time
meant chauffeuring husbands to their commuter trains and children to school in the mornings; spending the afternoons with
other wives at luncheons and then playing bridge; and attending
dinner parties and country club dances on the weekends. Lylah
truly wanted to live where Red felt most at home for his treasured
time away from work, and she was determined to forge a meaningful life for herself wherever that was. Fortunately, there were
opportunities for her to do that in Scarborough. For several years
she served on a three-member committee to oversee the resto-
ration of St. Mary's, the town's historic Episcopal Church, which
she and Red joined when they moved to Scarborough. For Lylah
it was a "labor of love."[28]

Lylah also developed a close and lifelong friendship with a
woman her age whom she met at a church rectory luncheon. Peggy
Bloch also was raised in the South and had a daughter a year older
than Sarah. Peggy helped Lylah adjust to her new community
and offered useful advice for easing the transition for thirteen-
year-old Sarah. Sarah had grown comfortable with the Spence
School in Manhattan and once again had some trouble getting
accustomed, this time to the public school she attended during
her first year in Scarborough. But a year later Sarah joined Peggy's
daughter at the Masters School, which she attended until her high
school graduation in 1955. During most of Red's and Lylah's years
in Scarborough, Lylah represented the local parish in the Episcopal Church's statewide social service program, Youth Consultation Services (YCS), designed to aid troubled teens and young
adults. Working to provide young people with resources to help
them through tough times gave "meaning and purpose" for her
life in Scarborough: "I think I am a more compassionate person
because of my work with YCS; certainly, I am less judgmental."

Lylah also reconnected with the pianist and painter Harry Crowley, who had been her piano teacher when the family lived in Scarsdale; it was a reunion that triggered a passion for painting that she pursued for many years. She converted a room in their home into a studio of her own and began painting for hours each day. One day after Red left home to cover a doubleheader, she began painting a scene imprinted upon her memory from when she had gone snorkeling in Bermuda—a beautiful underwater world full of brilliantly colored fish gliding softly by. When she finally was pleased with the composition, she turned from her easel and discovered Red standing in the doorway of her studio; he had been silently watching her at work. It was nighttime, the doubleheader was long over, and she had given no thought to dinner. Lylah painted for many years, selling some of her work; one of her paintings, a folk-art style portrait of a Mexican couple on their wedding day, currently hangs in the living room of Red's niece, E. V. E. Joy.

The Son He Never Had

While Red Barber wrote often about Branch Rickey and his own father, he had no son of his own. The closest candidate was the great Dodgers' broadcaster Vincent Edward Scully, who completed his own Hall of Fame career in 2016. Vin Scully's sixty-seven-year career as a baseball play-by-play broadcaster is the durability record for all sports broadcasters. After Scully graduated with a degree in English from Fordham University in 1949, he papered East Coast radio stations with applications. CBS radio affiliate WTOP in Washington DC hired him as a summer fill-in. In November 1949 Barber needed a *College Football Roundup* reporter in a pinch to cover the University of Maryland–Boston University game in Fenway Park. Scully, who had impressed Barber in an earlier CBS interview, was called at the last minute. His mother answered the phone and took a message. She later told Vin that "Red Skelton" wanted to talk to him about a job.

Unfortunately, Scully brought to the game only a light topcoat to defend himself against the cruel New England elements. When he got to Fenway Park for the November 12, 1949, University of Maryland–Boston University game, he discovered there was no room in the press box for him. He would need to call the game from the roof, facing the wind on a chilly fall day. Since the contest was close—Maryland won 14–13—Barber's *Roundup* kept returning to Scully for more reports. The rookie announcer was growing colder by the minute, with only a sixty-watt light bulb to warm his hands. Scully never mentioned his discomfort during his game reports or when he returned to New York. Barber only learned of it from a Boston University official who apologized for not providing space in the booth for Scully. Barber immediately hired Scully to cover another game, Yale-Harvard, one of college football's greatest rivalries.

When Ernie Harwell left Brooklyn to take the New York Giants' number-two broadcaster slot for the 1950 season, Barber recommended Scully to Branch Rickey. Rickey interviewed him for three hours, concluding with the standard "Mahatma" advice for all young men: "'You married?' [Scully] said, 'No, sir.' [Rickey] said, 'Engaged?' [Scully] said, 'No, sir.' [Rickey] said, 'Going steady?' [Scully] said, 'No, sir.' [Rickey] chewed that cigar of his for a minute and then he snapped, 'Get a girl, go steady, get engaged, get married. Best thing in the world for a young man.'"[29] After spending three hours with Scully, Rickey called Barber at his CBS office to say, "Walter, this is Branch. I don't wish to trespass upon your time, but you sent the right young man; good day."[30]

In Vin Scully, Red Barber had a nearly perfect pupil. Scully was bright, verbally gifted, hardworking, and, happily for Barber, inexperienced—in Red's words, a "green pea." But Scully was "a pretty appealing young green pea. . . . You could tell this was a boy who had something on the ball." Unlike earlier associate broadcasters—Connie Desmond, Ernie Harwell and Al Helfer— Scully had spent almost no time as a professional broadcaster and none as a professional baseball announcer; he had little reason to question Barber's directions. Barber told Creamer, "I'd never gotten over the idea of being a schoolteacher in some form or fashion. I'd always had a secret dream of taking . . . a piece of clay and seeing what I could do with it."[31]

When Barber critiqued Scully, the rookie would grin and bear it. During one game Scully announced that a starting player was out of the lineup and would be replaced. After the broadcast Barber asked him why the regular was out of the lineup. When Scully said he didn't know, Red wanted to know why not. Barber was teaching his apprentice his lesson that "sports broadcasting is 75 percent preparation." At first Scully's time before the mic was limited; he did more gofer-ing than announcing. Red told him, "You do whatever we don't want to do or find inconvenient to do," and Scully would "be presented to the public for exactly what you are, a neophyte. . . . If you make a mistake over the air, we will correct you on the air."[32] But under Barber's supervision, Scully blossomed more robustly than the camellias that the Old Redhead cultivated in his later years.

Throughout his career Scully credited Barber with giving him his first big break and instilling the discipline and values of a professional baseball announcer. Still, some of Barber's barbs must have stung. Tom Villante remembered incidents that made him doubt Scully would ever have much good to say about Barber.[33] But Scully's personal letters to Red show that despite any tensions during his early years with Red, Scully deeply valued Barber as a teacher and mentor.

One conflict over which Scully stewed concerned a glass of beer. In the press lounge before a game, Scully was having a beer with his sandwich. In the Scully household, beer with a meal was not "drinking"; it was a beverage, like cola or iced tea. But to Barber it was a drink that, before a game, was forbidden. Perhaps one beer would not cloud Scully's judgment or affect his speech, but when he made a mistake—and all announcers made mistakes— the reporters who observed him drinking a beer before the game would connect the dots: Scully was drinking, and his work suffered. Barber recalls that Scully was angry about his rebuke for several weeks, but Red saw no repetition of the pregame pour.[34]

Although Barber had the influence to enforce his will on Scully, he was powerless to control the alcohol abuse of the more experienced man in the Dodgers' booth, Connie Desmond.

The Pains and Joys of Drink

Connie Desmond was a lifelong lover of alcohol, and the passion ultimately cost him his career. In his writings, Barber discussed the drinking problems of Bill Munday and Waite Hoyt, describing how their recovery efforts gave Munday a second chance as a broadcaster and Hall of Fame pitcher Hoyt a second career as the voice of the Cincinnati Reds. But Barber appears never to have discussed Desmond's problem in public. It was likely that he did not want to embarrass his colleague and had persuaded himself that Desmond's habit was still manageable during their years together in the Dodgers' booth. Desmond was also a fine announcer, and some fans, although they were a minority, preferred him to Barber. In his interviews with Robert Creamer for *Rhubarb in the Catbird Seat*, Barber told Creamer that his taped comments about Desmond's alcoholism should not be in their book: "His drinking was not a sudden onslaught; it was just finally the ultimate weight that tilted the scales. . . . What possessed him to drink, I don't know, but nobody was going to stop him. . . . He drank up a career and a good one. Desmond in condition was the best fellow I ever worked with. . . . Drank up his family, marriage, everything."[35]

One night in St. Louis, Connie's drinking forced Red to innovate quickly. Desmond and Barber were to do a night game from St. Louis that would be aired on both radio (Desmond) and television (Barber). At the time, televised road games were a rarity and, Red noted, "a big deal. . . . And son of a gun, [Desmond] didn't show up. You keep waiting and you say he's going to come in the booth any minute."[36] But he didn't and Barber, to protect his colleague, improvised. Tom Villante remembered the moment: "Red was terrific. [He] turned to the engineer and asked, 'Will that radio microphone reach in this booth?' The radio mic just made it. So we get on the air and Red opens up with, 'Today we're going to do something brand new; you're going to love it. It's called a simulcast. I'm going to do radio play-by-play at the same time that's going to be the audio for television. Let us know how you enjoy it.' [Barber] made it sound like the whole thing was planned."[37] Desmond finally arrived at the booth in the seventh inning, but he was too late to contribute to the broadcast.

Desmond's career with the Dodgers ended when Walter O'Malley fired him after the 1955 season. O'Malley gave him repeated chances to reform, more opportunities than Barber would have, but Desmond could not give up his habit.[38] Three and a half decades after Barber left the Dodgers, he received a letter from Desmond's son Jim. The younger Desmond had written the Baseball Hall of Fame asking it to consider his father for the Ford C. Frick Award and wanted Barber to send a letter of support. In his letter to the Hall, Jim Desmond admitted his father "was an alcoholic," but "his problems were baseball's too, back then." He argued that three of Connie Desmond's Dodgers colleagues—Red Barber, Ernie Harwell, and Vin Scully—were in the Hall of Fame and that his father deserved to join them. In his personal letter to Red, he wrote that his father "was a confusing person who screwed up a lot of things, but I feel there should be a place *there* for what he did well." Connie's son also implied that Barber had intervened in other ways to help the Desmond family, thanking Red "for all your thoughtfulness & concern when I needed it back then; I will never forget it."[39]

Red Barber was far from a teetotaler; drinking had always played a prominent role in his social life. He met Lylah in the University of Florida infirmary after his friend's bakery truck had rolled over during a moonshine procurement expedition. Lylah writes of the boisterous parties she and Red had as a young couple in Gainesville, and alcohol enhanced social occasions in Cincinnati. Barber did not object to drinking so long as it did not interfere with professional or family obligations. To convince Creamer that his dressing down of Scully's press box beer was not about abstention, Barber spontaneously offers what could pass as a commercial testimonial selling the joys of mixed drinks:

> I've had my share of drinks, enjoy drinking. . . . In its proper time and proper place, I don't believe a human being ever lived that enjoyed a drink more than I enjoyed it. I enjoyed the anticipation of coming to the time and place to have the drink. . . . I enjoyed making the mental decision maybe an hour or so in advance as to whether it would be a martini or an old fashioned or a Manhattan or a highball. And I enjoyed the preparing of the drink; the clean, cool glass; the ice, sound, smell; the anticipation. And I have always had a very good sense of smell. And I always enjoyed the smell of the drink before I even tasted it. And for some years, I believe I could make about as good a martini as anybody. I could have been a professional. So I had no quarrel with alcohol.[40]

But the pleasures of drink must never compromise the quality of one's work. Red explains: "I had a quarrel with the abuse of alcohol and misuse of it. And I've had some rather rough times with some other people about it. But I've had such a complete respect for a microphone and such a complete respect for alcohol that I've known there can be no wedding there, ever."[41] While there is no evidence that alcohol ever compromised Red Barber's work, his daughter Sarah experienced problems it caused during her parents' later years.

Permission to Preach Original Sermons

While drink provided its diversions, Red drew more profound satisfaction from a new avocation after he moved to Scarborough, one that reflected his intention to use his voice for purposes beyond broadcasting ballgames. Early in 1951 the rector of St. Mary's Church in Scarborough informed Barber that he would soon be receiving from the bishop a license to perform as a lay reader in the church. Red was surprised: "The last thing in my mind was to be a lay reader."[42] Even Lylah laughed at the thought of ballplayers' reactions to Red's "dressing up in all those petticoats and getting up there reading the lessons." Red wrote Bishop Donegan a letter detailing all the solid reasons he could not perform this function, but Donegan's reply was the lay reader license itself with a strategic handwritten amendment: "With permission to preach *original* sermons." Contemplating that addendum weakened Barber's resistance; he accepted the offer and began to ponder on his travels back and forth from the ballpark what, exactly, he would preach about if the occasion arose.

Red formulated in his head a short homily on The Lord's Prayer—specifically the line "as we forgive those who trespass against us." He wanted to dwell on the significance of the fact that it was "the only clause in the prayer that 'we' as humans say what *we* would do." One Sunday morning, when he was a little hung over from wine he had consumed while singing and dancing at a Saturday night country club affair, he received a call from his rector. The reverend had an eye infection, and Red would need to cover the eleven o'clock service. He rose to the occasion, spinning out glibly his half-formed thoughts about the implications of "we forgive" in The Lord's Prayer. "My years in the broadcast booth helped me," he later recalled, "and I got through it." Barber would continue to preach "original" and well-received sermons for many years. He employed the excellent advice of Sidney Sweet, dean of the cathedral in St. Louis, who told him to "preach on something you know about." Red realized he knew very little about theology and a lot about athletes, an honest assessment that influenced the content of most of his sermons.

Barber would develop almost all of his best sermons, as well as other public addresses, by using experiences and lessons from the world of sports as metaphors for the "right" and "wrong" way to live. In church sermons, a player's sacrifice hit evolves into a symbol for the spiritual virtue of "losing one's self."[43] Or the matador's use of his cape in a bullfight to confuse the bull is a metaphor for the way most of us spend our time "charging at capes" instead of looking into the real source of our problems.[44] Barber's sermons are carefully adapted to audience and setting, but they are all designed to promote a theology of a "civic spirituality" focused upon concern for others and honesty with oneself. The sermons are not rigidly doctrinal; their aim is to nudge listeners to move toward, and be activated by, a deeper experience of the spiritual dimensions of life. Barber saved print copies of some of his sermons, and some of them are included in his book *Show Me the Way to Go Home*. But recordings and firsthand newspaper accounts also document how Barber's delivery intensified the engagement of his congregations. His use of sports metaphors allowed him to "act out," with the expert broadcaster's sense of timing, the dramatic stages of a bullfight or a player's last-minute magnanimous sacrifice that wins the game for a team. Church audiences enjoyed a spirited celebrity sporting event while absorbing, perhaps unawares, an uplifting spiritual message.

"The Old World Was New"

Both Red and Lylah loved to travel. Starting in the early 1950s, when he eased his way out of some of his CBS responsibilities, Barber cleared more time in his schedule for the pleasures of non-work-related travel with his family. Red had first traveled to Europe to cover the 1948 Winter Olympic Games, but in February 1953 he and Lylah enjoyed several weeks in Italy and Spain—Lylah's first trip across the Atlantic. The Barbers' travels were generously subsidized by felicitous connections that their Dodgers-loving travel agent had forged with European hoteliers, as they happily discovered when they went to check out and pay their bills. Lylah tells the readers of her memoir that she and Red were surprised to be paged by the loudspeaker when they stepped into the Rome airport. They soon discovered that a car and chauffeur were waiting to drive them to their hotel and that the car would be theirs to use throughout their ten-day stay. Their itinerary was exhausting, as they covered Florence and Umbria in their first few days and planned to travel to Naples, Sorrento, and Capri before touring Rome. But Red caught a touch of the flu that had gripped much of the country, so they focused the remaining five days of their trip in Rome. They were swept away by their long drive through the Umbrian countryside; by the fine dining, museums, and galleries; and by the Colosseum, which they visited both by day and under a full moon. Lylah surrendered, also, to her weakness for the fashionable shoes she saw in shop windows.[45]

Lylah admits that her assumptions about Spain were influenced by childhood stories of castles, Moors, and gypsies, but she and Red discovered in 1953 "a land of uneasy truce," as the tension of Franco's dictatorship was palpable throughout their travels. Their tour guides were guarded when answering questions, and one of them told Lylah to "be careful what you say in public buildings; they are listening everywhere." Her experience at a bullfight outside of Seville was educational but discomfiting, particularly when a fighter cut off an ear from his bull and threw it into the crowd, where it landed near her seat. She was surprised that parents brought their young children to witness the bloody spectacle. But it occurred to her on the ride back to town that her disgust at the cruelty of the sport was hypocritical, considering her own country's obsession with prize fighting. Recalling the one prize fight she had attended in New York City, where the crowd began roaring when the blood began flowing, she says, "[It] put my thoughts in perspective." Ed Murrow had given Red a letter of introduction to the governor-general of Gibraltar, where their European vacation ended—not before the governor took them on a private tour of "the Rock."[46] Lylah and Red were bitten by the travel bug, and many more journeys to parts unknown soon would follow.

Critical Rumblings

The press generally had been kind to Red Barber so far in his career, but by the early 1950s some criticism was emerging. One early pushback was a rare example of the press chiding Barber for expressing his opinion over the air. Here it was on a matter unrelated to sports. The 1950 New York gubernatorial race was between Republican Thomas E. Dewey and Democrat Walter A. Lynch.

The race was not close; Dewey won re-election by over eight hundred thousand votes. But in September 1950 Barber reportedly gave "an out-and-out political plug for his favorite candidate for governor during the telecast of a Dodgers-Giants baseball game on WOR-TV." *Radio Daily*, historically an enthusiastic supporter of Barber, questioned "the good taste" of the endorsement, arguing that "politics and baseball should be kept in their respective places."[47] While the trade periodical does not name the candidate he endorsed, it most likely was Governor Tom Dewey, a fellow Episcopalian, whom Barber knew personally through his fundraising work. The political plug was perhaps a momentary lapse in judgment; there is no evidence Barber repeated it.

Barber also was working more rarified references into his reporting. An amusing example of Barber's confounding his audience was his reference to two dangerous monsters in Homer's *Odyssey* who guarded the opposite banks of the narrow strait that Ulysses had to navigate carefully. Barber used the reference when the team's opposing pitcher had to select between the lesser of two Dodgers evils. During his TV call of the fifth game of the 1952 World Series, right before Duke Snider hit a home run, Barber proclaimed that Yankees pitcher Ewell Blackwell "now finds himself for the second time between Scylla and Charybdis." Murray Robinson of the *World-Telegram* reported, "We like to fell off our bar stool in a Brooklyn gin mill when Mr. Barber made that crack and the man next to us swilled the beer in his glass nervously and muttered: 'Between *who*?'"[48] Red's Homeric reference showed up in a *New York Times* "Fifteen News Questions" quiz: "At one point during the world series, TV announcer Red Barber said Ewell Blackwell, the Yankees pitcher, was 'between Scylla and Charybdis,' and a number of fans wanted to know what positions they played. Do you know?"[49] Citing the Scylla and Charybdis reference, populist sportswriter Dick Young of the *New York Daily News* playfully mocked what he considered Barber's professorial aspirations: "Sometimes he broadcasts the play-by-play of the ball games, but mostly he raises the intellectual level of Flatbush and environs."[50]

Barber's aversion to profanity was also gently spoofed. During the 1950 season he took issue with players using profanity during a game at such a loud volume that field mics picked up the wayward words. During one of his broadcasts, Barber told his listeners: "I don't believe masculinity and profanity are in any equal ratio. Attendance has improved because of the interest of women, and owners and players should do everything to keep women interested, not revolted. The best way to control the spoken word is to control the player who might use profanity. No one will hear any profanity if no one says it."[51] *Newsweek* columnist John Lardner thought Barber's reaction was overly solicitous of women, who, "even in a state of shock, are generally able to re-form their lines and strike back." Lardner noted that "Mr. Red Barber, the Brooklyn broadcaster, implied very strongly that the guilty mouths should be washed out with soap." To help with the profanity crisis, Lardner, who had "made a wide study of clean language," offered a "glossary" of words that players could use in the heat of the moment, including "Oh, fudge," "For goodness' sake," "Oh, sugar," "Oh, dear," "Drat it," and "Tsk, tsk."[52]

But the press really went on the offensive when Barber, representing his sponsor, ESSO, created an award to recognize sportswriters who were successful in predicting football winners. As Barber explained, "I felt it would be proper and fitting to award them so that they would have something to show for successful predictions and a record of consistently good reporting."[53] For sportswriters, any radio man who deemed to set himself up as a judge of newspaper scribes was guilty of unforgivable presumption, as we learn from Milton Gross of the *New York Post* when he identified Barber as a "Southerner who has contentedly remained transplanted in the North for lo these many years while peddling beer, tobacco and breakfast cereals through the medium of Dodgers baseball broadcasts. . . . As a sort of kickoff for Barber's latest huckstering adventure, an enterprising press agent thought up a gimmick which was tried on for size at Toots Shor's eating emporium yesterday when Barber condescendingly handed out what was modestly termed a 'Barber Poll' award to sports writers." Gross wondered "how Barber was qualified as one who sits in judgement of reporters who make objectivity the creed by which they live and work." According to Gross, Barber showed his team bias when he questioned Robinson's loyalty to the Dodgers after Jackie predicted, during a close pennant race, that the Dodgers would trade him after the 1950 season. "Baseball broadcasters would like to leave the impression that they comment objectively. That is so much pap." Gross argues: "The broadcaster's first allegiance is not to [his] listeners, but to the ball club or an advertising agency or sponsor." While the press often applauded Red Barber's "objectivity" in calling the game, Gross regarded Barber and all broadcasters as structurally incapable of neutrality in controversies that surrounded the teams they covered. His assertion may have been colored by envy of the much higher salaries paid to top broadcast talent. For Gross, radio men were hucksters first and reporters second, even on their best days.

Barber's critics weren't always mainstream, and their criticism wasn't always about sports. When he filled in for columnist Bill Corum at the *New York Journal-American* in 1950, he wrote one column that drew a sharp response from sports columnist Lester Rodney of the Communist newspaper *Daily Worker*. Using boxing rhetoric, Barber seemed to urge the United States to throw "the first punch" against Soviet aggression. Rodney quotes Barber, who wrote, "I wouldn't think it would be news to anyone that Russia is going to knock off anybody and everybody—if she can. That ought to be as obvious as a punch in the kisser. But it seems time to take stock about an attitude in this country of waiting until we get bashed over the head before we make a move." Barber supports his point with a baseball example. After an on-field fight, Leo Durocher told his player, "Why did you let him hit you first? Don't you know enough, when trouble is going to happen, . . . to get in the first punch?" Of course, a baseball fight is not exactly a nuclear war, where the other player's return "punches" can annihilate entire cities. Rodney tells Barber, "Red, they got that thing too." He then offers a critique of U.S. policy toward Russia, the failure of the American press to acknowledge the devastating consequences of World War II for the Russian people, and the economic benefits of war to arms manufactures.[54]

Red's first-strike position was not that unusual in midcentury America. The nation was just coming to grips with the rise of the Soviet Union as a Cold War rival with its own devastating weapon of mass destruction. But Rodney argues, "[For] other warriors of the microphone and typewriters like [Walter] Winchell and [Drew] Pearson . . . this stuff has become routine." But Red Barber, whom Rodney calls "*the very good* Dodger announcer with the mild-mannered voice," was swimming in water that was a bit deep for a sports broadcaster.[55]

As Barber's fame and income rose, it is not surprising that his moderately conservative, sometimes moralistic, and employer-supportive public pronouncements were criticized. Barber *was* striving to develop a weightier and more meaningful voice. He made a conscious decision to move more to the "editorial" side of sports reporting, involving himself in CBS's prestige radio program *Hear It Now* as its sports correspondent. He appeared on the network's Sunday morning program *Lamp unto My Feet* for a series of four episodes that were designed to teach abstract moral values to children by staging puppet shows enacting biblical parables. Barber's role was to discuss with other guests the meaning and contemporary relevance of the parables. His determination to use his voice to address matters beyond the ballpark was vying with his work as a broadcaster; baseball announcing, and the travel it required, was starting to seem less personally salient. But not everyone cared to hear Barber preach. Tom Gallery, his sports director counterpart at NBC, was particularly irritated: "I hate that Psalm-singing, sanctimonious son of a bitch."[56]

A Bitter End to the Dodgers Years

According to the New York press, Red Barber was always leaving the Dodgers. After his first season, the story was that General

Mills would drop the Bums' broadcasts, transferring Barber to Philadelphia. When his three-year contract with General Mills was up in 1942, rumors that the Dodgers would lose the "Barber of Flatbush" resurfaced. Craig Smith tried to convince Barber to abandon the Dodgers and begin covering the Yankees and Giants for Gillette in 1944. The end of the 1945 season brought the most serious threat. New Yankees boss Larry MacPhail wanted Red Barber, and the Old Redhead was set to join the Yankees until an intervention by Branch Rickey and a substantial raise kept him in Brooklyn. When that three-year commitment expired after the 1948 season, the press reported Barber might give up play-by-play to devote himself to his position as director of sports for CBS, a position that brought more responsibilities as network television expanded. But Barber re-upped with his favorite boss, Mr. Rickey, for another three years. In 1951 new rumors emerged that Red would leave Brooklyn's Bums for the Bronx's Bombers. Rickey was gone, and O'Malley was a very different employer. For one thing, he believed in one-year contracts. Barber signed for the 1952 season, but the glue binding him to the Dodgers was drying up.

Meanwhile, to handle their pre- and postgame shows, the Yankees had hired one of their greatest legends, Joe DiMaggio, after the Yankee Clipper retired in 1951. Although he would make millions as the TV spokesperson for Mr. Coffee, DiMaggio was reserved and never comfortable hosting a television interview show. He also did not want to travel with the team, as the producers sometimes expected him to do. After the 1952 season the host role would be open. Barber had years of experience and exceptional skills as an interviewer. He knew he would never replace Mel Allen as the lead Yankees broadcaster, so the pre- and postgame gig would be a way of establishing a role with the broadcast team that was his alone. But leaving the Dodgers was a big step, and after some consideration Barber signed one more of Walter O'Malley's one-year contracts to continue as the lead play-by-play broadcaster for the 1953 season. Joe E. Brown, comedian, former professional baseball player, and star of several baseball movies in the 1930s, took over DiMaggio's TV assignment with the Yankees.

Barber's problems with Walter O'Malley had accumulated steadily from the point of Rickey's departure. Three incidents irked Barber. At their first meeting after O'Malley took control of the Dodgers, Barber offered to leave his post if O'Malley wanted to name his own broadcaster. Barber also wanted O'Malley to know that he and Rickey would always remain close friends. O'Malley assured Barber that he understood his value to the team and certainly wanted him to remain the voice of the Dodgers. He respected Barber's bond with Rickey and vowed that his own conflicts with Rickey would have no bearing on his relationship with Red. As the conversation moved on, the topic of the Dodgers' manager came up. Burt Shotton was one of Barber's favorite managers, and he told O'Malley he should remain the Dodgers' skipper. O'Malley quickly dismissed this suggestion, wanting to know who else Barber would recommend. Red offered two names, including Dixie Walker, one of his favorite players from his early Dodgers years. Barber later wrote that O'Malley "smiled, thanked me, and said: 'I've been talking with Harold Parrott and the boys in the front office—we are naming Charlie Dressen as the manager tomorrow.'" Barber was stunned. During his days in Cincinnati, he developed a deep respect for Dressen as a baseball man. So O'Malley's choice to lead the team was no issue, but why had he sought Barber's counsel if he had already made his choice? Red believed he knew the answer: "Walter must amuse himself by playing games. He plays people like they are markers in a checker game. . . . He is a graduate lawyer, and it is a constant challenge to him to get you to think he said this when legally he said that."[57]

The second incident was a rumpus over the foot speed of Dodgers right fielder Carl Furillo. Barber acknowledged that MacPhail and Rickey had spoiled him for future owners by "giving me the supreme compliment of saying that I was a grown man who knew his business and then leaving me alone to do it." MacPhail told him, "When you're broadcasting and you think this club should be burned, you burn it." O'Malley rarely intervened in Barber's broadcasting, but when it happened it was "one of the first real straws in the wind" that a Barber-O'Malley marriage might not last. In a close game, Barber told his listeners that the Phillies were playing the infield back on Carl Furillo because he was not a fast runner; knowing this, they were preparing for the double play. Furillo did indeed hit into a double play. Barber thought nothing of the call; it was his job to know the strengths and weaknesses of the players on both teams and report how what he knew affected game action. But Red states: "The next day in Brooklyn, I got word from O'Malley wondering, 'What was I trying to do, deprecate his ball players? Was I trying to alert the league that Furillo was a slow man afoot?'" According to Barber, O'Malley chided him in "such a cute way," saying, "Gee, yesterday were you just trying to tell everyone how slow Furillo is?" Barber resented the remark, cute or not, finding it hard to believe that O'Malley did not know what everyone else in the National League already knew: Furillo was not likely to win many foot races.[58]

Then there was the *boina* beef incident. When Red and Lylah were in Spain in February 1953, Barber bought a black Basque beret, a *boina*, as a souvenir. He wore his cherished *boina* for a spring training Dodgers yearbook photo featuring the "two Walters": O'Malley and Barber. Barber did not wear his favorite new hat at spring training in Florida—it was too hot. But in the cool Brooklyn April, it felt just right, and he began wearing it to the ballpark. One day O'Malley told Barber that his sponsor, Schaefer Beer, was not happy about the beret. Barber asked him why O'Malley, and not the sponsor, was telling him this. Later, when the team was flying home from Milwaukee, O'Malley observed, "I see you are still wearing that cap." Finally, Bill McCaffrey let Red know that BBDO, Schaefer's ad agency, did not want him to wear the *boina* when he broadcast Dodgers games. Although Red wrote in *The Broadcasters* that Lylah threatened to divorce him "if I took that *boina* off," he conceded he should not wear his beloved cap when appearing in Schaefer's commercials, representing the sponsor's product. But he would wear it during the rest of the broadcast whenever he wanted. He felt he had earned the right to top his thinning locks as he pleased: "I wore it. And every time I ran into O'Malley, his eyes went straight to the *boina*." Interestingly, Red's fans were not as enamored with the *boina* as he was.[59] According to *The Sporting News*, Barber's call-in request to fans during a game to name their favorite section of Ebbets Field produced mostly pleas to "tell Barber to chuck that beret of his."[60]

In a recorded conversation with Robert Creamer for his memoir *Rhubarb in the Catbird Seat*, Barber made it clear that he wanted his version of his rupture with the Dodgers told: "I want O'Malley's reaction when I quit the Series. Where if I had had any doubt about staying in Brooklyn, that [O'Malley's reaction] would have finished it."[61] After the 1952 World Series, Barber received a check from Gillette for $1,400, or $200 for each game. By 1952 national television networking was established, and the World Series was one of the biggest events on the tube. As one of two principal Series broadcasters, Red Barber received a payment that was more an honorarium than a fair compensation. But what bothered him more was that he had not negotiated the fee. Staring at the insignificant check from Maxon, Gillette's advertising agency, he told Lylah and his agent Bill McCaffrey that next year would be different. He would not do the Series unless he had the right to negotiate his fee before the Series: "I had gotten ashamed of myself." Red's father had told him, "Every night when you go to bed, you're going to wind up sleeping with yourself, and, Red concluded, "I couldn't take that thing from Gillette and sleep with myself anymore." The *amount* of pay wasn't the sticking point. Barber simply did not want to yield in a "take it or leave it situation." NBC's John Royal had confronted Barber with one in his 1935 network interview. Even though the young broadcaster had little leverage at the time, he still walked away.

After the Dodgers wrapped up the 1953 pennant with a week to go in the season, Barber received a call from Ed Wilhelm of Maxon Advertising; Barber saw Wilhelm as a "hatchet man" and "dog runner" for Gillette's Craig Smith. Wilhelm informed Barber that Gillette had just announced that he and Mel Allen were doing the World Series. Barber was vexed that Gillette had made a public announcement without his agreeing to broadcast the Series or even being informed of his selection. He told Wilhelm to contact his agent, Bill McCaffrey, immediately. After their conversation, McCaffrey called Barber to confirm that Red still wanted to reject the Series offer if he could not negotiate his fee in advance. Angered by Gillette's precipitous announcement, Barber was firm: no negotiation, no deal. When Craig Smith found out, he fumed, telling Wilhelm to deliver a message through McCaffrey to Barber: "You'll get the same as you got last year; take it or leave it." Barber told McCaffrey to call Wilhelm and "tell him we leave it." Barber's rejection of Gillette's offer fell on Sarah's sixteenth birthday. He flew back from St. Louis in time to join a surprise gathering he had arranged for her at the Birdland jazz club. In between the lively sets, Barber told his daughter, "I gave you the best sixteenth birthday present I could give you today; I gave you your father's self-respect." We don't know how she reacted, but it is easy to imagine that teenaged Sarah may have had some quibbles about her father's idea of a "best gift."

Even after the story of Barber's stiffing of Gillette had broken in the press, he still wanted to call his boss to explain why he had rejected the assignment. Walter Barber, who would have appreciated this boss's support, was not pleased when Walter O'Malley said, "That's your problem." Red promptly hung up, satisfying himself with the thought that "anything connected to O'Malley and the Brooklyn ball club as soon as I finish my contract . . . that's his problem.'" When his contract expired after the last game of the season, Red let it lapse. The Barber of Flatbush was a Dodger no more.

Gillette was contractually obligated to use a Dodgers announcer on the Series. Connie Desmond's problems with alcohol were no secret, so Vin Scully, who had just completed his fourth season as the Dodgers' number three announcer, was offered the

World Series national showcase. It was a major turning point in his career. After he got the offer, Scully called Barber to seek his approval. It touched Barber that his former pupil, now a colleague, had called. Barber told him, "You get my 100 percent blessing. . . . I'll give you my score book, and if necessary, I'll come up to the booth and rub you down before the first game." At least one play-by-play colleague, however, believed the Old Redhead had made a mistake. Washington Senators announcer Bob Wolff thought Red's ego had gotten the better of him, claiming that he and most other announcers would gladly have traded the modest Gillette fee for the grand exposure that came with covering the biggest sporting event of the era.[62]

The New York press generally endorsed Barber's principled dismissal of a World Series assignment that he had had no voice in negotiating, and some columnists assumed tensions with O'Malley, at least in part, had triggered his move to the Yankees. *Brooklyn Eagle* sportswriters poignantly lamented Barber's departure; coming just after the World Series, it constituted Brooklyn's "second loss to the Yankees" that October. They lauded Red's many contributions to the borough almost as much as his valuable expertise in the broadcast booth. *Eagle* editors opined that his sudden and "surprising" move likely was a choice he had made to curtail travel trips with the team and to engage more fully in pre- and postgame interview work: "It's nice to know that his new contract is a desirable bit for Barber and was made with the blessings of O'Malley." Tommy Holmes speculated that Barber would "humanize" the Yankees "and thereby provide a terrific lift to the public relations of that club." According to Holmes, Barber's move fit the tradition that "the Yankees always get the best." At least a few Dodgers fans, however, asserted that Red's going over to broadcast Yankees games was an act of "rank desertion."[63]

Ironically, Barber's sudden departure from Brooklyn overlapped with a project he had been working on for months with Dodgers photographer Barney Stein: a picture book called *The Rhubarb Patch: The Story of the Modern Brooklyn Dodgers*, covering Barber's years broadcasting for the team. Barber wrote voluminous captions for the photos, telling poignant stories behind some of the pictures, profiling lovable and feisty figures in the organization, and narrating memorable moments of play that Stein had captured. When *The Rhubarb Patch* was published during Barber's first summer with the Yankees, the *Brooklyn Eagle* recommended the book, "a wonderful collection of Ebbets Field's personalities during the Old Redhead's regime." Dodgers fans could "not afford to miss Red Barber's spritely text."[64]

When Barber left the Dodgers, they were still the best team in the National League. They would lose the 1954 pennant to the Giants but rebound for their first World Championship in 1955 and a return to the Series again in 1956. But their most beloved announcer would never call their regular season games again, nor would he call another World Series. Red Barber is linked forever to the Brooklyn Dodgers. His name is bound permanently to the greats of the "Bums" golden age: managers Leo Durocher, Burt Shotton, Charlie Dressen and players Jackie Robinson, Pee Wee Reese, Roy Campanella, Duke Snider, Dixie Walker, Pete Reiser, Don Newcombe, Clem Labine, Carl Erskine, and so many others. In his fifteen years with the club, the Dodgers won five pennants; they were in the race nearly every year, finishing lower than third only once. The pennant races of 1942, 1946, 1947, 1950, and 1951 all came down to the wire. The 1946 and 1951 races were decided in playoffs; the 1951 playoff ended with perhaps the most dramatic home run in baseball history: Bobby Thomson's "Shot Heard Round the World." His Dodgers days were Red Barber's zenith as a play-by-play broadcaster. When he moved up the East and Harlem Rivers to the Bronx, he entered "the Stadium," the Yankees' cavernous arena that Red saw as a stark contrast to the intimate Ebbets Field. Barber would never feel fully accepted at "the Stadium," and he would never again be the "Voice" of any team.

PART 4

YANKEE YEARS

Never at Home

12

Stadium Work

When Barber left the Brooklyn broadcast booth, he was no longer the Dodgers' play-by-play announcer, but he was not unemployed; his position as counselor for CBS Sports was secure and paid well. He also had reason to believe that he would not be without a baseball team for long. There were discussions with the Yankees before both the 1952 and 1953 seasons, and Joe E. Brown's contract for the pre- and postgame television programs was up for renewal. The Old Redhead was not that old, only forty-five; he was at the apex of his craft, and as he made clear to Sarah at her sixteenth birthday dinner, his self-respect was intact. His confidence was far from shaken. As he said years later, "I'm the best play-by-play baseball man in the history of mankind."[1] For the first time, however, he bought his own ticket to the World Series. The 1953 early October contest brought the Dodgers and Yankees together for a fifth subway series. Barber needed to go to Yankee Stadium and see his old friend Arthur "Red" Patterson about tickets for Lylah and himself to the Yankees' home games. By the time the Series was over, yet another Yankees victory, Barber had agreed to steam up the river to the Bronx. Getting a job with the World Series champs was a snap, but settling in at "the Stadium" was his most challenging professional transition.

The Bronx Barber

Patterson was happy to secure two Series tickets for Barber from the personal reserves of his boss, Yankees general manager George Weiss. After giving Patterson a check for the tickets, Barber reminded him, just as he entered the elevator, that the former "Barber of Flatbush" was available: "Arthur . . . I own myself." A few days later, while Red was dining with Buzzie Bavasi and Harold Parrott before Game Three, Weiss and Yankees owner Dan Topping walked into the room and invited Barber to join them for a brief chat. Weiss said that he and Topping were interested in Red's "coming to work at the Stadium . . . to do the pre- and post-game shows."[2]

The parties came to an agreement quickly. For $50,000 a year, Barber would do the pre- and postgame shows for all Yankees home games, replacing Joe E. Brown. But Barber also insisted that he continue to do some play-by-play. "Some" play-by-play turned out to be five innings equally split between radio and television. Barber's day would be strenuous. He would broadcast the pregame from the dugout, locker room, or other stadium location and then move quickly up to the booth to work with his broadcast partners. Before the end of the seventh inning, Barber would make his way to the stadium's TV studio to watch the rest of the game and then do the postgame summary and interview. The intense home stands, however, would be followed by long breaks when the team hit the road. Jim Woods, who joined the team in 1953, and Mel Allen handled the road contests. While Red made it clear to Weiss and Topping that he would travel as needed, during the years Barber and Allen shared the booth, he rarely went on the road with the team. In New York, Barber could pursue other potentially lucrative projects and retreat most evenings to the comfort of his beautiful home overlooking the Hudson River.

Barber's relationship with Mel Allen was always professionally solid, if not personally close. Since they both were from the South, the press often grouped them together with other baseball voices from the region, but their experiences of growing up in Dixie were different. Barber's family, on both sides, were Protestants of the middle and working classes. They were private folks but well integrated into the white culture of their region. Mel Allen *Israel*'s family was Jewish and merchant class. They were successful small business operators but always ethnic outsiders.[3] Allen had more formal education—both undergraduate and law degrees— while Barber completed only two years as an undergraduate. Still, Walter *Lanier* Barber was the lover of high culture. He treasured reading, the visual arts, opera, travel, and fine dining.

There also was little overlap in the social worlds of Red and Mel. *Walter* Barber was devoted to his family and close friends but comfortable with his own company. He rarely spent his free time with colleagues and players, preferring to socialize at his country club, Sleepy Hollow, and the Lambs Club, a Broadway show-people hangout. Allen was a lifelong bachelor, committed to the care of his parents but enjoying the pleasures of the single life in the nation's largest city. He hungered for social stimulation from his workmates, enjoying the company of Yankees players. Mel Allen was friendly, loud, and colorful. With no family of his own, the travel requirements for the "Voice of the Yankees" were not troubling. Barber was adamant in his commitment to objective reporting, while Allen was the classic "homer," the announcer who pulls for his team. Chronicler of the voices of the game, Curt Smith summed it up: "Barber was white wine, crepes suzette, and blue grass music. Allen was beer [Ballantine, naturally], hot dogs, and the United States Marine Band."[4] Jim Woods, the third man in the Yankees' booth, vividly captured his partners' differences: "After a game, [Barber would] go up to his room; Mel would circulate in a restaurant table-hopping; he loved the attention. On the air, yes, both were professionals—one was a machine-gun; the other, a violin. But privately, Mel had a more exuberant sense of fun, sort of on the corny side. Red's humor was more, well, sometimes you had to think for a moment and wonder, 'What the hell did he say?'"[5]

The 1954 Yankees broadcasts featured two superstar announcers, teammates who would both win the Hall of Fame's Ford C. Frick Award in 1978. Superstars often have superstar egos, and superstar egos often clash head-on. Who would be the Voice of the Yankees: the incumbent, Mel Allen, or the Brooklyn legend, Red Barber? In Red's mind, it was never a question: Mel was the Voice of the Yankees; Red Barber was his colleague. The son of a railroad engineer, Red honored seniority, and Mel had seniority in the Yankees' booth. Barber was upfront about what he considered his place in the new Yankees hierarchy: "At Brooklyn, I was the boss broadcaster, the principal announcer who gave the orders, assigned the innings, called the shots. At the Stadium, Mel Allen was the established Voice of the Yankees. He had earned his position. But I was not to be his assistant. I came in as an associate—as Ed Murrow used to say of so many people on his staff, as a 'colleague.'"[6] Mel Allen was the Voice of the Yankees, but he was not to be Red Barber's boss. Allen's obliging personality facilitated their professional accommodation. According to Bob Prince, the longtime voice of the Pittsburgh Pirates, Mel Allen "had almost a total lack of ego." Allen "was tremendously sensitive and had a humanity that isn't always true of broadcasters."[7] Barber's ego was strong, but his sense of fair play was even stronger. It also helped that the Yankees paid him $50,000 a year—as much as Mel Allen. Money has charms that soothe the savage ego.

One-Sided Hearing

Barber long had noticed a weakening of his hearing in his left ear. Like many men's physical and mental declines, the problem was first detected by his spouse. When Lylah accused Red of not listening to her, a not uncommon spousal complaint, Red suggested she needed to stop mumbling. But they both soon realized Red's hearing, not Lylah's speech, was the problem. Red's hearing loss had not affected his Brooklyn play-by-play work. Between his good right and weaker left ears, he could pick up all the ball-park sounds during the games. The problem came when he interviewed. If the player stood on Red's left side, Barber would miss some of his responses to questions. Since the Yankees hired him to interview players in front of a live TV camera, Barber knew his weakening left ear would become a serious issue. As he had always done in the past, he turned to the best medical experts he could find.

Barber worried he would lose hearing completely in his left ear and encounter problems with his right ear. His father had "died deaf, so hearing was something I was alerted to, aware of, and fearful of." As he recounted in *The Broadcasters*, "All by my little self . . . full of vanity, fear, and ignorance . . . I reasoned that because my hearing was going down, I needed to get the bad ear working and normal again. Yet I could not afford to be seen with an earpiece. I owed this new job and myself my very best. And I thought that you could believe whatever a doctor told you."[8]

The "experts" in the 1940s and 1950s recommended fenestration, a relatively successful surgical procedure used to improve lost hearing caused by abnormal growth of bone in the middle ear, the very growth that was weakening Barber's hearing. When successful, the operation significantly improved the patient's hearing but did not completely restore it.[9] Since the surgery was not always successful, Barber wanted assurances from his surgeon, one of two prominent New York specialists in the procedure, that he would be no worse off: "I asked him one question. 'Is there any chance of the operation doing any damage to the nerve, so if in the future I want to wear a hearing aid, it wouldn't do me any good?' He said: 'Absolutely not.'" The surgery was scheduled for January 14, 1954, leaving Red enough time to recover before the Yankees' spring training began.[10] When he awoke the day after his procedure, however, he was *totally deaf in his left ear*. At first the surgeon hoped that his hearing would come back, but it soon became clear that the nerve that would "absolutely not" be damaged was damaged beyond repair. Red Barber was disabled but not in any obvious way.

Newspapers, wire services, the broadcasting trade press, and *The Sporting News* covering Barber's surgery reported that he would have a delicate ear operation at the New York Eye and Ear Hospital. He planned to recuperate at his Scarborough home, and later in Florida, before joining the Yankees at spring training.[11] But the press did not report that the operation left Barber deaf in one ear because Barber did not want anyone to know. He did not tell the Yankees' leadership—not Weiss, Topping, or manager Casey Stengel. While his one-sided hearing was not immediately apparent, Barber worried that his lack of balance, a side effect from his surgery, would convince everyone he was drunk. Then the ear became infected, dripping with pus. When Barber took penicillin, he had an allergic reaction during a game broadcast. When he switched to cortisone, his friends told him he looked strained on television; he *was* straining—to understand his interviewees. He sought another specialist who told him what he already knew: his nerve was dead, and nothing could be done to bring back hearing in his left ear, an outcome he might have avoided had he opted for an earpiece. For Red, "The worse part was what I did to myself. . . . I was bitter about it. I went into an inner rage if anyone referred to my lack of hearing. I could not speak about it. I gave anyone who had to sit on my left side a cold, rude time. . . . All I thought about was what I had lost." Barber quit going to the theater and live music venues he loved. He gave most of his record collection to a veterans' hospital. He consulted a psychiatrist because he thought his complete deafness in his left ear might be a mental block, not a physical disability. Finally, as he often did when sinking into anger and depression, Red turned inward to find his way out. "Nobody could help me," he says; "I had to do it. And quick."[12]

The solution was simple but difficult for such a self-reliant and private man. He began to heal when he forced himself to "tell everybody I met that I was *deaf* in my left ear." When he did not respond to someone's question, the person now understood why, got his attention with a touch, and repeated the query into his good ear. Barber's focus turned from "what *I had lost*" to "how much *I had left*." Always a strong interviewer, he became a better one because he needed to listen more closely and pay more attention to a guest's face. Reading those nonverbal facial cues helped Red "hear things I never heard before." Now he was picking up "what people leave unsaid."[13] When Barber confessed to Stengel at the beginning of the 1954 season that he could not hear much of the Yankees manager's conversations with reporters, Casey pulled him aside and gave him a thirty-minute comprehensive rundown of his 1954 team. There was none of the "Stengelese" nonsense for which he was famous. Barber learned most of what he needed to know about his new team in that half hour.[14] Stengel's accommodation to Red's delicate condition helped to forge a lifelong bond between the two baseball legends.

A Scooter in the Booth

Once Barber adjusted to his hearing loss, his transition to the Yankees went more smoothly. Although he did not value the Yankees owners Dan Topping or Del Webb, he believed both George Weiss and Casey Stengel were tops in their professions. Weiss had learned his craft from Ed Barrow, builder of the great Yankees teams of the 1920s, '30s and '40s. Barber considered him a straightforward, trustworthy negotiator. Stengel was a sly fox who camouflaged his real genius by developing an entertaining persona. But he was no clown. He understood the strengths and weaknesses of his players, using platoon hitting and defensive substitutes freely so they could excel. Both men were deeply experienced and in full command of the latest Yankees dynasty, which had won five straight World Series before Barber jumped to the Bronx in 1954. Gradually, Red sensed the anxiety he'd felt under O'Malley melting away. The Yankees leaders, just like Powell Crosley, Larry MacPhail, and Branch Rickey, were men in whom he could believe. Unfortunately, the Yankees still needed sponsors who were, by constitution, relentlessly intent upon scrutinizing the broadcasts.

The Yankees' broadcasting team performed well together. Allen and Barber developed a comfortable working relationship. Jim Woods, who jumped to the Yankees from the Minor League Atlanta Crackers, was a pleasant, professional number-three man. In 1956 the *New York World-Telegram and Sun*'s "Saturday Magazine" profiled the three Yankees broadcasters, who all hailed from the South: Allen from Alabama, Barber from Mississippi, and Woods from Missouri. While dubbed the "Rebels in the Yankee Camp," the three booth partners were absolved quickly of their Dixie roots: "Truth of the matter is, though, that except for occasional lapses in idiom by Messrs. Allen and Barber, there is little to remind one that they came out of the South. As for Woods, he looks and sounds as Yankee as a nut-megger from Connecticut."[15] After three years together, the announcing team seemed complete, but the team's primary sponsor, Ballantine Beer, wanted something new. The pleasant professional, Woods, was not rehired for the 1957 season, and his replacement, though also pleasant, did not satisfy Barber's definition of a professional.

The Yankees released Phil Rizzuto in 1956 after thirteen seasons as their shortstop. He was a five-time All-Star and the American League Most Valuable Player in 1950. The Yankees won seven world championships in his thirteen years. But in the pre-free-agency era, players, even future Hall of Famers like Rizzuto, needed a second career, and Phil wanted to stay in baseball. The broadcast booth seemed like a possible new home. In his last years as a player, when Stengel rested him, Mel Allen would invite Rizzuto to do play-by-play for a half inning. Phil told *The Sporting News*, "That got me excited and I never missed when Mel asked me upstairs. I began dreaming that somebody who thought I had a chance might hear me."[16]

Red Barber always considered sports broadcasting a profession. He believed teams should hire announcers based on their professional credentials, not their popularity as players. He recognized that some ex-players had made a successful transition from player to broadcaster; Waite Hoyt became an excellent broadcaster once he kicked a drinking problem. Barber also understood there were exceptions, like Dizzy Dean, whose natural ability to entertain listeners compensated for his rough language skills and professional lapses. Rizzuto was an engaging personality and a good interview; he had a bit of experience thanks to Mel Allen, and he had potential. The Baltimore Orioles had offered him a spot in their booth. While he considered that offer, the Giants told him they planned to add another broadcaster, opening an alternative possibility. Phil Rizzuto was suddenly a hot commodity. Ultimately, Ballantine Beer and the Yankees won the Rizzuto competition. Phil could stay with the Yankees and keep his home in Hillside, New Jersey, with his wife, his four children, and his "golf clubs and movie-camera."[17]

Both Barber and Allen, however, found it hard to accept trading a seasoned professional like Jim Woods for an untried rookie like Phil Rizzuto. More unsettling, the change had been forced, not by their Yankees bosses, but by a sponsor. In Brooklyn, Barber had nominated Vin Scully to replace Ernie Harwell, and Branch Rickey had quickly hired him, but the Yankees' brass apparently did not consult Barber or Allen about a replacement. Rizzuto owed his job to his popularity as a player and his friendship with New Jersey country club golf partners: Ballantine president Carl W. Badenhausen and his sons. As Mel Allen biographer Stephen Borelli observed, "Rizzuto had a gregarious nature and name recognition that could potentially sell an awful lot of beer."[18]

From the start Barber and Rizzuto were a poor match. Barber was a cultured reader; a dedicated, demanding professional; self-reflective; and, at times, dismissive. Rizzuto was likeable, easygoing, and, usually, worry free. Pressure for him was playing in the seventh game of the World Series; providing an entertaining description of a game was not serious stress. As soon as the day game ended, he could trip lightly off to the golf course and join his friends. For Barber 75 percent of the broadcast was pregame preparation; for Rizzuto preparation was his thirteen years at the center of the Yankees' infield—already over. But Rizzuto still recognized that he had much to learn about his new craft, as he told *The Sporting News*: "When I started, I found myself umpiring and scoring, as well as trying to tell what had happened. . . . On a pitch, I would yell, 'That's a strike,' and then the umpire would call it a ball. On a grounder, which might be a hit or an error, I made the mistake of giving my opinion spontaneously instead of waiting on the game scorer's judgment. . . . I was anticipating the play, which I learned later was a common mistake for a rookie in my business." Rizzuto added that both Allen and Barber said he was "improving" but warned him not to take negative comments from fans "to heart right off the bat."[19]

Although Barber resented Woods's firing, once the Yankees had hired Rizzuto, Red "was there to help."[20] Even though he knew the answer, Barber would ask Phil questions so that his new colleague could impress listeners with his knowledge. Once when Rizzuto noticed that Billy Martin had a big lead off of third and was set to steal home, he whispered his insider tip to Red. But instead of forecasting the steal of home himself, Barber told Rizzuto, "Here, Phil, you take the mike." And, Rizzuto said, he "came off smelling like roses."[21] Columnist Red Smith, a Barber enthusiast, thought the Old Redhead helped bring Rizzuto out, producing little chats that were instructive and capitalizing on Rizzuto's experience as an ex-player.[22] In a 1991 interview Red remembered that after Phil's first season, "Mrs. Rizzuto gave me a beautiful pair of gold cufflinks with a diamond in each one" because, she said, he had been so good to Phil.[23] Rizzuto wanted to meet the expectations of New York's two most famous play-by-play men. He summed up his plight: "Can you imagine? Two guys with Southern accents speaking the king's English, and here comes this guy from Brooklyn busting up the language. It was brutal! I almost quit."[24]

Barber shared a booth with Rizzuto for a decade. After his apprenticeship with Allen and Barber, Phil continued to develop his own casual, appealing style that was the antithesis of Barber's highly detailed and focused accounts. Barber was not his boss; he could not make Rizzuto copy his approach, but he still could not stomach Rizzuto's nonchalant slant. His resentment triggered the persnickety side of his nature. According to Borelli, "[Red] would go out of his way to try to embarrass Rizzuto on the air. He asked questions he knew would stump the Scooter. What states border on Nevada? What is Michigan's state rock? . . . When the Scooter shared with listeners that he craved a 'pizza pie,' Barber retorted, 'Pizza *means* pie.'"[25] Marty Appel, executive producer of Yankees telecasts and Rizzuto's friend, thought that Barber was not helpful in developing him as a broadcaster: "Phil eventually became a terrific and beloved sportscaster, but not with the help of Red Barber, who had a disdain for former players going into the booth."[26] Rizzuto's casual, gregarious personality connected with fans throughout his forty-year career, the longest of any Yankees announcer, becoming, perhaps, the team's most cherished voice. Yankees fans would remember Red Barber as the complete professional, but they never developed the same fondness for him they felt for Mel Allen or the Scooter.

The Many Voices of Red Barber

During the 1946–51 period, when Barber was both the Voice of the Dodgers and director of CBS Sports, his time for outside activities was limited. His CBS contract also restricted paid appearances on other networks. He lent his voice to a few films and continued volunteer work with the Red Cross, fund-raising for St. Barnabas House, and hosting charity events. But his professional work focused on the Dodgers' broadcasts and his varied CBS assignments. In 1951 Barber became sports counselor at CBS, reducing his management responsibilities. After his first year with the Yankees, Barber was ready to leave CBS altogether, resigning his position effective March 1, 1955. According to *Variety*, "[Barber] couldn't see himself deskbound any longer." He planned to concentrate on his work as a radio/TV performer and to pursue a deferred writing project. *Variety* noted that Barber was mimicking "Ed Murrow's [resigning CBS's] news and special events vee-peeship a few years ago to return wholly to broadcasting."[27] A year and a half later, Barber told a New York newspaper, "Getting rid of the executive duties was one of the smartest things I ever did. It's made me years younger."[28]

Barber also recognized that television's increasing importance in network sports demanded a full-time sports executive for CBS. Red knew that the radio announcer–network sports executive model he had inherited from Ted Husing at CBS and that Bill Stern practiced at NBC was obsolete in the television age. In a meeting with CBS president Frank Stanton, Barber made the case for change: "You and CBS need a full-time executive—a desk man who doesn't go on the air—as Director of Sports. Television alone demands a skilled negotiator. I'm a broadcaster, not an office man. In fairness to both of us, I have to resign. I intend to go back to broadcasting . . . and do nothing else."[29] In 1956, at the request of Larry MacPhail, Red endorsed his son Bill for the position of CBS Sports president. The younger MacPhail remained with CBS until 1973.

Red Barber did not reveal publicly yet another reason for his leaving CBS: *money*. While Barber's compensation at CBS was generous—estimated in the six figures—his network contract limited the programs he could broadcast and the companies he could endorse on other networks. In fall 1954, when Barber wanted to do commercials for NBC-TV's *Donald O'Connor Texaco Show*, CBS denied his request, costing Barber approximately $40,000 in additional income (about $385,000 in 2020 dollars). Barber assumed that since this was not a sports assignment, it did not violate his exclusivity clause in his CBS contract. When Camel Cigarettes spots he had recorded for his Yankees broadcasts later were used on other networks, CBS had not complained.[30] But CBS saw Texaco spots on the O'Connor show as directly aiding its major competitor, NBC. Barber and his agent could see that his opportunities beyond CBS were increasing. With the Dodgers, he had been "the Voice," but Brooklyn was just one borough.

The Yankees were baseball's most successful brand. Red may not have been their number-one announcer, but his place in the Yankees' booth brought more corporate interest to his door. His Scarborough neighbors, country club friends, and membership in the Lambs Club also provided useful connections.

A year after Barber left CBS, *Variety* estimated that Barber, "who is known not to hate money," made $200,000 (about $1.9 million in 2020 dollars) from his freelance work. *Variety* speculated that although Barber told the press he had quit CBS "to be relieved from the rigors of 'administrative duties,'" the key to his resignation was "the pocketbook," referring to Red's loss of "all sorts of lucrative bids while a captive of Columbia." Barber's new opportunities included doing Fluffo TV commercials for Procter & Gamble, appearing in a corporate film for Johnson & Johnson on safety, narrating a Ted Williams film on fishing, and taking on a wide range of speaking engagements. Barber earned $75,000 from the Fluffo ads alone. Once Barber's Wednesday night postboxing sports show on CBS ended, his program, now sponsored by State Farm Insurance, moved to NBC-TV. It followed the Friday night boxing matches sponsored by Gillette. Barber continued his radio work on the CBS *College Football Roundup* for "a flat fee." He also was under consideration as the host of several panel shows, including one with Branch Rickey.[31] Of course, while Barber's income was high, so was his tax rate; most of his big bucks bump did not go into his pockets. The 1955 federal income tax rate for incomes over $100,000 increased on a sliding scale from 75 to 91 percent.[32]

As Barber was reaching his financial peak, he gave a little back to the university and radio station that launched his career. In February 1955 he sponsored an annual Red Barber WRUF Award; a sterling silver bowl and $100 check would go to a WRUF student announcer who best demonstrated Barber's "4 I's: industry, improvement, initiative, and integrity." Red told the *Gainesville Times* that "intensive preparation" is a "must" for broadcasting success. "But the announcer must not be bound completely by the chains of tradition." A broadcaster "must be a servant of the truth as best he sees it and must not be swayed by public opinion." On March 6, 1955, Barber presented the award to Ralph Goodwin on the twenty-fifth anniversary of Barber's first day at WRUF. Major Garland Powell, still the director of the station, was on hand for the presentation.[33]

Regular program commitments were difficult to fit into Barber's busy professional and personal schedule, but Red and his agent, Bill McCaffrey, seized other opportunities as they arose. In 1957 Red appeared as a Yankees announcer on an episode of Phil Silvers's Sergeant Bilko program *You'll Never Get Rich.* The plot involved a super talented GI, a "hillbilly wiz," from the South that Bilko planned to sell to the Yankees for $125,000. The GI, played by Dick Van Dyke, wouldn't sign with the club unless his girlfriend could get a job with the Yankees and come north with him. Yankees players, including Whitey Ford, Gil McDougald, and Yogi Berra, and broadcaster Phil Rizzuto donned Southern garb and accents to convince Van Dyke's GI that the Yankees, despite their name, were "Southern Gentlemen" just like he was. The ultimate solution was to create a new position for the hillbilly wiz's beautiful blonde Southern gal as Red Barber's new broadcasting colleague, bypassing the profiteering Bilko. At the show's conclusion, Bilko lamented, "They brought in Red Barber on me, a real Southerner." Barber, the "hillbilly wiz," and his girlfriend formed "the solid South. You can't beat 'em."[34]

Barber continued to make guest appearances on television in the late 1950s. His old boss and friend, Ed Murrow, came for a visit to Barber's Scarborough home on national television in January 1958, when Red, Lylah, and Sarah appeared on Murrow's CBS program *Person to Person.* Barber's release from CBS enabled his lucrative "traveling ambassadorship" for Gulf Oil, with Red appearing in television commercials and a series of print ads for the company. NBC tapped Barber for a prime time "Aqua-Spectacle" on its *Saturday Spectacular,* an "amazing performance of the four world champion water skiers as they were towed around a pool at speeds that well could have been break-neck for any less skilled athletes."[35] Red also appeared on David Susskind's *Open End*, a syndicated TV talk program. The episode, titled "Interesting People with Strong Opinions," also featured Shelly Winters, Anthony Quinn, Richard Tobin (editor of the *Saturday Review*), and writer Leo Rosten. On the show that night as well was Red's distant cousin, with whom he shared a middle name and a hometown in Columbus, Mississippi: Thomas Lanier "Tennessee" Williams. The *Oakland Tribune* wrote that Barber seemed comfortable with the show's controversial subjects and fast verbal company: "For those who know Red, it is not too surprising that the sportscaster speaks with clarity and wisdom on many topics."[36]

In his years with the Yankees, Barber continued to cover football, but his broadcasts were limited. Barber called the 1955 and 1956 Orange Bowl games on CBS Radio. In 1963 he returned to regular-season college football, covering five regional games with Johnny Lujack for CBS-TV. That same year CBS Radio used him to host *Sport-A-Rama*, a series of sports specials where Barber did "on-the-scene" interviews with athletes and coaches on "topical sports of the month."[37]

Look magazine featured Barber in a protracted profile for a second time, now capturing the wide parameters of his public life in the late 1950s. The photo spread revealed "The Double Life of Red Barber." Predictably, *Look* showed Red at work with the Yankees, doing play-by-play, interviewing Yankees personnel, and signing autographs. But the story also featured photos of Barber in his Episcopal robe, readying himself for the pulpit. Barber's charity work also was highlighted, including his fund-raising for St. Barnabas House. Red also is shown charming potential donors to Youth Consultation Service, the Episcopal agency for which Lylah volunteered her time, helping troubled teenagers and unmarried mothers. Barber, who chaired its board, told *Look*, "I'd do anything, go anywhere, if it would mean something to YCS." *Look* also included a photo of Red and Lylah sorting through "mad-hatter" Barber's "zany" hat collection. When asked what it was like to be married to the Old Redhead, Lylah replied, "He's wonderful, a deep and complex man. I've been married to him 26 years and *still* I can't predict what he'll do next."[38]

The *Look* article highlighted Barber's preaching. His scrapbooks from the 1950s contain dozens of newspaper accounts of his sermons in Cooperstown, the New York area, and other Major League cities (including Cincinnati, Pittsburgh, St. Louis, and Chicago), as well as Florida and other parts of the American South. In August 1954 Barber spoke at the Christ Episcopal Church in Cooperstown, joined by Warren Giles, president of the National League. As we know, Red often wove baseball themes into his talks. In his Cooperstown sermon he spoke of God as "the Good Manager" who often must wait for a player in a slump to ask for help. For Barber, "God and man is a two-way street, just as it is two ways between manager and player." God, like a good manager, "never blames the player, who tries, for making a physical error." He knows his best hitters hit safely only three times in ten at bats and understands that "his team at best is still going to lose about one-third of its games."[39] Barber's "Good Manager" talk became a go-to sermon.[40] In June 1958 Hobart College, affiliated with the Episcopal Church, recognized Barber's work as a lay reader and a public servant with an honorary Doctor of Humanities.[41] The University of Florida dropout, denied an honorary degree in 1953 from Branch Rickey's alma mater, Ohio Wesleyan University, now had a doctorate.

Resigning as CBS sports counselor freed Red Barber to pursue vigorously his spiritual mission while also satisfying his entrepreneurial instincts. He made more money and paid more taxes than at any earlier point in his career. But he also lost control of his broadcast booth—not to Mel Allen, with whom he had developed a comfortable working relationship, but to Yankees sponsor Ballantine. During this same period, while Barber was weathering shake-ups in his professional pursuits, at home he and Lylah were navigating life-altering challenges triggered during their daughter's college years.

Sarah's Journey

In the fall of 1955, having graduated from prep school in Dobbs Ferry, Sarah left the suburbs of New York for Rollins College in Winter Park, Florida. This was the same private college that thirty years earlier had offered her father a full-tuition athletic scholarship with a guarantee of an on-campus job to cover his living expenses. But his friend had talked him out of attending that school because it was full of "rich men's children wearing racoon hats and driving roadsters.... You wouldn't be happy there." Sarah attended the school at a point when it had begun to attract students from New York and other northeast cities.[42] In 1960 Sarah graduated from Rollins with a BA in English; by this time, she also had come out to her parents as a lesbian. She moved from college in Florida, to Greenwich Village, and she remained in New York City until she retired in 1992 and moved to Santa Fe with her longtime partner, Gloria Donadello, a Fordham University professor. After graduating from Rollins, Sarah worked for a brief stint at *Look* magazine and took courses preparing her for a job as a second- and third-grade teacher in Harlem. She taught there from 1962 to 1969, when she accepted a teaching position at LaGuardia Community College.[43]

Neither Red nor Lylah wrote or talked publicly about their daughter's coming out to them or about her sexual orientation. But material from several sources enables us to sketch steps in Sarah's awakening to her "difference" and her successful embrace of it during her college years. First, she struggled to forge an identity unconnected to her status as Red Barber's daughter. Then she wrestled with the potential loss of the loving support she had always enjoyed from what she later in life described as her "very *closed*" family.[44] Persuaded by her parents, she endured a tough therapy that, rather than "curing her," validated who she really wanted to be. In 1945 Branch Rickey had challenged Red Barber to confront the lessons he had been "carefully taught" about race in American life, before most of the country had fully awakened to the issue. A decade later Red had to navigate in a much more personal arena the controversial issue of lesbianism, rarely whispered at the time in public forums. Well-meaning physicians still classified and treated homosexuality as a psychiatric disorder, for which well-situated parents sought professional advice and therapy.

During the 1954 Yankees' spring training in Florida, the Barbers took Sarah, then a high school junior, for a campus visit at Rollins.[45] Red also wrote a letter to an academic dean at the college, expressing his interest in teaching a short course or workshop on radio announcing for a few weeks while he was in the area.[46] The course did not materialize, but two years later Barber would return to the campus for a full week during the winter term of Sarah's freshman year. He would be a highly visible guest speaker for the college's annual forum, "Animated Magazine." At this week-long event, widely covered in the local press, leaders in various professions were invited to address a general theme. Barber spoke at the campus forum along with, among others, U.S. Senator Margaret Chase Smith, the president of the New York Stock Exchange, and a nationally syndicated comic strip writer.[47]

Lylah Barber believed Sarah resented her father's "infringing on her territory" at Rollins. At the time of Red's appearance on campus in March 1956, she was doing well in college, getting good grades, joining a sorority, and singing in the Chapel Choir. Lylah suggests that after Sarah had left home and forged her own identity on campus, it might have been disheartening to be back in the shadow of her celebrated father and having to revert to her status as "Red Barber's Daughter."[48] In his address "As a Man Thinketh," which he delivered during the week-long event attended by five thousand guests, Barber mentions his daughter directly: "I am delighted to follow our daughter to Rollins. She got here a few months ahead of her father."[49] One article covering the event was a protracted profile of Red's successful life, published in the Rollins' campus newspaper, *Sandspur*. It was based upon an informal "talk fest" that Red volunteered to conduct with Rollins's students on "Sunday morning in the Fox Hall living room."[50] The acclaimed announcer, it seems, was finally experiencing the student life at Rollins he had once scorned, as well as the long-discarded ambition of becoming a college teacher, but perhaps, unwittingly, at his daughter's expense.

College administrators may have contributed to Sarah's malaise regarding her father's presence on campus during her college career. Memos and letters between the college's president, its fund-raising staff, and one of Sarah's professors discuss Barber's past and potential future donations to the school. A letter from the professor to Red describes Sarah's excellent work in his class, expressing concern about her recent cold and praising Red's own remarkable achievements.[51] Rollins, like most private schools, attempted to cultivate generous "friends" and donors out of their students' famous parents.

"Twisted Streets"

The summer after Sarah's sophomore year was transformative. She interned for *Look* at the magazine's editorial headquarters on New York City's Madison Avenue, absorbing the diversity of big city life on her own for the first time. This experience would find expression in poems that Sarah began contributing the following fall to the Rollins literary magazine, *Flamingo*, for which she also served as one of the three editorial board members. Most of her poems feature a first-person speaker who, like many introspective young English majors, attempts to navigate contradictions and ambiguities that plague the passage from youth to adulthood. One of her poems won a regional college student poetry award, and another, a national award.[52]

Sarah's 1957 regional award-winning free-verse poem, "Greenwich Village," expresses contradictions experienced in the "twisted streets" of this then bohemian community and perhaps during her own past summer in the neighborhood, where she would soon live. The speaker compares the people in Greenwich Village to its "twisted streets that are/warm inviting beckoning / to those that dream they / are different with a purpose/to fulfill." The Village community reinforces her creative spirit, and she has learned "love" in these twisted streets. But she has lost and found love so many times that after "too much drink and words unguarded said/and into beds, [she] wakes in morning lost / with no identity." The poem expresses both an attraction and a fear of twisted streets that are associated with love—sometimes reckless, and creativity—sometimes wasted. It ends by formulating troubling alternatives: being "twisted" and inspired or "straight" and safe. But however threatening the neighborhood seemed, within the next decade Sarah would forge a home on those twisted streets and a social justice mission that fueled the rest of her life.[53]

Another of Sarah's contributions to the fall 1957 issue of *Flamingo*, "Sonnet for You," is a love poem in which the speaker is more confident of her "dreamer" side. Like a courtly gentleman, she invites her lover to walk with her into the woods, "a private place that only lovers see." She tells her lover: "Have faith in me / Look through the eyes of this sad dreamer, and perhaps / We'll find a love that lasts, longer than a day."[54] Copies of both these poems were saved in one of Red Barber's scrapbooks. Published at the end of 1957, they may have provoked conversation with her parents after the winter holidays. In her only poem published in *Flamingo*'s next issue, winter 1958, entitled "As Days Pass," the speaker expresses despair at her ruptured dreams, her lost naïveté that "I thought was me." She longs "to lie upon the cold unyielding floor / of some great cathedral and have the music / of some un-played organ / cleanse me of my sin / and let me live my dreams again."[55] The discouraged speaker seems to seek an unshakeable authority that will wash her clean and return her to the innocence of her childhood. At the end of her winter term in 1958, Sarah took a year-and-a-half sabbatical from Rollins College, from March 1958 to September 1959, when she began her senior year, which she completed in May 1960. Lylah Barber mentions in her memoir that Sarah had satisfied all her junior-year requirements by the end of the 1958 winter term, but she does not explain why her daughter did not return to Rollins until a year and a half later in fall 1959.[56]

"Best Practices"

The events in the Barber family after Sarah's junior year reveal her movement toward affirming what she "thought was me" and away from the dictates of "unyielding" authority. Several friends who were close to her in New York and Santa Fe recalled Sarah's telling them she came out as a lesbian during college and that her parents encouraged her to undergo what was considered within the psychiatric community at the time to be one of the "best practices" for dealing with what was then understood to be the "disorder" of homosexuality: electroconvulsive therapy (ECT).[57] Friends also recall Sarah's occasionally being haunted by her memory of the experience.[58] Lacking the research that since has confirmed genetic and physiological influences upon sexual identification, practitioners at the time believed that ECT—electronically induced seizures—could help treat homosexuality as effectively as it appeared to do for other "mental disorders."[59] Red and Lylah both had sought psychological counseling at different points in their lives, and we know Barber actively sought the top medical experts for his own and Lylah's issues.[60] They likely would do the same for what they perceived to be their daughter's "aberrant" affliction, one that could burden her future with painful social stigma. As Red said regarding the celebrated specialist of ear fenestration, he had always thought "you could believe whatever [the experts] tell you," and he felt obligated to follow their advice.[61]

Evidence indicates that Sarah underwent her therapy over the spring or summer after her junior year. Lylah tells us that her husband surprised her that spring with the gift of a European travel tour for her and Sarah. He cashed in the college insurance policy that he had taken out when Sarah was born to pay for her travels with her mother; these included short visits to Italy, France, and Germany before their brief terminus in Edinburgh, where arrangements were made for Sarah to pursue some course of study at the university, beginning in September 1958.[62] Lylah acknowledges "a few rough spots" between them during the trip, but "[it was] on the whole pleasant. . . . Sarah was twenty and I was fifty-one. We were both growing up."[63] September 1958 records of the *Queen Elizabeth* ocean liner list Sarah as a passenger, the only "Barber" on a ship sailing from New York to the port of Southampton, and they cite her destination as Edinburgh, for the purpose of study for a period of nine months.[64] Her college senior yearbook photo caption indicates that she "attended University of Edinburgh," and a 1960 *Sandspur* piece on Sarah's poetry mentions that she spent the 1958–59 academic year in Europe.[65] The sequence of events beginning with Sarah's abrupt departure from Rollins suggests that there was a quickly arranged plan for a change of location in Sarah's life—one of those real, as well as symbolic, voyages that signal a break from the present and a testing of new possibilities.

The outcome of that test was apparent when Sarah returned to Rollins in September 1959 to pursue her senior year. She lived in her own apartment near campus and resumed her position on the board of *Flamingo*.[66] Her national award-winning poem, "Awake Remembering," first appeared in the fall 1959 issue of the magazine and was accompanied by a drawing of a large hand reaching out to a toddler. The speaker narrates a dream in which she rocked her mother in her arms and smoothed her hair throughout a dark night. She hears the voice of her mother whispering, "My child is gone."[67] The haunting poem suggests the speaker saw herself as the care-taking adult, attempting to comfort the bereft mother who cannot recognize her child as the mature person she had become. Remarks by some of Sarah's English professors on her senior year course grade cards also describe a successful transition for a student they had come to know well; one professor observed that "she has learned to think for herself and has achieved stability as a person." Another remarked that "she has matured a lot since her freshman year."[68]

Sarah was advised to endure a procedure that would make her "straight," but the treatment failed, just as surely as the expert's remedy for Red's hearing loss in his left ear would leave it deaf.

Like her father and his deafness, Sarah found peace in accepting and publicly acknowledging what medical procedures had failed to "fix." Her anxiety about her sexual identity appeared to dissipate. Within a decade of her college graduation, she was comfortably settled in Greenwich Village, where, according to one of her friends during that period, "she was a role model for all of us who never believed we could conduct our lives openly as lesbians. She gave us courage."[69] In that sense Sarah was following the advice that Red Barber had received from his own mother—to respect the quality within himself—and that he had received from his father—to be true to the person one was instead of acting a part. Before her death from a virulent brain disease in 2005, Sarah wrote that her parents "never fully accepted [her] lifestyle."[70] However, existing letters from Sarah to her father, interviews where she describes his influence upon her, texts published by both of her parents, and interviews with Sarah's close friends still residing today in Santa Fe, attest that there remained, throughout their lifetimes, deep and abiding bonds among this "very *closed*" threesome.

"What Happened to Milwaukee?"

Between 1958 and 1961, at the invitation of the Department of Defense, Barber took part in three USO tours at military installations in the Far East and the Mediterranean, two of them with Lylah as a teammate. Barber later wrote that typical USO shows were not like Bob Hope's exceptional Christmas extravaganzas— with bands, singers, television crews, props, lighting, and sound equipment. Most acts went to entertain without fanfare or publicity, accompanied by only one military escort to guide them from location to location and through a rigorous schedule of performances, ideally with no special equipment to lug around. Lean acts like Red's could be transferred from place to place by helicopter or small plane, could easily navigate "handshake tours," and could move gracefully from bed to bed in a hospital without creating a disturbance. Once the tour began, military orders completely controlled the entertainers' lives; the entertainers traveled, ate, and slept in troop facilities. They could perform in tents or in large auditoriums, or they could spend more time interacting spontaneously with troops in small groups or individually, depending upon the size, resources, and preferences of the installation. Entertainers averaged three "shows" a day at three different installations. Red was always scheduled for a "sports talk" based on his experience as a broadcaster, and if the military chaplains requested, an installation could also use him as a lay reader licensed to preach sermons.[71]

Barber's first visit to the Far East in 1958 took him to South Korea, Japan, Iwo Jima, and Okinawa. In an interview with *Variety* after his tour, Barber observed that the greatest problem for the troops he met in Korea was loneliness, which was exacerbated during leisure time, even though many healthy diversions were available—movies, libraries, sports programs, and even academic courses. Red had discovered in his first visit with troops in Germany in 1948 that the men most wanted to reconnect with home; they were most responsive when he strung together stories that would bring home closer to them. Accordingly, in all subsequent tours, "All I ask for is a mike and a pitcher of water; I don't even want to go on stage." The first question the men asked in Korea in October 1958 was, "What happened to Milwaukee?" He just told them, "'They didn't win the fourth game,' and went on from there."[72]

On the flight from Tokyo to Iwo Jima, Red experienced the frightening effects of being aloft with a typhoon in the neighborhood: "Man, it rained!" His gig in Iwo Jima was only a one-night stand, and Red had to perform his "sports show" in a Quonset hut, "already leaking like a sieve in the storming rain." Barber was deeply disappointed that there was no time in the itinerary to visit the top of Mt. Suribachi, where U.S. Marines had engaged the Japanese in a major battle, ultimately raising the American flag on the mountain's peak. But late in the evening a colonel asked him if he could get up at 5 a.m. "to see our mountain" before his early morning flight. At the break of day, Red recalls, "We stood up there and looked down in the quiet of dawn, in the smell of sulfur, in the midst of the ghosts of thousands of men. The Colonel said that the largest force of Marines ever committed to action took thirty-six days to capture this island fortress."[73]

When he arrived for a four-day visit on Okinawa, Barber learned to his surprise that he was to preach a sermon that very afternoon, an appearance that had been added to the itinerary at the last minute. His audience would be Marines stationed at a small camp with another Quonset hut for a chapel. The chaplain informed Barber that he had also invited the men in the brig to attend the sermon; *every one* of the brig troops planned to be there. Red later wrote that the prospect of preaching to tough Marines—to "*brawling* Marines so tough they had gotten themselves locked up"—provoked him to ditch the sermon he had prepared to give several days later to troops at Okinawa's Main Chapel.[74] That sermon focused on themes of peace and love based on lines from the *Beatitudes*. He suspected the prisoners were coming to his sermon merely to get out of the brig. He felt he needed to preach a tough sermon, hurriedly jotting down notes on an envelope during the ride to the Marine camp.

Barber included a reconstructed text of that performance in his book *Show Me the Way to Go Home*. The sermon "enacted" the tough moments of esteemed military leaders throughout modern history who turned to prayer or pertinent passages of scripture at desperate moments in war. He movingly broadcast the words of these tough men experiencing the toughest of perils—George Washington; Stonewall Jackson; Field Marshal Montgomery; Eddie Rickenbacker, who got lost on a raft in the Pacific; Robert E. Lee; Dwight Eisenhower; Winston Churchill; General MacArthur; and even Jesus. We see them rallying their troops or themselves by turning to the faith that sustained them. Red records that his audience grew increasingly attentive, he thinks, because he was channeling the indomitable spirit of men "the troops knew about, and respected—men even tougher than themselves."

A year later Barber made a similar USO trip, this time to the Mediterranean, including Lylah in the act, "on the basis of merit, as an entertainer in her own right." Lylah told the stories she knew firsthand from the wives of baseball players: "Why Mrs. Yogi Berra would not let Yogi hang pictures; what Mrs. Jackie Robinson said to Mrs. Don Newcombe in Philadelphia the last day of the season when the Dodgers had to beat the Phillies to win the pennant; why Mrs. Preacher Roe said pitching was such a hard way to make a living." Red admits: "[After Lylah] did the Mediterranean and a full swing of the Far East, I woke up to the fact that she was stealing the show."[75]

When Red and Lylah were conducting a "sports talk" during the Mediterranean tour at a radar base in Spain, an air force sergeant inquired, "May I ask a question?" Red assumed it would be a sports question, but instead the man pointed out that the radar installation was too small to have its own chaplain, and he asked, "Would you say some prayers for us today?" He later said the sergeant's request moved him and made him realize that "many of our men in the armed services have a deep religious need." He believed he could "provide solace in language the chaplains do not possess"—presumably the earthier, grittier nouns and verbs of the bullpen, the dugout, and the broadcast booth. Red, along with Lylah, made a third USO tour back to the Far East in 1961, this time at installations in Japan, Korea, Taiwan, Guam, the Philippines, and Hawaii. Red made a final, more unsettling tour to Vietnam in 1967, after his baseball announcing career was over.[76] On that visit he would "provide solace" in a live war quite different from those he'd lived through as a civilian or read about in his history books.

Troubled Times

Red and Lylah Barber's military trips combined two experiences they valued: public service and travel. But the trips preceded some disquieting years. Red experienced more health issues as his high-mileage body moved into its fifties. The first problem was recurring ulcers. His 1948 hospitalization had both saved and transformed his life but had not cured his stomach traumas. His ulcers became so bad that he needed additional surgery. In January 1960 Barber underwent an operation at Northern Westchester Hospital in Mt. Kisco, New York. The press, including columnist Walter Winchell, offered only a brief report of the what and where of the surgery and no sign of its extent.[77] Red Barber lost two-thirds of his stomach that day. He wrote: "[The gastrectomy] sent me into a severe decline. Food became repugnant, repulsive. I lost weight and strength."[78] With only a third of his original stomach capacity remaining, Barber would struggle for the rest of his life to maintain a healthy weight, an effort that became even more difficult as he aged. When his NPR *Morning Edition* partner Bob Edwards met him in person for the first time in the early 1980s, the slight build of his legendary radio companion struck him: "He was so frail it seemed a gust of wind might take him away. I sensed that if I wasn't careful, I might accidentally bump into him and knock him down."[79]

With much less stomach, Barber returned to the microphone for the 1960 season. His greatest thrill for the year was the 1960 World Series, which ended with the only walk-off, Game Seven home run in Series history: Bill Mazeroski's blast off Ralph Terry, which flew over the left field wall at Forbes Field.[80] The World Series was thrilling, but Barber's year ended sadly when the two members of the Yankees' management he respected most, George Weiss and Casey Stengel, were both fired at the end of the season, increasing Barber's isolation at "the Stadium."

The Bronx Bombers regained their composure, slugging their way to the 1961 pennant and a four-games-to-one World Series victory over the Cincinnati Reds. Their success was fueled, in part, by the race between Roger Maris and Mickey Mantle to break Babe Ruth's record of sixty home runs in a season. Barber always respected Maris's strength as he overcame a hostile press and Commissioner Ford Frick's threat to place an asterisk in the books if Maris beat the Babe's mark using more than the 154 season games during which Ruth had established the record in 1927. By 1961 both leagues had increased the number of regular-season games to 162. Barber told *The Sporting News* his biggest thrill in 1961 was "watching Roger Maris in September. . . . Not only watching him hit the home runs, but also seeing and knowing the constant pressure he endured. He stood up."[81] It was Barber, on WPIX-TV, who made the television call of Maris's sixty-first home run on October 1, 1961, the last game of the season. In the fourth inning Maris took two balls. With the fans booing, Barber begins: "The crowd is reacting negatively. They want to see Maris get something he can swing on." On the third pitch, Maris swung. "There it is." Crowd cheering. "Sixty-one—five thousand dollars for somebody." More cheering. "He got his pitch, five thousand dollars. Here is the fella with 61; you've seen a lot today."[82] Barber's reference to $5,000 reminded his viewers of a restaurant owner's offer for the sixty-first home run ball. Barber added only the barest of descriptions and context, letting crowd sounds and the video images tell most of the story. In vivid contrast, Rizzuto's call of number sixty-one on radio came in waves of words and a flood of feeling: "Here's the windup. Fastball hit deep to right. This could be it. Way back there. *Ho-lee-cow*, Roger Maris. *Ho-lee-cow*, what a shot. Another standing ovation for Roger Maris. Sixty-one home runs. And they're still fighting for the ball out there. People are climbing over each other's backs. One of the greatest sights I've seen here at Yankee Stadium."[83] Both announcers got it right; each adapted his calls for his medium and personal style—Barber, for television simplicity; Rizzuto, for radio detail. Barber was ever the dispassionate reporter; Rizzuto, the ever-passionate fan.

In February 1964 Red's increasingly frail health took another dramatic turn.[84] On their annual drive to the Yankees' spring training in Florida, Red and Lylah spent the night at a motel in Emporia, Virginia. That evening Red walked to his car, stamping out a cigarette on the ground. As he opened his car door, Bang! What felt like a heart attack struck him down. He passed out. When he came to fifteen minutes later, he had an oxygen mask on his face.

In a fortunate break that Barber saw as the "provenance of God," medical help arrived quickly. Amazingly, the motel staff had just summoned a doctor and a rescue squad to help another patron with heart attack symptoms. The doctor, having determined that the first person was fine, went to the motel's restaurant to have some dinner. When Barber dropped to the ground beside his car, the doctor was on site and ready to help. When the rescuers arrived, they gave Red oxygen within two minutes of his passing out. Red proclaimed: "I fell in the dirt in Emporia, Virginia, and there he [God] was with the oxygen and a doctor."[85] While Barber's symptoms had all the markings of a heart attack, the episode had actually been acute fibrillation—an irregular heartbeat—and there was no lasting damage to his heart. But he stayed in the hospital for three weeks until he fully recovered.[86] Barber set as his goal to be ready for work on Opening Day 1964, and he succeeded.

Barber's heart episode may have added decades to his life. His scare convinced the man who had hawked Old Gold, Camel, and Lucky Strike cigarettes on baseball broadcasts and in print ads throughout the 1940s and 1950s to stop smoking. He did so cold turkey, ending the two-to-three-pack-a-day habit he had enjoyed for decades. Both his father, and later his brother Billy, succumbed to cancer, probably brought on by decades of smoking. The same fate likely awaited Red Barber had he continued the habit. At a time when the powerful addictiveness of nicotine for many people was not fully understood, Red could not empathize with others who would not "just stop" as he had. It seemed to him a simple matter of willpower. "Nobody's ever told me not to smoke any more," he states; "I knew not to smoke any more, and it hasn't been any problem. It's just that simple. So when somebody tells me, 'I'm thinking about quitting,' well you ain't gonna quit."[87] Red's heart episode also got him to stop drinking—temporarily.

Unfortunately, Barber's renunciation of tobacco did not end his 1964 health issues. In late May Barber felt a soreness in his left leg calf that he dismissed as a slight muscle pull. But the pain only got worse. When Red consulted his doctor, he was told he had phlebitis, caused by a blood clot in his leg. One morning at about four o'clock, Barber woke up with a fierce chest pain. "Boy I thought I was a goner," Barber later confessed. After an ambulance ride to the hospital, Barber found out that the clot in his leg had broken away and moved to his lung. During his three weeks in Doctors Hospital in Manhattan, two more clot pieces swam to his lungs, which his doctors described as a close call. Barber had to stay off the leg, treat it with a hot pack, and take blood thinners. Because the Yankees were on the road two of the three weeks, he missed only a week's broadcasts. Red worked to recover his strength during the summer, and in late September volunteered to replace Rizzuto for some road games. In Cleveland he challenged himself to work doubleheaders two days in a row; he wanted to show beyond a doubt that he was fully recovered, "a pretty positive, tactical, public exposition that I was back in health."[88] The Yankees won all four games, part of an eleven-game winning streak that helped carry them to the 1964 American League pennant.

During his final Yankees years, Barber's health was not the only source of change and challenge. In 1962 Lylah and he moved back to New York City. Sarah was working as an elementary school teacher in Harlem now and living in Greenwich Village. They no longer needed a Hudson River estate. Red's busy schedule kept him in the city most days, and Lylah wanted to get back to Manhattan after fifteen years in the suburbs. They struggled to find a buyer for the dream home they had struggled to build in 1951. When the sale finally came, Lylah and Red had only a few weeks to find their new home in the city and dispose of a sizable chunk of their possessions.

Lylah found a two-bedroom, two bath, end-of-the-hall apartment in a new building at 420 East Fifty-First Street. From the second bedroom they could see the United Nations building. The new apartment suffered by comparison to the spacious thirteen-room, five-bath residence across from the Metropolitan Museum of Art they had enjoyed the last time they lived in Manhattan. They were forced to make quick decisions about what to discard, sell, and store from a lifetime of family treasures. They even had to downsize their pets: two cats came to the city apartment, but their dachshund and poodle, Lylah's constant companions, moved to new homes in the country. Except for the limited space, the new unit seemed fine until they moved in. The building was poorly soundproofed; they were treated to a regular symphony of bathroom sounds from their neighbors above and below. Still, Lylah enjoyed easy access to the city's cultural life once again, and her Scarborough friends would sometimes join her for afternoons in Manhattan. Red, however, resented the small apartment and the noisy neighbors. Both the state of his health and the satisfactions of hearth and home seemed in decline.[89]

In 1963, before his heart fibrillation and blood clot scares, Barber's ego, not his body, suffered a painful blow. Ballantine wanted to add a fourth announcer to the Yankees' crew: another former player—Jerry Coleman, a Yankees infielder from 1949 to 1957. Ballantine's advertising manager told Barber that Coleman's salary would come from a reduction in the Old Redhead's Yankees pay. Ballantine wanted Barber to renegotiate his contract, accepting a $15,000 a year pay cut for extending his contract an additional year. "It was ice water when he handed that to me," Barber protested, and he flatly refused: "I have a contract for this year to be paid, and I'm going to be paid every cent of it." Ballantine's advertising manager "was mad, but I was madder."[90] It also was a clear signal to Barber that he was on shaky ground at "the Stadium."

Ballantine hired Jerry Coleman for the 1963 season but not at Red Barber's expense. Coleman did only road games his first season, but he became a full-fledged member of the broadcasting team in 1964, alternating among Red, Mel, and the Scooter. Despite Coleman's background as a player, his relationship with Barber was comfortable: Red held his welcome role as teacher, and Coleman was his willing student. In his autobiography Coleman wrote, "Red took me under his wing and he taught me things that I've used to this day." Barber told "Jayee," his Southernization of "Jerry," "Don't eat anything mushy or creamy or sugary before the game. It'll make it hard to talk." Mushy food aside, Red's more important lesson was that what a broadcaster said, he couldn't unsay: "Make sure, Jayee, that you know something is right when you say it. There's no guessing in this game—you got to be right." Coleman accepted his place in the booth's pecking order: "As for our interactions on the air, Red told me, 'You can talk when I ask you a question.' My response was, 'Okay, Red, whatever you say.'" Coleman respected Barber as "a stubborn guy, but a brilliant broadcaster." "Jayee" "never thought Red had a broadcaster's voice," but he believed the Old Redhead "was far superior to any of them intelligence-wise."[91] In 2005 Coleman would win the Ford C. Frick Award, joining Vin Scully as the second Barber protégé to enter the announcer's wing of the Baseball Hall of Fame.

Ballantine's plan to hire Coleman at Red's expense was still on Barber's mind when Yankees president Dan Topping and general manager Ralph Houk called him in for a meeting late in September 1964. Barber's contract was up. He was prepared for the worst; after his pushback in 1963, Ballantine might not want the Yankees to renew his contract. His last days at "the Stadium," where he never felt at home, might have arrived. Indeed, the axe fell, but not on the Old Redhead. Instead the "Voice of the Yankees" was silenced.

13

Breakfast in Manhattan

The sacking of Mel Allen never made sense to Yankees fans. When the team did not renew his contract at the end of the 1964 season, the Yankees were on their way to another pennant. The team was aging but still intact, primarily because in the era before free agency their stars had nowhere else to go. Most businesses and most baseball teams do not mess with success; Mel Allen had been the voice of success for a quarter century. There were complaints that Allen was becoming too long-winded. Some writers claimed that he just talked too much, especially when he invaded the press box. *New York Times* reporter John Drebinger would sometimes publicly turn down his hearing aid during one of Allen's monologues in the Yankees' press box and, banging on his device, announce to his peers, "All I ever get on here is Mel Allen." In retired *New York Times* writer George Vecsey's version of the story, Drebinger demonstrably pulled out his earpieces, telling the group: "Oops, here comes that f—king Allen again." These press box jabs were most likely good-natured teasing, one media brother to another. According to Len Faupel, Ballantine Beer's advertising manager, Mel Allen's chattering did not turn off beer downers. Company surveys showed that "beer drinkers loved Mel and his down-home delivery. . . . From a marketing perspective, he was one of the best in the business."[1]

"How About That!"

While Allen may have satisfied beer drinkers, those holding power over him were growing more distant. Among Yankees personnel, other than players, Allen was the highest profile link to the Weiss-Stengel Yankees and a regular storyteller of the golden age. But the Yankees' leadership was changing; Dan Topping and Del Webb decided to sell the franchise. First, to make the team more attractive, they cut expenses by firing some of their most highly paid staff, George Weiss and Casey Stengel among them. Then to save themselves some money, they reduced the funds available to sign players for development. By August 1964 they had a buyer when CBS purchased controlling interest in the Yankees. Topping and Webb each kept 10 percent of the club, with Topping remaining president through 1966. After three successive pennants, Ralph Houk moved from manager to general manager in 1964, and Yogi Berra became manager. For two years Topping and Houk ran the team for CBS until the network took complete control in 1966, buying out Topping's and Webb's remaining shares.

It was Topping and Houk who were most concerned about Mel Allen's verbosity. According to Allen's biographer, Stephen Borelli, "The charges that Mel was too chatty mostly trickled in from what Faupel calls the 'country club' crowd." Houk, who was around Allen much more than Topping, grew especially weary of the Allen blather. Marty Appel, who later became executive producer of the Yankees' telecasts, opined that it was just "Mel fatigue" that led to the nonrenewal: "When you hang around so long, people get tired of you, and they cross the street when they see you coming; I think Mel had just worn out his welcome."[2]

Allen's firing played out over parts of three months, September–November 1964. On September 21, Allen went to what he believed would be a routine contract renewal meeting with Topping and Houk. But when he saw Topping lighting repeated cigarettes,

Mel wondered why he was so nervous. He soon found out. The Yankees' brass dropped the bomb: the team would not renew his contract. Topping told the Voice of the Yankees, now "silent and stunned," that "the decision wasn't based on anything he did."[3] But at a meeting later that same day, Topping told Red Barber, "I had Mel in here this morning and told him he is through . . . that I was tired of his popping off," although it was not clear whether the "popping off" occurred during broadcasts.[4] The parties agreed to keep the decision in house until after the season. When the Yankees clinched the pennant, Allen assumed he would still represent the team at the World Series, as he had every time that they had played in it during his career. But the second shoe dropped on Allen when Topping gave NBC's World Series assignment to Phil Rizzuto. Despite his seniority in the Yankees' booth, Red Barber apparently was not considered as Allen's replacement. Allen, however, did not passively accept Topping's decision. He wired Topping, asking him to change his mind, but Topping would not budge. Allen then wired baseball commissioner Ford Frick, requesting he overrule the Yankees' selection, but Frick preferred to honor the team's choice. Perhaps this was no surprise since team owners, not baseball announcers, hired and fired commissioners.

When the press found out that Phil would replace Mel for the World Series, Allen's future with the Yankees became an open topic for discussion. Rumors everywhere speculated that Allen either had been or would be let go. But Allen confirmed the cover story that the Yankees were planning to rotate announcers for the Series.[5] Finally on November 25, the *New York Times* quoted two anonymous sources who said that the Yankees would not renew Allen's contract. The *Times* reported that both Rizzuto and Coleman would return and that negotiations between the Yankees and Red Barber were continuing.[6]

At his September meeting with Topping and Houk, Barber had indicated that he might leave the Yankees for Atlanta after the 1964 season if the Braves moved there from Milwaukee. He was still furious with Ballantine Beer for trying to cut his salary when it hired Jerry Coleman. He fumed: "I got this thing down inside me from [Ballantine] which bothered me a lot more than that fibrillation or the phlebitis. That's where the focus of infection was."[7] When Topping told Red that Allen's days with the Bronx Bombers were over, the Old Redhead's emotions were mixed. Allen had been his respected professional partner for thirteen years. Barber also knew that the job was everything to Mel Allen: "His job was his life . . . the wife and children he never had. It was that much to the man."[8] But the position of lead Yankees broadcaster was now open.

Although he never openly complained, Barber likely missed being in charge, as he had been in the Brooklyn broadcasting booth and at CBS Sports. He told Topping and Houk, "I can smooth out the announcing booth if I am given the authority to do it." Red wanted to "order Rizzuto to go into the dugouts and do his preparation," but even more ardently, he wanted "to find a young announcer, who [was] eager, willing to listen"—the next Vin Scully. He might be able to enjoy once more the professional control that had been slipping from the locomotive engineer's son's hands for a decade. Barber told Topping and Houk that he could get a list of potential Allen replacements from Gordon Bridge at Armed Forces Radio and Television Service (AFRTS); Bridge knew every sports announcer in the country. Topping told him to wait until after the World Series. Barber and Topping quickly agreed on a new salary, including a raise and a stipulation that Red would now travel with the team for at least half of the road games. They shook hands on a new two-year deal.[9] The opportunity for the fifty-six-year-old announcer to revive some of his broadcasting glory days seemed within his grasp.

It did not take long for Barber to discover that Topping and Houk were only entertaining possibilities for the Old Redhead. A few weeks after the September meeting, Topping sent word to Barber that the Yankees were changing how they managed their announcers. They had created a new position for a supervisor who would manage their radio and TV rights and oversee their broadcasts. That new supervisor was Perry Smith, former assistant sports director at NBC, who was available because NBC had lost its *Game of the Week* contract to ABC for the 1965 season. Barber's hope of controlling the broadcast booth was dashed. Also, NBC's most popular baseball announcer, Joe Garagiola, wanted to continue covering baseball. A week after the Yankees hired Smith, Barber learned at a Toots Shor's Restaurant gathering that Garagiola was his new broadcasting teammate. This new teammate was the antithesis of the Vin Scully clone Barber wanted to mentor.

By 1964 Joe Garagiola was as well known and more popular nationally than Red Barber. And he was clearly his own man. Garagiola started broadcasting St. Louis Cardinals games in 1955 and held his own working alongside one of the game's strongest personalities, Harry Caray. In 1960 he published *Baseball Is a Funny Game*, a best-selling, self-deprecating look at the game drawn from his years as a Major League catcher. The book's success brought Garagiola national attention and then national exposure when NBC hired him for its *Game of the Week* in 1961. Garagiola had the insider knowledge that many ex-players, particularly catchers, brought to the broadcast booth. But he was also a skilled raconteur, adding large doses of entertainment to his baseball acumen. At one of the first 1965 spring training games, Garagiola watched Mickey Mantle hit a long home run that landed far into the adjacent baseball field, and he told his listeners, "They ought to score that hit two ways, a home run on this field and a double on the other one."[10] *Fort Lauderdale News* columnist Bill Bondurant was impressed: "Maybe Garagiola doesn't do it with the finesse of Red Barber, whose soft and southern tones slide smoothly into the ear. . . . Garagiola is another combination. Mostly baseball player, even though he is retired, and a student of broadcasting."[11]

When the Yankees hired Garagiola, he had just worked the World Series with Mel Allen's replacement, Phil Rizzuto. While most viewers probably enjoyed Garagiola's knowledgeable and witty patter, some heard an ex-ballplayer with too much to say. When Barber covered the World Series for the AFRTS, as he had since 1954, Barber's and his partner's job was to offer summary and comment before and after the contest and during the commercial breaks, as AFRTS did not carry the messages of commercial sponsors. During the game Red and his AFRTS colleagues would listen to the Series voices. For the 1964 Series, Garagiola's frequent interruptions of his colleague, Phil Rizzuto, disturbed Barber, who groused: "It was difficult for him to let his associate broadcaster finish a sentence without Joe just cutting in on him. Apparently, Garagiola felt whatever he had to say was so much more interesting and colorful and funny. . . . I would say he demonstrated a public lack of concern for his colleague."[12] AFRTS producer Gordon Bridge and Barber's broadcast partner Jerry Coleman concurred. Bridge reported that Garagiola had a reputation for cutting in: "Joe does it all the time to everybody he works with. . . . [He] had trouble with Harry Caray in St. Louis about it. . . . Caray stopped him. . . . They don't like each other."[13] But would Garagiola interrupt the nation's most senior baseball voice? Barber found out in Boston early in their first season together.

At a Yankees–Red Sox game, Barber and Garagiola were teamed. In *The Broadcasters* Red tells the tale: "Joe was consistent. For the first time in my life, I sit in a booth with a fella, and he cuts in on me. I can't finish what I'm saying." The next morning Barber showed Garagiola a few notes on the upper left-hand corner of his scorebook for stories he had wanted to work into the preceding day's broadcast. He had finished none of them because Joe had cut him off each time. "You are not to cut in on me," Red insisted, instructing his broadcasting partner to hold up his hand he if needed to say something while Barber—the proverbial schoolteacher—was verbally engaged. "When I get around to it, if I feel like it, I will bring you on."[14] Garagiola was not happy with the dressing down, but Barber's demand considerably reduced Joe's interruptions.

New Home in Key Biscayne

The hiring of Perry Smith and then Joe Garagiola alerted Barber that his future with the Yankees was far from certain. At the same time, Red wanted out of the noisy, cramped East Fifty-First Street apartment where he and Lylah now lived. One morning in early 1965 he asked Lylah, "Where do you have the most friends?" She answered, "Miami, I suppose," sensing the question was not just academic. Red and Lylah had a special connection to the Miami area, where they frequently had stayed when Barber covered the Orange Bowl games, and now, when they went nearby to Fort Lauderdale for spring training. Red concluded, "Good, let's look for a house to buy when we are there this spring."[15] While Red never admitted the plan was related to his shaky standing with the Yankees, he had to know that his time in New York might be limited to his current contract. Perhaps a new start in a new market would revitalize his career.

When Lylah went house hunting in Miami during spring training, her agent persuaded the Barbers to look in Key Biscayne, a nearby community that they had dismissed as too touristy. They bought a functional but bland house there with a fine view of Biscayne Bay and Smuggler's Cove and hired an architect to add some "finesse." Much impressed by the home designs they saw during their USO visit to Japan, the Barbers challenged their architect to turn a pedestrian three-bedroom, three-bath structure into an American version of a Japanese farmhouse, complete with a replica of the veranda in a Kyoto temple.[16] They had found their new home, but what was Red to do in the off-seasons in Florida?

After the 1965 season, Barber parleyed his Gotham fame into television work in Miami, home to thousands of retired New Yorkers with fond memories of the Old Redhead. He signed on with WTVJ-TV for four weekend sports reports as part of *News Weekend*, the station's aggressive move into prime-time news.[17] Barber was a big-name star who would help the station establish a beachhead against prime-time programs on NBC and ABC. Handling interviews on *News Weekend* was a young Miami broadcaster who would become much richer and more famous: Larry King. But at the time King was just a local reporter on a new show. When his boyhood idol, Red Barber, introduced him after covering the sports news, King was in awe. He recalled the moment in his introduction to the 1985 re-issue of Barber's *The Broadcasters*: "As Red neared the end of his segment, my hands clenched the embroidery of the seat cover on my couch. Then he turned to his monitor and said, 'Now, here's Larry King.' Tingles shot up my spine. I will carry that memory as long as I live." King also noted that Barber helped launch a successful franchise; *News Weekend* was the most popular program in each of its four time slots for six years running.[18]

King also did interviews for Miami radio station WIOD. Just before Red began his work at WTVJ, King featured his sportscasting hero in an extensive interview that touched upon some issues on Barber's radar. They covered Red's personal history, his time at WRUF and WLW, his years in Brooklyn, and his transition to the Yankees. When asked about Jackie Robinson's coming to the Dodgers and the fateful 1947 season, Barber prophetically told King that he "could write a whole book on that year."[19] King also inquired about Barber's religious work. When asked if religion was in decline, Red argued it was not because humans wanted "the answers to three basic questions: where did I come from? what am I doing in this life? and when this life is finished, then where do I go? And I know of no place where you can begin to get those answers except in religion."

King asked if Red's daughter Sarah was married, and Red replied that she "is married very much to a job that is quite demanding and her mother and I are very proud of her." She was teaching second grade in the heart of Harlem, which she saw as her "Peace Corps." Red proudly added, "I think that it requires, for this country to get straightened out, more people of genuine, practically implemented good will doing the work that our child is doing." King asked if Red worried for her safety. Barber said he was not unduly worried, asking, "Where on the face of this earth is any human being safe?"

King and Barber ended their conversation discussing whether Leo Durocher would return to managing—as he soon did for the Chicago Cubs. King told Barber that he thought Durocher belonged in baseball. Barber, however, challenged him on the point. "Larry, I may say something very bitter. There is no such thing [as "belonging"] in this world populated by human beings. . . . They *don't* need any of us tomorrow." Shortly after the King interview, the Yankees renewed the contracts for Barber and the other Yankees announcers for the 1966 season.[20] Nonetheless, Barber's uncertainty about his future with the club may have been on display for Miami radio listeners in his interview with King. Barber continued alongside King on *News Weekend* through the winter and early spring of 1966, leaving WTVJ after a spring training special to resume his work with the Yankees. Red never returned to the show.

A Chapel for Ballplayers

Barber was returning to a Yankees team in steep decline. The 1965 club had finished sixth in a ten-team league. Now its aging core was a year older, and the team had few promising rookies or prospects. The 1966 Yankees looked like a team in need of prayer and divine intervention. During spring training Barber and Bobby Richardson, the much-respected Yankees second baseman, began thinking about the team's spiritual needs.

Barber regretted that Protestant players could not attend Sunday church services when they were on the road. Catholic players could go to early mass, but most Protestant services took place as the players were departing for the ballpark. Barber, an Episcopal lay reader, and Richardson, a devout Baptist who had done some preaching as well, felt that they could develop a half-hour, nondenominational Christian service that would give Yankees players an opportunity to worship while away from home. As they deliberated the idea, both men knew that religion was rarely a topic for clubhouse discussion. Barber observed that "ballplayers talk about everything under the sun—sex, politics, news of the day, baseball, golf, horses, travel, taxes, family life," but debates over deeply held and differing religious beliefs were off limits.[21] Ever respectful of the manager's role in controlling the team, Barber knew they needed manager Johnny Keane's acceptance of their plan if they were to proceed. But they did not give Keane much time to decide. They approached him in his office the Friday before they hoped to hold their first Sunday morning service.

Keane, a committed Catholic, ruminated a bit and then opined, "This will be a good thing for the ball club—the way I know you and Bobby will run it—good for the players individually, good for the team as a whole." But Keane added that he, as a representative of the Yankees' management, should not come to any meetings. There also could be no public announcements or postings of the meetings on the team's bulletin board or on the team's traveling itinerary. Players were to find out about the meetings by word of mouth. It must be clear it was not a team-sponsored event and "[it] must stay strictly outside the clubhouse."

Barber and Richardson's first service was at a Baltimore hotel; it was an informal setting with no lectern. Barber removed the ashtrays to prevent any smoking; he believed the service should not be too casual. Sixteen men—fourteen players, one coach, and Barber—attended the first service. Barber was especially pleased when Mickey Mantle arrived just before they started: "When I saw Mickey, the Big Guy on the club, come in the room quietly and take a chair, I knew this was serious business."[22] Mantle continued to attend the services as long as they didn't interfere with his notoriously active night life. In a 1968 article celebrating his extraordinary career, *The Sporting News* reported Mantle's reaction on the team bus one Saturday evening when it became clear that the prayer meeting would need to be earlier on Sunday morning because of a doubleheader that day. He told his teammates, "It's going to be a short night if we get up that early. . . . I suggest we have our meeting right now, so let's all sing." The Yankees icon then "launched into a revivalist hymn and soon had the others singing with him."[23]

In 1966 the players' "church" held services on eleven road game Sundays, with Barber conducting the meeting nine times.[24] Red wrote that reporters were invited to the service, but none attended. While he could not prevent reporters from writing about what was a potentially interesting story, he told Yankees public relations head Bob Fishel to convey to them that the gatherings were personal, and "We would just as soon be left alone, without publicity, to hold our meetings." His friends in the press got the message. According to Barber, during the 1966 season, "Not one word was ever written about those meetings . . . not one word."[25] Richardson says that Barber's idea helped to launch what became "Baseball Chapel": "You can't really see it. No actual physical chapels exist, but today nearly every team throughout the major and minor leagues, both at home and on the road, holds Baseball Chapel on Sunday mornings before batting practice."[26] Whenever he thinks of those Sunday services, Richardson says, "It reminds me of Red Barber, a great man with a great idea and great faith."[27]

"Oh, Yes, There Were Bells Going Off"

After his initial concerns about the hiring of Perry Smith and Joe Garagiola, Barber adjusted to the new reality. While he continued to criticize Rizzuto's lack of preparation, he reached an accommodation with Garagiola.[28] Because Coleman always showed Barber appropriate respect, the two worked well together. Barber's relationship with his new boss, Perry Smith, was another matter. Initially, Barber found Smith to be "scrupulously fair" in assigning the broadcasters. While Barber was not called the "principal broadcaster," a privilege Mel Allen had insisted upon in his contract, he saw himself as senior "because [he was] a professional broadcaster."[29] But the supervisor of the broadcasting crew seemed interested in putting Barber in his place. In the middle of the 1965 season in the Yankees' pressroom, Smith broke one of Barber's unwritten rules: he *publicly* criticized him.

Barber recognized that discouraged fans were tuning out because the team was floundering, and he worked hard to cull interesting material to enrich his broadcasts. When he got back from a mid-season road trip, Barber said, "[I] was in a glow, feeling I had done a pretty good two weeks' work for a club that needed it." In Barber's account of the "public dressing down," he was sitting in the pressroom with a few members of the WPIX-TV crew when Smith came in and joined the group. He told Barber—and everyone in earshot—"Red, you really are talking too much out there on this trip. Dan's getting letters saying you talk too much. A sportswriter up in Buffalo . . . called me and complained that you're talking too much." Furious, Barber got up and walked away. When he saw Houk on the stairs, he complained to him about the "impropriety of Smith's remarks in front of strangers." In response, Houk profanely berated Barber for bothering him with a triviality when his ball club was in a downward spiral.[30] Smith's public complaint and Houk's dismissive response were a sharp blow to the pride of a broadcaster who still viewed himself as the best play-by-play man in the game. His Yankees bosses seemed to regard him as just another employee.

The Yankees' rapid decline meant changes were coming. The first upheaval was the firing of manager Johnny Keane in early May 1966, with Ralph Houk assuming that role once again. Topping's son, Dan Jr., became the interim general manager. But the team continued to play poorly. By the middle of the season Dan Topping's dissatisfaction spread to the broadcast booth. He sent a copy of a memo to Barber, Garagiola, Rizzuto, and Coleman that he had originally sent to Perry Smith:

> We have, by far, the best broadcasting crew in baseball. However, of late all four have been horrible. I would just as soon you relayed this message to them. I realize it was a mighty tough job during our losing streak to give an interesting broadcast, but certainly the way the club has been doing recently there is no excuse for all the talk about everything but reporting the game. It has gotten so bad that I am tired of having to answer all the letters of complaint and trying to find excuses.[31]

Topping added that he was not singling out any one broadcaster but was reminding all of them of their obligation to focus on the game.[32] He also had a habit of dropping notes to broadcasters with complaints and suggestions, as did Yankees PR man Bob Fishel.[33] Barber likely felt his extra work unearthing interesting stories to cover for the on-field doldrums of a last-place team was being criticized as part of the "everything but reporting the game" that Topping was slamming.

Perhaps the clearest sign that Barber was in trouble was a *Radio Daily* piece reporting that the Yankees planned to shake up their booth by firing one or two broadcasters at the end of the season. Barber figured he might be the one to go: "Topping is a fellow who seems to sour on people when he gets ready to. He soured on Mel, didn't he? And I had been there longer than the others." The Yankees also paid him more than $50,000 a year at a time when the average player salary was about $19,000. He heard nothing personally–only "silence from Olympus"–but he was aware of rumors that "Topping was like a wild man" because of the team's collapse.[34]

Barber still believed he might survive an announcer purge if he was not fired before CBS took full control of the club. Red was well respected for his time as a CBS executive and sportscaster and still had many friends at the network. However, one CBS friend warned him not to turn his back on Topping's replacement, Michael Burke, who had "the fastest knife on or off the CBS television screen."[35] But Red's July 1966 meeting with Burke at the Lambs Club produced no red flags. Barber remembers that they barely talked about the team but "just sort of looked each other over."[36] When Michael Burke assumed control of the club in September, Barber wrote him a welcome greeting, as he had for Rickey and then O'Malley when they had assumed control of the Dodgers. On September 20, 1966, Burke briefly replied on his personal stationery: "Dear Red, Thanks very much for your most thoughtful note. I appreciate it greatly. Sincerely, Mike."[37]

Perhaps Barber's greeting to his new boss was triggered by stories that had appeared in the press days earlier suggesting that the Yankees might fire both him and his protégé Jerry Coleman. One columnist speculated that Barber, with his home now in Key Biscayne, would become the voice of the Dolphins, the new Miami franchise in the AFL.[38] Soon after, when Red was away on a road trip, *Boston Traveler* columnist Cliff Sundberg fanned rumors that there was an open conflict in the Yankees' booth: "Don't invite Jerry Coleman and Red Barber to a party with Joe Garagiola and Phil Rizzuto. The Yankees' broadcasters have been feuding, and word is that Coleman and Barber are out."[39]

When Barber got back to New York, he confronted Perry Smith about the Sundberg story. Smith clarified that the powers that be were reviewing the makeup of the Yankees' announcing team for 1967. He informed Barber about a meeting at CBS that included Topping, Burke, CBS president Frank Stanton, and William Paley. They asked Smith if he could get along with three announcers next year. Smith told them, "If I have to, I can get along with two." On September 17 a *New York World Journal Tribune* columnist reported that while it first appeared the Yankees would not change their broadcasters, the situation had reversed, and "Red Barber is out for next year."[40] With rumors mounting, the announcing team got a very tepid endorsement when Burke told the *New York Times* news service, "At the moment, I don't have any plan to make changes in the broadcasting staff. The question is premature. I haven't dealt with the matter in any serious way."[41] In fact, the decision about Barber's future with the Yankees had already been made, probably at the meeting between the CBS and Yankees' brass that Smith had described to Barber.

Dropping the Black Spot

The firing of Walter Lanier Barber by Edmund Michael Burke on September 26, 1966, has been viewed as a turning point in the history of sports reporting in the United States. While Barber's stature with his bosses was in decline, his standing as one of the greatest baseball broadcasters was well established, especially with the New York press. Burke was an accomplished executive with a background as a decorated naval officer, OSS and CIA agent, and general manager of the Ringling Bros. and Barnum & Bailey Circus. The team that Burke was about to control had reached its nadir. Burke and CBS, a diversified corporation with no experience running a baseball team, would somehow have to lead it back to the pennant-draped promised land its fans thought was theirs for eternity. Barber's firing would become, variously, a symbol of the triumph of entertainment over information, shilling over honest reporting, the corporation over the individual, and the moldable future over the calcified past.

When Barber provided Robert Creamer with his account of the morning meeting in which Michael Burke, who had been president of the New York Yankees for only a few days, "dropped the black spot" on him, his memory of the event was still painfully fresh.[42] In Barber's telling, he had convinced himself by the time of that morning meeting, despite signs to the contrary, that the departure of Dan Topping—a move that left CBS in full control of the Yankees—would not only save his job, but would also give him an opportunity to help rebuild the historically rich franchise. Drawing from the Larry MacPhail playbook for turning around baseball clubs, Barber put together, in his mind, a list of suggestions he would share with the new Yankees president.

First, he would recommend painting the stadium outside and in. The Yankees were "stuck" with an aging ballpark, but so had MacPhail been in Cincinnati and Brooklyn. Painting made the old look a lot newer. He would advise Burke to remove the advertising on the outfield fences and paint them "a nice restful green." Fans would see that some class was returning to the Yankees and that CBS, a rich corporation, didn't need to squeeze for every dollar. Then he would move the "three tombstones" in center field: the granite slab monuments honoring Babe Ruth, Lou Gehrig, and Miller Huggins. Barber felt a last-place team did not need three symbols of death in plain view. He would also make the bullpens more visible by fencing off some of the stadium's vast center field and placing bullpens behind it. He would revitalize the Ladies' Day promotion: "Every lady would get a little Hawaiian orchid as she came into the park, or a carnation." The Yankees also should remove the chains around the club president's box seats. Like fan-friendly Bill Veeck, the Yankees' president should mix with his paying customers. Changing the Yankees' cold corporate image would help to keep fans coming even as the team rebuilt.

With his ducks all in a row, Barber felt prepared for his meeting with Michael Burke, scheduled for September 26, 1966, at Barber's suite at the New York Hilton, which he had been renting for the 1966 season. He was eager to play host for his new boss. Instead of breakfast from room service, Red would prepare coffee and offer Burke casaba melon and English muffins with butter and orange marmalade. When Burke arrived, he would serve the light breakfast on "lovely blue-and-white china" with stainless steel tableware from a Japanese shop on Fifth Avenue. Barber even borrowed linen napkins from one of the hotel's restaurants. The two Yankees colleagues, old and new, could discuss the future of the team as they enjoyed Barber's view of Central Park. Like the white linen suit and new shoes Red had brought to his interview at WLW in 1934, Red Barber was rolling out his finest for a new boss. But Burke would not play his part in Barber's breakfast show.

At about ten thirty on Sunday evening, Perry Smith called Barber to tell him that Monday morning's plans had changed. Barber would join Burke for breakfast at the Edwardian Room at the Plaza Hotel. Red knew the change meant something. First, it meant that Perry Smith knew about the meeting. It also meant something that Smith rather than Burke had called about the location change. As he gathered his coat and hat to leave for the 8:30 a.m. meeting, Barber happened on a copy of *Best Sport Stories of 1966*; Red was honored to serve as one of the three judges for the stories selected for the volume, which he hoped would be a gracious gift for Burke's son. When he got to the Edwardian Room, Burke was waiting for him. Red gave him the book and recommended several of his favorite stories in the anthology. After some small talk, Burke introduced the topic of broadcasting philosophy, a subject Barber had written and talked about throughout his career. Barber launched into how his approach to calling games was like Bill Klem's approach to umpiring them: just report what you see, not what you or the fans might want to see. Burke cut him off, alerting Red: "There's no reason for us to be talking about these things. What I have to say is not very pleasant. We have decided not to seek to renew your contract."

Given Mel Allen's dismissal in 1964, all that had unfolded during the summer of 1966, and the last-minute change of venue for the meeting with Burke, Barber could not have been surprised. But he was deeply disappointed and would become more disturbed in the weeks that followed. After Burke's announcement, Barber asked him why his contract was not being renewed. Burke told Barber, "There has been a growing feeling that you were getting disinterested—bitter. No, bitter is not the word." Burke revealed that the decision had been made "some time ago" and that Topping had wanted to drop Red after the 1965 season, but CBS officials had changed his mind. He clarified the timeline: the decision had come down two weeks ago. He explained, "Topping was supposed to have told you, but he didn't. So, I am telling you." Barber acknowledged that relaying the decision could not be a pleasant task but then offered a rebuttal to Burke's claim: "I have not been disinterested. These past two years, broadcasting for a ball club that was crumbling on the field and off, I regard as the best two years of work I ever did.... I have never been more interested in broadcasting in my life." Barber then told him, "You have made a mistake. You have fired the wrong broadcaster." When Burke asked him whom he should fire, Barber told him but never publicly revealed his choice.

Burke expressed concern about rumors that the Old Redhead planned to "rip everybody to shreds" in his last broadcasts—three road games with the Washington Senators. Barber acknowledged that he occasionally had joked about how his last day broadcasting would liberate him "to talk about a ball club and its ballplayers—dames, debts, dumbness, drunkenness—that you don't talk about." But he insisted he would never seriously consider "throwing the least bit of discolor" on his thirty-three-year career by doing so. He vowed, "I'm a professional broadcaster, and I'll broadcast these three games in Washington the way I'd broadcast any other three games in Washington."

While Barber has offered the most detailed account of his breakfast with Burke, sportswriter Jack Mann interviewed both Barber and Burke within a year of the event for his 1967 book on the decline of the Yankees. Burke's version of the story included two significant additions. First, Burke told Mann, "I made the decision. I inherited it, but I agreed with it. I even sat in on the discussions." While Barber was "probably the best ever" at broadcasting baseball, Burke continued: "I believe that for every man there is a time to come and a time to go. In my opinion, it was Red's time to go." Burke also said that Barber told him at their breakfast that he "expected to be made captain of the broadcasting team," correcting a mistake he thought the Yankees had made after Mel Allen was fired. When Mann told Barber that "there was a story that Red had demanded that he, as senior man, be made captain of the broadcast team" with the right to fire one of his colleagues, Barber jumped on him: "Anyone who told you that story is a liar. There was no friction with any of the other broadcasters, as far as I know, and none with anybody in the organization, until Burke gave me the black spot."[43] The source of the disparity in these two accounts might have been the word "demanded." Barber admitted telling Burke he would fire one of the other broadcasters rather than himself. His pre-breakfast ruminations on the future of the Yankees also included a leadership role for himself in their renaissance. But he had never, in his mind, "demanded" anything.

Burke did not want to engage in a back-and-forth with Barber over what was said at the breakfast, but newspaper and public criticism of his firing Red Barber clearly bothered him. When distinguished baseball historian Lawrence Ritter reviewed Burke's 1984 autobiography, *Outrageous Good Fortune*, he ended his positive review by noting that Burke did not include any mention of Red Barber's dismissal: "We never learn whether Mr. Burke has ever had second thoughts about the firing. . . . It would have been nice if he had admitted his misjudgment and offered a belated apology to Mr. Barber and New York's baseball fans."[44] Burke contacted Ritter and complained about his mentioning the Barber firing in his review but soon felt remorse about doing so. In a letter to Ritter written on Hotel Algonquin letterhead, Burke lamented: "We Irish are forever striding through the fairground dragging our capes behind us. Forgive my bad manners, protesting about Red Barber. I should not have let that distress me. Rather, I should have thanked you very much for your generous review in *The Sunday Times*."[45]

Over fifty years after the day the black spot dropped, retired *New York Times* columnist George Vecsey found it uncanny that a single meeting over breakfast in Manhattan would link Red Barber and Michael Burke, two men he deeply respected. "For Burke to fire Red Barber is one of the great contradictions," Vecsey thought. "[Burke] didn't like to be identified with that; he had to fire Red Barber, and he knew that was never going to look good on his resume."[46] Burke even sent a conciliatory telegram to Barber while he waited to cover his last games in Washington, games that ultimately were rained out. Burke told Barber, "YOU ARE A MAN, MAY THE WIND BE ALWAYS AT YOUR BACK."[47]

Controlling the Story

After his meeting with Burke, Barber went to his physician for a scheduled checkup and learned that his blood pressure was normal, despite his dramatic breakfast. He and his agent, Bill McCaffrey, then moved to shape the narrative of his firing. Barber called the *World Journal Tribune*'s Jack O'Brian, a firm supporter of Barber's over the years, and gave him his version of the story. He told O'Brian, "I feel completely free." Barber was proud of his work with the Yankees, but if they did not want him, he "did not wish to be there. You only work for willing buyers." Red noted he was a year younger than Casey Stengel had been when he began managing the Yankees and won ten pennants in twelve years. He said he wired Stengel: "I stayed up there one year longer than you did, dear Casey." Minus the Stengel references, Red repeated the story to the *New York Times*. He gave the *Daily News* the exact time of his axing wrapped in Ecclesiastes: "There is a time to come and a time to go. My time came at 8:40 a.m." The *New York Post* reported that the Yankees had begun their rebuilding program "by firing the veteran broadcaster." Barber, the paper said, planned to continue broadcasting baseball and quoted him as saying, "That's what I want to do, that's what I love to do."[48]

Barber saved copies of the three dozen newspaper accounts of his firing in a folder titled "1966 Retirement Clippings." The day after his dismissal, the *New York Post* reported Barber was interested in staying in New York and would welcome an opportunity to broadcast for the Mets, working for his old Yankees boss, George Weiss. According to the *Post*, Barber said, "I don't have affection for New York, I love it—L-O-V-E—and I have reason to believe the people here love me."[49] Weiss said that if he had an opening, he would be interested in hiring Red but was satisfied with his current broadcast team of Lindsey Nelson, Ralph Kiner, and Bob Murphy.

The *New York World Journal Tribune* got Casey Stengel's point of view on Barber's termination: "Red's Broadcastin' wasn't the thing put the Yanks in last place. He isn't the reason the team can't find the public anymore, even though the Stadium is open every game."[50] Red particularly appreciated Red Smith's wry take on the firing of Barber as Burke's and CBS's first move in their attempt to turn the team around. Mocking the canning of the broadcaster for poor team play, Smith facetiously suggested that Baltimore's broadcast team, Chuck Thompson and Frank Messer, "took the lead way back last spring and coasted to a pennant," while Vin Scully and his associates deserved some credit for taking the Dodgers to the NL crown but dragged the race out: "If Scully had any class, he'd clinch the championship by Sept. 1." Smith added, in the same vein, "CBS was right to get rid of [Barber], though. He hadn't been winning lately. And a great big corporation can't hold still for a loser, even if he's the best reporter who ever covered baseball on the air."[51]

The press reaction to Barber's forced unemployment must have provided Red some emotional compensation. According to sportswriters, CBS and the tenth-place Yankees had booted baseball's best broadcaster, turning the booth over to three ex-jocks while the only serious reporter was shown the door. Joe Garagiola, who said he was happy to be a "house man," was now the gold standard for baseball announcers.[52] As for Barber, a new team would snap him up, and the Yankees would regret their rebuilding's opening blunder. But it is critical to note that nowhere in the coverage of those first post-breakfast days was there any mention of what eventually would become the "received truth" about why the Yankees fired Red Barber.

On September 22, 1966, Red Barber told his WPIX-TV viewers that there were only 413 paid customers at Yankee Stadium. But that was *not* why he was fired. By then the decision to fire Barber had already been made. The 413 myth seems to have surfaced about two weeks after Barber's dismissal by Burke. In a Sunday, October 9, 1966, *New York Times* article, Jack Gould observed that television does not apply his high standards for news coverage to the reporting of baseball and football games. His first example was Red Barber's struggle to show the empty seats at Yankee Stadium: "During a game between the Chicago White Sox and the Yankees, it struck Mr. Barber as pertinent that there were only 413 paid spectators in the mammoth Yankee Stadium. It was the smallest crowd in the history of the house that Babe Ruth built. But on specific orders of the representative of the Yankees, Mr. Barber said, the cameramen were told not to pan around and show the wide-open spaces that qualified as news in newspapers and on other broadcasting stations."[53] While Gould does not directly connect the incident to Barber's firing, it occurred only four days before the news of Red's termination. *Sports Illustrated* connected the dots, writing the following in its October 10 issue: "In recent days the Yankees played to 413 customers at home, finished 10th and last, and canned Red Barber—which is not wholly a non sequitur." But the magazine quickly added that Barber "was not dismissed just because the Yankees had a lousy season with him at the mike, but because they had one broadcaster too many; because he was at times imperious; and because he had gone out of style."[54] *Newsweek*, however, bolstered the 413 myth with more national coverage when it claimed that Barber's candor in trying to call attention to the empty seats had "upset the lately lowly Yankees."[55]

The story took permanent roots after the *Newsweek* piece was published, becoming one of the enduring Yankees myths. It became a way quickly and dramatically to explain the unexplainable. How could the fast-sinking Yankees throw away one of their remaining assets so callously? Barber's doggedness in telling his viewers, despite clear direction not to, that the real story of the game that day was the historically poor attendance, and that the Yankees had no way to go but up, *must* have been the last straw for his employers. When asked about why he was fired, Barber generally referred to earlier complaints that he was talking too much or Burke's perception that he had lost interest in his broadcasting. In a radio interview the year before his death, Red told Bob Costas, when he repeated the 413 myth, "Some people said that was it. But I think maybe I had just lived my time."[56] When Burke finally opened up about the Barber affair, he laid the blame directly on the Old Redhead and himself: "I fired Barber personally because he was giving us a terrible time in the broadcast booth, squabbling with Rizzuto, going out of his way to embarrass Garagiola on the air and make him look stupid. Moreover, he began to wander, parading his own erudition—his own insecurities—on the air."[57] But Burke's justification for firing Barber rarely saw the light of day. The press portrayed Barber as the heroic victim and his firing as another example of CBS mismanagement, signaling the ascent of public relations over professional responsibility. By the start of the 1966 fall classic that Red Barber had announced thirteen times, his thirty-three-year career as "the best reporter who ever covered baseball on the air" was over. A new career, which paid much less money but afforded more of the control he so valued, awaited him in Key Biscayne.

PART 5

RETURN TO FLORIDA

A Writerly Broadcaster

14

A Developing Writer, A Darker Vision

Barber's transition from sports announcer to writer was neither sudden nor smooth. We know that during his years as a full-time baseball broadcaster, he began to consider authorship a valuable alternative medium for delivering messages he most wanted to communicate. He bristled under the limitations that television imposed upon his conversations with his audiences, and there was no way to avoid television if he wished to remain in sports broadcasting. Also Red was eager to broaden his messages from those of the "reporter" to those of the journalist, the social commentator, the teacher, and the spiritual adviser. His release from the Yankees and his permanent move to Key Biscayne would seem to have provided the perfect "testing grounds" for the fifty-eight-year-old broadcaster who wanted to begin a serious writing career. But there was a weaning process.

Lylah reports in her memoir her satisfaction that "after over three decades of life in Cincinnati and New York, we were home again in Florida." Red was liberated from his tight play-by-play schedule, she adds, "for the first time in our married years." She says her husband was worn down from the tensions he had endured in his later years with the Yankees but asserts that "with the help of our pool, in which he swam at least twice and often three times a day, he soon regained his health."[1] Shortly after Red and Lylah settled into Key Biscayne, a local newspaper article, entitled "The Frustrated Professor," informed readers that Barber wanted to draft his philosophy of objective sports broadcasting into a series of lectures that he would offer as a course for university journalism programs.[2]

However, Red was not yet ready to give up broadcasting altogether, likely due to the force of "economic determinism," as well as his enduring interest in being heard in some regular forum. In early October, just weeks after his breakfast with Michael Burke, ABC snapped up the recently released Barber to broadcast two Los Angeles Dodgers exhibition games in Tokyo, an offer that was just what he needed at the time. Red admitted: "After I was fired, I wasn't the happiest guy in the world. After all, I had never been handed my walking papers before. . . . That was a most wonderful thing ABC did for me—picked me up and turned me around."[3] The following August, ABC asked Barber to return to Japan—a country that first intrigued him on his USO tours to the Far East—to broadcast the Japanese All-Star Game for a taped telecast.

Barber soon secured a radio gig on Miami's WGBS, giving brief sports summaries three times per day from Monday through Friday at 7:10 a.m., 8:10 a.m., and 5:10 p.m. The job did not even require a commute to the station, as he arranged for a radio wire hookup that enabled him to speak from a microphone on the desk of his office in Key Biscayne. His former CBS colleague Walter Cronkite admired Barber's ingenuity in appropriating technology to conduct his radio work at home. In a 1971 letter, Cronkite tells Barber that when CBS installed a broadcast line in his own New York brownstone, he never thought to use it. It has become "a constant reminder of how one ought to work, and now, of Red Barber."[4] Lylah believed that this was the perfect job, enabling Red to avoid a "cold turkey" exit from broadcasting and from "missing too much the intense activity of play-by-play."[5]

In fact, evidence suggests that Red had not given up entirely the prospect of returning to full time play-by-play if he could find "a willing buyer" for his talents. Barber repeatedly mentioned in interviews after his breakfast with Burke that he was expecting opportunities with several teams.[6] He pushed Bill McCaffrey, still his agent and "one of his three closest friends," to find a new spot for him as a team announcer. McCaffrey failed, telling Red in May 1967, "I've been aware for some time past that you have been restive and frustrated in regard to the lack of broadcasting employment . . . and I think I have approached every broadcasting situation where I thought your services could be employed—without too much success, I'm afraid, . . . due to a drastic transition in sports broadcasting." By "a drastic transition," McCaffrey was referring to the development Red himself had been criticizing: the appeal to owners and sponsors of replacing professionals with popular ex-players in the broadcast booth. A disappointed Barber replaced McCaffrey, his longtime agent and friend, with Lester Lewis, an agent much less accommodating to Barber than McCaffrey had been and no more successful in putting Red back behind the baseball mic.[7]

During a taped conversation with Casey Stengel, Barber shared a revealing account of his immediate and subsequent reactions to having been let go by the Yankees. He frankly admitted that even though he now was happy with the way things had turned out, he would not have been able to leave the Yankees' broadcast booth if they had not fired him: "I was not a big enough person to get out of Major League ball. I'd been it in thirty-three years and going to spring training camp just naturally followed the end of the season. I was in a cycle like a monkey or a squirrel going around in a cage. And they paid me $50,000, and I thought it was a big job, and I was smitten with the importance of it." But, Barber observed, "[After] the Yankees quit me, I suddenly found there was another world than baseball all summer long, year after year." Instead of spending the summer "in ten hotels, I was living at home with my wife." He enjoyed being at home more, "going to Japan for ABC, coming . . . to L.A. for a TV commercial," and writing columns and new book proposals. He would fill in at the broadcast booth for ten days if someone got sick, "but my whole life dominated again from March to October, no."[8]

By 1970, when Red had become fully engaged in completing the last two of three books he would publish between 1969 and 1971 while also penning a weekly sports column for the *Miami Herald*, Barber was reported to have turned down a baseball broadcast offer from Jack Buck to do play-by-play for the St. Louis Cardinals, with equal status on the broadcasting team. Barber declined the job with thanks, explaining that he had no interest in returning to announce baseball play-by-play.[9] While he was speaking to Buck on the phone, Lylah was listening. After Red hung up, she told him, "If you had said yes, you would have had to get another wife."[10] A short time later, during a taped interview of New York Giants great Bill Terry, Barber affirmed his satisfaction with his transition to a career as writer and local radio sports reporter: "Bill, you know if you hang around a place long enough you find out they don't need you. . . . Now I've never been happier and I wouldn't change. I'm in my fifth year doing a weekly column for the *Herald*, syndicated. . . . I broadcast fifteen times a week on WGBS, and I've written three books since I've been down here. I've never been as busy and I'm my own boss."[11]

"A Toe-Hold in the Column Business"

In early 1967 Barber connected with some experienced editors who would help sharpen his journalistic skills. The first were John McMullan, Larry Jinks, and Ed Storin of the *Miami Herald*. McMullan was the executive editor who signed up Barber for a weekly column, "The Old Redhead." Jinks was the managing editor, and Storin, the executive sports editor. Jinks taught Red the importance of the opening sentence, while Storin warned him against "detours" that would take him and the reader on a pointless side trip. Storin also made it clear "The Old Redhead" would be edited. Barber was paid the modest fee of $25 for each article and received $200 every three months to cover expenses. For Barber, who was used to receiving $1,000 for a single speaking engagement, the financial reality faced by a rookie columnist was a shock. McMullan apologized "for these piddling amounts, but we both recognize that the really important thing here is to give you a toe-hold in the column business and bring your name before the public in a new role."[12] The relationship would last from 1967 to 1971 and produce approximately 240 columns.

Realizing his limitations as a relatively inexperienced newspaper columnist, Barber accepted the editing of his original copy, even if the cuts were sometimes painful. His *Miami Herald* articles covered all sports but focused on baseball; the exploits of former and current New York–area players received the most ink. In a recorded interview with Paul Richards, then general manager of the Atlanta Braves, Barber explains what his goals are in the column and why it provides such gratification at this point in his life: "I'm trying to write something in the tempo of people's minds but not hinged merely to yesterday's game. . . . Mine is a feature column that goes in depth with personalities and points of view, like you might pick up in a magazine. It's another world for me; like an old pitcher, you hurt your arm and come up with another pitch." The transplanted voice of the Dodgers and later the Yankees would appeal to tens of thousands of transplanted New Yorkers in Miami and south Florida. Initially, Barber's *Miami Herald* columns appeared in the first few pages of the sports section, but as time passed and his broadcasting fame beyond his Miami audience faded, offerings slid further from the front, sometimes appearing after the horse racing, bowling, and fishing news. The Miami columns were syndicated by Columbia Features to a handful of papers, mostly in smaller markets, although some columns were taken by the *New York Knickerbocker*. Columbia features president Robert Pearsall would frequently write to Barber about the company's desire to better market Red's work, but the efforts did not significantly improve circulation. Pearsall also gently urged Barber to remain topical: "Try to keep as close to current events as possible. . . . I am no spring chicken myself, but I am terribly afraid to talk about anything that happened yesterday."[13]

Barber did not always follow Pearsall's advice; he sometimes fondly invoked ghosts of "baseball past" in recalling the skills and character traits of players who must have been unfamiliar "old timers" for some of his current readers. But his strongest pieces among his *Miami Herald* columns were based upon on-site interviews or compelling current events. They remind readers today that Barber was at his best as a writer when he combined perceptive commentary—supported by an admirable system of values— with his gifts as a play-by-play radio reporter who brought a scene to life for listeners who could not see it except through the lens of Barber's keen descriptive powers.

For instance, in one effective piece, Barber combines past, present, and a look toward the future in a column drawing upon an afternoon he shared with Jerry Lucas, then a Cincinnati Royals NBA star. Red begins by evoking James Naismith and his invention of the game of basketball in rural New England, with images of hoops hanging on every barn door and "small agile boys who could duck, dodge and get loose" as they played the new game in sleepy small-town America.[14] Then, awakening the reader with vividly contrasting imagery, Barber slides into the afternoon he recently spent in Harlem talking with and observing Lucas as he interacted with African American children at a YMCA gym on 135th Street. We get a series of facts and images characterizing the game that Lucas plays—the one that Barber's readers recognize.

Lucas explains to Red that players as tall as he "are coming in faster and even taller—we live in a different world. All our clothes and shoes and even our beds have to be made for us." He tells Red that professional basketball rookies first learn how "to hold and push and shove—do all you can get away with, anything to keep your opponent away from the basket." Pro basketball, Red concludes "is a world of flying elbows under the basket," noting that most players eventually end up buying additional sets of teeth. Readers are drawn into the contrast between the ghost of Naismith's pacific rural game and what it has become by 1970, and they assume the Old Redhead is implying some loss of cultural innocence. But gradually we sense the writer's underlying awe for the talents, gifts, determination, and eloquence of Jerry Lucas: "He is a big, strong man who makes a violent living in physical combat with other big, strong men. And he does quite well."

The piece comes to a moving conclusion when Red steps back and watches Lucas play with the young boys on the court at the YMCA in the same neighborhood "that houses Roy Campanella's liquor store and Wilt Chamberlain's restaurant and bar." Lucas had come to the gym to tape a television commercial, working with "seven little boys aged 11 and 12 from the immediate area." As Lucas suits up, the "seven kids, already in their shorts, wait patiently, for in a moment this giant would soon step on the same floor they were standing on." Barber describes Lucas patiently working with the kids all afternoon, taking time to answer their questions and give them tips, so "the TV director was hard put to get Lucas to quit playing with the boys." There was a break for lunch, and "on his way to eat, Lucas stopped in at Campanella's store where Roy was sitting in his wheelchair, . . . You should have seen Campy's face light up." In this piece Red dramatizes his own movement from comfort with an idealized past to an experience of a "different world" and a new energy, suffused with brotherhood and cultivating disciplined values for the future, nurtured with strength and kindness.

One of Barber's most intense *Miami Herald* pieces, written in response to recent events, displays his powerful empathy for Jackie Robinson as he endured the trials of his son's tumultuous life. Published after Barber saw television coverage of Jackie Robinson Jr.'s arrest for drug possession, Red describes the young man being led away by police and then juxtaposes the image he recalls of the toddler, meticulously dressed and just learning to walk, during the Dodgers' spring training twenty years earlier. He looks at the television screen again and sees Jackie Robinson Sr., "grey-haired and heavy faced," answering the relentless questions from reporters, "his head down, with barely the strength to lift it." Barber recalls for his readers scenes of Robinson's strength and courage—episodes that could not make him bow, as this trial had forced him to do. He imagines what Robinson might be thinking during this sad moment. In the list of possibilities, we hear some of Barber's own regrets about being too competitive professionally, too often inaccessible to his family. Even after his baseball career ended, Robinson worked tirelessly as an advocate for change, for charities, and for youth movements. Barber records Robinson's heartbreaking response to a reporter's piercing question, "How will this experience enable you to help other young people?" Jackie raised his head and answered bitterly, "How can I help them when I couldn't help my own son?" Barber concludes the piece by quoting King David's response when Absalom was killed: "Oh my son, would I had died for thee, oh Absalom, my son."[15]

Barber spoke about the column in a taped conversation with Walter O'Malley, with whom he had mended some fences since 1953. On the tape, which focuses upon baseball in Japan, Barber segues off the record to tell O'Malley about the Robinson piece he had just written. His comments suggest the unanticipated intensity and self-discovery that writing has provided, different from the daily gratifications of the broadcast booth. He explains to O'Malley that the Robinson column "was inspired by what I saw on television about the problems with Jackie's boy, and Jackie with his head bowed down. I cried. I did. . . . I went right around to the typewriter—this is another thing about writing. I went to the typewriter and this piece came out of me. It wasn't what I planned to write."[16]

Barber also writes several columns lamenting the "big business" of college athletics, which, he believes, exploits too many players by robbing them of a meaningful education and the genuine opportunities college should provide its students to advance in life. In one of his most effective pieces on this theme, rather than indict the schools that run such programs, he provides a refreshing description of life at a relatively new campus, the University of South Florida, which at that time did not participate in intercollegiate sports but still had a thriving athletics department. Barber interviews the college president, who has worked at schools with "big time" athletics, and also with the "young athletic director." Both describe a healthy program of intramural golf, tennis, soccer, swimming, cross-country, and baseball. The public is welcome to attend all games, free of charge.[17]

One of Red's columns is based upon an interview with a teacher working at an elementary school in Harlem who educates him about the valuable work that Black Muslims are performing in that neighborhood. The teacher helps Red understand why Muhammad Ali is such a hero for Black children and why so many Blacks oppose the Vietnam War: their children, who can't get deferments, are being forced to die in a "white man's war." Ali, she argues, speaks for the children who have a hard life in Harlem. She then explains why Black Muslims are so highly respected in the neighborhood: "They are taking troubled young men and women off the streets and working with them to improve the quality of their lives." For many children in Harlem, they are valuable role models. Red concludes his piece on the lessons he has learned from the young teacher by informing his readers that she is his daughter, Sarah, whom he has interviewed at her school in Harlem.[18]

"It's Like Wearing a Hair Shirt"

Ambitious to make progress in his new career as a writer, Barber was eager to expand beyond the newspaper column business. He wanted to find a forum in magazines where he could publish occasional longer pieces. After moving back to Florida, he also had outlined chapters for several books. He found a literary agent and a mentor in Malcolm Reiss, who soon became a close friend. Reiss was an agent at Paul R. Reynolds, Inc., a New York literary agency. He also was a very experienced editor/writer, serving as managing editor of *Fiction House* and penning articles for the *Saturday Evening Post*, *Colliers*, and *Boys Life*. The protracted correspondence between Reiss and Barber shows Reiss providing considerable advice and support for Barber's development as a writer, helping him through rejections and revisions. Barber regularly sent Reiss his newspaper columns, and Reiss offered him encouragement, at one point telling Red that his writing now "is 100% better than anything you were able to do five or six months ago. . . . When you said you were determined to work out a second career, I must admit I was dubious, but at the rate you are going, you should turn out to be as good a writer as you are a broadcaster."[19]

Reiss connected Barber to *Reader's Digest*, where Red struggled and finally succeeded in adapting his writing to the expectations of the popular magazine's editors. The magazine rejected several pieces, but he finally got articles accepted during his time in Key Biscayne. The first was a detailed and prescient piece asking, "Can Baseball Be Saved?," in which Barber fully embraces innovations of the game. His critiques are still current fifty years after his analysis: baseball has become too slow, like "watching paint dry." Batters merely swing for the fences, batting averages are falling, and pitchers dominate. According to Red, "Baseball was never intended to be a pitcher's game. It was meant to be a hitting, running, base-stealing, throwing game." The Old Redhead recommends deadening the ball to reduce home runs, shortening the season so that players can perform at their peak, adding a fifteen-second pitch clock to force pitchers into action, and eliminating on-field arguments. Players should just take first for an intentional walk—no need for the pitcher to throw four balls. If a game is tied after twelve innings, the contest should end and each team be awarded a half game in the standings. Eliminate doubleheaders or cut them to seven innings. He also offers one solution, drawn from football, that was indeed radical: unlimited substitution. He endorses the idea because "with unlimited substitution, fans would get to see the best batters batting, the best runners running, the best fielders fielding." Pitchers would no longer hit. While unlimited substitution has never been considered, several of Barber's suggestions have been implemented in some form. Just as Barber was writing his recommendations, the Major

Leagues lowered the pitching mound and shrank the strike zone to increase hitting. In 1973 the American League virtually eliminated pitchers hitting by approving a designated hitter. Starting in 2017, intentional walks no longer required four thrown balls. Baseball has also experimented with pitch clocks, reining in extra-inning games, and using seven-inning doubleheaders. But critics still are waiting for a livelier game and more on-field action.[20]

In October 1968 Barber was invited by the Authors Guild to become a member. In time the guild recruited him to write an article for its newsletter about his transition from full-time broadcaster to mostly full-time writer. His 1971 piece, "Confessions of a Broadcaster Studying His Typewriter," clearly captures Barber's challenging transition to his new career. First, the pay is poor—for Red it is a 90 percent cut in salary. Red foresees that "at the rate I am earning money from my typewriter, I'll write at least ten years to equal one year's income from the microphone. Were it not for having Malcolm Reiss of Paul R. Reynolds as literary agent and friend, I would have thrown the whole writing thing into Biscayne Bay, which is very handy—just across the street." Although broadcasting had its limitations—the inflexibility of the schedule for sure—Red admits that "the broadcaster has no pains of creation. The work is done as the game is played—for better or for worse—but the writer's work is never done." It's "like wearing a hair shirt," and yet, Barber insists, "it is exciting."[21]

Red's need for quiet concentration as he wrote led to at least one legal dispute with a neighbor and his dog. A letter from Barber's lawyer claimed that the neighbor's chained bowser had for several months "barked more or less continuously from the early morning hours until 10:00 or 11:00 o'clock at night." The neighbor sent Barber's lawyer a detailed response, supplying the exact and limited backyard schedule of the offending pooch, apparently absolving the canine defendant.[22]

Another barking critter that probably annoyed Red was Leonard Shecter, formerly a prominent member of the irreverent New York sportswriters' group dubbed the "Chipmunks" and editor of the hottest baseball book of the moment, Jim Bouton's *Ball Four*. Barber's criticism of Yankees colleagues Phil Rizzuto and Joe Garagiola in his 1968 memoir, *Rhubarb in the Catbird Seat*, drew Shecter's attention. By May 1970 Shecter, now sports editor for *Look* magazine, wanted Barber to "do a piece . . . on the jock broadcasters." He asked Barber to consider four questions: "What's wrong with Phil Rizzuto? What dumb things did Koufax say? Why will Mickey Mantle never be a broadcaster? What do you find so irritating about Joe Garagiola?" Shecter insisted that if Barber was "interested in doing such a specific cutting job [he] would be most interested in seeing it."[23] Although Barber actually liked the Bouton book and interviewed the Bulldog for his *Miami Herald* column, he never considered doing a *Ball Four*–like "cutting job." The Old Redhead was too much of a gentleman for such a spiteful task.

"Spiced with Love and Salted with Bitterness"

Barber published four books between 1968 and 1971, the first co-authored with Robert Creamer, biographer and longtime writer for *Sports Illustrated*. For all these works Barber drew upon his own experiences as a boy growing up in the South, his career as a broadcaster, and his evolving ethical and spiritual persuasions. The rapid rate of publication reflected Barber's impatience to establish his voice as a writer and to get his stories told his own way. He also seemed motivated to articulate, via storytelling and before it was too late, a cherished set of values he felt was imperiled. *Rhubarb in the Catbird Seat*, published in 1968, was compiled and drafted by Creamer, based upon many hours of tapes he recorded of Red Barber telling the stories of his life and his work.

The first third of the book is a loosely connected series of tales about Red's experiences in Brooklyn, the two men who most influenced his career—Larry MacPhail and Branch Rickey—and memorable episodes and controversies during his Brooklyn years. The rest of the book traces his life chronologically from his humble childhood all the way through his career with the Yankees, which ended shortly before Creamer's tape recordings of Barber's story were completed. Red tells readers about his accomplishments as well as his setbacks, his mistakes and his conflicts with some managers, sponsors, and colleagues in the broadcast booth. Throughout the narrative chapters are separated by short "Between Innings" discussions of random but specific facets of baseball, broadcasting, sports personalities, Barber's career, and people he admires.

The sales of the book, published by Doubleday, disappointed Barber, probably because his expectations were unrealistic. Red had been absent from the broadcast booth for two years before the book came out, and he was relatively unknown to a national audience as a writer. Still, reviews of the book were generally favorable. Critics praised Red's colorful narrative style and were intrigued by his insider's knowledge of baseball greats such as Larry MacPhail, Branch Rickey, and Casey Stengel. Many reviewers were impressed by what they described as Barber's principled refusal to accept shabby treatment by management or sponsors. For one critic, Dick Young, the book was so engaging because it was both "spiced with love and salted with bitterness." Most reviewers commented on Barber's deft and penetrating exposure of the influence of advertising upon the world of broadcasting and the careers of its talented voices. According to reviewer Mark Stuart, "There [were] red faces in the sports world and on Madison Avenue now that the book [was] out, but those depicted must have known Red was going to do it sooner or later."[24]

One reader, however, Joe Garagiola, was not pleased with Barber's depiction of him in *Rhubarb in the Catbird Seat*. Garagiola said that when he read Barber's comments about him, he "met a new Garagiola" that he did not recognize. He was furious about Red's claim that he rudely broke in and cut Barber off when he was speaking on air. Garagiola also assumed that Red was speaking about him in the book when he argued that Burke should have fired "another announcer," and he accused Red of "being scared to name me."[25] The rhubarb resulted in Garagiola's pulling out of a planned "reunion" with Red on the *Today Show*. As the show's sports specialist, he had been scheduled to interview Barber about the book upon its release, but Doubleday canceled the segment when Joe refused to play ball. The discord between Joe and Red would ease over time, mellowing into mutual appreciation.

"People Don't Start Off Writing Good Books"

Barber's first single-authored book, *Walk in the Spirit*, consisted of twenty profiles of sports figures who exhibited uncommon strength of spirit in facing tough challenges. Each profile is introduced with a scriptural passage that evokes Barber's sense of the sort of "spirit" that animated each man. His controlling idea is that self-knowledge and self-discipline, coupled with strong character and moral convictions, provide the outstanding athlete with "a quiet confidence" that fuels success. The men profiled include some athletes and managers that Red had written about earlier in newspaper or magazine columns, such as George Sisler, Roger Bannister, Ben Hogan, and Branch Rickey, and others who reached their goals despite serious obstacles, who maintained uncommon tranquility in perilous circumstances, or who bravely faced and wrestled with their demons to overcome them.[26]

Although in each case Barber dutifully documents and dramatizes the virtues of his subject, several of the pieces seem uniquely inspired, including his profile of Lou Gehrig. At the close of this piece, Barber movingly narrates a meeting between New York mayor Fiorello LaGuardia and the ailing Gehrig that took place late at night in a darkened train car returning to New York after the winning game of the Yankees' 1939 World Series victory over Cincinnati. Red, fortunately for his readers, was present at this stirring scene. He juxtaposes the mayor's fidgety quickness to Gehrig's quiet strength, as LaGuardia tells Bill Dickey, Gehrig's roommate, that Lou has just agreed to take a job on the New York City Parole Commission. Red describes LaGuardia's dark eyes burning with excitement because rather than singing a dirge for Lou, he is offering him another challenge. But it is Red's awe in the moment that the reader absorbs when LaGuardia "said to a man who'd just taken off his last Yankee uniform, 'Here, think about some men in the city prisons. . . . Give your remaining strength and life and interest by going to work for them—not for money, but for them.'" Red tells his readers: "Lou, by the window, nodded as the Mayor poured out his news to Dickey. . . . It was dark inside the train, but there was a special light in Gehrig's face. It was a glow from inside him. His strong face was radiant. He was illuminated. There was a sweetness on his face as he sat there, a sweetness I had not seen on a man's face before—and I haven't seen since."[27]

Red's agent, Reiss, worked hard to find a publisher for this book and landed upon Dial Press after rejections from Knopf and from Lippincott, who found it "somewhat fragmented." Reiss urged his client not to be discouraged, and when Red's spirits sank after rejections from several other presses, Reiss admonished him: "You are being too negative. People don't start off writing good books, they learn the trade, which is what you have been doing."[28] Barber swallowed some pride and accepted a smaller advance from Dial than he had expected—$3,000. Even after the advance, the editor at Dial, Donald Hutter, wanted several of the profiles to be "meatier, fuller, more unified and coherently presented," requiring significant revisions.[29] Red persevered accordingly but found the work challenging: "Writing a book is the hardest work I've ever been tangled with." The struggling author catalogs the leisure activities he's been forced to abandon: "When I began *Walk in the Spirit*, I was trying to play golf, go fishing in my outboard, enjoy the Atlantic Ocean. By the time the book was finished, I had resigned from the golf club and sold my sticks, resigned from both the yacht club and the beach club, and managed to strain my relationships with a lot of 'friends' who had nothing else to do but get on the telephone or give cocktail parties."[30]

Walk in the Spirit was less widely reviewed by the press than *Rhubarb in the Catbird Seat*; most critics, such as Larry King, described the book as uplifting, praising Barber's "old fashioned morality," which a *Variety* reviewer claimed "should be just the thing for the youth of America in this post-Christian time." Many reviewers, including the book critic for Florida's *Brandenton Review*, enjoyed the "easy informal style, written almost in column format." However, Marley Soper, reviewer for *Library Journal*, who labeled the book a "sports devotional," thought it would have been better "with less theology and moralizing."[31] Barber distributed copies of the book to friends and to celebrated but distant acquaintances, including Billy Graham and Frank Sinatra, two men, one might imagine, of quite disparate literary tastes. The blue-eyed "rat packer" sent his copy back to Red, asking him to "autograph and return it for my personal library."[32]

Barber's 1970 book *The Broadcasters*, also published by Dial Press, was written as a tribute to the pioneers of radio broadcasting who were the first to experiment with the new medium and who became the mentors for all practitioners who followed. Barber attempts to evoke the excitement and energy that radio triggered and to paint enduring pictures of the first two generations of sportscasters, providing honest assessments of their strengths and weaknesses, both on and off the air. Re-purposing some material from earlier texts, he shares lively stories of his own development in the business, profiles the mentors he most admired, and critiques the overuse of former players in the broadcast booth. Always the teacher, he concludes the book with practical advice for aspiring broadcasters, including ways to preserve one's voice and tips on the arts of interviewing and keeping efficient but detailed scorecards.

Reviewers of *The Broadcasters* who loved the topic also raved about the book for its insights into the highs and lows of the business and for the up-close assessments and comparisons of its celebrated pioneers and more recent practitioners. Many reviewers echoed what *The New Republic* critic John Yardley saw in Barber's account: the sad demise of the "quirky, flamboyant, unique and lovable" broadcasting pioneers who now were being "edged out by glib cookie-cutter voices" and the "empty babble and labored witticisms we hear on television." Some reviewers also agreed with Yardley's critique of the "haphazard organization" of the text that resulted in occasional repetitions. But even critics of the book, his best seller to date, agreed with Yardley that as "the most honest and the most influential sports broadcaster of any era," only Red Barber could have written this story.[33]

Reiss and Barber hoped that Dial Press would also publish Red's next book, *Show Me the Way to go Home*, but Donald Hutter rejected the manuscript because it was "a personal religious book" outside the purview of the press. Harper and Row also rejected *Show Me the Way to Go Home*.[34] It was accepted for publication by Westminster Press, which specialized in scholarly works on religion and theology but also published books about living a life of faith written for the general public. *Show Me the Way to Go Home* is indeed a very personal book—and a most valuable resource for a biographer—as Barber traces his own compelling spiritual journey. Curious readers discover detailed accounts of the events in Red's life that tested, weakened, and renewed his faith. Barber exposes what he believes have been his errors, his sources of shame, his longtime fear of death, and his gradual opening up to and acceptance of a rational faith. Readers learn that Barber's religion, founded upon his intuition of a "personal God," is an ecumenical spiritual commitment that incorporates concern for others, civic duty, and an unstinting quest for self-knowledge and personal growth.

Show Me the Way to Go Home was primarily promoted and briefly reviewed in religious publications. The book was recommended to church leaders and pastors, and it was sold with guides for its use in the pulpit or for group discussions among church members. A cassette tape of Barber reading two of his sermons printed in the book could be purchased for $3.95. Red's sister Effie Virginia wrote to tell him that the section on their father's death moved her deeply, adding, "This is your finest book, Walter, and I'm proud of you and your work."[35]

Barber stopped working on books for a decade, and he would not publish another one until his 1982 account of *1947: When*

All Hell Broke Loose in Baseball. He may have resisted another book-length project at the time because of his concern about exceeding annual income limits imposed by the Social Security Administration. Repeatedly in correspondence and interviews, Barber expressed anxiety about the possibility of losing his Social Security benefits—as a penalty for exceeding the annual earning limits—until he was seventy-two, the age at which the earnings limits were removed from Social Security regulations. After he left the Yankees, Red apparently was earning an adequate income from his radio job; his newspaper column; his pensions from the Screen Actors Guild and the American Federation of Television and Radio Artists (AFTRA); his Social Security checks; and additional money he earned for speeches, occasional broadcasting gigs, and commercials. Royalties for the four books discussed above, which sold between six thousand and sixteen thousand copies each in their first printings, also provided supplemental funds.

Still, although Barber's income was substantial during his peak broadcasting years and although he and his small family had lived extremely well during his full-time employment as a broadcaster, there is no evidence that he ever invested savings or that he had accumulated great wealth over the years and apparently did not wish to risk losing his Social Security checks.[36] The Barbers seemed to take some small cost-cutting or revenue-enhancing measures during their years in Key Biscayne. Several letters from a jeweler in Coral Gables document that Barber had given him both a ruby and an emerald bracelet to sell. Red also let the College of Journalism and Communication at the University of Florida know he was changing the terms of the annual "Red Barber Award," given to the top student broadcasters at WRUF. It would no longer include the $100 stipend that he had been donating for the award each year since it began.[37]

"Babies Learn to Walk with Pigeons in Paris!"

In addition to developing his skills as a writer, Barber also continued to work as a broadcaster in Miami, doing weekday sports summaries for WGBS. His contract with the station included the option of working on "special programs," including audio documentary work. Barber used this option to help subsidize his and Lylah's favorite avocation: traveling overseas. They took an extended spring vacation in 1970, touring around France, specifically in Paris, Provence, and the French Riviera. Red tape-recorded his observations, interviews, and reflections throughout their travels and occasionally asked Lylah to share her impressions with the listeners. Then Barber would mail the cassettes to WGBS, where they aired on radio every Monday, Wednesday, and Friday at 12:15 p.m. The twenty-four fifteen-minute episodes provide a delightful opportunity for listeners to hear Barber's insights into French culture, his skills in eliciting refreshingly honest and informative responses from his interview subjects, and the unmitigated joy he takes in being footloose, especially when he gets behind the wheel on winding roads along the Mediterranean or in the mountains. He seems committed to three objectives in his travel reporting: pointing out and attempting to account for cultural differences and similarities, drawing edifying moral lessons from his observations, and providing useful tips and advice for American listeners who might be planning their first trips abroad at a time when European travel was becoming more affordable for the middle class.[38]

Red's interview with the owner of a high-end French auberge in Provence provides listeners specific details about the eighteen-hour days the man happily devotes to maintaining his highly rated inn. We learn exactly how many chickens he buys each week for his restaurant, how he selects his wines, and who arranges the beautiful flowers that decorate all the sitting rooms. Barber tries to elicit from him information about the relationship between staff and management at inns like this one, inquiring how employees can keep moving up in their careers. The owner cannot provide satisfying answers because, he says, his employees have worked with him for years and are like family; they are not obsessed with moving up. They actually love the work they are doing, which comes with many benefits, even beyond material rewards. Throughout this interview, Red speaks as if he is absorbing an interesting new understanding of "labor." He wants to share with his American listeners the greater respect accorded to service employees in Western Europe at that time: waiters, cooks, and housekeepers are regarded as professionals and are rewarded as such.

The listener is struck by some of Barber's seemingly spontaneous descriptions of what he is seeing along his drives, from his train window or just walking the streets. He supplies a vivid description of the mistral, the northwesterly wind that blows through the Rhone Valley and south to the sea. Barber now understands for the first time why "the grasses and leaves in Van Gogh's paintings always blow in one direction." He is delighted when he notices that "babies learn to walk with pigeons in Paris." When they see a pigeon running ahead of them and then stopping, the toddlers try to catch up, and the game continues until their stumbling presumably develops into a steady gait. On an airplane he is struck by the loveliness of a flight attendant, but his gaze refreshingly evolves into a more poignant appreciation of how skillfully she helps a blind passenger make his way to the restroom. He later tells her how impressed he was by her care and patience with the man. She appreciates the compliment but tells Barber how much easier it is to assist blind people because "they listen to you so much more attentively, and they trust you because they have no other choice." Barber, who worked closely with the American Federation for the Blind to record portions of his books for the visually impaired, then delivers a tribute to the blind for his radio audience: "[They] do not give up on life; they choose instead to engage deeply in it—they fight to have a full life, which takes guts."

Throughout his travels in France, he is awed by the efficient, spotless, luxurious trains that so reliably connect tourists in Europe from one destination to the next. They evoke his memories of riding trains as a child and his nostalgic lament over the decline of railroading back home; the celebrated 20th Century Limited on the New York Central line had been terminated three years before Red and Lylah's travels in France.

Lylah was pleased after their move to Key Biscayne that she and Red were finally free to take long road trips, and one of their favorites was a protracted drive to the Rockies, her first cross-country adventure. Red realized his dream of buying a brand-new car—a green Lincoln Continental—and they hit the road as Barber conducted interviews along the way, this time to write up and send to the *Miami Herald* for his weekly column. They loved driving through the farmlands of Iowa and Nebraska and witnessing the slowly emerging expanse of the Rockies. They took in a stirring recital of Utah's Mormon Tabernacle Choir but were less impressed by their detour to Las Vegas; along the way their new car's air conditioning died, and they both arrived at Caesar's Palace "hot and crabby." After several days of walking through "aesthetically ugly and crowded casinos" and "sold out claustrophobic theaters," they made an early-morning exit from the Palace. Lylah noticed the gamblers still gaming in the casino; it seemed "so sad, so empty."[39]

"Come What May, This War Is Already Lost"

Red took his final USO tour to Vietnam in 1967, early in his Key Biscayne years, his first tour during live conflict and a trip that altered his view of the war. He tells us in *Show Me the Way to Go Home* that he was inspired to make the tour after meeting wounded soldiers at Walter Reed Hospital. Near the end of his last year with the Yankees, the team visited with the injured from Vietnam. Barber was surprised and genuinely moved watching Mickey Mantle's patient and warm interactions with the wounded men, and in no time, he'd gotten himself booked on a USO tour for January 1967. He volunteered again to serve as sports commentator and lay preacher.

Barber's later description of his Vietnam tour begins with a dismal episode in the village of Camau, one of the early stops on his itinerary. Shortly before his arrival, the pilot of a spotter plane had been shot though the head by the enemy, and the observer assigned to accompany him did not know how to fly or land. He could only circle around the airport as ground control tried to provide instructions. He apparently could not absorb them and crash landed instead. Then he crawled out of the cockpit, drenched in the blood of the dead pilot. Barber was flown to the scene the next day in a single-engine plane, "a square set, ugly little brute" that suffered at least one rifle hit during his flight. "In Vietnam, the idea is to get up fast to a safe elevation over what you believe to be friendly ground; every bush or tree shelters a rifle if you tempt it."[40]

When Barber finally arrives at the tiny Camau airport, he sees the crashed spotter plane and someone tells him that "the body of the pilot had been zippered into a rubber bag and already flown out . . . and a notice had been sent to his wife." Red realizes that his audience for the Sunday morning sermon he was scheduled to deliver the next day would be young men who had just witnessed the crashed plane and bloody remains of one of their brothers. He makes a snap decision to ditch the text he had composed and cut to the chase with a sermon addressing the one reality he knew each one of his listeners had directly in his sites: his own death. Barber talked about how death binds us all as the universal condition for our being alive. He attempted to persuade his audience—by analogy and metaphor, scripture and scientific study—that death cannot be the end for our beautiful souls—even chemistry confirms that "man can neither create matter nor destroy it; it merely changes its form."

During the tour, Red tells his readers, he becomes convinced that "come what may, this war is already lost." He bases his conclusion primarily on what he saw as potentially irreversible psychological effects upon the men who were fighting it. Soldiers were dehumanized by the unsustainable rigors of guerilla warfare that they had not been trained to master. He witnessed what for him were the worst effects of these demoralizing conditions: "[These are the] skills our men have learned in South Vietnam: the placing of big red ants with savage, searing stings on a man's testicles . . .

having a woman while having [one's] jeep washed clean . . . the constant availability and cheapness of dope."

Red received several military commendations for his 1967 USO tour and his four earlier tours between 1948 and 1961. His Certificate of Appreciation acknowledging all five tours commends Barber "for patriotic service providing entertainment to members of the armed forces in Vietnam, the Pacific, the Mediterranean and Germany."[41] Whenever he spoke to the press about his observations in Vietnam, Barber always supported the men who had been sent there to fight: "Whether they're hungry, muddy, shot at or wounded, there's never a complaint."[42]

Several months after Red returned from Vietnam, he received a letter from Captain Edward Heffelfinger, the pilot who had flown him by helicopter to several of the installations he visited. Heffelfinger recalls that Red graciously bought a tortoise shell necklace for him to give to his wife, and he also thanks Red for kindly calling her when he returned to Florida after his USO tour was completed. Red assured the woman that when he left Heffelfinger, her husband was safe and well. Heffelfinger wants Barber to know that flying him "throughout a portion of Vietnam was a distinct privilege and pleasure. Being able to do this was a highlight in my life. . . . We were very fortunate to see so much and learn so much."[43]

In June 1971 Red received a letter from U.S. Senator Edward Gurney of Florida, thanking him for his recent communication urging Gurney to support the "recent proposal to establish a date for the total withdrawal of American troops from Indochina." He explains to Red that he cannot support the measure because establishing a date "would foreclose all possibility of a negotiated settlement of the war," an eventuality that would "put the United States at a disadvantage." Barber's pressing the senator to support an end to U.S. engagement in Vietnam marks changes in thinking for the man who, in one of his 1950 *Journal American* pieces, had urged an American first strike on the Soviet Union and who voted for Goldwater in 1964.[44]

Broadcasters Have Forgotten That "Radio Belongs to the People"

Red Barber's other time-consuming activities during his years in Key Biscayne were the many lectures and sermons he agreed to deliver. After leaving the Yankees, he contracted with the Keedick Lecture Bureau to manage the arrangements for all of his paid appearances, for which Keedick received one-third of his fee.[45] He also applied for and received his certification in Florida's Episcopal Dioceses to practice as a lay reader with the authority to preach original sermons.[46] Between 1967 and 1972 he spoke at Rollins College and University of Florida graduations, preached sermons at two large churches in New York City and at others across Florida, and was guest speaker at advertising company events and advertising club luncheons. Barber also spoke at libraries, bookstores, and book clubs when his own publishers scheduled promotional tours for his publications. He spoke at area country club and golf club affairs, Rotary International clubs, Boy Scout banquets, and denominational church convocations. Red was a guest speaker for Rollins College's 1968 Baseball Week, and in 1967 and 1972 he also appeared in satirical sketches at the annual New York City Sportswriters dinner and follies. He was featured on the *Mike Douglas Show* and occasionally was interviewed on radio.

Two of Red's speeches during these years—a controversial 1970 speech delivered at the National Association of Broadcasters (NAB) Annual Convention in Chicago and a 1970 graduation speech at the University of Florida in Gainesville—are notable for the dark vision that Barber painted of current American culture and values. Many commentators at the time also were describing a country painfully divided over the Vietnam War, racial discord, drug use, the women's movement, and other challenges to traditional "family values." But Barber's speeches may also have reflected personal frustrations in his efforts to be an influential civic voice. His NAB speech was delivered by a man who still believed that persuading listeners to contribute their blood for the war effort "was what mass communication was intended to be . . . selling life, not baseball, not tickets, not cigarettes."[47] By 1970 he was convinced that sports broadcasting and commercial broadcasting in general were hostile to honest critiques of contemporary American society and its values. They were evading the role they could perform so effectively—educating the public about the essential values and duties of citizenship.

On April 13, 1970, *Broadcasting* reported that Barber was asked to speak at the NAB conference on "the broadcaster's role in his community and the dependency listeners have on his best efforts." The program for the conference indicated that, in a presentation entitled "Radio from the Catbird Seat," attendees would get "sage advice from Red Barber compiled in a long career as major league announcer." But when he came to the podium, Red asserted: "This talk has caused me more disturbance and pain than any I have ever delivered." Then, according to *Broadcasting*'s account, Barber "began firing pitch after pitch at the economics of today's radio programming." He claimed that the broadcasting business had "grown selfish and forgotten that the air belongs to the people and not to the station operators," whose licenses supposedly were renewed because of their service to the public and not because they were the most profitable. There should be limits, he concluded, on how much money stations could make.[48]

In its coverage *Advertising Age* reported that Barber critiqued radio and television for lowering their standards for commercial advertising, as well as for the poor quality of their programming: "I have to ask the question, what product now, what potion or patent medicine is not acceptable?" He reminded listeners that when the connection between smoking and cancer first was exposed, no one whined more about potential advertising losses than radio and television. Station managers, he told his audience, once selected the shows that were aired, but now it was the advertising "time salesman" who determined the content that stations delivered to their audiences on the sole basis of "ratings and the strictly mercenary demands of advertising agencies," who were merely pawns of their clients. Channeling Edward R. Murrow,

Barber also reminded his audience that programmers at one time had been "the top men" in the station, committed to "stimulating the imaginations of their audiences with great poetry, music and drama. . . . They understood their job was to lead their audiences" rather than weakly pandering to them.[49]

The *New York Times* claimed that as Barber "pummeled television and radio" some attendees walked out before his speech was over. However, it reported that Barber was not the only speaker who triggered departures from the audience. The African American speaker who followed him also provoked walkouts when he documented the lack of opportunity for minorities in radio to advance to management and ownership.[50]

Four months later, in his summer commencement address at the University of Florida, Barber probed other deep sores in the nation.[51] His speech challenged the graduates to assess their qualifications for achieving excellence in their life's work. Midway through the address, he shifted into an intimidating depiction of the world in which they would be working. Red admitted: "Tonight I am afraid for our country and our civilization," which was still living in the shadow of Hiroshima and the horrors of Vietnam. He believed that we were "killing ourselves in our own trash," that our system of laws was breaking down, that drug consumption was widespread, and that we have "overpopulated our good earth beyond its ability to sustain us." He linked these threats to debilitating psychic and spiritual ailments, "doubt and despair" and addiction to television: "We watch and do not think. . . . We have lost the refreshment of quiet in the constant noise of our world."

To this weighty catalog of contemporary social ills that these graduates must address, Barber added modern medicine's project to "take away from us the dignity of death by prolonging life in the vain pretense that death is not inevitable." Barber was touching upon a new concern that had become more pressing to him with age and the ravages that his illnesses had already wrought on his body. Committed to believing that the finest part of each individual is not of the flesh, he worried that our medical and legislative communities may unthinkingly insist upon trapping our aspiring souls in a useless shell when they are longing to be free. Around the time of this speech, Red was writing in *Show Me the Way to Go Home* that he had repressed the inevitability of his mother's death but also the possibility that she might have preferred death to protracted years of pain and immobility. Still, Barber supplied a hopeful conclusion to the speech, encouraging the young people to trust the powers within them, recalling the examples of Jesus and Jackie Robinson, who both had faced powerful obstacles and "who went up against the world" with their hearts full of hope and an unwavering conviction that they would succeed. He wants the young graduates to remember that "when Rickey asked Jackie if he thought he could take all the blows he would encounter day after day, he replied simply, 'I *have* to.'"[52]

"MacPhail in the Pulpit Was Big News"

One project that delighted both Red and Lylah during their years in Key Biscayne also reconnected them to their old friend Larry MacPhail. Red once again signed up to serve on a fund-raising campaign, this time to build a church for the increasing number of Episcopalians on the Key who currently were worshipping in a repurposed one-room building originally constructed to house migrant workers. Red invited Larry MacPhail, who was wintering in Key Biscayne at the time, to preach a sermon in the current church; the unlikely choice would create a stir, ensure newspaper coverage, and draw a sizable crowd that might be eager to contribute to the new building campaign. MacPhail agreed to do it if an unnamed good friend would donate $1,000 toward the new church building, and the man agreed to do it. As Lylah noted, "MacPhail in the pulpit was news."[53]

Edwin Pope of the *Miami Herald* records that MacPhail spoke to a crowd of seventy people in the tiny one-room church, beginning his remarks with the confession that he had "no right or reason to be here" except that a friend offered to donate to the building project if Larry accepted the challenge to preach. He admitted to his audience that he likely was not a real Christian, "even if others think so, because you have to prove it by your actions, and I have not done much. But I want to tell you about a few people who have." MacPhail offered the example of New York mayor LaGuardia, who had agreed to serve a fourth term even after he'd been diagnosed with cancer, continuing, nearly until the day he died, his humanitarian efforts to revitalize New York City for all the people who lived there, including the poorest. Pope reports that after MacPhail's speech, "a lot of people came up and told Larry how much his heart-felt homily meant to them."[54] Lylah Barber notes in her memoir that "MacPhail spoke well, and in his choir robe, he looked 'born again.'"[55] After he left the church, MacPhail "did something" himself. He threw an enormous cocktail party at a new and very expensive oceanfront condominium complex as a fundraiser for the new church building. Pope assures readers that "Larry MacPhail is still pitching, this time in a church by the sea."[56]

By the summer of 1971, however, the Barbers were growing disaffected with Key Biscayne because of the rapid development of the island; Lylah says that it had begun "to look like Miami Beach, a solid expanse of hotels and condominiums."[57] New housing had blocked their beautiful ocean view, and they were tired of endless summer; they wanted to experience at least a slight change of seasons. In a letter to his sister, Red bluntly remarked that Key Biscayne had become "too crowded, too rich, too cocktail party-ish and too expensive."[58]

Red and Lylah had been planning a driving trip north during the summer of 1971 to Sarah's vacation cabin in the Adirondacks. She would join her parents for a few weekends during their stay at her mountain retreat, where they had vacationed from time to time in recent years. The Barbers took a detour to Tallahassee early in their trip north. Lylah had spent her college years there and always considered it a friendly town with beautiful springtime flowers; she recalled being happy and busy. They shared with a Tallahassee real estate agent the type of house and setting they were seeking, and he showed them a property that seemed the perfect fit. It was a large ranch house set in a grove of pine trees with an ancient live oak towering among them. By the time they reached South Carolina, they had made an offer, Lylah says, "and by the time our visit in the Adirondacks was finished, the house was ours."[59]

15

Hall of Fame Broadcaster

The Barbers' move to Tallahassee launched their retirement together but not the end of Red's stature as a national celebrity. The Old Redhead would spend his last two decades in Florida's capital city, but he was never out of the public eye. In his last decade, because of his celebrated role on NPR's *Morning Edition*, his media shadow would extend further than at any time since his glory days as the voice of the Brooklyn Dodgers. His first decade in Tallahassee initially seemed to follow the path of many men of media fame, gradually narrowing with time. He transferred his newspaper column from the *Miami Herald*, a major regional daily, to the more modest *Tallahassee Democrat*, changing the column name from "The Old Redhead" to "The Catbird Seat." His days of regular radio work seemed over once his contract with WGBS in Miami expired. In addition to his weekly column, Barber continued to write feature articles for *Reader's Digest* and other national publications, but his next book remained a topic of discussion with his literary agent, Malcolm Reiss, rather than a process of production in his study at 3013 Brookmont Drive, Tallahassee, Florida.

When the anniversary of a significant milestone in baseball history arrived, reporters often asked Red to comment as he evolved into a human reference book on the national pastime. Recognizing his place in baseball history, NBC came calling. In August 1973 Barber joined longtime admirer Curt Gowdy and former Yankees shortstop Tony Kubek, whose play Barber had described in his Yankees years, for an NBC Monday Night Game from Pittsburgh. The next year on August 26, the thirty-fifth anniversary of the first televised Major League baseball game, broadcast by Red, he joined the NBC team again, this time in Cincinnati to cover the Reds-Phillies contest. Gowdy featured Barber on his PBS program, *The Way it Was*, where the Old Redhead provided a nostalgic look at the 1947 World Series. Barber seemed to transition into a comfortable retirement, seeking neither fame nor fortune but receiving enough of each.

The Catbird Seat

Between 1972 and 1982 Barber wrote over 550 weekly "Catbird Seat" columns for the *Tallahassee Democrat*. Like his *Miami Herald* posts, his new column continued to focus on the connections between the present and past. A typical column seized on a sports rhubarb (such as a lockout or a strike), a notable achievement (such as Hank Aaron's breaking Ruth's career home run record), the death of a sports figure, or a mega-sports event and then related the current event to a past episode he had observed or taken part in, drawing meaning from the juxtaposition. He also offered reflections on key events in his own life. In his introductory piece on February 20, 1972, Red tells his readers how he "bought" the phrase that named his new column in 1934, after he lost a penny ante poker pot to his friend Frank Koch.[1]

While some themes and issues recur throughout the decade, Barber's point of view on the subjects he engaged was nuanced and not always predictable.[2] He could be an old-school conservative on some issues and a clear advocate of change on others. Like many elder observers of the game, he saw the current generation of players as unappreciative of the difficulties endured by the golden age icons he had covered. He was critical of second-generation African American players, including Reggie Jackson, who, he believed, had ignored Jackie Robinson when he visited their locker room at an All-Star Game. Barber also soundly criticized the flamboyant and—from Red's perspective—self-centered Dick Allen. Current players and owners also underappreciated the contributions of Branch Rickey to the integration of the game. In 1982, when both Hank Aaron and Frank Robinson were inducted into the Baseball Hall of Fame, Barber wrote to remind his readers that each owed a debt to Mr. Rickey for integrating baseball. As Aaron approached Ruth's 714 career home run record in 1972, Barber offered a convincing statistical analysis to support his argument that the Bambino was the better player. He believed replays had no place in sports. Officials and umpires could not be replaced; they had to be trusted.[3] Barber also continued to criticize the commercialization of sports, arguing that big money had corrupted college sports and turned players into mercenaries. A casual critic of some columns might dismiss Barber as just another "old fart," living in a glorious past that never was. But that was not the case.

While he often privileged the wisdom of the past, Red Barber also embraced change. He saw Marvin Miller as a sharp negotiator who was helping players finally escape the bonds of the reserve clause. In any confrontation between Miller and the owners, Red's money was always on Miller to get the best of the bosses. At each player-owner impasse—there were five during the years Barber wrote "The Catbird Seat" column—Red supported the players. He ridiculed claims in 1978 that six teams would have to fold if owners didn't get a better deal. He supported the end of the reserve clause, assuming that player salaries would spike when it was removed but incorrectly predicting they soon would drop to reasonable levels once the owners realized they could not buy a winning team.[4] The players may be greedy, but the owners had always been far worse. While he accepted the earthiness of player talk, Barber was critical of the "adult" language used by Roger Kahn in his 1972 celebration of the Brooklyn Dodgers, *The*

Boys of Summer, believing that publishers encouraged salty talk to sell books. But he tolerated Jim Bouton's much more profanity-laced *Ball Four*. For Barber, Bouton had accurately reported the truth about how players behaved; given the language used in the Nixon White House, as revealed in the Watergate Tapes, why should sports books be held to a higher standard?[5] It also probably made a difference that Bouton wrote about the Yankees in his tell-all, while Kahn was "talking out of school" about Barber's fondly remembered Dodgers.

Although he objected to video replay reviews, Barber often welcomed changes to the game. In 1980, seventeen years before its introduction, Barber argued interleague play would be a valuable innovation; a Yankees-Mets series would rekindle baseball excitement in Gotham not seen since the Dodgers-Giants grudge matches of Barber's Brooklyn broadcasting days. He argued that the length of a player's hair should be a personal choice. In 1978 Barber celebrated the implementation of Title IX, the federal law barring discrimination in any educational program (including sports) that received federal money and opening the door for significantly increased participation by women in sports. He applauded the *New York Times* for hiring LeAnne Schreiber as the first woman to edit its sports pages.[6]

When he had the opportunity, Barber lauded many conservative political and military figures, including Winston Churchill, Herbert Hoover, Thomas Dewey, Mrs. Calvin Coolidge, Dwight Eisenhower, and General William Westmoreland, reflecting the traditional political leanings of his earlier years. But his experiences on his Vietnam USO tour in 1967 significantly qualified his political views. Barber's columns celebrated Muhammad Ali, a pariah for many white Americans, while Richard Nixon's Watergate scandal was duly referenced. Barber criticized Ronald Reagan's tendency in his early broadcast years to "fudge" on-field action during wire delays when he did baseball re-creations for WHO. But for the most part, Barber avoided overt discussion of politics, focusing on the personal qualities of individual leaders rather than their ideology.[7] He recalled his memories of Pearl Harbor Day, the 1948 Winter Olympics, his own bout with a ruptured vocal cord in 1942, and fond memories of first witnessing the skills of Major League players as a youngster in Sanford. The Old Redhead even narrated his personal history with house cats.[8]

Barber often sent copies of his columns to his literary agent, Malcolm Reiss, and other friends in sports and the media, a self-selected audience whose responses were consistently encouraging. But one column on the early-season umpires' strike in 1979 triggered a stinging rebuke from the son of one of the men he most respected in baseball, Larry MacPhail. Leland Stanford MacPhail Jr. (Lee MacPhail), as president of the American League, was in charge of the league's umpires. Always a champion of the men in blue, Red criticized baseball in his column for using Minor League and amateur umpires to replace striking umpires, noting that top NBA officials earned more than MLB umpires for officiating a shorter season and far fewer games. Barber implied that both NL president Chub Feeney and AL president Lee MacPhail, influenced by their earlier experiences in the front offices of the Giants and Orioles respectively, were hostile to umpires. Red alleged that when MacPhail was president of the Baltimore Orioles, he "learned to mark down those umpires who ruled against him."[9] Lee MacPhail attached a Gannett News Service article quoting Barber's column to a short but blunt April 18, 1979, letter on AL stationary in which he unloaded on his old family friend: "I was amazed at your comments. I expected the majority of the press would back the umpires. . . . If they feel the umpires are entitled to what they seek and have acted morally, that is their right. I do object to judgments such as voiced in this column and you are probably the very last person on earth I would expect to hear it from." In a handwritten note at the end of the letter, MacPhail told Barber, "There are two umpires in the League today who were on the staff when I was at Baltimore," implying that his dispute with the current AL umpires was not about any personal vendetta.[10]

Starting in June 1972, Newsco Press Features syndicated "The Catbird Seat" column and initially sold it to thirty papers, mostly in North Carolina, Virginia, Maryland, and Delaware. But just as with Red's earlier syndicated *Miami Herald* column, the response was tepid, and Newsco quickly dropped "The Catbird Seat" at the end of 1972.[11]

At the *Miami Herald*, Barber had been open to editing. But no longer a novice, he resisted some changes requested by his new editors. After occasional battles during a decade of columns, Barber resigned in a huff in the middle of 1982. The paper's executive editor, Walker Lundy, was "saddened and disappointed." In a letter to Barber, Lundy noted he had been out of the office when Red submitted his resignation and regretted that Red hadn't given him a chance to solve any problems he might have. Deeply disappointed by Red's departure, he hoped Barber would still "suggest occasional special pieces for [the *Democrat*]."[12] Respectful of hierarchy, Red always treated Lundy like his boss, a courtesy that felt awkward to the young editor, given their difference in status in the larger world. When Lundy introduced his father to Red, his dad reacted as though he were meeting the Queen.[13]

In his farewell column, Barber did not refer to any tensions but expressed his joy at being freed from the relentless pressure to produce a weekly column: "No matter where I have gone, Europe, around South America, to various places in the United States, the typewriter has been an extra piece of luggage, and the weekly column has always been on my mind." He also revealed that "the personal satisfactions of writing columns do not begin to equal those of writing books," but each column cost him one day's work on a book. He also mentioned his new NPR Friday morning spot, his upcoming assignment to do play-by-play of the Crackerjack Old Timers' Classic, and a guest lecturer gig on a cruise ship, implying that new opportunities were emerging for him. Barber ended his last column, as he had done when he was let go by the Yankees, quoting Ecclesiastes 3:1: "To everything there is a season."[14]

The Next Book?

Although Red mentions his satisfaction in writing books in his final *Tallahassee Democrat* column, he continued his hiatus from book projects well after his move to Tallahassee. We know the sales of his earlier books disappointed him, but his reticence did not deter his literary agent, Malcolm Reiss, from encouraging Red to pursue another book-length project. Reiss wrote to Barber regularly, often in response to a "Catbird Seat" column Red had sent him. He frequently recommended a biography of a baseball figure whom Red had known personally. Tom McPherson at G. P. Putnam's Sons had convinced Reiss that Putnam's series on famous baseball players targeted for young readers were always "sure-fire" sellers. Reiss sent Barber recent biographies of Ernie Banks and Tony Conigliaro, apprising him that such titles paid "a better than average advance" and had the potential for a much longer shelf life than adult sports books. While Putnam would not pay for any travel money, which Barber had requested, it might add $500 to the $1,500 advance typical for such books.[15]

But Barber would never take up the challenge of a book-length biography. Almost all of his writing drew from his own experiences, memory, and point of view on life. Emersion in the life of another and the protracted research such a task would require apparently did not appeal to him. His final book, *1947: When All Hell Broke Loose in Baseball,* published in 1982, required some research, particularly concerning the Yankees' race to the American League pennant, but he based much of it on his own experience of that historic season. Barber also learned that books rarely produced much revenue for their authors. Writing brief pieces, while not as emotionally gratifying, could earn him almost as much money as a book, with a fraction of the effort. For example, Red earned $1,500—as much as the advance for a book—for simply writing a "signed" introduction to *Closest Shaves in Sports,* a booklet released by the Schick Safety Razor Company. Barber's name still had commercial appeal, and it was likely that asset that Schick was buying, not the Old Redhead's literary skills.[16]

Still Reiss persisted, hoping Barber would send him "an outline for a big new Red Barber book": "What have you got curing down there in your Tallahassee smokehouse?"[17] Reiss put together a collection of Barber's *Tallahassee Democrat* articles to circulate to publishers for a compilation, but he warned Red that "publishers rarely ever get enthused by collections of short articles."[18] Don Hutter, Barber's editor at Dial Press, now at Holt, Rinehart and Winston, read Barber's columns and saw "a sharpness and control which I think represent quite an improvement," but he did not see "the makings of a book." The topicality of the columns made them a poor choice for an anthology.[19]

Barber's highest profile pieces during the decade were his contributions to the *New York Times*. In November 1972 Barber reviewed for the *Times* Jackie Robinson's autobiography, *I Never Had It Made*. Robinson's book was published not long after he had been honored in Cincinnati by the commissioner of baseball at the second game of the 1972 World Series for integrating Major League Baseball and for his work to prevent drug addiction among young people. Red emceed that historic recognition ceremony; in a *Tallahassee Democrat* article profiling the event, Red noted that Robinson at the time was "not in good health and his hair [was] snow white." Then, in a moving column just two weeks later, Red eulogized the man whose example had so profoundly affected the broadcaster from the Deep South.[20] In his review of Jackie's autobiography, penned shortly after Robinson's death, Barber asserted that "no baseball player was ever forced to fight so hard as Jackie Robinson." Barber also celebrated Robinson's attacking "with all his strength, racial intolerance and drug use by young people."[21]

Although Barber knew some of Robinson's story from firsthand observation, the book still moved him deeply. Red understood the guilt Robinson expresses over the price his family paid for his very public career. Robinson felt it was his first-born, Jackie Jr., who bore the brunt of his father's absenteeism, a "lack" that made him vulnerable to the drug addiction he later contracted in Vietnam. Barber ends his *Times* review by recounting the tragedy of Robinson's lost son, who, after freeing himself of drug addiction, died in a car crash. While not a detailed book review, Barber's personal ties to Jackie Robinson makes his essay compelling reading and helps cement the tie between Barber, son of the Old South, and Robinson, the only player whose number, 42, was retired for all teams in the Major Leagues.

One of Barber's most powerful *Times* columns during these years appeared in the sports section. On the day it was published, the op-ed editor, Harold Goldberg, wrote a letter to Red saying how much he regretted sending the article to the sports editor instead of printing it in his own section.[22] Barber's piece, entitled "Ernest Hemingway and the Tough Dodger," tells a true story about Hemingway and suggests Barber's malaise with macho mentality and the inner demons that fuel it. The piece also demonstrates his skill in uncovering fatal and haunting links in the tragic lives of two men who had only one brief encounter.[23] Red recalls the Dodgers' 1947 spring training in Havana, where Hemingway enjoyed hanging around other "mighty" men at the ballpark, taking some of them out to shoot pigeons, and inviting "the strongest" back to his place. One evening, Hemingway dominated a heavy drinking session at his favorite bar with some players, including relief pitcher Hugh Casey, a big man with a paunchy stomach and "rosy apple cheeks" who had become a killer on the mound. Hemingway invited Casey, "who looked so innocent," and a few others back to his home, where he brought out two pairs of boxing gloves and insisted upon sparring with Casey. Casey later told Red he refused, admitting he'd had some experience with boxing when he was younger, but he tells Red that Hemingway "wouldn't let me alone, until I finally put on the gloves. Hemingway started belting me as hard as he could. I told him to cut it out. He didn't and so I just knocked him down . . . and that ended the boxing for the night."

Barber flashes forward to twenty years later, after he was fired by the Yankees and took his first long road trip west with Lylah. They pulled off the road on a sunny mid-morning, turned into a cemetery in Ketchum, Idaho, and drove to the spot where Ernest Hemingway was buried, the only two visitors. Staring down at the grave, Red recalled Hugh Casey and pondered unfolding parallels. Hemingway could have written "a novel on the famous relief pitcher," Red muses. Casey, too, was "big and rough and deeply troubled inside, consumed by doubts and fears, hidden to all, except his roommates." After a game, he'd return to his room alone and "drink whiskey by the water glass, without the water." Driving late one night in Brooklyn, Casey accidentally killed a blind man. Subsequently, he was convicted of a paternity charge and later fell down some stairs, hurting his back and ending his pitching career. Each setback further inflamed repressed inner fires. Then his wife left him, and, on July 3, 1951, ten years almost to the day before Hemingway's July 2, 1961, suicide, Casey also "blew his brains out" with a shotgun. "That ended the fire." Barber concludes by observing that "both were big, rough men," and both "knew how to handle their weapons; It gets hot in early July."

Losses Mount

The year 1975 was a challenging one for Red Barber. He made the last visit to the town of his birth, Columbus, Mississippi, where he was saddened by the loss of so many of the beautiful antebellum mansions that once had lined the downtown streets. He had been invited by Father Comer, the rector of St. Paul's Episcopal Church in Columbus, to conduct Sunday services and deliver a casual Tuesday evening supper talk, with time allotted for informal conversation with the town's native son. In his letter accepting the invitation, Barber reports that by this time he had lost his lay reader vestments: "For some years now, I have preferred to preach in street attire. I came to feel strongly a layman should always be one and should look like one." Even more surprising, he tells the rector that he will give up his lay reader license "should next year's Episcopal General Convention deny women the right to be priests." In 1976 the Episcopal Convention approved the ordination of women.[24]

But Barber was far more shaken in 1975 by the loss of his only brother, of the Yankees' leader he most admired, of his first great boss, and of the literary agent and dear friend who had worked tirelessly with him in his transition from broadcaster to writer. Billy Barber died in April; Casey Stengel, at the end of September; Larry MacPhail, two days later; and Malcolm Reiss, at year's end.

In his October 5 "Catbird Seat" column, Barber lauded Stengel's devotion to his wife Edna, serving as her caretaker after she had suffered a series of strokes. It was a responsibility that Red would assume with his own beloved partner once Lylah began her struggle with Alzheimer's disease a few years later. He recalls Casey's kindness to him when he was joining the Yankees and adjusting to the loss of hearing in his left ear. But as Barber was writing his Casey Stengel eulogy, Lee MacPhail called to tell Red that his father, Larry, had died. Mid-column, Barber's Stengel piece shifted to a double memorial as he wrote: "Larry MacPhail . . . take him out of my life and I have no idea what my life would have been." He told his readers that "MacPhail was a man who repaired broken-down enterprises. He healed them, made them work, did it in a hurry, and provided storms of sound and fury." The proximity of the deaths of these two baseball giants struck Barber: "Two men, who were men, both 85, within two days."[25]

During their adult years, Red's relationship with his brother Billy remained emotionally close but geographically distant.[26] Billy spent his adult life in Tampa while Red was in New York, but at key points they visited one another. Red was Billy's best man at his first wedding. On furlough from the army, Lt. Billy Barber visited Red at the studio of the Sammy Kaye *Old Gold Show*. Billy and his second wife spent part of their honeymoon with his older brother and his family at their Fifth Avenue apartment. After that marriage also ended in divorce, Billy finally found his life partner, Olli Lenuweit. Red and Lylah hosted their wedding at their

Scarborough dream home in the summer of 1956. Slides in Red's personal photo collections capture the joyful couple at the wedding ceremony and the celebration that followed.

Red and Billy seem to have had a typical relationship for an older and younger brother nearly seven years apart. In school Red was the high achiever, while Billy occasionally had to see the principal, who sometimes was his own mother. Red's niece E. V. E. Joy, his sister Virginia's daughter, saw in Billy the playful mischief of her grandfather, Bill Barber.[27] Physically Red and Billy could easily be recognized as bothers, but the adult Billy was three inches taller, 5 feet 11 inches to Red's 5 feet 8 inches, with striking red hair, compared to Red's gradually receding reddish-blond locks. Red was clearly the family's star, but Billy had a lucrative career in advertising. He went to work for his maternal uncle, John Martin, in his outdoor advertising firm in 1934 and, except for his service in the war, stayed with the company in Tampa, eventually becoming president. Billy was a leader in the Tampa business community and a generous supporter of the city's arts.[28] He loved boating and hosted Red, Lylah, and Sarah on fishing trips in Florida during their visits when Red covered the Orange Bowl and during spring training.

Conchita Benito, an advertising colleague of Billy's in Tampa, wrote to Red shortly before Billy's death. She thanks Red for a book he gave her and then fills him in on Billy's morning schedule, letting him know how bravely his brother was holding up: "All of us marvel at the strength and faith that he has displayed these past six months. He has brightened our lives in so many ways."[29] Two weeks later Benito writes again to thank Red for sending another book and reports on Billy: "He was in such good spirits. Your visits mean a lot to him." Billy got "a big bang" out of Red's taking home one of his suits.[30] Two months later Billy Barber, at sixty, succumbed to lung cancer.

Before he died, Billy promised to leave his older brother a windfall that he could enjoy. By this point Red and Lylah were living on Red's modest AFTRA and SAG pensions, his Social Security, and the unexceptional amounts he earned from his writing and speaking engagements. Perhaps Billy was pleased that he could give his older brother, far more famous but likely not as wealthy, something better than a used suit. According to Red, Billy told him, "Blow the money, take a trip, buy something special." Red "blew" the $25,000 on a light green Mercedes with a cream interior. He would drive that car for the remaining seventeen years of his life.[31]

Cooperstown Comes Calling

By 1978 Barber had settled into a comfortable routine. He still had his weekly column, an occasional speaking engagement, and his gardening to enjoy. When reporters came calling, he offered his thoughts on the state of baseball and its history but remained aloof from the national pastime. In February Red learned the Baseball Hall of Fame would soon honor Larry MacPhail. He sent his congratulations to Lee MacPhail, and Lee wrote back to Red: "As you know, you were one of my father's favorite people. As far as I know, maybe the only one he never fought with." He apparently did not know that his father had threatened to have Dodgers workers rip Red from his broadcast booth in a 1940 dispute. Lee invited Red, if he could make it to Cooperstown in August, to "join any gathering of the family."[32] Five months later, on July 21, 1978, Ed Stack, president of the National Baseball Hall of Fame, called Red to assure him that, indeed, he *would* be visiting Cooperstown that August: "Red, *You* and Mel Allen have been selected to be honored by the Hall of Fame as the first broadcasters."[33] Barber was astonished, not because the Hall had selected him—he knew he was a great sportscaster—but that it would recognize any broadcasters for their contribution. As Red saw it, "Elections to the Hall of Fame have been conducted primarily by writers and not all writers wanted to pass the time of day with broadcasters."[34]

The news release from the Baseball Hall of Fame stated that Allen and Barber "were among numerous nominees solicited from former and active major league broadcasters." A screening committee condensed those nominations into a list of finalists, after which "a selection committee consisting of baseball officials and broadcasters" then chose Allen and Barber from the narrowed list. Ed Stack gushed that "the Committee couldn't have made two finer selections than Mel Allen and Red Barber. Both their voices became synonymous with the World Series and baseball in general." According to the release, the Hall of Fame created the Ford C. Frick Award to honor the late commissioner, who was a baseball broadcaster early in his career. It was designed to recognize baseball broadcasters for "their vital role in creating fan enthusiasm."[35]

The decision to create the award to honor Frick and the selection of the first recipients took place over only a few months: Frick died in April 1978, the Hall announced its creation of the award to the press in June, and it revealed the first recipients a month later.[36] The selection process was mysterious since the Hall did not publicly identify the committee members. The inaugural selection was the only time the Hall chose two winners in the same year. Perhaps Allen and Barber were so close in the committee's evaluation that it decided not to choose between them.

Barber saved dozens of congratulatory letters and telegrams he received in the days following his selection. Many were from personal friends and longtime Barber fans, but they were also from the famous, including George Steinbrenner, baseball commissioner Bowie Kuhn, Peter O'Malley, Gabe Paul (president of the Cleveland Indians), U.S. Senator Dick Stone of Florida, and Florida governor Reubin Askew. Steinbrenner wrote, "Being named along with Mel Allen as the first two recipients of this prestigious award is a great thing. But then again, you are a great man, announcer, and a great credit to the Yankees." Gabe Paul acknowledged Barber's "great contribution" but also "the moral standard you have followed, which has rubbed off on a lot of people." In his handwritten letter, Bowie Kuhn told Red: "How delighted I am that you will receive the Ford Frick Award. I think he would be too." After Barber sent him some articles, he received belated congratulations from the prince of baseball royalty, Ted Williams, who told Red he was "extremely pleased to know that you were rightfully honored."[37]

Barber also heard from two other members in the pantheon of baseball announcers. Vin Scully sent his congratulations on a hand-written note that conveyed the genuine devotion of a favored for-mer apprentice. Barber's selection was "an honor justly deserved, and as one who sat at your feet and observed and tried to learn, I know as well as anyone alive what a true artist you were behind the mike. There is a great deal of you in anything I do well in play-by-play, and it will live in me as long as I am working. For all of that, I am eternally grateful." In a 1978 Christmas card to Red and Lylah, Mel Allen added a note expressing how much the honor he had received along with Red meant to him: "Red, sharing with you the Ford Frick Award at Cooperstown made a priceless hap-pening even more rewarding."[38]

Given the attention of the baseball world for a few minutes on a warm August day, Red chose not to talk much about him-self in his acceptance speech but to educate his Cooperstown listeners.[39] First, he taught them about Larry MacPhail, whose contributions to the game he mentioned only briefly. His lis-teners likely already knew that MacPhail had turned around the Cincinnati and Brooklyn teams, pioneered night baseball, and brought radio coverage to New York. Instead, Barber spent his MacPhail moments reviewing his contribution to the building of a new Episcopal church in Key Biscayne, a side of the "Roar-ing Redhead" that few had ever witnessed. Next, he told his "stu-dents" that it was MacPhail who, despite the taboo prohibiting the word "blood" on air, urged him to promote those Red Cross donations: "Hell, there's a war on isn't there?" Most in the Coo-perstown crowd knew MacPhail had his flaws, but Red Barber wanted them to know that Larry had a solid moral center as well.

Barber devoted the second act of his talk to a history lesson. Drawing from his book *The Broadcasters*, he provided a detailed account of Harold Arlin's first broadcast of a Major League game.

He told his "students" that there was no radio announcer at the first broadcast of a World Series in 1921. The announcer, Thomas Cowan, had to receive a telephone report from the field and then parrot it out to his listeners on WJZ in Newark, New Jersey. He recalled Graham McNamee, "the greatest voice radio ever had," and his broadcasts of the World Series starting in 1923, and he reminded his audience of Hal Totten's pioneering regular-season coverage of Chicago baseball. Barber's lecture then acknowledged Cubs owner Phil Wrigley's role in blocking the baseball owners when they wanted to ban radio in the early 1930s. He moved to Larry MacPhail's role in ending New York's baseball broadcasting embargo and his ushering of a young Red Barber to Brooklyn in 1939, prompting the Giants' unfulfilled threat to get "the greatest radio announcer in the country and blast the Dodgers broadcasts into the East River."

Barber then emphasized how important radio and television were to the game. Broadcast coverage "has taken baseball into the homes. It has made baseball a family game. It was radio broadcasting that taught the women of this country what this game was all about." And since dollars speak loudly in America, Red had asked his CBS friend Harry Feeney to contact his sources at *Broadcasting* magazine to find out how much money the electronic media had brought to the game. Barber reported to his listeners that in the previous twenty years, "Broadcasting has poured into baseball 700 million dollars." In his conclusion, Barber extolled the contributions of pioneering sportscasters, offering the dedication he used in *The Broadcasters*: "This is for Graham McNamee and for those others who first went into the new land called radio armed only with carbon microphones." Barber's focus on the contributions of others rather than himself moved his Florida friend Bob Kennedy to write, "Your acceptance remarks were . . . reflective of the humble, unselfish human being your privileged close friends know you to be."[40]

Red Barber was now a Hall of Fame broadcaster. He and Mel Allen were the first broadcasters acknowledged in Cooperstown, a distinction that cemented their places in baseball history. For Barber the Ford C. Frick Award confirmed his substantial contributions to his profession and also triggered new opportunities, which seventy-year-olds rarely enjoy. In the months following the induction, at the invitation of Peter O'Malley, Barber would throw out the first pitch at a National League championship series game; be interviewed in Los Angeles by his prize student, Vin Scully; and emcee a banquet celebrating the life of Roy Campanella. He would also serve as guest of honor at the Evolution of Sports Journalism conference at LaGuardia Community College, where Sarah was an assistant professor; be honored with Mel Allen on Opening Day at Yankee Stadium; and work another baseball world series with his old colleague: this time Mel and Red would call the Little League World Series.[41] Ken McCormick, senior consulting editor at Doubleday, was now interested in an idea that Barber had discussed with Malcolm Reiss back in 1973: an anniversary book on the 1947 baseball season. He let Barber know that "the 1947 book absolutely fascinates me."[42]

In January 1979 Ed Stack invited Barber and Mel Allen to serve on the Ford C. Frick Award selection committee. The nominees for consideration that year included Jack Brickhouse, Harry Caray, Bob Elson, Curt Gowdy, Russ Hodges, Ted Husing, Lindsey Nelson, Bob Prince, and two former Barber booth partners, Ernie Harwell and Vin Scully. The committee selected Bob Elson, but everyone on the list, except for Ted Husing, would eventually win the Frick Award.[43]

During their first decade in Tallahassee, the Barbers had settled comfortably and relatively quietly into the city's life. But Red's selection for the Hall of Fame's Frick Award, and his liberation from Social Security restrictions on his income when he turned seventy-two in 1980, sparked a late-life renaissance. He dedicated himself to researching and writing 1947, fortifying his role as the firsthand authority on that pivotal baseball season. Barber also returned to radio, his medium of choice and the one that best channeled his distinctive talents. A brief interview on National

Public Radio led to newfound fame. His commentary on NPR drew a national audience of four million, thousands of times the number that read the columns and books he'd worked so hard to write. But while his audience grew, his body shrank, his health declined, and Lylah's mind faded. In his last decade, Red Barber would reap rich rewards and confront compelling challenges.

PART 6

RED'S RENAISSANCE

"Red Barber Moved People"

16

National Public Radio

ed Barber's twelve-year tenure on NPR's *Morning Edition* with Bob Edwards elevated him once again to a stimulating catbird seat where he was free to speak his mind, tell his stories, and paint his vivid word-pictures while winning over an entirely new generation of fans. He began a new monthly column, this time for the *Christian Science Monitor*. Throughout the decade Barber was showered with countless accolades and honors, from prestigious national awards to a myriad of regional recognitions. He engaged in a prolific correspondence during these years, occasionally renewing or repairing old friendships. Barber traveled less during his final ten years, but he still regularly accepted speaking engagements and guest appearances on television and radio.

Red was a pioneer in working from home via electronic media. He conducted his live *Morning Edition* conversations with Edwards from the comfort of his office at home in Tallahassee; a line was installed connecting his voice to the local public radio station, and then uplinked to NPR. During these years, whenever requested, he agreed to tape fund-raising promotions for local public radio stations, both in Florida and nationwide. He also taped from home narrations and interviews for documentaries, including

Ken Burns's *Empire of the Air* and *Baseball*. Finally, newspaper and magazine writers flocked to Red and Lylah's home in Tallahassee to record conversations with Barber for the many profiles of his life published during his last decade.

Fridays with Red

Red's twelve years sharing a segment of NPR's *Morning Edition* with Bob Edwards have been fully and delightfully documented by Edwards himself in his book *Fridays with Red: A Radio Friendship*. Edwards tells us that when the sports producer on *Morning Edition*, Ketzel Levine, interviewed Red in February 1980 for a Black History Month story focusing on Jackie Robinson's integration of Major League Baseball, she realized that Barber "had it all" as a radio personality—"the knowledge, the charm, the wit, the accent and the storyteller's sense of drama and timing." She promptly invited him to do a weekly commentary for *Morning Edition*. He accepted her offer the following December when Levine again interviewed him for a radio obituary for Elston Howard. He began his morning gig on the show in January 1981. The format was a four-minute conversation between Barber and Edwards every Friday at 7:35 a.m. Eastern time, a good slot for a man who claimed to be at his peak early in the morning. His contract with the station stipulated that he would be paid $150 per broadcast. Each Thursday at 10 a.m. the sports producer would call Barber at his home in Tallahassee to discuss possible topics for the next day's program—a current sports story or issue; a good sports book he'd recently read; or an important "anniversary" in sports, in his personal life, or in human history. Sometimes no compelling topic surfaced on Thursday; on Friday, the two would simply "wing it."[1]

A January 30, 1981, letter from Edwards to Barber suggests the new couple's "marriage" had gotten off to a good start, although a reader senses Bob's consciousness that the bond is still new and fragile: "I think we're rolling now," Edwards notes; "the last two weeks have been perfect. It sounds spontaneous and conversational. My only regret is that we don't have twice the air-time." Edwards congratulates Red on having secured Doubleday as publisher for his new book, *1947*, and then throws out an idea for an upcoming Friday. He would ask Red to compare Ronald Reagan's approach to wire re-creations of baseball games—using artificial sound effects and "fudging" foul balls to fill up time when the wire went out—to Barber's own commitment to debunking any illusion that he was broadcasting from the field of play. But the young broadcaster assures the elder that if he hates the idea, that's okay: "I wouldn't dare tell you what I think you ought to say in a broadcast." He concludes by expressing his excitement to be working with Red: "The only thing that could top it would be to meet you in person."[2]

The two met in person from time to time, but their relationship developed primarily by their over six hundred four-minute Friday radio conversations and the correspondence that enveloped them. In their fan letters, listeners occasionally wrote that observing the warm bond that developed between Edwards and Barber over time was one of the most appealing dimensions of their *Morning Edition* segment; one listener reported, "I am happy to note that there is no generation gap between two people whose culture, education and good manners are the same.... There is a magical chemistry to your friendship." Another listener thought the conversations represented the ideal "evolution into friendship" that can occur between sons and fathers when they reach middle and old age, "providing some of life's best moments."[3]

Edwards admits, however, that his working relationship with Barber at first required significant adjustments on his part. Over time listeners would come to admire his patient willingness to play the role of usher, whose job was to elicit Barber's spontaneous gems, the products of his years of full engagement in hard work, extensive reading, and protracted thinking and writing about life's pains and pleasures, both in and far beyond the arena of sports. Edwards's earlier radio work had not schooled him in the art of "unscripted, free-ranging, open-ended conversation that Red had been doing on air for fifty years." Now Red was asking him questions on a live segment for which he had no prepared answers. Red even wanted to know his opinions, but as a "straightlaced news guy," Edwards "was not supposed to have any opinions." The young host "went to school on Red Barber and learned how to relax and join the party," as the four-minute segment gradually became the most popular on public radio, carried on 385 stations.[4]

The reasons for the show's popularity are clear in letters from listeners that Edwards quotes in his book and those that Barber saved. In the most general sense, the segment was a favorite for NPR audiences because it was *not* committed only to "sports talk"; audiences loved listening to an old man who made no pretensions at this stage of his life to being an expert on any single subject but who was clever, lively, and comfortable just being himself. He would talk to listeners about the weather, the squirrels in his yard, or the cats he'd adopted just because they were *interesting* to him, and his camellias just because they were so beautiful.

Many younger NPR listeners in the 1980s had never connected intimately to a *radio* voice, one who became their friend over time; "a voice they wanted to hear more often, bring home and introduce to their family."[5] Many of his older listeners were thrilled to hear Barber invoke the distant glory days of the Brooklyn Dodgers, but for others the experience of hearing his voice reminded them that Red had always been talking about more than baseball. In his letter to Barber, one *Morning Edition* fan tells him that listening to his Friday conversations always brought back a particular 1940s Dodgers' broadcast that affected him more than any other, even though he couldn't remember a thing about the game:

> You commented on two news bulletins you had received during the game, one announcing the death of Herbert Pennock and the other announcing the birth of Shirley Temple's first child. Those two events, the birth and the death, evoked in you what I can only describe as a beautifully articulated reverie on life's mysteries which remains vivid to me today. Somehow, you managed to capture, in the midst

of what was probably not a very enthralling game, a sense of the wonder and sadness of human experience, and I will never forget it.[6]

As Edwards sums it up, "Red Barber moved people."[7]

Letters from his fans and tapes of those four-minute segments also suggest why the NPR gig was so valuable for Barber. It provided him a low-stress, structured, time-limited forum for reaching a wide audience while also supplying the intimacy of a small, close-knit "family" of mutually reinforcing colleagues who encouraged him to say whatever he wanted. It was like being back in the broadcast booth at Ebbets Field before the onset of television—before the visuals and intensified advertising agendas invaded and limited his conversation with his listeners. For Red the four-minute slot was not an interview but a widely overheard chat with a friend where one of the two begins by asking "What ya been up to?" or "How's the family?"[8] A Southern gentleman knows that one eases into a topic of conversation via the warmth of small talk lubrication. But more than just breaking the ice, by describing the weather in his town, Red was drawing his listeners closer to him. There was no distance between him and them once they all were looking out of his office window at his azaleas, dogwoods, and bird feeders.

The affection that tied Barber to the much younger members of the *Morning Edition* production staff is palpable in their periodic correspondence with him over his twelve years working with the program. Staff members showered him with birthday, anniversary, and get-well cards, signed by all, and their congratulations for his receiving prestigious awards, including the Peabody Award in 1991. On his seventy-fifth birthday the staff arranged a two-day *Morning Edition* celebration with tapes of his play-by-play reporting and testimonials from notable figures he'd worked with or for throughout his broadcasting career, including, among others, William Paley, Don Newcombe, Pee Wee Reese, and former baseball broadcaster and current president Ronald Reagan. A similar extravaganza aired for Red's tenth anniversary on NPR.

One suspects that the workplace collegiality Barber enjoyed with his young *Morning Edition* crew revived pleasures he'd experienced much earlier in his life with his close-knit peers at WRUF back in Gainesville, with the bachelor professors who had welcomed their young janitor into their circle at the University Club, or with Connie and Vin in the broadcast booth. Letters he received from some of his young *Morning Edition* colleagues suggest how deeply Red touched them, in ways that would leave his mark upon their future selves. In a March 1991 letter, the show's young producer, Mark Schramm, expresses the entire staff's pride over Barber's Peabody Award and his personal pleasure in having "shared in some of [Red's] 60 years in broadcasting." He closes by describing how he and his wife spent the early spring afternoon in Washington DC that day, "walking around the tidal basin, soaking up the warm sunshine and admiring the cherry blossoms, white and pink and delicate at their peak. We thought of you and Lylah and your sixty years together, and we felt very happy inside. A day you and Lylah would have enjoyed." Upon the occasion of his father's death, Bob Edwards wrote a brief note saying it all on a postcard to Red: "Your comment on my Dad produced a small flood of sympathy cards. Many thanks. They're a comfort to my mom and to me. Your letter was the best."[9]

"Shooting the Bull"

In *Fridays with Red* Edwards describes the wide range and types of topics Barber and he discussed over their twelve years of conversation—recollections of celebrated people, anniversaries of outstanding achievements, obituaries of famous figures, striking moments or current issues in baseball, social issues, and one of the many books that Barber had recently read and was all too willing to plug.[10] Barber frequently brought the past to life for his *Morning Edition* audience but not merely to evoke a comforting nostalgia; he *used* the past as a stern measure of the present and relied on its significant moments of moral clarity for direction in assessing current quandaries. For instance, in a 1990 Friday conversation with Red, Edwards brought up a recent controversy regarding Baseball Commissioner A. Bartlett Giamatti's tough suspension of Pete Rose for shoving an umpire over a call and his subsequent placing of Rose on the game's permanent ineligibility list for betting on games. Barber's response was to summon a voice from the past to confirm his own rigid stand on the exceptionally gifted player's punishment. For Red the grounds for Rose's expulsion were articulated seventy years earlier when Commissioner Landis made his landmark decision to ban from baseball eight players in the Black Sox scandal for "jeopardizing the integrity of the sport."[11] Similarly, on the day after the start of the Persian Gulf War, Barber invoked the wartime wisdom that Franklin Roosevelt delivered to settle a dispute fifty years earlier. Edwards began his Friday segment by asking Red where he stood on the debate over whether the coming Sunday's NFL playoff games should be canceled because of the war. In response, Red described the shock of Pearl Harbor, the NFL's decision to complete its season in its wake, and Landis's appeal to President Roosevelt to decide whether Major League Baseball should continue during the war. Listeners heard Red's rendition of Roosevelt's reply: "So long as you don't withhold anything from the war effort, I think the game is important for the morale, not only of the people at home, but for the armed forces." Barber's recollections of how passionately the troops he visited on his USO tours wanted to talk baseball validated the long-term relevance of Roosevelt's judgment.[12]

Other Friday conversations reflected Barber's genuine esteem for women who were making their mark in the competitive world of professional sports. In a 1998 broadcast, Barber identified Susan Butcher, winner of the recent Iditarod, the demanding annual long-distance dog sled race from Anchorage to Nome, Alaska, as "one of the greatest athletes of all time." Butcher sent Red a photograph of herself and the dogs in action and a letter thanking him for his assessment of her skills and for "getting the word out about this great sport, which is starting to be noticed."[13] NPR's Susan Stamberg, guest hosting one Friday in 1991, asked Red for his opinion of the new book *Baseball in America,* a collection of photo essays edited by Karen Mullarkey, then photography director for *Sports Illustrated.* Red strongly endorsed the book, saying it contained the "best baseball photos I have ever seen."[14]

But Barber also received an eloquent letter from Alexandra D. Sandler, "a devoted fan," criticizing him for his comments on another Friday segment in which he discussed some of his favorite baseball books. Sandler is dismayed that Barber recommended books for "fathers to give to their sons" as Christmas gifts. "What about their daughters?" she asks Barber. "On behalf of all female baseball fans, I feel compelled to object to this archaic, if inadvertent, chauvinism." In the rest of her letter, just as Barber himself might do, she delights her reader with an engaging anecdote— her story about how the love of baseball bound the generations of women in her family. For years her grandmother listened to Red Sox games on radio but, raising six children, never had the time to *attend* a Major League game. One of Sandler's "greatest baseball joys" was taking her grandmother to Opening Day at Fenway in 1980, where they sat, drenched and undaunted, through a long rain delay, "a young woman and an old lady, separated in time by more than 50 years, but united in our love of the only true sport."[15]

Red also triggered strong listener responses from his critique of what he considered inflated player salaries and the fortunes being spent on network broadcasting deals and advertising minutes. Although we know Barber commended the successful efforts of Marvin Miller in the fight to obtain collective bargaining rights for players, he grew increasingly uneasy with million-dollar contracts, especially at a time when homelessness was surging and AIDS victims were dying, in part because of inadequate funding for anti-poverty initiatives, medical care, and research. Red's attention to these social problems may have been inspired in part by his daughter's activism during these years as an advocate for AIDS victims and funding for research on effective treatments. After his general indictments of deadly disparities in the country's distribution of wealth, the problem of homelessness, and the needs of those suffering from AIDS in several Friday segments from 1989 through 1991, Red received heartfelt letters from listeners.

Although no one offered a concrete solution for narrowing wealth disparities, many correspondents agreed that Red's focus upon the human misery it caused was a necessary consciousness raiser. One writer was pained that legislators and too many community leaders had put these issues "in the back drawer" and thanked Barber for focusing upon them. Other listeners thanked Red for adding "a spiritual dimension" to the discussion of the "enormous needs of the world's poor," while another correspondent lamented the misguided slashing of school budgets where funds were most needed: "This is a culture," he said, "that hates its children. . . . Thanks for speaking the truth." A Jesuit priest teaching at Berkeley lauded Barber for raising on his broadcast the question, "How does an unemployed head of a family feel hearing that a ball player earns $851,000 a year?"[16]

Even listeners who had grown familiar with the Old Redhead could still be stunned by his insights. One of them expressed his wonder concerning Red's late-life perspective on baseball in a *Morning Edition* segment that aired during the 1991 World Series: "You said your wife had to undergo a serious eye surgery and so you had to miss a few of the games. And then you said, quite seriously 'Baseball, Bob, after all, is just a game for people with idle time.' I was astounded by the poignancy of such a remark coming from a man whose whole life was devoted to the sport, and I was moved by the depth of feeling that must have caused him to make it."[17] Blessed with a forum so generous as *Morning Edition* turned out to be for him, Barber never stopped "moving people."

Writing as Reviewing

Throughout the last decade of his life, Barber continued to publish articles, both for a monthly column in the *Christian Science Monitor* and occasional pieces. Among the occasional pieces, Barber wrote a substantial series of book reviews for major newspapers—

the *New York Times, Boston Globe, and Miami Herald,* among others. His reputation as a credible and lively commentator on the world of sports and media was still strong enough for book review editors to seek his assessments of new publications, primarily on baseball but also on radio, media coverage of sports, and sports reporting. For biographers his book reviews also provide insight into his values during the last decade of his life as he assessed the work of others. For instance, his *New York Times* review of the lavishly illustrated *Radios: The Golden Age,* by Philip Collins, provides readers with a summary of Collins's history of vintage radio design and construction from the 1920s to the 1950s and radio's role in binding the nation during war and depression. In his review, Barber recalls the first radio his father brought home and the first table-model that Red himself bought just after he and Lylah were married, evoking early radio's power to nurture and preserve, for a lifetime, shared domestic memories.[18]

Also for the *New York Times* Barber reviewed former umpire Ron Luciano's *Remembrance of Swings Past* and David Falkner's *Nine Sides of the Diamond.* The former is an account of the umpire's job in baseball up to the present, enlivened by Luciano's amusing firsthand experiences. Barber's review informs readers about the source of his own empathy with and respect for umpires throughout his career. When he began Major League broadcasting in Cincinnati, he recalls, he would eat with the umpires in the pressroom, where he would pummel them with his questions, tapping their "deep knowledge of the game. . . . It was like baseball graduate school in that kitchen." In his review of Falkner's book, Barber admits he would have been a better baseball announcer and a better interviewer of players had he been able to read *Nine Sides of the Diamond* early in his career. The book analyzes the defensive demands and strategies of each of the nine fielding positions in the game as executed by master fielders in each position—for example, "Robinson at third, Kaline in right field." In a rare acknowledgment of the value of the video industry, Barber is pleased that

television's slow-motion replays are "helping viewers to appreciate defensive play, as will this book."[19]

In some of his reviews, Barber's assessment is riveted upon an
issue raised in the book that is most crucial to him. His review of
Jules Tygiel's *Baseball's Great Experiment: Jackie Robinson and His
Legacy*, published in *The New Republic*, applauds the scope and
accuracy of the book, which chronicles the successful struggle
to integrate American baseball. But Barber focuses heavily upon
Tygiel's treatment of Branch Rickey's role in the Jackie Robinson
story because Red believes the author has "under-emphasized"
it. Until the end of his life Barber was convinced and sought to
persuade others that Rickey's motives were essentially "spiritual";
he wanted to address a tragic injustice that he had powerfully
been moved to recognize as a young man. Tygiel, like some other
researchers who have examined Rickey's historic initiative, supplies evidence that Rickey's motives were mixed—a combination of moral conviction, competitiveness, personal ambition,
and economic pragmatics. After Barber's review was published,
however, Tygiel wrote a personal letter thanking Barber for his
mostly positive critique and even for the suggestion that he may
have understated Rickey's central role: "Your comments provide some new [to me] and interesting insights, none of which
my sources revealed."[20]

One of the most poignant of Red Barber's book reviews was
the one he wrote on Ira Berkow's *Red: A Biography of Red Smith*,
published in the *Houston Times*. Barber praises Berkow's skill in
making the life of famed New York sportswriter Red Smith so
compelling that "it reads like a novel."[21] It is clear to those who
know the story of Barber's life why he would be so moved by a
well-told version of Smith's. Barber saw many of his own aspirations and struggles in Berkow's story of Smith, far beyond their
both being called "Red." Barber revered Smith's talents as a sports
columnist and was touched when Smith wrote "a beautiful column" on him when Red was let go by the Yankees. When Barber
began writing sports columns, he likely gauged his own success

by how close he might advance toward Smith's level of excellence, even though Barber had begun his career as a writer so much later in life. Berkow describes Smith struggling to pay his way through Notre Dame and, fueled by his determination to be a newspaperman, scraping to find work during the Great Depression, when he had a young family to support. The account triggers Red's recollection of his own protracted pursuit for a "shot in Cincinnati" and his accepting better broadcasting jobs for less money in order to reach his long-term goals. Barber recommends that all fledgling columnists study Berkow's account of how Smith "learned to polish his work until in 1976 he became the first sportswriter to receive a Pulitzer Prize."

Barber was writing this review around the time that Lylah's health was failing. He says that for him the most compelling part of Berkow's book addresses the terminal illness of Kay, Smith's first wife of thirty-three years, and his subsequent courtship of Phyllis, his second wife, "saving him from complete despair, loneliness and alcoholism." Smith, Barber concludes, "was a gifted professional; he knew the people in his world, a man of strong opinions that he expressed beautifully. He loved the English language, loved his family. . . . He was a man of strict integrity." Writers commenting on Barber's virtues would make similar claims after he died. Smith once told Barber that the most important thing about writing a column was "[to] be there." Barber affirms that Smith "was there: he saw for himself, wrote for himself and he was his own severest critic."

A Voice in the *Monitor*

On January 13, 1986, the features editor of the *Christian Science Monitor* wrote the soon-to-be seventy-eight-year-old Barber to express his delight that Red had offered to send the newspaper some pieces "with the possibility of something regular, perhaps a monthly column." He let Barber know that his proposed piece on the money to be spent in the upcoming Super Bowl "sounds great to run in the week before the game."[22] The piece, "Pro Football from $25 Franchise to Gold-Plated Super Bowl," was in fact published in the January 26, 1986, issue of the *Monitor*, the first of the monthly columns Red wrote for the paper through December 1988. Red begins the piece by associating the competitors in the ancient Roman Bread and Circus with the "two sets of gladiators" that football fans are eagerly waiting to watch in the upcoming contest. The former contestants were "fortunate to escape with their lives," while each of the latter will walk away with $36,000 if their team wins the Super Bowl and with $18,000 if it loses. For today's competitors, Red concludes, it is "Beer, Circus and so much money."[23]

That first article employs the template Barber had used for earlier columns and continued to employ for his three-year run in the *Monitor*. A current event or issue in sports and beyond triggers his return to the past for a comparison that reveals changes in our culture's values. In his fourth and final commitment to a column, Red publishes his cultural "report card," evaluating how effectively sports and the country have been navigating the issues that have concerned him since he was a young announcer: the qualities of an effective broadcaster, the character and spirit of a great athlete, the need for better safety protections in baseball, increasing violence in sports, and the impact of changes in the game of baseball and in the broadcast industry over time. But occasionally readers familiar with Barber's voice in print and on air encounter a piece in the *Monitor* that surprises—an unfamiliar but moving insight or anecdote or his naming of an influence upon him that readers do not recall his ever mentioning. In his 1986 column "Rickey Recognized the Invaluable Contributions of Baseball Wives," for instance, Barber repeats his familiar concern over burdens imposed upon a ballplayer's family by his protracted absences from home during the better part of a year. But it surprises the reader when his commentary about "baseball wives" prompts him sadly to confess, "I did not realize just how *completely* lonely it was for my wife until she wrote her book," *Lylah*, published in 1985.[24]

In a piece titled "Mirror, Mirror on the Wall, What Do Sports Tell Us All?" surveying what he sees as increasing levels of violence in American sports, Barber tells us that his understanding of the culture of American sports was powerfully influenced early in his career when he read Foster Rhea Dulles's 1940 book, *America Learns to Play: A History of Recreation.* Red explains that in this comprehensive book, a groundbreaking study of leisure in American culture from 1607 to 1940, Dulles, a historian and public intellectual, develops the argument that "the games a nation plays, the sporting events a nation attends, tell us much about the values of a people and their times." This early influence may, in part, account for Barber's career-long focus upon and critique of the cultural impacts of the sports that engaged him, that he broadcast, and about which he wrote.[25]

Still Moving and Shaking

Throughout the final ten years of his life, Red still engaged actively in public speaking, frequent live and telephone interviews, and sporadic, "one-time" broadcasts. His favorite one-time broadcasting gigs included annual Old Timers Baseball Games at various ballparks in the country. In 1982 Red broadcast the Cracker Jacks Old Timers Classic at RFK Stadium, where seventy-five-year-old Luke Appling hit a first-inning home run off Warren Spahn. According to Thomas Oliphant of the *Boston Globe,* seventy-five-year-old Barber, "the king of radio sportscasters, was succinct and accurate as ever." Red wrote a column about the 1987 Memorial Day game at Shea Stadium pitting 1969 Mets World Series All-Stars against former players from Ebbets Field. Red's job in that broadcast was to introduce all the returning Dodgers; he reported being touched by the invitation to perform that role. In his *Monitor* column, he describes with unabashed awe and affection the aging stars who showed up for the game, still in fair to excellent shape.[26]

Perhaps the most moving experience for Red that day was his reunion with Joe Garagiola. Barber later revealed in an interview that even though he had said some tough things about Joe in the past, the broadcaster, in Red's eyes, had really changed: now "Joe does his preparation." At the 1987 Memorial Day Game, Red was surprised and pleased when Garagiola approached him with a confession of his own when he admitted, "You know, I've been remiss, Red. I've been meaning to tell you that I've always had a deep appreciation for your professionalism. You taught me a great deal. Naturally, I don't like some of the things you wrote, but I just want to tell you I'm grateful to you." Barber recalls, "Well, that was pretty big. That's quite a compliment."[27] A year later Garagiola responded to a letter Red had sent him after Joe's retirement from NBC. Joe wanted to thank him for the many lessons he had learned from Red Barber: "I feel that my leaving NBC might have been another one. . . . When conditions are putting you in a position you would rather not be in, it's time to declare yourself. That's what *you* did. Don't compromise; make a decision and leave with head held high."[28]

When Red visited the booth at another Old Timers Game in San Diego, Padres broadcaster and Red's one-time apprentice with the Yankees, Jerry Coleman, invited him to announce the first inning, but Red shook his head. The game moved on until it was the fifth inning, when Barber piped up, "I'm ready." According to Coleman, "Red, like the old pro that he is, had been studying the players, getting the feel, the flow of the game. He was ready *now*. He takes the mike and that voice of his was as stirring as ever. On the first play, Red calls it, 'here's a line drive to right field—just as clean as a hound's tooth.'"[29]

Barber also continued to make appearances for interviews on network television throughout the 1980s. After the publication of *1947* he appeared on *The Today Show, Good Morning America,* and on a CBS *This Morning* sequence on aging. In 1987 Barber taped an interview for a controversial episode on *Nightline* focusing on the fortieth anniversary of the integration of Major League Baseball. Barber's taped interview for the segment, describing Robinson's trials and fortitude, aired before a phone interview with Dodgers general manager Al Campanis, who, according to Red, had been invited to appear on the program by phone hookup along with Don Newcombe, who could not show up. The two were chosen because they had been Robinson's friends and teammates.

Red knew Campanis when he had played with, befriended, and actively defended Robinson in 1947. In a *Tallahassee Democrat* interview with Bill McGrotha, Barber addressed Campanis's struggle when asked on *Nightline* why there were so few Blacks in baseball's hierarchy. Red acknowledged that Campanis stumbled into what struck his interviewers, and likely most of the program's viewers, as a racist response when he answered: "Maybe they lack the necessities." After botched attempts to explain himself in follow-up questions, Campanis was sorely pummeled by his *Nightline* hosts. Barber, however, tells McGrotha that the aging and not particularly articulate old-timer should be forgiven, but not for the *content* of what he said. Barber believed that Campanis, anticipating questions about his firsthand experiences with Jackie, was unprepared to unpack the range of systemic institutional practices that had long kept Black Americans from fair representation in sports management. Campanis was fired as the Dodgers' GM within days. But when Red was questioned about the episode, he felt obligated to report what he considered a relevant context and to foreground for readers the virtues of an old friend who was incapable of ad-libbing on live national television a cogent response to a serious issue.[30]

"This I Know"

Among Barber's most widely touted media events in the latter years of his life was his role as expert commentator for Ken Burns's eighteen-hour Emmy-award-winning celebration of the national pastime, *Baseball*, arguably the most significant, and certainly the longest, television documentary on America's game. Burns and his co-producer, Lynn Novick, contacted Barber in spring 1990, and he, Novick, and their crew met with him at the end of April at Barber's home in Tallahassee. They offered Barber a $350 honorarium for his contribution to *Baseball*, and Burns informed him of their plan to "concentrate on the years you were announcing. We will want you to talk about the highlights on the field during that time, as well as the changes the game underwent. . . . Of course, the integration of major league baseball will be very important."[31]

Although Barber had died by the time *Baseball* aired in September 1994, he is very much alive in some of the most critical moments of the series. Burns used Barber's commentary at several points, including the sections on MacPhail's efforts to promote the broadcasting of baseball on radio, the Dodgers' capturing of the 1941 pennant, the intimate joys of Ebbets Field and its colorful fans, and Mickey Mantle's struggles to play baseball with a deteriorating body. Most significant, Burns and Novick relied on Barber to tell much of the story that many consider the most important development in the history of baseball: the coming of Jackie Robinson.

In the documentary's episode entitled "Inning 6: The National Pastime," Barber calls Robinson the greatest gate attraction since Ruth and the most competitive ballplayer since Ty Cobb. He marvels at Robinson's ability to control himself in the face of blind bigotry. Barber tells the story of Rickey's signing of Robinson, Jackie's pledge not to fight back against his attackers for three years, and Red's own struggle to surmount the prejudice he had absorbed from his youth in the Deep South. Barber also recounts Durocher's reaction to the Dodgers' player petition objecting to the signing of Robinson and vividly describes Pee Wee Reese telling his teammates, "If he can take my job, he's entitled to it." The Old Redhead recounts the rabid race baiting Robinson received from Phillies manager Ben Chapman and describes how Chapman's attacks provoked Eddie Stanky, who had opposed the signing of Robinson, to defend his teammate. Then Barber recreates the moving scene when Reese offered his arm in friendship to Robinson in front of a hostile crowd in Cincinnati. In *Baseball* the octogenarian Barber embodies the persona of a man who came of age in the Deep South early in the twentieth century and who had evolved into a more racially enlightened American. In his soft, elegant but passionate voice, Walter Lanier Barber describes the key moments of baseball's greatest civic accomplishment. Barber tells Burns's PBS audience and future generations of baseball fans: "Robinson did more for me than I did for him; he 'matured me'" and, by implication, he matured the nation.[32]

In a September 1994 interview just before *Baseball* premiered on PBS, Burns told PBS's Charlie Rose about a moment when Barber "describes a conversation he had with Branch Rickey telling him about why he was going to bring a black man and he goes, 'This I know.'" Apparently, at that moment Burns realized just where Barber's narration of the conversation with Rickey would go in the film: "I know there will be a title that says 'This I Know,' and it will initiate what will be the dramatic centerpiece of this series, which is the arrival of Jackie Robinson." Burns also knew that as Barber was not in good health, he needed to film Red while he still could. Burns told Rose that for his documentary, featuring fifty-three interviews, Barber "was the person that I needed to go and see first. And he is fantastic."[33]

Barber continued to make regular public-speaking appearances until his last years for gigs which paid him up to five thousand dollars plus all expenses. He signed up with Branson Entertainment to be guest speaker and talk baseball on cruises sailing to Alaska and to the Bahamas. One of his most widely reported appearances was at the 1984 Denver Athletic Club Baseball Symposium, arranged partly to stimulate support for a Major League baseball team for the city. It was a two-day event for which Red was the featured speaker. Barber received scores of letters heralding his performance, including raves from Bowie Kuhn and Denver Bears GM James H. Burris, who wrote, "Red, you may be the single most articulate baseball speaker I've ever heard."[34] Part of his address featured, of course, the spellbinding re-creation of the fourth game, last half inning of the 1947 World Series. Red also apparently was the "life of the party" when he appeared at a 1986 White House luncheon, hosted by President Ronald Reagan, "in honor of baseball reporters and sportscasters."[35]

A president pressed for Barber's presence, but so did an elementary school teacher. Red accepted an invitation to talk with a fourth-grade class at Tallahassee's Sealy Elementary School in November 1990. The students had just read Bette Bao Lord's classic children's book, *In the Year of the Boar and Jackie Robinson*, which includes references to Red Barber's broadcasting for the Dodgers. The book tells the story of a young immigrant girl who is so inspired by baseball that she sets out to form a team of her own. Red brought some of his favorite books, and his wife, to class along with him. When her Alzheimer's disease progressed, Barber would not leave Lylah at home alone if he could avoid it. The fourth graders wrote a thank-you letter to their octogenarian guests, promising that they will "remember many things you said, like 'words once spoken can never be taken back,' and the story you told about Mr. Branch Rickey and the young black catcher that was so sad we almost cried."[36]

Finally, Red Barber's activities during the last decade of his life included his unyielding commitment to local and national civic and political causes. A longtime contributor, Barber became a member of Planned Parenthood's Board of Advocates, which included, among others, Steve Allen, Pearl Bailey, Harry Belafonte, Judy Collins, Ed Asner, Leonard Bernstein, Norman Lear, Betty Friedan, and Joanne Woodward. In a 1990 letter to Barber, Planned Parenthood president Fay Wattleton thanked Red for his generous and timely gift to the organization's Freedom Fund, a gift that would "ensure that our basic rights of individual decision-making and privacy are protected."[37]

Red generously recorded tapes and sometimes spoke on air for NPR fundraising campaigns when stations asked for his support. An October 1990 launch of a major campaign for a second public station at Florida State University—one that would carry all NPR programs—brought Bob Edwards and Red Barber together physically for the first time for one of their four-minute Friday *Morning Edition* conversations. The celebration began with a gala Thursday night party for donors, featuring local classical music performers, and, of course, Barber and Edwards. The festivities continued the next day with a "Breakfast with Bob and Red." Those who had snapped up one of the 140 tickets to the breakfast would be invited to watch the live *Morning Edition* conversation between Edwards and Barber in person, at a campus venue set up for the broadcast.

Lifetime Achievement Rewarded

Red Barber did not decorate his home office with the many awards, certificates, and honors he received throughout his career; most of them he gave to broadcast museums, friends and relatives, and libraries. During the last decade of his life, after having won the new Hall of Fame's Ford C. Frick Award and rebooting his broadcast career for NPR, he was showered with recognitions of his professional achievements, as well as a few of his less publicized accomplishments. In 1984 he was inducted into the American Sportscasters Hall of Fame during its inaugural year, along with the distinguished company of Don Dunphy, Ted Husing, Graham McNamee, and Bill Stern. Red had agreed to share some remarks about Husing and McNamee at the October induction ceremony, held in New York City. But, unfortunately, he could not attend because, according to a UPI press release, he needed to "be with his wife, who was recovering from surgery." Still, Red must have been gratified that it was Ralph Branca who presented his award at the Sportscasters Hall of Fame banquet and Rachel Robinson who accepted it for him.[38]

Closer to home, in 1984 Barber was presented with Tallahassee's Fourth Annual National Easter Seal Achievement Award, designed to honor professionals who had demonstrated distinguished public service throughout their careers. Barber received the award at a dinner held at the Tallahassee Civic Center, where his portrait was unveiled and placed on a wall next to the those of the three former recipients, including former Florida governor Leroy Collins and Florida A&M coach Jake Gaither. The president of the Easter Seal board of directors welcomed the attendees, and Pat Summerall, one of Barber's favorite broadcasters, served as emcee for the event. According to one reporter, "No one was prepared for the magic of Red's performance that evening, even though *Tallahassee Democrat* Sports Editor, Bill McGrotha, had promised it would be worth the $50 dinner tab." Just as he'd done in Denver, Red stunned the Tallahassee audience with his dramatic recreation of the last half inning, Game Four, of the 1947 World Series.[39]

In 1985 Barber received the prestigious George Polk Career Award for his work as a sportscaster. Bestowed annually by Long Island University since 1914, the Polk Award honors influential work of reporters and journalists throughout the country. At the Roosevelt Hotel in New York City, Barber was lauded for "lifelong distinction" and for "making sportscasting history by narrating, with a calm eloquence that made it all seem so natural, the dramatic arrival and success of [Jackie Robinson] to break big league baseball's racial barrier."[40]

In 1986 Red Barber was pleased to learn from the dean of liberal arts and sciences at the University of Florida, in response to his inquiry, that he would be awarded an undergraduate degree, fifty-six years after he'd withdrawn from the school. "Your long wait for the sheepskin from the University of Florida," Dean Sidman wrote to Red, "will soon be over."[41] Red likely had winced throughout his adult life when some doors were closed to him—teaching a college course or receiving an honorary degree from at least one institution—because he was not a college graduate, as were many of the people who had strongly influenced him: Larry MacPhail, Branch Rickey, Edward R. Murrow, his wife, and his mother.

The next year the Old Redhead was named to the National Baseball Hall of Fame's Veterans Committee, where his experience, recall, and eloquence would play a strong role in determining which overlooked players from the past would finally be recognized in the game's most exclusive club.[42] Also in 1987, at the sixtieth anniversary of WRUF, the station established its own Hall of Fame, inducting Red Barber among its first members. Two months later, WRUF dedicated its new newsroom at the University of Florida to its most famous broadcaster, and it remains the Red Barber Newsroom. On Red's eightieth birthday, the state of Florida recognized Red in a reception at the capitol in Tallahassee, where the secretary of state, by formal resolution, declared February 17, 1988, "Red Barber Day."[43]

But the most prestigious recognition during Red's last decade, and perhaps of his life, was the distinguished Peabody Personal Award for 1990, which he received in May 1991. The Peabody Awards are generally considered the "Pulitzer" of broadcast journalism and mass communication. Barber was honored for his career as sports announcer from 1934 to 1966 and for his ten years at NPR. Upon learning of his selection, he told a reporter, in a characteristically understated but sincere response: "I was pleased to have sixty years' worth of work—and I think it was good work—recognized."[44] Once again, Barber could not travel to New York to receive the award. Bob Edwards, who received it for him, wrote Red: "It was a great honor to accept the Peabody award on your behalf. The only flaw is that you were not included before."[45]

"Twenty-Five Years in the Writing"

Since Barber was a prolific letter writer throughout his life, he received many letters in return. Although the letters he wrote are scarce, Red fortunately saved thousands of those he received. Correspondence during the last decade of his life documents instances of his generosity, a healing of some past conflicts, a renewed connection to old friends, and heartfelt responses to reflections he'd recently shared in the electronic or print media. Letters from the agency Futures for Children document that Red Barber sponsored a Native American child, Rhonda Begaye, born in 1976 and living in California.[46] From the time she started school until his death, when Rhonda was sixteen, Red donated $300 at regular intervals to help her family cover expenses for her clothes, books, shoes, and school supplies. From time-to-time Rhonda wrote letters to him, though there is no record of their ever meeting. In one letter an adolescent Rhonda informs Red that she likes "rock and roll, and baseball," and in a later missive she apologizes for not having written for a while: "I didn't get you a valentine card because you deserve the best and the store didn't have the best kind." In early 1992 she lets Red know, "I am doing my best to get on the Honor Roll, but Geometry is really hard. I think I will be able to get a B plus." She includes a recent photo and signs the letter, "Your true Indian Friend."[47]

Red's letters also document other examples of his magnanimity. Two years before he died, Red received a letter from Joan Willoughby Shattuck, whom he and Lylah had once heard sing at a recital in New York City when she was in high school. They were so impressed with her talent that Red offered to pay for her education at the Julliard Music Academy, the school she so wanted to attend, if she would accompany their young daughter from time to time to the symphony and opera. Her parents wanted Sarah to experience and learn more about these arts from a friend closer to her own age. Shattuck was not prepared to accept Red's offer at the time; her life took her in a different direction. But forty years later she wanted him to know that she had never forgotten his generous offer and thought about him often.[48]

Barber also received letters from people thanking him for kind words he wrote to them on a recent accomplishment, including William Paley, Bill Moyers, and Tom Brokaw, to whom he had written concerning his 1987 Gorbachev interview.[49] Others wrote to thank Red for favors he had performed, including Pee Wee Reese, after Red had supported his nomination for the Hall of Fame. Reese's revealing response conveys the depth of his bond with another man who had also learned about the fleeting value of public recognition: "Thanks for all of your help in trying to get me into the Hall. For some reason or other, Red, it doesn't mean that much to me anymore. Shouldn't say that, but I can to you."[50] Audrey Woods, widow of Jim Woods, the Yankees' broadcaster who was replaced by Phil Rizzuto, wrote Red to thank him for the kind words he'd recently spoken about her husband in an obituary: "They were a special tribute to my dear husband; I always felt Jim was never really appreciated for the many years he devoted to his craft, but I am finding I was mistaken. There are those like you who did appreciate his special talents and do have fond memories of days gone by. . . . We both treasured your friendship throughout the years."[51]

Staff members he had worked with early in his professional life also reconnected with Red now that he was speaking to them on the air again. Harry Moorman, Red's first telegraph operator back at Cincinnati's WSAI, decided to send him some old clippings reporting stories he might have forgotten and also reminded him of the very hot day in the studio when two "society ladies" were shocked when stumbling upon Red Barber broadcasting bare-chested.[52]

Bob Pasotti, another broadcast assistant from Red's past, wrote a moving letter to Barber in the 1980s to explain Red's powerful impact on his life. Pasotti was Red's young statistician in the Dodgers' broadcast booth in the early 1950s who was occasionally assaulted by pencils that Barber would throw at him when he was underperforming on the job. Pasotti left the broadcast booth, later pursued a PhD, and eventually became a philosophy professor at Adelphi University. He struggled for years with alcoholism, but now he was sober. He tells Barber that the "letter has been 25 years in the writing." Pasotti thanked Red for "teaching me discipline." When he worked with Barber, Pasotti said, "I was too smart-ass, know-it-all young to appreciate what was happening. But I've come to realize what a tremendous impression for good those years with you . . . stamped upon my arrogant spirit."[53]

As we have noted, Red received scores of letters from *Morning Edition* listeners and also in response to articles written by and about him. When Barber was profiled in a 1988 AARP *News Bulletin,* an article that focused upon his active engagement in life after his "retirement," he received a stream of letters from other retirees who admired his buoyancy. Barber's comments in the AARP piece prompted a poignant letter from Janet Murrow, Edward's widow, about her efforts to keep herself engaged during her life in a retirement community in Needham, Massachusetts. Murrow had corresponded with the Barbers from time to time since her husband's death, and she caught them up on the lives of her son and his family. She noted that she was "hobbling about" because of a recent knee surgery. She liked her retirement apartment, "but it is hard to fit into three rooms after life in a five-bedroom house . . . too many boxes of papers and photos which I hope to get at this summer. Are you worn out reading this letter? I hope you are both well; I am sure you are both happy. All best wishes and love to you, Janet."[54]

Finally, many other correspondents tried to convey what listening to Barber's voice when they were younger had meant for their lives over the years, as we read in a letter to Red from former *Washington Post* sportswriter and novelist Jane Leavy: "In 1981, I wrote an opening day story for the *Post* about a little girl who slept with a Sam Esposito glove under her pillow and the sound of Red Barber's voice in her dreams. A few days later I got a note postmarked 'The Catbird Seat.' I have treasured that note ever since. . . . I have it in the box with my first baseball cards." Leavy tells Barber that she turned that story into a novel: "I am taking the liberty of sending it to you, with hopes that you read it and it makes you laugh. Thank you for having a look and thank you for all those years of whispered inspiration."[55]

There is no Hall of Fame for those who have significantly and favorably influenced the lives of others. But it is not hard to imagine that Red was moved deeply by the appreciative letters he received during the decade before he died. They may have eased his mind when, summoned by his favorite psalm, he would at last "lay me down and take my rest."

17

A Closed Family

I n their profiles of Red Barber published in newspapers and
magazines during the last decade of his life, writers sketch Barber's later years in Tallahassee with mellow shades of autumnal contentment. The richness of this final phase of Barber's life,
according to reporters, is rooted in his invigorating release from
externally imposed assignments and a life-enhancing involvement with the comforting rhythms of the domestic and the natural worlds as they surround and uplift him at home in Tallahassee.
He completely controls the use of his talents and the pursuit of
his interests, now occupying his crowning catbird seat.

"Your Daily Work Should Never Be Completely Finished"

Most of his profilers share with their readers Barber's delight
with having been unwittingly "liberated" by Michael Burke. As
the story now goes, by ending Red's career as a full-time sportscaster, the new Yankees president actually enabled Barber to pursue the rigorous but satisfying life of a writer, an ambition long
considered but deferred. Now, whenever he likes, he can comment upon pressing issues or tell engaging stories without being
cut off by the whim of a producer or director, and he can take his
audiences well beyond the realm of sports. Barber reports that

he no longer watches most sports broadcasts, except for championship and World Series baseball games, if he can find the time.[1] He asserts that he no longer recognizes Major League baseball today, with its designated hitters, artificial turf, endlessly chattering announcers, and million-dollar contracts.[2] Red told columnists who asked about his favorite teams or players that as a broadcaster, he had forced himself to remain detached from any team or player, so why would he want to get "close to the game" at this stage of his life?[3] However, he enjoys watching golf tournaments on television because "each player performs by himself, tension builds slowly, and the coverage is superb; it affords time to savor the play," the way Barber himself once liked to call his games on radio.[4]

In late life conversations, Red told his interviewers that his contentment was partly the result of his being "probably the richest man you've ever known," in the sense that he no longer is in debt to anyone.[5] According to a letter from the banker who negotiated Red's purchase of his house in Tallahassee, he had, in fact, paid off the balance for the home not long after he and Lylah had moved in, probably just after he got cash from the sale of his property in Key Biscayne.[6] So now he doesn't have to do any work that does not interest him. He told one interviewer that he had recently been offered a lot of money to do a commercial for dentures but declined the opportunity because he still had most of his own teeth. When the advertiser told him, "You could pretend," Red replied he was "not that hard up."[7] Barber always claimed that he used the products he endorsed and appears to have honored that vow, at least when it came to promoting false teeth.

In 1989 Barber may have sabotaged another invitation to capitalize upon his famous voice by providing a taped opening for that year's Yankees broadcasts on wpix-tv. Marty Appel, then vice president of public relations at the station, wanted to alternate Barber's and Mel Allen's "Hi everyone, this is Red Barber/Mel Allen. Welcome to today's broadcast." Allen had taped the friendly and popular "welcome" for 1988 game broadcasts, and

Appel thought it would be fun to integrate Barber's welcome into the 1989 game openings: "What a wonderful reaction this would have in New York, especially for all of us baby boomers," he wrote to Red. Barber tentatively accepted the invitation when they discussed the project over the phone, but Appel sensed Red had misgivings, and never followed up with him on the proposal, concluding that "perhaps Barber's was not the best voice for that purpose."[8]

Profile writers note that the slower pace of Red's life belied his still intense energy: "He always addresses life with the relish and vigor of a much younger man."[9] When Barber was invited to speak or write about aging, he focused upon the difference between "being old" and "aging," a comparison that aligns with the difference between body and spirit. Just as some of the most outstanding athletes compensate for any deficits in their physical gifts by a powerful commitment to performing at their best, so seniors can continue to thrive even with weaker bodies if the spirit is willing.[10] One reporter interviewing Barber at his house in Tallahassee recorded Red's disgust when, having just arrived home from a visit to New York a week earlier, he discovered his swimming pool covered in pine needles swept from his trees by hard autumn winds. But immediately after his whining about nature's untidiness, a hard breeze again began blowing through the trees by the poolside where he and the reporter were standing. As the branches began to rock and moan, in an impetuous leap from weak body to inflamed spirit, Red proclaimed, "Isn't nature wonderful! There is nothing like a hard wind blowing through tall pines to make a fella feel really back home."[11]

Barber's seamless integration of old age with the spirit of youth is contagious: one profile writer recalls the response of an aging college professor who tunes in Red on *Morning Edition* whenever he jogs on Fridays: "I've heard his baseball stories before, but what I love about the guy, what I envy him for, is his wonderful content in retirement. He not only smells the flowers; he *grows* them."[12] Barber's autumnal focus upon the renewing cycles of life was reflected in his latter-day fondness for housework, which drew him closer to his wife. Housework, he gushed, as if it were a blessing, never ends; he and Lylah wake up each morning to "muddle around" with daily chores, and then they wake up the next morning to start the cycle anew. Once a week they go out grocery shopping together, selecting their favorites at Publix, and the next week they enjoy the same delight all over again!

In almost all of his interviews during the final eight to ten years of his life, Barber mentioned his "sixth book," on which he was gleefully working. One reporter, frustrated with his inability to convey Red's excitement about the project, tells his readers, "If only you could hear his voice when he talks about it!"[13] The book was never published, and no manuscript survives, but we have Red's animated descriptions of its prospective content. In some accounts the book will be titled "Odds and Ends," and in others it will be called "Extra Innings." According to some descriptions, it will include a chapter on the "therapeutic pleasure of silently watering the yard with a garden hose" and another on the series of cats that he and Lylah had adopted. One chapter, called "The Art of Indirection," will link the strategy of Casey Stengel's speaking style and the tricks of Blackstone the Magician.[14]

In one interview in which Barber described the recurring cycle of his day's activities, he concluded: "Your daily work should never be completely finished. You should always go to bed thinking what you will need to do when you get up."[15] "You need to keep the cycle going," Barber was telling his listeners and perhaps explaining why this "sixth book" never got *terminated* in the form of publication. He just kept writing it in his head and perhaps typing it on leaf after leaf of paper, leaves recurring every spring. That way, he knew each night there was always something to work on the next day. In his moving obituary for Red Barber, *New York Times* sports columnist George Vecsey recalls the day near the end of the 1950 Dodgers' season, when the team lost the pennant and all the fans began mourning. He remembers vividly, as if it were yesterday, what Red said softly, definitively, to his audience: "Things didn't quite work out this season; still, it was a good one. We'll begin another one soon and it will probably be good too." Vecsey describes the effects of that simple, unadorned encouragement as "more than just a vehicle for selling tickets"; for Red's listeners it was "prophecy"—an irresistible intimation of renewal. Vecsey recalls years later he heard an inspired Black Baptist preacher in Brooklyn delivering an Easter sermon with a message about rebirth "so vital that it reminded me of Red Barber that autumn afternoon."[16]

"Nothing Like a Hard Wind Blowing"

Bob Edwards writes that "the last two years of Red Barber's life were hell." It is true that during his last few years Red was experiencing gastric episodes, a deteriorating intestinal system, bladder infections, and hearing and vision loss. Having lost much of his stomach, he could not eat substantial meals to maintain his weight. Lylah was gradually succumbing to the incurable manifestations of Alzheimer's disease—including dementia and unpredictable behavioral and personality changes. Barber was unwilling to share Lylah's diagnosis with anyone except Sarah, not even with his only living sibling, Effie Virginia, with whom he periodically corresponded. Edwards sent letters to Red, talked to him every Friday for twelve years, and spent time with him and Lylah on several occasions, but he did not learn about her Alzheimer's disease until after Red died. After he learned of Lylah's condition, it occurred to Edwards that during the final years of their weekly four minutes together on air, "Red must have been nervous that she may have been walking out their front door while he was chatting with me."[17]

According to Sarah, due to her "very closed" family's penchant for privacy, her father never entertained the thought of having caretakers come into the house to help him look after her mother. During the last years of his life her father would occasionally collapse and have to be rushed to the hospital. Sarah then would fly down from New York or from Santa Fe—where she moved in

1991—to care for her mother until Red returned home, remaining during his recovery. She tried to persuade him to move with Lylah into a "total care community," where they could have their own apartment and remain independent, but Lylah vetoed each one they visited. According to Sarah, after that point, whenever the subject of moving to a care community was raised, "Mother would get hysterical and we could not talk about it any longer."[18]

After her father died Sarah shared her experiences of caregiving for her aging parents with two professional psychotherapists who were writing a book to help friends and family members navigate the challenges of that role; she allowed the authors to use her name and transcriptions of their interviews with her for their book. Sarah describes difficulties she encountered when she came home to stay with her parents during their later years, particularly when her father was recovering from his own bouts with ulcers and intestinal problems. She was concerned about the "pitchers of martinis" her father would regularly share with Lylah.[19] According to one of her friends in Santa Fe, Sarah was disappointed when, as soon as she walked into the house in Tallahassee, her mother would say, "Sarah's here, Red; let's have some drinks!" because she knew the conversation could easily deteriorate.[20] She thought her father may have been attempting to "medicate" Lylah, but dementia and alcohol would sometimes send her mother into a "tirade" that was difficult to temper. When Sarah tried to persuade Red not to accommodate Lylah's drinking, he would take out his hearing aid "and that would pretty much end the conversation."[21]

Sarah suggests that her mother's mix of dementia and martinis unloosed the long unresolved issue of her "lifestyle" that simmered just beneath the surface of their mutual efforts to be good friends. Even before her mother's first symptoms of Alzheimer's appeared, Sarah acknowledges, her relationship with her mother was fragile.[22] Edwards recalled that upon first meeting Red and Lylah in person in the early 1980s, he asked about their daughter and then inquired about grandchildren. "Lylah rolled her eyes and said dryly, 'Well, that will never happen.'"[23] We know that Lylah once had longed for continuance of the Scarborough family line, wanted grandchildren, and perhaps continued to believe that Sarah's lesbianism was a choice that she could "unmake" rather than the person she really was.

Sarah affirms, however, that her relationship with her father "was not conflicted in that way. I think he generally found my presence comforting."[24] A part of the actual hell for Barber during these tough years must have been hearing the two women he most loved in conflict; removing his earpiece was an act of self-preservation, his only way to assert control. But even during the final two years of his life, he was still successfully airing his Friday broadcasts on NPR; visiting, along with Lylah, an elementary school classroom; attending a Camellia Society affair honoring the couple at Tallahassee's Dorothy B. Oven Park; continuing to work on what he referred to as "my sixth book"; and caring for his wife, who wanted to keep living with him at home.

Based on his public reflections, at this point in his life, Barber likely was less concerned about his and Lylah's dying than about the grim possibility of their living beyond any potential for what Red's mother called "quality," the purpose for living. In a 2020 interview, Bob Edwards recalled Sarah's telling him that in the months before her father died, one of their neighbors in Tallahassee had passed away. Barber's response was a subdued, "At least he is out of it now."[25] Sarah Barber absorbed her father's concern about honoring the quality of human life. When she moved her mother to a long-term care facility in Tallahassee after her father's death, she left a "Do Not Resuscitate" directive with administrators; she was horrified to learn that at one point, Lylah was put on life support in violation of the directive that would have enabled a natural death. Several years after Lylah's death, Sarah, afflicted with a rapidly progressing brain disorder, began losing mobility, balance, verbal and manual skills, and the ability to read. She, too, expressed to her friends in Santa Fe her fears about a life protracted without quality.[26]

"In the Middle of Five Camellia Plants . . ."

Bob Edwards poignantly recalls the closing weeks of Barber's life. On Red's final Friday broadcast, October 2, 1992, he thought Barber's voice sounded raspy and signed off by telling him to "take care of that cold, or whatever it is. . . . It was our last conversation." Red could not take part in the Friday, October 9, broadcast because, in what must have been terrible pain, he had driven himself and Lylah to the hospital. When he arrived at the Tallahassee Memorial Regional Hospital with Lylah, staff there realized they had two seriously ill patients.[27]

That morning Barber underwent emergency surgery for an intestinal blockage, which was removed, but after the surgery he did not regain consciousness and remained in critical condition. According to Sarah, Lylah was placed in the hospital's psychological unit with Red next door under intensive care.[28] On October 16 Edwards told NPR listeners that Red's condition remained critical and let them know where to send messages for him. Edwards prepared a statement to be released by NPR should Barber die. The show's producer then drafted an obituary to record for use on air and urged Edwards to write another, more personal piece to deliver to Red's Morning Edition audiences. On the following Thursday, October 22, Red died of "complications resulting from surgery, pneumonia, and kidney and lung problems related to age."[29] At that point Sarah moved Lylah into the hospital's nearby nursing home facility, where she continued to live until her death in 1997. According to Sarah, Lylah was disoriented, and did not resist the move.[30]

Although Edwards was out of town on Friday, October 23, the station ran his reading of the producer's obit during the first hour of Morning Edition, and during Red's four minutes in the second hour, listeners heard Bob's personal eulogy. He described the many dimensions of Red Barber, his wide-ranging interests, and then regretfully reflected upon things Edwards wished he had asked his Friday partner about but now would never be able to.

He invoked the amazement he felt the first time he heard Red, in his late seventies, energetically perform his celebrated re-creation of that riveting last half inning from the 1947 World Series. Finally, he summarized succinctly all that Barber has taught "three generations of broadcasters," but he wondered, "Who will teach us now?" His loss is palpable, but he remains rich in memories to sustain him and fortunately has secured a Barber audiotape because for this Kentucky Colonel, "listening to that voice was better than a julep on Derby Day."[31]

Edwards and two of his *Morning Edition* producers made it to Barber's home in Tallahassee on Sunday, October 25, the day before Red's funeral, where they were greeted by Sarah and a "collection of Red's friends and relatives," including his sister, Effie Virginia. A little later in the day they were joined by Mel Allen. Sarah generously invited everyone to take part in the project of "emptying Daddy's liquor cabinet," starting with about "fifteen bottles of booze on the kitchen counter." According to Edwards, "It looked as though Red had prepared for any eventuality. Irish wakes have always been my favorite." The lively afternoon was punctuated with memorable Red Barber stories: "They treated us as if we had been a part of the family all of our lives," Edwards recalls. The best storyteller, he says, was Red's animated sister. When Bob's producer "heard her talk, he wanted to give her Red's Friday spot on *Morning Edition*." The next morning, a crowd of two hundred mourners assembled for Barber's funeral service at St. John's Episcopal Church, where attendees sang "Joyful, Joyful, We Adore Thee," "A Mighty Fortress," and "Amazing Grace." "There I was," says Edwards, "a one-time Catholic altar boy, standing next to the former Melvin Israel, and belting out Protestantism's greatest hits!"[32]

According to the *Tallahassee Democrat*, the thirty-minute memorial service "was as concise and lyrical as a Barber broadcast." Dr. J. Stanley Marshall, former Florida State University president, spoke the eulogy, hailing Barber as "the forerunner, the pioneer, the Prometheus" of impartial sports broadcasting. After the service, fellow mourners greeted one another; among the crowd were Vin Scully, Duke Snider, Ralph Branca, Pee Wee Reese, and Peter O'Malley, Walter's son. Vin Scully told a reporter that on October 22, just after he'd learned about Red's death but just before the fourth game of the World Series, which he was scheduled to announce, he could hear Red Barber saying, "'Now, don't you talk about me during the game. These people aren't tuning in to hear about me. Talk about the game.' It was a difficult night. It helped that Red was in the booth with me."[33]

The *Tallahassee Democrat* confirmed that among the many amusing and poignant stories they told after the service, "The main thing the former athletes recalled about Barber was his decency as a human being, each remembering the Ol' Redhead as a 'class act.'" Pee Wee Reese recalled: "When I was a young player, and had a bad game, he'd come down to the clubhouse afterward and say, 'Hang in there. You're going to have a long career in the majors.' He helped me a lot that way. He was a good friend."[34] Edwards tells us that after the service he and his two colleagues joined Red's family in Barber's backyard, "to a spot in the middle of five camellia plants. There was a pile of red clay about a foot high next to a hole some eight inches in diameter. Inside the hole were the ashes of Red Barber." Sarah sprinkled in some blossoms and other mourners took a handful of dirt and placed it over the ashes. Then, in the "finest of old Southern traditions, everyone entered the house, filled with food of all kinds," including Mississippi mud cake, "one of those heavenly confections that makes you feel the blood rushing up to your face." Five years later, the subsequent owners of the Barber home would kindly allow Sarah to lay her mother's ashes in the same backyard site among the camellias that Red and Lylah had planted.[35]

"His Was a Voice That Made Walls Tumble"

Personal letters delivered to Edwards and newspaper obituaries document what individuals from diverse audiences considered important to remember about Red Barber. Letter writers frequently mentioned ways in which Barber had changed their perspective on important matters, whether in his conversations with Bob or in his earlier work as a sports broadcaster. One writer admitted that as a youngster in Brooklyn during the early 1940s his impressions of the South were stereotypical and negative: "[The South was] a land of racist senators and a *Gone with the Wind* society. The Mason Dixon Line was as impenetrable as the Berlin Wall. The voice of Red Barber was instrumental in breaking this barrier. His southern voice was full of compassion and decency. It had no bounds. When Red Barber solicited for blood donors in World War II, I realized a bond of decency tied people of all cultures together. He was more than a ball and strike announcer. His was a voice that made walls tumble." Another writer also believed that Barber's broadcasts, at least temporarily, dissolved cultural barriers. His affecting words and images recreated for first- and second-generation immigrants "a more genteel America, steeped in arcane traditions and embodied within the confines of the ballpark—an America where we all belonged, no matter where we started from."[36]

Scores of obituaries published in the days after Red's death recount the story of Red Barber's life as sportswriters assessed his accomplishments and attempted to articulate the hallmarks of his character. They recalled Barber's many "firsts" as a broadcaster, described the unique strengths of his announcing style and recounted his role in introducing Jackie Robinson to Major League Baseball. Some repeated handfuls of Red's folksy "Barbarisms," more perceptive writers insisting that he actually used them sparingly because he knew how repetition easily slid into "schtick." Many were laced with nostalgia: "He was representative of an earlier time when announcers textured the game, magnified it and made it unforgettable."[37]

In his nostalgic October 23, 1992, obituary, George Vecsey describes Barber as perfect for a time when baseball was played in daylight and on radio. Barber's "soft-spoken voice and meticulous intellect conveyed baseball as a rural game being played by men outdoors, who should not be taken too seriously." Vecsey wrote a piece for the *Times* two days later, lamenting that some of the recent World Series games had aired into darkness—into midnight, too late for kids to stay up and watch, and even Vecsey himself would fall asleep before the final out. How different it was for him when he listened to the October climax as a boy. While raking leaves on a sunny fall afternoon, he heard the game's story from the lips of "mellifluous Red Barber . . . and stentorian Mel Allen." The passing of Red Barber two days earlier, at least to this fan of the game, seemed coterminous with the last chapter of Major League Baseball.[38]

We get a different sense of Barber's impact, however, from James "Scotty" Reston, who was interviewed by Craig Basse of the *Tampa Bay Times* on the day that Red Barber died. Reston saw Barber as a "pioneer of both national radio and national television sports reporting." By bringing baseball on television into the American living room, "he helped to save the game into its present glory days."[39] From this perspective, Barber's death in 1992, rather than signifying the demise of baseball, marked the survival and vitality of a game that his technical and verbal skills helped popularize, disseminate, and nationalize.

The most frequently recurring adjective among the Barber obituary writers is "decent." Although one writer who worked with Red at the *Tallahassee Democrat* acknowledged that his "shy and serious" nature prompted some to view him as "standoffish or egotistical," almost all accounts reference a deeply rooted and "gentlemanly" integrity, honesty, and generosity. In the comments they shared with the *Tampa Tribune* upon Red's death, the two friends who worked with him most closely expressed, simply and concisely, their experience of his solid decency. Vin Scully told reporters that the Red he knew "was not only a man from the south with great southern expressions, but a highly moral and extremely intelligent man." And Bob Edwards reported that his Friday morning partner was "a spiritual man who never let games or athletes have more importance than the wonders of God and nature."[40]

18

Legacies

For twenty-first-century readers, Red Barber's enduring influences extend beyond twentieth-century baseball and broadcasting, for which he is primarily remembered today. Although not as widely touted, Barber also left a literary legacy documented by the testimonies of those who have acknowledged his influence upon the products of their own love affair with the English language, which, they claim, were inspired by listening to Red's engaging commentary. He left a third, biological, legacy in the person of his daughter Sarah, who demonstrated, by her most intense engagements in life the influence of her father. But any analysis of Walter Lanier Barber's legacy must start with his enormous influence on generations of sportscasters.

"Like Watching Michelangelo Paint or Olivier Act"

Red Barber honored the contributions of Graham McNamee, Ted Husing, Bill Munday, and others in his books and articles. For him these were the true pioneers of sports broadcasting; he stood on the shoulders of these giants. But for the generations of baseball broadcasters that followed the Old Redhead, Barber was the trailblazer. In some respects it is difficult for twenty-first-century baseball fans to recognize why Barber's style of broadcasting was so influential in his time: he was the first to exercise habits for calling a game that we assume had always been standard practice. The strongest and clearest statement of his influence on his profession comes from Pat Hughes, the longtime radio voice of the Chicago Cubs and creator of *Baseball Voices*, an impressive CD series celebrating Hall of Fame announcers. For Hughes, Barber "is simply the most influential play-by-play man in the history of our country, and nobody else is even close." Ernie Harwell, the Detroit Tigers' announcing legend, agreed with Hughes's assessment: "Probably more than any other announcer, we learned from him [Barber], every one of us."[1]

Hughes summarized what he saw as Red's unique and pioneering contributions to the professionalizing of baseball broadcasting: "[It was] just the way he approached the job: the preparation, the detailed description of what was transpiring on the field in front of him, the background knowledge, the filling in between pitches. Nobody had ever done that before he did. The allowance of letting the crowd roar after a big play instead of trying to shout over it."[2] In his commentative CD on Barber, Hughes traced the route by which Red's disciplined habits of professional practice were passed on to the generations of baseball broadcasters who followed him, starting with Vin Scully. Barber mentored Scully, and Scully influenced the next generation: "Since so many current baseball announcers have learned from Vinny, fans in many towns still hear a trace of Red Barber every single baseball day."[3]

Vin Scully, the baseball broadcaster rated the best by many and the one with the longest run, acknowledges the exclusive, career-shaping influence of Barber upon his success by claiming Red as his "father." In a recorded message for the one hundredth anniversary celebration of Barber's birth in Columbus, Mississippi, in 2008, Scully told the crowd honoring the Old Redhead: "The simplest way for me to describe my relationship with the great Red Barber is to say that he was like a father to me, and I believe I was a son to him."[4] When Vin joined Barber and Connie Desmond in the Brooklyn Dodgers' booth, he learned quickly about Barber's passion for excellence: "The biggest thing about Red was the fact that he cared. I wasn't just another kid in the booth. I wasn't just another announcer. He made sure that my work habits were good, and he rode me if I indeed drifted off away from what he felt was the ideal way to work." After Barber died, Scully wrote in a *Reader's Digest* tribute to him that Red was "radio's first poet" and "the most honorable man I ever met." For Vin Scully, Red Barber "was more than a sportscaster. He was the voice of truth."[5]

In addition to his star pupil, Scully, Barber also directly influenced several more of the game's greatest voices. Dick Enberg, a 2015 Frick Award winner, saw Barber as "a teacher to his contemporaries over thirty-three years of broadcasting" and "a man who showed all of those who followed how to report a baseball game." Just as radio had linked a young Barber in Florida to the legendary Graham McNamee, it connected Enberg, as "a twelve-year-old farm boy unloading apple crates from the barn" in rural Michigan to Barber broadcasting from Ebbets Field in Brooklyn. Enberg and his father were listening to Game Four of the 1947 World Series when Lavagetto's hit ended Bevens's no-hitter, delivering a heart-stopping victory to the Bums and etching for Enberg "a Series that will live in my memory as the most exciting ever."[6]

Ernie Harwell, hired by Branch Rickey to fill in while Barber recovered from his near-fatal bleeding ulcer, had also listened to Barber from afar. At the Columbus centennial celebration, Harwell recalled, "When I was growing up, down in Georgia, Red Barber was my hero, and later on I had the privilege of working with him at Brooklyn, . . . He was a mentor, and most of all a friend." Harwell succinctly sums up the practices that Barber invariably executed: "Red was the consummate professional, the classic baseball announcer. He'd come to the ballpark and he'd talk to players, managers, coaches, umpires, and have a complete knowledge of the game before he even got to the booth. And then he knew how to describe, he knew how to be sincere; he knew how to be fair."[7]

In his centennial remarks, Bob Picozzi of ESPN Radio offered a touching personal reflection on the breadth of Barber's contributions to sportscasters:

> Red Barber wrote the book on play-by-play, literally and figuratively. How often should you give the score when doing a baseball game on the radio? Well, it's simple; let the sand make its way from the top of the three-minute sized hourglass to the bottom, and then it's time to give the score and flip over the hourglass. Simple and genius. I learned that one from Red. And when I listened to games as a kid, it wasn't only because I wanted to see if my team won, but because I wanted to hear how Red described the game. It was like watching Michelangelo paint or Olivier act.[8]

Picozzi also internalized Barber's passion for professional responsibility. Sportscasters, like the players on the field, needed to work for excellence in every broadcast and push themselves to improve. Picozzi explains: "Every time you go on the air, you owe it to give your best; you owe it to the sponsor, you owe it to the folks who pay you, more importantly, you owe it to your audience. Most importantly, you owe it to yourself."[9]

For other sportscasting greats, Barber's dogged insistence on impartiality was an essential takeaway from the Old Redhead. In his book *You Can't Make This Up*, Al Michaels, the 2021 Ford C. Frick Award winner, credits Barber and his protégé Scully with his passion for objectivity: "I have always taken my cue from Vin Scully and Red Barber and shied away from being a 'homer.' I wanted to be impartial and call games in a straightforward fashion. If the opponent did something well, I praised them. If the Reds didn't do something well, I addressed that."[10] Curt Gowdy, the most prominent national sportscaster of the 1960s and 1970s and another Frick Award winner, also absorbed Barber's belief in impartiality as part of his own legacy. In his 2006 *New York Times* obituary for Gowdy, Richard Sandomir reported that Gowdy "modeled his objectivity on Red Barber," proudly announcing, "I'm no cheerleader.... You have to instill confidence in your listeners."[11]

Barber's peers and the generation that followed him learned directly from the master, but third-generation listeners also absorbed Barber's skills from old recordings. Barber's detailed descriptions impressed Bob Costas, yet another Frick Award winner: "I've heard tapes of Red Barber in the 1930s and '40s where he tells you there's a line single to left center and he tells you how many times it bounced before the center fielder picked it up. . . . Today, even the very good announcers will very rarely describe a guy's stance or the peculiarities of a guy's windup, because they've been subconsciously influenced by television, even though they're on the radio."[12] Chris Berman, Costas's generational peer, developed one of his most famous catch phrases and learned a crafty announcing tactic from a Barber recording. When the ESPN Sports Center star heard a replay of Barber's "Back, back, back, back, back, back" call of Gionfriddo's catch of DiMaggio's left field shot in Game Six of the 1947 World Series, he thought to himself, "Back, back, back; you know, I'm going to try that tonight on Sports Center when I do some baseball highlights. Now that it has become my staple I owe Red Barber a huge thank you, but it's become a way to describe a ball when you are doing live play-by-play. It goes back, back, back, and I'm covered whether it goes over the fence or the outfielder makes the catch. Red Barber was truly a genius."[13]

While other sportscasters influenced the next generation of announcers who had listened to them on radio, television, or recordings, Red Barber, unlike most of his peers, also *wrote* extensively about the mechanics of his profession. Before such textbooks were common, college instructors used *The Broadcasters* as both a history of and practical guide to sportscasting. Bob Costas, for one, read Barber's *The Broadcasters* while in high school.[14] Jon Miller, arguably the most critically acclaimed baseball announcer of the past twenty-five years, learned at least two valuable lessons from Barber's writing. The first was that an egg timer could remind an announcer to give the score frequently: "The score is the most important piece of information in any broadcast. Nothing else you say has any relevance until the listener knows the score."[15] The second lesson was that a play-by-play announcer has to maintain a healthy social distance from the men on the field.

Monte Moore, longtime Oakland Athletics broadcaster and Miller's mentor, lent the twenty-two-year-old novice a copy of *Rhubarb in the Catbird Seat*. Moore had always respected Barber and knew Miller could learn much from the master. For Miller *Rhubarb in the Catbird Seat* was a game changer. He wrote in his own 1998 book, *Confessions of a Baseball Purist*: "I devoured that book. I was totally absorbed. . . . As someone just starting in the business, I took very seriously [Red's] advice not to get too friendly with the players. The job demands that you report on them, and at times, even report negative things about them, Red wrote. And if they're close personal friends, he warned, that could be difficult. . . . To a twenty-two-year-old, Red Barber's advice made a lot of sense. I took his words to heart."[16]

But it took a little time to fully absorb the message. Miller tells us that he and his wife became good friends with Jim Sundberg, the great Texas Rangers catcher, and his wife. One day Sundberg confided to him that his arm was sore and that the pain was affecting his throwing. Sundberg was known for his powerful throws, which kept the opposition's running game in check. Without thinking much about it, Miller shared this "inside information" on the air, much to the chagrin of Sundberg when he heard about it. If they were listening, the Rangers' opponents for upcoming games were no doubt delighted to receive Miller's hot tip. The meaning of Red's advice became clear: "Mr. Barber had a rule he employed to avoid such misunderstandings: When he spoke with managers and general managers, he'd make it very clear they should not offer any information that could not be put out on the broadcast. Don't tell me something if I can't use it, Red would warn; in a live-broadcast situation, where snap decisions must be made, it would be too confusing to have to remember which information can be used and which can't."[17]

Barber's passion for professionalism, as he defined the term, rubbed off on even his most unwilling pupil. After Phil Rizzuto was elected to the Baseball Hall of Fame as a player in 1994, Richard Sandomir of the *New York Times* asked him if he thought he also might win the Ford C. Frick Award for his years of work as a Yankees announcer. He told Sandomir, "I'd refuse it. I'm not a professional broadcaster. I've been told that over and over. I'm a homer. I'd really be embarrassed to accept something like that."[18]

Barber's legacy for the field of broadcasting was his articulation of rigorous professional standards and habits that he formulated for himself and tirelessly practiced but that he also impressed upon those who worked with him, listened to him, and wrote about him. Tom Villante, Barber's Brooklyn broadcast producer, insisted that "of all of the announcers I've met in baseball, without a doubt, Red Barber was the craftsman. . . . I always refer to him as the master. He was the master radio play-by-play man."[19] Barber's call for objectivity, accuracy, and preparation survived him and has influenced the work of several generations of sportscasters who have inherited his legacy, even those who found it difficult to execute his directives. A surprising range of American writers also has identified Barber's way with words as an inspiration for their own careers as storytellers.

"He Was Instructing Me in the Beauties of Creation and of Order"

Throughout the pages of this biography, we have quoted stirring passages written by sports columnists inspired by the voice, the poetry, and the music of Barber's words, uttered in pleasing tones that melded assurance and promise with authority and accuracy. Philip Roth, a writer who had much to say about baseball, always maintained that as a youngster, he loved the game better than football because it could be described more effectively on radio, particularly "by announcers like Red Barber, a respectful mild southerner with a subtle rural tanginess to his vocabulary and a soft country parson tone to his voice." For Roth the fact that such an "alien but loving" voice could have captivated boisterous fans of the Brooklyn Dodgers, "the very symbol of urban wackiness and tumult," constitutes proof that for this sport, it is the unique perspective and gifts of the storyteller that so powerfully impact the appeal of the game.[20]

Red Barber, the skillful storyteller, left a trail of professional writers who have attributed to the mellifluous broadcaster their initial awakening as future authors—for example, Jane Leavy, who as a young girl went to sleep "with the voice of Red Barber in her dreams." Their testimonies to his influence represent an unrecognized legacy of the gifted sportscaster. Writers beyond the realm of baseball have attributed their birth as wordsmiths to their childhood hours absorbing Red Barber's speech and the values his words seemed to instill, an effect that deeply pleased him. In a 1987 interview, Red mentions, self-effacingly, "Some people have been very generous . . . when they talk about me. I have had some college professors tell me I had a good influence upon them as boys, but all I did was speak correctly and try not to foul up my tenses."[21]

In 1989 a college literature professor, Richard Costa, sent Barber his recently published book, along with a letter that suggests it was much more than Red's correctness with verb tenses that influenced fledgling writers among his listeners. Costa writes that it was Red's genius in describing action and his felicitous command of language that woke him up as a college freshman to the wizardry of words when they are mindfully arranged. Costa still remembers Barber's exact words on one broadcast just after right fielder Carl Furillo made a great throw to third to cut down streaking runner Bill Werber: "Werber, who is proud of his consummate skills as a baserunner, now knows that audacity has its place in life, but not on the base paths when Carl Furillo's strong right arm is the antagonist." The young college student was awed that "such grace with language could find its way into baseball commentary. . . . I was mesmerized by how well [Red] combined command of the action with command of the language." He decided to major in English, explaining, "Red, I knew early on I had to devote my life to a calling in which language and literature were uppermost." He is convinced that listening to Red had inspired him.[22]

Another university instructor sent Barber a section of a novel written by college professor and fiction writer Alan Lelchuk. Entitled *Brooklyn Boy*, the book is based upon the author's youth in Brooklyn as an avid Dodgers fan and the influences that shaped him as a writer. Red Barber is the focus of one chapter in which Lelchuk describes the eloquent broadcaster as an inspiration for the novel's young protagonist, "Aaron," who would become a writer. The narrator tells us that Barber was "the voice and maybe the conscience of the borough. This Mississippi born gentleman talked to us, sang to us. Soft-spoken, scrupulous, knowledgeable, humorous, always eloquent, his voice suffused us with its sweetness and moral light. . . . In Aaron's childhood Red was the gravelly interpreter of baseball. He'd paint Slats Marion "out there at shortstop, movin' easy as a bank of fog." Aaron would think about that image for a long time after the game. Red was his earliest teacher."[23]

Among the surprising number of other authors' testimonies claiming Red Barber as a seminal influence is a compelling article included in *Diamonds Are a Girl's Best Friend*, a 1994 collection of essays on baseball written by women. Journalist and award-winning fiction writer Barbara Grizzuti Harrison reflects deeply upon the encouraging role the Dodgers broadcaster's soothing, reliable voice played in her tumultuous childhood and her subsequent development as a professional writer. A survivor of a Brooklyn household splintered by parental sexual abuse, mental illness, and overbearing fundamentalist religiosity, she later wrote feature articles for the *New York Times*, *Los Angeles Times*, *The New Republic* and the *Village Voice*, among other leading publications. She is best known for weaving autobiographic testimony into compelling articles that explore in depth American society's response to traumas that she had experienced. Harrison refers to her essay in *Diamonds*, published two years after Red's death, as "a very respectful love letter" to Red Barber, whom she first met in person and interviewed for a newspaper piece in 1990. She described Red at that time as "a graceful, stubborn, prayerful, charming, wise old southern gentleman in whom curiosity and ardor breathe as steadily now as they did when he was my eyes, the poet of my childhood."[24]

Harrison then tells us that when she listened to Barber's broadcasts as a child, "He brought the gold of summer into an attic apartment in the bowels of Brooklyn." Throughout the essay she wants readers to understand what was happening when she listened to Red Barber's voice, "soft and clear, cadenced and authoritative," calling a ball game: "He was instructing me in the beauties of creation and of order, the necessity of law, and the transforming power of grace. He brought order and he brought joy. He didn't know he was doing all this or if he did, he was too modest or contained to say so." Harrison accentuates the contrast between rowdy loud-mouthed Brooklyn fans and Barber's measured vocal rhythms, his vivid evocation of atmosphere and action, and his magical use of metaphor—but rarely hyperbole. She also was schooled by his "little homilies—chatty back fence asides on character, time and fate, urging us to charity and understanding: 'I don't want you to judge Pee Wee too harshly—only pop fly he's missed in eleven years.'" Hearing Barber fill dead time by talking about a coach who failed twice before he admirably beat his addiction and other demons assured her and "made [her] feel safe": "When Red Barber broadcast the ball games, I was home safe every time."

Harrison evokes Red Barber as her role model for a storyteller whose thoughtful handling of words could tame what is wild at the core of human nature by foregrounding all that is civil. The evocation echoes Robert Frost's description of poetry as a "momentary stay against confusion." It persuades us that the Old Redhead really did plant the seeds for a writing career in which Harrison could transform a violent and chaotic childhood into texts of hope and change. How many other young listeners were moved by Barber's way with words to develop their own voices as storytellers, poets, professors, and broadcasters? It is impossible to know the extent of Red Barber's literary legacy. But it is easy to imagine that some of the threads of civility, however frayed, that still bind American culture have been stitched by those who inherited the lessons "of creation and of order" that Red Barber passed on to his acolytes. Barber also passed on another legacy for the generation that followed him—an articulate and civically engaged daughter who, like her father, moved people.

"A Fully Formed Person"

According to a good friend, Sarah Barber's favorite book was a novel, *A Wreath for the Enemy*, by Pamela Frankau, first published in 1954.[25] The novel depicts the trials of a precocious teenager, Penelope, the only child in her family, whose father, a celebrated poet, runs a bohemian hotel on the French Riviera. The lifestyle of this family of three is unconventional, including frequent relocations and irregular schedules that preclude the formation of long-term and stable relationships. Penelope longs for a life she believes "other people" live—one that is calm and orderly, where the family has meals together at the same table and the children, along with their brothers and sisters, attend the same schools until they graduate. Sarah's favorite piece of fiction may suggest that as a young reader she was dissatisfied with a life influenced by a celebrity father. But parents have a way of passing on to their offspring valuable gifts, even if it takes a lifetime to recognize them.

Red Barber's influence upon his daughter's values, projects, and avocations compels us to regard her accomplishments as his third significant legacy. Red played a key part in generating Sarah's lifelong commitment to promoting social justice in her work as a teacher. He provided a role model for her tireless fundraising in support of causes to which she was deeply committed; he fostered her lifelong interest in the fine arts and encouraged her love of travel as a means for understanding cultural differences. He also passed on to his daughter some of his prickly character traits.

When Sarah was a child, Red introduced her to baseball, frequently taking her to spring training, allowing her occasionally to sit with him in the broadcast booth, and introducing her to players and managers. In a 2001 interview she recalled vividly the drama of her father's Brooklyn years when Jackie Robinson was challenging the color line and "there was a whole kind of human warmth at Ebbets Field." She lamented that baseball now lacked the "social impact" that it had had for her as an adolescent.[26] According to her mother, Sarah had absorbed and understood the significance of the integration of Major League Baseball; she believed that witnessing Robinson's struggle inspired her daughter's passion for social justice and equality for minorities and led her to begin her teaching career in Harlem. The child of the Brooklyn Dodgers' popular announcer absorbed lessons in the practice of "agape," her father's term for "opening one's self up to the 'other.'" Sarah was eager to teach in Harlem at the beginning of her career because she felt that was where she was most needed. She learned the neighborhood and enjoyed taking her second- and third-grade classes down the block to Roy Campanella's liquor store for a visit with him. The children were in awe of the celebrated catcher, who would tell them stories and always remind them to pay attention in class.[27]

After nine years, Sarah left her job in Harlem to teach writing and literature at LaGuardia Community College because she was offered an opportunity to work in a new interdisciplinary program designed to accommodate the needs of a wider range of minority groups whose academic needs were not being accommodated: recent immigrants, working mothers, and first-generation college students. Realizing that her ethnically and racially diverse students struggled with class materials that were detached from their own experiences, she designed courses that engaged them in reading and responding to stories written by people like themselves. Her efforts to effectively integrate reading and writing assignments to empower her students resulted in several publications designed to engage and instruct other teachers in her project.[28] During the late 1970s and 1980s, when the AIDS crisis triggered gay and lesbian minorities to demand equal rights and resources, Sarah began her second career as an activist and fundraiser for the community to which she belonged.

As a child, Sarah had listened as her father tirelessly urged Brooklyn fans to give blood for the Red Cross and dauntlessly persuaded people of means to provide funds for rebuilding a crumbling shelter for homeless women and children. When she retired from teaching at the age of fifty-three and moved to Santa Fe, Sarah, like her father, redirected her energies into impressive fund-raising roles. The ease of her transition reminds us of her father's embarking, at the age of fifty-eight, upon a new career focused upon writing and speaking. In both cases, skills that father and daughter had developed in their primary professions enabled them to advance in their new projects.

Soon after she moved to Santa Fe, Sarah became a founding member of the Hope House initiative, which raised money to buy a large home that would be converted to a welcoming hospice accommodating the needs of those afflicted with AIDS. In 1999 Sarah was empowered to implement some of her most significant contributions for the lesbian and gay community when she was invited to serve as a member of the board for the Santa Fe Community Foundation (SFCF), the organizational heart of all nonprofit fund-raising in the city.[29] According to her friends, at the time Sarah joined the SFCF board, there weren't any other openly lesbian or gay people among its relatively conservative members. Sarah's goal was to create a subcommittee of the foundation, to be named the "Santa Fe Lesbian and Gay Community Funding Partnership." The partnership would focus its efforts on working with area-wide agencies and organizations seeking funds to develop programs that would address the needs of the lesbian and gay people they served. According to Sarah's close friend Liz Bremner, also a member of the foundation, she knew her proposal would be controversial.[30] But like her father, Sarah had learned how to please and persuade her audiences and "make walls tumble."

Within a few years the Gay and Lesbian Partnership was flourishing, and the SFCF had awarded grants to a myriad of Santa Fe organizations concerned with integrating and meeting the needs of lesbians and gays. These included, among many others, a local college that wanted to hire counselors to work with the issues faced by

LEGACIES

gays and lesbians on campus, a rape crisis center working to prevent sexual violence against gay youth, and a media group that wanted to launch a campaign on prejudice reduction.[31] A year before her death, Sarah was recognized as the "Treasure of the Gay Community" by a local chapter of the Human Rights Alliance.[32] Just as her father had worked tirelessly to become the "Voice of the Red Cross" in New York City, Sarah is remembered by the lesbian and gay community in Santa Fe as a fearless leader where her voice was most needed.

While Red Barber's lifelong engagement in civic affairs clearly provided a role model for his daughter, he also passed on to her his and Lylah's love and support for the fine arts. In an interview in Santa Fe, after speaking about her father's popularity in Brooklyn, "Sarah grew silent and pensive and then shared that she was recently 'listening to a *La Boheme* broadcast and I thought about the first time I saw it. My father took me. I wore a baby blue formal. We sat in a box and my mother was there too; my first opera. It is a dimension of my father many people don't know. He loved music, and this was so formative in my growing up. It stunned me that he mixed the two disparate loves of opera and baseball.'"[33]

Like her parents, Sarah was an avid collector of art and committed to supporting local artists, whom she knew personally. That way, she thought, each painting or sculpture or piece of pottery "has a story," enriching the value of the work and the narrative of a relationship. She saved some of her parents' favorite paintings from their home in Tallahassee: "Even if you think your taste has changed, you may return to what has been gone from your palette for twenty years." In 1997 she saw a painting that enabled her to reconcile herself to her mother's recent death: "I was surprised to come upon a painting with soft blurred triangles against a grey, thin, white horizon line. It reminded me of the reflection of landscape in water, a serene, ideal place. My mother had just died when I saw the painting; it had been a long dying. I saw this piece and had to buy it because it spoke to me about where she has gone, which gave me peace."[34]

Sarah's friends testify to her love of travel, a passion she also

432

inherited from Red and Lylah, and several of them occasionally joined her and her partner Gloria on their trips, including an exciting African safari "into the wild." They recall how carefully she prepared for the trips, "always identifying the best places to stay and the most interesting sites and activities to pursue in each location."[35]

Listening to her friends' detailed descriptions of Sarah's personality, one is struck by her similarities to her father. They say, like Red, she was a private and serious person but always able to "wax eloquent" when advancing her beliefs and her projects in public forums. Like Red, she was an avid reader, a "fully formed person," with strong opinions. She also could be demanding and critical. Liz Bremner says that even though she sat on the SFCF board alongside Sarah, she often felt as though Sarah was her boss because of her command of all the issues. Bremner recalls Sarah's critique of one of her board presentations, an evaluation that concluded with a humiliating assessment of Bremner's worn and dated footwear: "And, Liz," Sarah exclaimed, "those shoes you had on your feet . . . how could you!" Like Red, Sarah was always a meticulous dresser, and, Liz admits, "She was right about those shoes."

In the weeks before Sarah died from the brain-wasting effects of cortico-frontal degeneration, she invited friends to visit for a last farewell. She could not read, write, or even pick up a fork when instructed to do so. On March 9, 2005, she was blessedly delivered "from a life without quality," which Red and his mother both had insisted was no life at all. One of her friends supplied her enduring image of the "fully formed" Sarah Barber they all still miss:

> Late one evening during our safari, I walked by Sarah's hut. Her candle still was burning. She was still at her desk, still perfectly attired in her Abercrombie and Fitch safari outfit, writing her daily notes in her diary. She was detailing the colors and sizes of each bird that she'd seen that day, drawing sketches from her memory.

Like her father, Sarah was attentive and focused; a reader, writer, and poet; a teacher and civic activist, disciplined and deeply engaged by the world around her.

Epilogue

Walter Lanier "Red" Barber, Revisited

In our prologue we associated three consistent threads of Barber's personality with his name: *Walter,* the ambitious achiever; *Lanier,* the humanist; and *Red,* the lively performer. The story we have told traces the genesis and development of these inclinations and their gradual integration, as reflected in Barber's choices and decisions. We can identify the influence of these powerful proclivities upon the trajectory of his life as we see a spirited child develop into a thoughtful man conscientiously attempting to fathom and perform his nature. The narrative of his time on earth suggests that Barber's constitution proscribed his becoming a lifelong specialist in any one field or endeavor. Such a single-minded agenda would have impeded his pursuit of what he came to believe was his purpose for living: to continue growing stronger and deeper in mind and spirit. We recall his quandary on his first day of college when he was told he had to choose a field of study: "I came to college with an open mind. . . . There isn't anything particular I came to study. I guess I will choose Liberal Arts." His progress toward fullness persuaded him throughout his life to sideline former ambitions when they were no longer challenging and to dismiss comforting assumptions when firsthand experience discredited them.

Lanier may have been first to awaken, stirred by the voice of Selena Barber as she read to her firstborn son the tales of Ulysses and King Arthur. They kindled his love of the English language and his intuition that stories passed down over time bind us to a common humanity because they continue speaking to every new generation. Such an intuition of connection to a larger realm of being was early reinforced by William Barber's reminding his son that true religion is reverence for "the living community of ourselves with our brothers and with our Maker," a reverence dictating that we concern ourselves with the well-being of others. Throughout his life Lanier would be attracted to mentors, belief systems, and firsthand experiences that encouraged self-transcendence on behalf of the greater good. He is spellbound when he first hears the voices from miles and worlds away speaking to him on radio—bridging the differences and distance between lives and cultures. Radio's purpose seemed noble. His rapid ascent in broadcasting projected his voice to a diverse community in Brooklyn, one that he could persuade to give its own blood and whatever spare change it could afford. It was a community that would rally behind a principled leader who welcomed Black players. As the world opened up to him, Lanier also discovered the joy of losing himself in beauty—the beauty of talented athletic performance, music, painting, sculpture, architecture, and the natural world.

Our narrative suggests that *Walter* emerged when he exercised his own agency in Sanford. When he sat by his father watching him in complete control of a powerful steam engine, the boy sensed that challenging work, performed according to the highest of standards, built self-confidence and self-respect. The young Walter graduated from high school with the highest academic average and performed some impressive feats on the gridiron, even while playing on losing teams. Self-disciplined, determined, and focused, he worked himself through two years of college to become chief announcer of the university's radio station and its leading sports broadcaster, never discouraged by and always learning from his mistakes. Walter's early commitment to an ethos of aiming high and working tirelessly to reach his goals eventually catapulted him at the age of twenty-six to the most powerful radio station in the country. A distinctive component of his drive to succeed, however, was his professional commitment to advancing only by following the rules.

In a relatively new field like sports broadcasting, where "rules" were just being standardized, Walter stood for objective and accurate reporting. His set of rules also demanded sufficient preparation before a game to provide consistently informative and interesting commentary for his audiences, no matter how absorbing or dull the activity on the field. His rigorous professionalism sometimes made the job tough for his colleagues in the broadcast booth. Walter also worked under the assumption that valuable and gifted employees should have some control over the terms of their employment, including their remuneration and the appropriation of and demands upon their time. Walter's determination to reach the top of his profession by hard work, intense practice, tireless preparation, and reliance upon exceptional mentors moved him from local to national acclaim in Cincinnati and paved the way for his arrival in Brooklyn. Assuming the microphone in Brooklyn, just at the point when a ban on live radio coverage of Major League baseball was lifted, Walter, the talented and experienced professional, found himself in the finest catbird seat of his career. Broadcasting awards and popular acclaim soon followed, as well as civic recognition for his tireless Red Cross wartime efforts, which he executed with the same persistence and energy that he devoted to his paying job. He worked through career-challenging setbacks, including threats to his voice and hearing and fears of recurring stomach hemorrhages. Ever the striver, Walter accepted even more challenges that would test his management skills as CBS sports director, where he introduced innovative programming.

Red, the performer, appears to have gained his walking legs in Sanford, perhaps also inspired by his father's amusing front porch anecdotes that grabbed listeners before they realized that the lively stories were actually conveying laughter-coated messages. Red hit the stage in high school, developing his skills in song, dance, and delivery. Minstrelsy provided him with a platform to develop his gifts, which he continued to exercise in college, where he performed his acts on live tours with the campus glee club and on WRUF. Red even upset Walter's plan to work hard at his library job to earn the money he desperately needed. He quit his job in the musty library to perform his minstrel act on the glee club's statewide tour because it was something he "really enjoyed." In Cincinnati, Red began performing the act that stunned audiences for the next five decades: breathtaking on-stage re-creations of the most exciting final innings he'd witnessed in baseball. He performed as radio showman, emceeing and taking part in live acts throughout his Brooklyn and CBS days. For the rest of his life, he employed his colorful language and performance skills to uplift church congregations, entertain convention audiences, and challenge graduates at their commencement ceremonies.

After a few years in Brooklyn, the increasingly integrated and "fully formed" Walter Lanier "Red" Barber wearied of using his voice primarily to narrate balls and strikes. He wanted to address more enduring topics and to stir audiences in a deeper way, which he only sometimes could do in the broadcast booth—between innings or during pitching changes. When television's visuals edited out Barber's stories, when he was criticized for "talking too much," the prospect of sports writing appeared a better forum for sharing his life-affirming stories and for advancing his word-smithing skills. Now he could write books on the significance of sports broadcasting; he could write articles, sermons, and public speeches in which baseball and football provided vivid manifestations of courage, heroism, humility, self-sacrifice, self-discipline, determination, loyalty, and love. Barber's midlife career changes clearly were impacted by external forces, including contract terminations, the dominance of television, and changing tastes in broadcasting personalities. But the *direction* in which he changed was tied to the blended aspirations of Walter, Lanier, and Red. He tells us it was the dryness of his spirit—spending all of itself in its relentless quest for professional advancement—that led him to swim into deeper waters. A comforting presence surrounding him during a near-death experience made him feel he had a debt to pay by employing his gifts more deliberately.

Barber directed all of Walter's virtues—determination, practice, persistence, focus—into becoming a writer worthy of his messages, relying upon wise mentors once again and learning from failures and disappointments. Free of sponsors, owners, and general managers, he could explore and critique sports, media, and the culture of his times from the perspective of his own rich experience, with only occasional revisions requested by editors. Although advertising once seemed an innocent and even playful resource to help subsidize the civic value of mass media, he now could expose in damning detail how the media's priorities enforced a callous evasion of public responsibility. Although he had first gained fame as a broadcaster by reporting college sports, he was now armed with a pen to blast college administrations for selling out their educational mission to fill their stadiums and train gladiators for the professional leagues. Lanier was tirelessly nudging the hard-working Walter to direct his efforts toward a more compelling goal. During his earlier work for the Red Cross blood and war fund drives in Brooklyn, Barber had been inspired by the public good that could be accomplished by the powerful partnership between media and sports. That work remained for him a shining model of what those institutions should always strive to accomplish.

In the end, the most satisfying points in Barber's long career were the seasons when Walter, Lanier, and Red all thrived. The war years in Brooklyn were a season when he exercised his voice most effectively in ways that earned him his own self-respect. In the last third of his life, after a period of declining influence during his Yankees years, Barber was finally in control of how he used his talents. He was composing and publishing articles up until the months before he died; he was speaking again to radio audiences, still engaging them with stories that conveyed meaning in life, still uttering vivid word paintings of trees and gardens and wild critters in his backyard, and still sharing lessons and judgments culled from a lifetime of thought and action. He was still showing up in person for appearances where his presence and voice would turn a mere occasion into an event. He was still raising funds for public radio and still contributing to libraries, agencies for the blind, and Planned Parenthood. And Walter Lanier "Red" Barber still was relishing with wonder the rough autumn winds howling through his pines.

NOTES

Abbreviations

BRP   Branch Rickey Papers
ERMP   Edward R. Murrow Papers
LCPL   Lowndes County Public Library
NBC Archives   National Broadcasting Company Records
NBHF   National Baseball Hall of Fame
OLRC   Olin Library, Rollins College
RBC   Walter Lanier "Red" Barber Collection
SM   Sandford Museum

Prologue

1. Quotations in this paragraph are from Edwards, *Fridays with Red*, 227.

1. Cultured Roots

1. "New Ice-House Being Built," "Dreary Weather Brings Discomfort," *Columbus Weekly Dispatch*, February 20, 1908, 1, LCPL.

2. "Food for Fans," *Columbus Weekly Dispatch*, February 20, 1908, 1, LCPL.

3. "A History of Racial Injustice," February 10, 1908, https://calendar.eji.org/racial-injustice/feb/10.

4. "Brookhaven Lynching," *Columbus Weekly Dispatch*, February 20, 1908, 6, LCPL.

5. Authors' interview with Rufus Ward, Columbus, Mississippi, historian, December 20, 2019.

6. "Education," in *Mississippi History: Lowndes County* (section XLIV, part 2), LCPL.

7. "Education," in *Mississippi History: Lowndes County* (section XLIV, part 2), LCPL.

8. Caudill, *Mississippi Oral History Program*, 21.

9. Authors' interview with Rufus Ward, Columbus, Mississippi, historian, December 20, 2019.

10. Vance, *Images of America, Columbus*, 108.

11. "The Negro," in *Mississippi History: Lowndes County* (section XLIV, part 2), LCPL.

12. Hammerstein quoted in Norris, "Six Words."

13. Medley, *History of Anson County*, 128.

14. Medley, *History of Anson County*, 130.

15. Caudill, *Mississippi Oral History Program*, 7.

16. Red Barber, "My Most Unforgettable Character," 161.

17. Red Barber, "My Most Unforgettable Character," 162.

18. Red Barber, "My Most Unforgettable Character," 162.

19. Red Barber, "My Most Unforgettable Character," 162.

20. Red Barber, "72-Year Old Red Credits His Parents," *Tallahassee Democrat*, February 17, 1980, 7F.

21. "Barber-Martin," *Columbus Weekly Dispatch*, March 8, 1906, 1, LCPL.

22. Effie Virginia Barber, typescript of Barber family memoirs, in personal collection of her daughter, E. V. E. Joy.

23. "Backwoods Poems," *Yazoo Herald*, April 26, 1878, LCPL.

24. Effie Virginia Barber, typescript of Barber family memoirs, in personal collection of her daughter, E. V. E. Joy; Edward Randolph Hopkins, "Recollections," ca. 1930, 17, LCPL.

25. Caudill, *Mississippi Oral History Program*, 5.

26. *Columbus Mississippi City Directory*, 1912, 85; 1918, 82; LCPL.

27. Caudill, *Mississippi Oral History Program*, 21.

28. Red Barber, *The Broadcasters* (1970), 13.

29. Caudill, *Mississippi Oral History Program*, 6.

30. Quoted in Caudill, *Mississippi Oral History Program*, 24.

31. "Motion Pictures Theaters," in *Mississippi History: Lowndes County* (section XLIV, part 2), LCPL; Vance, *Images of America, Columbus*, 53, 108.

32. Quoted in Effie Virginia Barber, typescript of Barber family memoirs, in personal collection of her daughter, E. V. E. Joy.

33. Quoted in Caudill, *Mississippi Oral History Program*, 20.

34. Red Barber, *The Broadcasters* (1970), 14.

35. Red Barber, "Christmas Time and the Owl Remind Me So of Billy," *Tallahassee Democrat*, December 21, 1975, 5D.

36. Quoted in Caudill, *Mississippi Oral History Program*, 10.

37. Quoted in Caudill, *Mississippi Oral History Program*, 11–12.

38. Authors' interview with E. V. E. Joy, December 19, 2019.

39. Quoted in Caudill, *Mississippi Oral History Program*, 12–13.

40. Quoted in Caudill, *Mississippi Oral History Program*, 19–20.

41. Red Barber and Creamer, *Rhubarb in the Catbird Seat*, 103–4. All citations from this book are from the 1968 edition.

42. Red Barber and Creamer, *Rhubarb in the Catbird Seat*, 104–5.

2. Celery Capital of the World

1. Schaal, *Sanford As I Knew It*, preface.

2. Sanford Historical Society, *Images of America: Sanford*, 7–8.

3. Schaal, *Sanford As I Knew It*, 26–50.

4. Cloyde Russell, "Farewell," *Salmagundi 1926*, Sanford High School Yearbooks, SM.

5. Flewellyn, *African Americans of Sanford*, 7.

6. Red Barber and Creamer, *Rhubarb in the Catbird Seat*, 271.

7. Quoted in Schaal, *Sanford As I Knew It*, 26, 41.

8. Schaal, *Sanford As I Knew It*, 57–81.

9. Red Barber and Creamer, *Rhubarb in the Catbird Seat*, 105.

10. Tygiel, *Baseball's Greatest Experiment*, 106–7.

11. Red Barber, "Red Barber Criticizes Stenstrom," *Sanford Herald*, April 28, 1991, SM, folder "Barber, Red."

12. Creamer, RITCS, tape 5, side A.

13. Letter from John C. Horner to Red Barber, December 16, 1982, RBC, box 7.

14. Letter from Julian Stenstrom to Red Barber, May 21, 1989, RBC, box 10.

15. Quoted in Marshall, "Interview with Red Barber," 50–51.

16. Red Barber, "Red Barber Criticizes Stenstrom," *Sanford Herald*, April 28, 1991, SM, folder "Barber, Red."

17. "A Fitting Tribute to a Local Treasure," *Sanford Herald*, June 27, 1999, SM, folder "Barber, Red."

18. *Salmagundi* 1923–26, Sanford High School Yearbooks, SM.

19. *Salmagundi* 1923–26, Sanford High School Yearbooks, SM.

20. Red Barber and Creamer, *Rhubarb in the Catbird Seat*, 113.

21. *Salmagundi* 1923–26, Sanford High School Yearbooks, SM.

22. Red Barber and Creamer, *Rhubarb in the Catbird Seat*, 106–7.

23. *Salmagundi* 1923–26, Sanford High School Yearbooks, SM.

24. *Sanford Herald*, 1924–26 columns on Barber's high school football games; RBC, boxes 1–3, vol. 1.

25. Red Barber, "The Games Children Don't Play," *Tallahassee Democrat*, March 16, 1980, 3F.

26. Red Barber and Creamer, *Rhubarb in the Catbird Seat*, 106.

27. Red Barber, "The Games Children Don't Play," *Tallahassee Democrat*, March 16, 1980, 3F; Austin, "Interview with Red Barber."

28. Red Barber, "Many Things Change," *Tallahassee Democrat*, July 1, 1973, 4D.

29. Red Barber, "Diamond Delights," *Tallahassee Democrat*, May 11, 1980, 4F.

30. Red Barber, "Memory of a Boy Manager," *Tallahassee Democrat*, February 23, 1975, 3D.

31. Schaal, *Sanford As I Knew It*, 48.

32. Quoted in Red Barber, "Memory of a Boy Manager," *Tallahassee Democrat*, February 23, 1975, 3D.

33. Rickey quoted in Red Barber, "Lance Richboug," *Tallahassee Democrat*, September 28, 1975, 9D.

34. Rickey quoted in Red Barber, "Lance Richboug," *Tallahassee Democrat*, September 28, 1975, 9D.

35. Data in this and the next several paragraphs are from Red Barber, *The Broadcasters* (1970), 12–15.

36. Carlson, *Show Biz*, 50–51.

37. Red Barber and Creamer, *Rhubarb in the Catbird Seat*, 107–8.

38. Unless otherwise noted, quotes in this and the following paragraph are from *Sanford Herald*, 1924–26 columns on Barber's minstrel show appearances; RBC, boxes 1–3, vol. 1.

39. "Plan Cabaret Review for Sanford Guild," *Orlando Evening Star*, February 7, 1928, 7.

40. Red Barber and Creamer, *Rhubarb in the Catbird Seat*, 108–10.

41. Red Barber and Creamer, *Rhubarb in the Catbird Seat*, 105.

42. Red Barber, "My Most Unforgettable Character," 165–66.

43. Red Barber and Creamer, *Rhubarb in the Catbird Seat*, 89.

44. Creamer, RITCS, tape 3, side A.

45. Red Barber and Creamer, *Rhubarb in the Catbird Seat*, 89.

46. Quoted in Red Barber, "My Most Unforgettable Character," 166.

47. Red Barber and Creamer, *Rhubarb in the Catbird Seat*, 106.

48. Authors' interview with Tom Villante, April 13, 2018.

49. Red Barber and Creamer, *Rhubarb in the Catbird Seat*, 110–11.

50. Red Barber and Creamer, *Rhubarb in the Catbird Seat*, 115–18.

51. Red Barber, "My Most Unforgettable Character," 166.

3. Bumming Corner

1. Quoted in Creamer, RITCS, tape 4, side A; emphasis added. For a representative example of Barber's preference for capsulizing sections of his life story by highlighting a series of coincidences that lead to a positive outcome, see Red Barber and Creamer, *Rhubarb in the Catbird Seat*, 165–66.

2. Red Barber and Creamer, *Rhubarb in the Catbird Seat*, 118.

3. Red Barber, *The Broadcasters* (1970), 15.

4. Red Barber and Creamer, *Rhubarb in the Catbird Seat*, 118.

5. Red Barber and Creamer, *Rhubarb in the Catbird Seat*, 120.

6. Red Barber and Creamer, *Rhubarb in the Catbird Seat*, 118–19.

7. Red Barber and Creamer, *Rhubarb in the Catbird Seat*, 119.

8. Red Barber, *Show Me the Way to Go Home*, 43.

9. Creamer, RITCS, tape 4, side A.

10. Gannon, "Interview with Walter (Red) Barber"; "Miamians Take ROTC Honors," *Miami News*, May 4, 1929, 5.

11. Red Barber and Creamer, *Rhubarb in the Catbird Seat*, 121.

12. Red Barber and Creamer, *Rhubarb in the Catbird Seat*, 122.

13. Caudill, *Mississippi Oral History Program*, 3.

14. "Around the Town," *Sanford Herald*, October 1928 pieces on Red's college life, RBC, boxes 1–3, vol. 1; "Bacchus Club Announces Pledges," *Tampa Times*, October 9, 1928, 4.

15. Quotes in this and the following paragraph are from Red Barber and Creamer, *Rhubarb in the Catbird Seat*, 123.

16. Genung, *Practical Elements of Rhetoric*, 7–8.

17. Genung, *Practical Elements of Rhetoric*, 17–19.

18. Genung, *Practical Elements of Rhetoric*, 40, 67; emphasis in original.

19. Genung, *Practical Elements of Rhetoric*, 96–102.

20. Documents on Red's college life, RBC, boxes 1–3, vol. 1.

21. Red Barber and Creamer, *Rhubarb in the Catbird Seat*, 123–25.

22. Red Barber and Creamer, *Rhubarb in the Catbird Seat*, 126.

23. Red Barber and Creamer, *Rhubarb in the Catbird Seat*, 127.

24. Red Barber and Creamer, *Rhubarb in the Catbird Seat*, 128.

25. Red Barber and Creamer, *Rhubarb in the Catbird Seat*, 128. In free time he carved out between his classes and his library job, Red also won an intramural fraternity boxing match—"a bout so close it was hard to say who won, but Barber was declared winner with a slight edge." See documents on Red's college life, RBC, boxes 1–3, vol. 1.

26. Quotes in this and the following paragraph are from Red Barber and Creamer, *Rhubarb in the Catbird Seat*, 131.

27. Red Barber and Creamer, *Rhubarb in the Catbird Seat*, 129.

28. Documents on Red's glee club minstrel performances, RBC, boxes 1–3, vol. 1.

29. Red Barber and Creamer, *Rhubarb in the Catbird Seat*, 129.

30. Quoted in Creamer, RITCS, tape 4, side A.

31. Red Barber and Creamer, *Rhubarb in the Catbird Seat*, 134.

32. Red Barber and Creamer, *Rhubarb in the Catbird Seat*, 133–34.

33. "Tampa Students at Gainesville Aid in Freshmen Week," *Tampa Tribune*, September 26, 1929, 4.

34. Unless otherwise noted, data in this and the following three paragraphs are from Red Barber and Creamer, *Rhubarb in the Catbird Seat*, 135–38.

35. Lylah Barber, *Lylah*, 70–71. Readers of this engaging story of love at first sight might wonder if Barber had ever been in love or at least had a steady girlfriend before he saw Lylah's beautiful brown eyes. There may have been one. In 1990 an acquaintance of Barber mailed him a photocopy of a page from a book entitled *Model T Days*, a memoir by Carl D. King about his life in Florida in the 1920s and 1930s. When King was a freshman at the university, Red would occasionally ask him to fill in for him at the dining hall. "Red was sweet on a gal in his hometown of Sanford, and every other weekend, when he took off to visit this young lady, I substituted for him at his waiter job." But the "gal in . . . Sanford" appears to have played no further recorded role in Red's life. See King, *Model T Days*, 193.

36. Red Barber and Creamer, *Rhubarb in the Catbird Seat*, 140.

37. "Couple Known Here Wed in Gainesville," *Tampa Tribune*, August 22, 1930, 10.

38. Red Barber and Creamer, *Rhubarb in the Catbird Seat*, 140.

39. Quoted in Gannon, "Interview with Walter (Red) Barber."

40. Lylah Barber, *Lylah*, 70–71.

41. Caudill, *Mississippi Oral History Program*, 35–36.

42. Edwards, *Fridays with Red*, 143–44.

43. In her book, *The Parables of Kahlil Gibran*, 27–28, Annie Otto notes Barber became interested in *The Prophet* when "a friend gave it to him while he was in the hospital in 1948." He regularly gave copies of the book to his friends; in 1957 the publisher presented Red Barber, who had bought more copies than any other customer, with the millionth copy to be printed.

44. Gibran, *The Prophet*, 25–26.

45. Red Barber and Creamer, *Rhubarb in the Catbird Seat*, 50.

46. Creamer, RITCS, tape 9, side B.

47. Lylah Barber, *Lylah*, xi. In a 1985 television interview, when asked, "Being around such a celebrity as Red, have you ever felt like a non-entity?" Lylah replied, "Sure, why do you think I wrote the book?" Wymore, "Interview with Red and Lylah Barber," 5.

48. Lylah Barber, *Lylah*, 4–7.

49. Lylah Barber, *Lylah*, 71.

50. Lylah Barber, *Lylah*, 8.

51. Lylah Barber, *Lylah*, 102.

52. Lylah Barber, *Lylah*, 171.

53. Lylah Barber, *Lylah*, 27.

54. Lylah Barber, *Lylah*, 19.

55. Lylah Barber, *Lylah*, 16.

56. Lylah Barber, *Lylah*, 52.

57. Lylah Barber, *Lylah*, 13–14.

58. Lylah Barber, *Lylah*, 28.

59. Lylah Barber, *Lylah*, 40–53, 160.

60. Lylah Barber, *Lylah*, 62–63.

61. Data in this and the next several paragraphs are from Lylah Barber, *Lylah*, 64–69.

62. Data in this and the following several paragraphs are from Lylah Barber, *Lylah*, 71–79, and Red Barber and Creamer, *Rhubarb in the Catbird Seat*, 180.

63. Lylah Barber, *Lylah*, 80–86.

64. "Death of Mr. C. C. Martin," *Columbus Weekly Dispatch*, May 2, 1907, 7; "John C. Martin Dies," *Tampa Morning Tribune*, July 15, 1936, 1.

65. Red Barber, *Show Me the Way to Go Home*, 42–46.

66. Red Barber, *Show Me the Way to Go Home*, 42–46.

4. "Certain Aspects of Bovine Obstetrics"

1. Red Barber and Creamer, *Rhubarb in the Catbird Seat*, 141–42.

2. Red Barber, *The Broadcasters* (1970), 62–64.

3. Burrows, "Interview with Walter L. 'Red' Barber," 31–32.

4. "State Radio," *Tampa Tribune*, August 21, 1930, 4. Reprinted from the *Miami Herald*.

5. Red Barber and Creamer, *Rhubarb in the Catbird Seat*, 144–45.

6. Burrows, "Interview with Walter L. 'Red' Barber," 33.

7. Burrows, "Interview with Walter L. 'Red' Barber," 29.

8. Burrows, "Interview with Walter L. 'Red' Barber," 18.

9. Burrows, "Interview with Walter L. 'Red' Barber," 26.

10. "Negro Quartette to Sing at Church Here Tonight," *Tampa Tribune*, June 23, 1930, 7.

11. Burrows, "Interview with Walter L. 'Red' Barber," 33.

12. Burrows, "Interview with Walter L. 'Red' Barber," 34.

13. Red Barber, "Old Orange Grove String Band—A Different Sort of Day," *Tallahassee Democrat*, June 23, 1974, 2D.

14. Red Barber and Creamer, *Rhubarb in the Catbird Seat*, 153.

15. "'Red Barber' Has Certainly," RBC, boxes 1–3, vol. 2.

16. Red Barber, "Old Orange Grove String Band—A Different Sort of Day," *Tallahassee Democrat*, June 23, 1974, 2D.

17. Red Barber and Creamer, *Rhubarb in the Catbird Seat*, 155.

18. Laurence Emanuel, "'RUF and Otherwise," *Florida Alligator*, October 26, 1930, 2.

19. Red Barber and Creamer, *Rhubarb in the Catbird Seat*, 155.

20. Burrows, "Interview with Walter L. 'Red' Barber," 20.

21. Laurence Emanuel, "'RUF and Otherwise," *Florida Alligator*, October 26, 1930, 2.

22. Red Barber, "Catbird Seat," *Tallahassee Democrat*, July 20, 1975, 4D.

23. Red Barber, *The Broadcasters* (1970), 269.

24. "By Unanimous Vote of Football Fans," RBC, boxes 1–3, vol. 2.

25. Red Barber and Creamer, *Rhubarb in the Catbird Seat*, 157.

26. Quotes in this and the following paragraph are from Red Barber and Creamer, *Rhubarb in the Catbird Seat*, 158.

27. Pete Norton, "The Sport Outlook," *Tampa Bay Times*, December 7, 1930, 17.

28. Frank S. Wright, "Florida University Dope," *Fort Lauderdale News*, December 9, 1930, 6.

29. Bill Duncan, "RUF and Otherwise," *Florida Alligator*, September 25, 1932, 2.

30. "WRUF to Broadcast Detailed Report of Series Clash Today," RBC, boxes 1–3, vol. 2.

31. "Red Barber Has Concluded Four Seasons on Air," *Sanford Herald*, December 2, 1933, RBC, boxes 1–3, vol. 2.

32. "Red Barber at Mike Saturday," RBC, boxes 1–3, vol. 2.

33. Russell Kay, "Too Late to Classify," *Tallahassee Democrat*, May 17, 1933, 4.

34. "WRUF Presents Radio Account of Ball Games," *Tampa Bay Times*, March 6, 1931, 4.

35. Red Barber and Creamer, *Rhubarb in the Catbird Seat*, 150.

36. "Red and Blue Sport Feature" and "'Red' and 'Blue' Hook-up Enjoyed by Sports Fans," RBC, boxes 1–3, vol. 2.

37. "Station WRUF Will Broadcast Local Game," RBC, boxes 1–3, vol. 2.

38. "To Be Broadcast," RBC, boxes 1–3, vol. 2.

39. McEachern to Barber, September 12, 1982, RBC, box 7, folder 1982.

40. Red Barber and Creamer, *Rhubarb in the Catbird Seat*, 166.

41. Red Barber and Creamer, *Rhubarb in the Catbird Seat*, 166.

42. Red Barber and Robert Creamer fictionalized the hospital and physician names in this section when they published *Rhubarb in the Catbird Seat*. We use actual names

here. We found them in Robert Creamer's manuscript draft for the book archived at the National Baseball Hall of Fame.

43. Data in this and the next several paragraphs are from Red Barber and Creamer, *Rhubarb in the Catbird Seat*, 169–77.

44. Red Barber and Creamer, *Rhubarb in the Catbird Seat*, 152.

45. Red Barber and Creamer, *Rhubarb in the Catbird Seat*, 183.

46. Red Barber and Creamer, *Rhubarb in the Catbird Seat*, 185.

47. Authors' interview with Tom Villante, April 13, 2018.

5. Pay Cut

1. C. L. Thomas to Red Barber, April 12, 1979, RBC, box 6, folder 1974.

2. Creamer, RITCS, tape 7, side B.

3. Quoted in Red Barber and Creamer, *Rhubarb in the Catbird Seat*, 187.

4. Quoted in Red Barber and Creamer, *Rhubarb in the Catbird Seat*, 188.

5. Creamer, RITCS, tape 7, side B.

6. Speed Johnson, *Who's Who in Major League Baseball*, 521.

7. Quoted in Red Barber and Creamer, *Rhubarb in the Catbird Seat*, 190.

8. Quoted in Red Barber and Creamer, *Rhubarb in the Catbird Seat*, 191; emphasis in original.

9. Quoted in Red Barber, "My Most Unforgettable Character," 166.

10. Quoted in Red Barber and Creamer, *Rhubarb in the Catbird Seat*, 194.

11. "Florida Announcer Joins WSAI," *Radio Dial*, April 12, 1934.

12. "On the Air Lines," *The Sporting News*, April 5, 1934, 5.

13. Lylah Barber, *Lylah*, 95–96.

14. Lylah Barber, *Lylah*, 100–101.

15. Red Barber and Creamer, *Rhubarb in the Catbird Seat*, 200.

16. Quoted in "'Round and About WSAI Studios . . ."; From Alley to Freshney, RBC, boxes 1–3, vol. 2.

17. DiMaggio, *Baseball for Everyone*, 205–9.

18. Red Barber, "Opening Day in Cincinnati—Then and Now," *Tallahassee Democrat*, April 11, 1976, 5D.

19. Quoted in Red Barber and Creamer, *Rhubarb in the Catbird Seat*, 205.

20. "Cincinnati Baseball," *Variety*, April 24, 1934, 36.

21. Red Barber and Creamer, *Rhubarb in the Catbird Seat*, 206.

22. Red Barber and Creamer, *Rhubarb in the Catbird Seat*, 202.

23. Red Barber and Creamer, *Rhubarb in the Catbird Seat*, 203.

24. Red Barber and Creamer, *Rhubarb in the Catbird Seat*, 211.

25. Red Barber, *The Broadcasters* (1970), 69.

26. Quoted in Smith, *Voices of the Game*, 20.

27. E. Paul "Jack" Davis to Red Barber, April 29, 1990, RBC, box 11, folder 1990.

28. Red Barber, *The Broadcasters* (1970), 69.

29. Red Barber, *The Broadcasters* (1970), 69.

30. Gary Hartman, MD, to Red Barber, December, 4, 1989, RBC, box 9, folder 1989.

31. "New Follies Make Premier as 90-Minute Show," RBC, boxes 1–3, vol. 2.

32. "Crosley Follies," *Variety*, October 9, 1934.

33. Creamer, RITCS, tape 10, side A; *Variety*, October 9, 1934.

34. Red Barber and Creamer, *Rhubarb in the Catbird Seat*, 212.

35. Creamer, RITCS, tape 13, side B.

36. Red Barber and Creamer, *Rhubarb in the Catbird Seat*, 214.

37. Red Barber and Creamer, *Rhubarb in the Catbird Seat*, 216.

38. Quoted in Creamer, RITCS, tape 13, side B.

39. Walker, *Crack of the Bat*, 27.

40. Quoted in Red Barber, *The Broadcasters* (1970), 82–83.

41. Red Barber, *The Broadcasters* (1970), 81–83.

42. Red Barber and Creamer, *Rhubarb in the Catbird Seat*, 224.

43. Red Barber and Creamer, *Rhubarb in the Catbird Seat*, 222.

44. Red Barber and Creamer, *Rhubarb in the Catbird Seat*, 245, 247.

45. Red Barber and Creamer, *Rhubarb in the Catbird Seat*, 247.

46. Quoted in Creamer, RITCS, tape 12, side A.

47. Lylah Barber, *Lylah*, 97–98.

48. Red Barber and Creamer, *Rhubarb in the Catbird Seat*, 29.

49. Red Barber, "The Catbird Seat," *Tallahassee Democrat*, February 20, 1972, 3D.

50. John Kiesewetter, "Tales from the Catbird Seat," *Cincinnati Enquirer*, February 23, 1988. James Thurber further popularized the phrase when he used "The Catbird Seat" as the title of his widely anthologized 1942 *New Yorker* story. The story's protagonist, a mild-mannered office worker, is driven crazy by his new and threatening female boss, an avid Dodgers fan who endlessly utters Red's "Barbarisms." Barber was kept from using the phrase for an anticipated book title in 1953, when Thurber's story was under contract for a Hollywood film (Red Barber and Creamer, *Rhubarb in the Catbird Seat*, 28.) He reclaimed the phrase, however, for the title of his later column in the *Tallahassee Democrat*.

51. Red Barber and Creamer, *Rhubarb in the Catbird Seat*, 226.

52. Red Barber and Creamer, *Rhubarb in the Catbird Seat*, 225.

53. Quoted in Red Barber, *The Broadcasters* (1970), 29.

6. Rising Expectations

1. Advertisement, *Union County Journal*, September 23, 1935, 2.

2. Red Barber, *The Broadcasters* (1970), 237.

3. Harold E. Miller, Howard Cuseck, and Martin Burns to Managing Director: Mutual Broadcasting System, November 4, 1935, RBC, boxes 1–3, vol. 3.

4. O'Hara to Barber, November 29, 1936, RBC, boxes 1–3, vol. 3.

5. Quoted in Creamer, RITCS, tapes 4, 9, side B.

6. Quoted in Creamer, RITCS, tapes 4, 9, side B.

7. Morton to Royal, July 15, 1936, interdepartmental correspondence, NBC Archives; Barber to Morton, September 5, 1936, NBC Archives.

8. Royal to Morton, October 6, 1936, interdepartmental correspondence, NBC Archives.

9. Red Barber, *1947*, 45.

10. Unless otherwise noted, data in this and the following paragraph are from Lylah Barber, *Lylah*, 101–2.

11. Quoted in Warfield, *Roaring Redhead*, 64.

12. Warfield, *Roaring Redhead*, 64–66.

13. Quoted in Warfield, *Roaring Redhead*, 58.

14. Red Barber, "The Night the Lights Came on in Baseball," 38.

15. Red Barber, "June Is the Month for Cincy No-Hitters," *Tallahassee Democrat*, June 25, 1978, 8D.

16. Chuck Gay, "Listenin' In," *Dayton Daily News*, June 29, 1938, 6.

17. Red Barber and Creamer, *Rhubarb in the Catbird Seat*, 218–19.

18. "Opening Reds' Game Broadcast," RBC, boxes 1–3, vol. 4.

19. "Sports Get Big Play at WSAI," RBC, boxes 1–3, vol. 4.

20. Chuck Gay, "Listenin' In," *Dayton Daily News*, RBC, boxes 1–3, vol. 4.

21. "Declaring Last Sunday a 'Holiday' for Baseball Radio Broadcasters," RBC, boxes 1–3, vol. 4.

22. "New Sportscaster at WLW as Barber's Aide," RBC, boxes 1–3, vol. 4.

23. "Dear Nix," *Cincinnati Times-Star*, RBC, boxes 1–3, vol. 4.

24. "Thursday, May 8," and "For the Benefit of Those," RBC, boxes 1–3, vol. 4.

25. Quoted in Chuck Gay, "Listenin' In," *Dayton Daily News*, August 2, 1937, 4.

26. Chuck Gay, "Listenin' In," *Dayton Daily News*, September 27, 1937, 6.

27. Quoted in "Postman Rings—Sports Editor's Mail," *Dayton Daily News*, October 3, 1937, 25.

28. Quoted in "Broadcasting Comment," *Dayton Daily News*, September 5, 1937, 30.

29. "Dial Lights," *Cincinnati Enquirer*, August 15, 1937.

30. "Sports Announcer Knows Statistics," RBC, boxes 1–3, vol. 4.

31. "Airing the Series," *Brooklyn Eagle*, October 11, 1936, 9C.

32. "One Way Stars Keep Cool during the Warm Weather," *The Microphone*, August 3, 1935.

33. Advertisements in this section are in RBC, boxes 1–3, vol. 4.

34. "Broadcast Sports by Portable Unit," *Radio Dial*, April 22, 1937, 13.

35. "On the Air," *Cincinnati Enquirer*, July 18, 1938, 17.

36. "On the Air," *Cincinnati Enquirer*, April 19, 1938, 10.

37. "Man in the Neighborhood," *Radio Dial*, October 29, 1937; "Use Mobile Unit on Home Program," *Cincinnati Times-Star*, October 20, 1937.

38. Lylah Barber, *Lylah*, 102–3.

39. Red Barber, *Show Me the Way to Go Home*, 49.

40. Red Barber, *Show Me the Way to Go Home*, 45.

41. Red Barber, *Show Me the Way to Go Home*, 49–51.

42. Marshall, "Baseball from the Catbird Seat," 53–54.

43. Lylah Barber, *Lylah*, 103.

44. "Scrapbook," Sarah Barber's birth, clippings, cards, letters, RBC, box 45.

45. "Scrapbook," Sarah Barber's birth, clippings, cards, letters, RBC, box 45.

46. "U.D. Alumni to Meet Wednesday," *Dayton Evening News*, November 4, 1935, 22.

47. "Social Activities of Greater Cincinnati," *Cincinnati Enquirer*, November 10, 1935, 93.

48. "Civic Group Hears 'Chuck' Dressen," *Cincinnati Enquirer*, February 4, 1936, 2.

49. Paul Kennedy, "Red Learns How It Feels to Face Them," *Cincinnati Post*, January 26, 1939.

50. Chuck Gay, "Listenin' In," *Dayton Daily News*, February 5, 1939, 18.

51. "Oil for the Cars of Cincinnati" (advertisement), *Variety*, September 14, 1938.

52. "John Hancock Deluge," *Minneapolis Tribune*, August 18, 1938.

53. "Will Offer Testimonials to 'Red' Barber on Valley Day at Crosley Field, Sept. 7," RBC, boxes 1–3, vol. 6.

54. "Listening In," *Cincinnati Enquirer*, September 4, 1938.

55. "WSAI Sports Staff Answers Heavy Mail on Special Program," *Radio Dial*, August 26, 1938.

56. "New Program for Baber," *Cincinnati Enquirer*, July 31, 1938.

57. Quoted in Red Barber and Creamer, *Rhubarb in the Catbird Seat*, 236.

58. Red Barber and Creamer, *Rhubarb in the Catbird Seat*, 236.

59. Nixson Denton, "Second Thoughts," *Cincinnati Times-Star*, August 22, 1938, RBC, boxes 1–3, vol. 6.

60. Walker, *Crack of the Bat*, 130.

61. Red Barber and Creamer, *Rhubarb in the Catbird Seat*, 238.

7. Making of a Legend

1. "Compliments of Wheaties et al.," 62–63.

2. Walker, *Crack of the Bat*, 155.

3. Red Barber and Creamer, *Rhubarb in the Catbird Seat*, 37.

4. "Brooklyn Grants Baseball Pickups," *Broadcasting*, December 15, 1938, 16.

5. "Three to Sponsor Gotham Baseball," *Broadcasting*, February 1, 1939, 84.

6. WHN also carried some Dodgers games.

7. Red Barber and Creamer, *Rhubarb in the Catbird Seat*, 34.

8. Red Barber and Creamer, *Rhubarb in the Catbird Seat*, 33–36.

9. John Chapman, "Mainly about Manhattan," *New York Daily News*, April 29, 1939, 22.

10. "How 'Gone with the Wind' Became America's Biggest Blockbuster," CNN Business, December 15, 2014, https://money.cnn.com/2014/12/15/media/gone-with-the-wind-anniversary/index.html.

11. Cosell, "Interviews Red Barber."

12. Walker, *Crack of the Bat*, 115.

13. Quoted in Orrin E. Dunlap Jr., "Behind the Plate," *New York Times*, September 1, 1940, 10X.

14. Authors' interview with Tom Villante, April 13, 2018.

15. Maxwell Hamilton, "The Old Redhead," *Cue*, September 14, 1940, RBC, boxes 1–3, vol. 11.

16. "Ruth Chatterton in Radio," *New York World-Telegram*, July 14, 1939, RBC, boxes 1–3, vol. 7.

17. Walker, *Crack of the Bat*, 155.

18. Ben Gross, "Listening In," *New York City News*, July 16, 1939, RBC, boxes 1–3, vol. 7.

19. "Tips on Baseball Radio," *New York World-Telegram*, May 23, 1939, RBC, boxes 1–3, vol. 7.

20. Edward Zeltner, "Over the River," RBC, boxes 1–3, vol. 7.

21. Robert Windt, "It's in the Wind," *Boro Park Herald*, March 29, 1939, RBC, boxes 1–3, vol. 7.

22. Jo Ranson, "Radio Dial Log," *Brooklyn Eagle*, May 22, 1939, 22.

23. Red Barber and Creamer, *Rhubarb in the Catbird Seat*, 28; Barber never indicates how the word "rhubarb" initially came to be used in Brooklyn for an argument, but in a 1946 book about an unruly cat named Rhubarb, H. Allen Smith supplies some sources for the association between the stringy vegetable and verbal or physical fights. Smith credits Barber for popularizing Schumacher's use of the word in his own Dodgers broadcasts and also posits that the vegetable originally may have been associated with discord because when it is stewed, it takes the form of loose tangled cords that are unruly and disheveled. Further, Smith reports that Brooklyn mothers made their sons eat bread spread with stewed rhubarb after school; the boys invariably threw their bread at one another, splattering each other's hair and neck with pureed rhubarb. In time they began referring to their rough play as "Wotta rhubarb!" See Red Smith, "Views of Sports," *Philadelphia Inquirer*, May 21, 1959, 46.

24. "Follow-Up Comment," *Variety*, June 21, 1939, RBC, boxes 1–3, vol. 7.

25. Jerry Franken, "Talking Shop," *Billboard*, May 13, 1939, RBC, boxes 1–3, vol. 7.

26. "Baseball So Far No Wow in N.Y.," *Variety*, May 17, 1939, RBC, boxes 1–3, vol. 7.

27. Robert Windt, "It's in the Wind," *Boro Park Herald*, March 29, 1939, RBC, boxes 1–3, vol. 7.

28. Eddie Brietz, "Sports Round-Up," RBC, boxes 1–3, vol. 7.

29. "Chandler to Go on Air," *New York World-Telegram*, May 19, 1939, RBC, boxes 1–3, vol. 7.

30. Quoted in J. G. Taylor Spink, "Three and One," *The Sporting News*, December 14, 1939, 8.

31. Red Barber and Creamer, *Rhubarb in the Catbird Seat*, 241–42.

32. Red Barber and Creamer, *Rhubarb in the Catbird Seat*, 45.

33. *Television's First Year*.

34. Walker and Bellamy, *Center Field Shot*, 3–4.

35. "First U.S. Sports Event Is Televised by NBC," 70.

36. Quoted in William O. Johnson Jr., *Super Spectator and the Electric Lilliputians*, 37.

37. Red Barber, "We Were Making History," 16–17. Barber also covered the first color telecast of a Major League game for CBS in August 1951. See Red Smith, "Views on Sports," *The Sporting News*, August 22, 1951, 10.

38. Roscoe McGowen, "First Day for the Small Screen," *New York Times*, August 26, 1939, https://archive.nytimes.com/www.nytimes.com/packages/html/sports/year_in_sports/08.26.html?scp=11&sq=%2522St.%2520Louis%2520Cardinals%2522&st=cse.

39. Red Barber, "We Were Making History," 17.

40. Alfred H. Morton, "Television Wants Security," *Broadcasting*, October 1, 1939, 72.

41. "First Workout for Commercials on Television," *Variety*, August 30, 1939, RBC, boxes 1–3, vol. 7; Jack Banner, "Banner Radio Lines," *Motion Picture Daily*, August 29, 1939, RBC, boxes 1–3, vol. 7.

42. "Florida 'Cracker Boy' Hits High Point as Radio Ace," *Florida Searchlight*, October 5, 1939.

43. Morton to Barber, RBC, boxes 1–3, vol. 9.

44. Walker and Bellamy, *Center Field Shot*, 14.

45. Walker, *Crack of the Bat*, 109.

46. "All Warmed Up," *Broadcasting*, October 15, 1939, 16.

47. "WLNH to Broadcast World Series," *Laconia Democrat*, September 14, 1939, RBC, boxes 1–3, vol. 8.

48. Walter Winchell, "The New York Scene," *Los Angeles Express*, October 10, 1939, RBC, boxes 1–3, vol. 8.

49. "Excerpt from Lowell Thomas' Broadcast," October 5, 1939, RBC, boxes 1–3, vol. 8.

50. Letter, Smith to Barber, October 24, 1939, RBC, boxes 1–3, vol. 8.

51. Telegram, Dad to Barber, October 4, 1939, RBC, boxes 1–3, vol. 8.

52. "Red Barber of WOR Named Radio's Top Baseball Announcer," press release, Bamberger Broadcasting Service, December 5, 1939, RBC, boxes 1–3, vol. 9.

53. J. G. Taylor Spink, "Three and One," *The Sporting News*, December 14, 1939, 4, 8.

54. J. G. Taylor Spink, "Three and One," *The Sporting News*, December 14, 1939, 8.

55. Cosell, "Interviews Red Barber."

56. "Hey You! Turn It Down!" *Broadcasting*, October 1, 1940, 79.

57. "Dodgers Giving 'Em a Fireworks Finish," *The Sporting News*, September 26, 1940, 5.

58. "On the Radio Air Lines," *The Sporting News*, June 6, 1940, 5.

59. Quoted in Red Barber and Creamer, *Rhubarb in the Catbird Seat*, 54.

60. "Behind the Mike," *Broadcasting*, December 1, 1940, 47.

61. "Barber's Status in Doubt," *The Sporting News*, January 30, 1941, 6.

62. "Big League Games Shifted to WPEN," *Broadcasting*, February 24, 1941, 54; "On the Air Lines," *The Sporting News*, February 27, 1941, 12.

63. "Campaign Widens to Retain Barber as Dodger 'Voice,'" *Brooklyn Eagle*, February 1, 1941, 3.

64. "Lever, Gen. Mills Plan Split Sponsorship for Brooklyn Dodgers Games," *Broadcasting*, March 10, 1941, 11.

65. R. W. Stewart, "One Thing and Another," *New York Times*, July 27, 1941, 10X; "Dodgers Are Subject of Symphony—'With Alleyaygrows and Stuff,'" Associated Press, RBC, boxes 1–3, vol. 12.

66. "Baseball Symphony," *Louisville Courier-Journal*, May 25, 1941, RBC, boxes 1–3, vol. 12.

67. Bob Considine, *New York Daily Mirror*, August 6, 1941, RBC, boxes 1–3, vol. 12.

68. "No. 1 Broadcasters of '41 Honored," *The Sporting News*, October 9, 1941, 10; "On the Radio Air Lines," *The Sporting News*, October 9, 1941, 4.

69. "On the Radio Air Lines," *The Sporting News*, October 9, 1941, 4.

70. George Tucker, AP *Feature Service, New York*, February 21, 1941, RBC, boxes 1–3, vol. 12.

71. "On the Radio Air Lines," *The Sporting News*, October 23, 1941, 2.

72. *Hackensack Republican*, November 23, 1939, RBC, boxes 1–3, vol. 9.

73. Red Barber, "Skull Practice," *Key: The Host's Guide*, November 1939, RBC, boxes 1–3, vol. 9.

74. "Pro Game on 9," *Broadcasting*, December 15, 1939, 26.

75. "The Winnah—Wheaties," *Variety*, December 13, 1939, RBC, boxes 1–3, vol. 9.

76. Eddie Brietz, "Kimbrough Hero of Bowl Games," *Peoria Journal-Transcript*, January 2, 1940, RBC, boxes 1–3, vol. 11.

77. "Another Novelty," *Broadcasting*, December 15, 1940, 20.

78. Red Barber, "Man in Conflict," *Tallahassee Democrat*, June 4, 1972, 3D.

79. Quoted in Creamer, RITCS, tape 11, side A.

80. Red Barber, "Man in Conflict," *Tallahassee Democrat*, June 4, 1972, 3D.

81. Red Barber, *The Broadcasters* (1970), 166.

82. Quoted in Marshall, "Interview with Red Barber," 65.

83. Quoted in Marshall, "Interview with Red Barber," 65.

84. Quoted in Red Barber, *The Broadcasters* (1970), 167; Marshall, "Interview with Red Barber," 66.

85. "Television Calling Signals," *New York* PM, November 11, 1940, RBC, boxes 1–3, vol. 11; "Left out of the Shuffle," *New York World-Telegram*, November 16, 1940, RBC, boxes 1–3, vol. 11.

86. Creamer, RITCS, tape 11, side A.

87. Quoted in Creamer, RITCS, tape 11, side A. Barber states that the *New York Times* writer who gave him the news of the Pearl Harbor attack was Lou Effrat (Barber, 1947, 47).

88. Quoted in Creamer, RITCS, tape 11, side A.

89. Authors' interview with Tom Villante, April 13, 2018.

8. "Blood" on the Radio

1. Hubler, "The Barber of Brooklyn," 34.

2. Hubler, "Barber of Brooklyn," 34; Willard Mullin, cartoonist, "It's on the Beam—All Over There," *The Sporting News*, October 7, 1943, 1.

3. Authors' interview with Chuck Yarborough, professor of Southern history, December 20, 2019.

4. Price, "Famed Broadcaster Is Interviewed," 17; emphasis in original.

5. Red Barber, "The 'Verce' of Brooklyn," *New York World-Telegram*, August 6, 1943, RBC, boxes 1–3, vol. 14.

6. Price, "Famed Broadcaster Is Interviewed," 17.

7. Red Barber, "Prescription for Baseball Players," *New York Times*, September 13, 1942, 13SM.

8. Red Barber, "The Fans Make Baseball," *New York Times*, October 3, 1943, 10SM.

9. Red Barber, "The Music I Want," *Victor Record Review*, RBC, boxes 1–3, vol. 14.

10. Red Barber, "It Isn't Work—It's Fun."

11. Red Barber and Creamer, *Rhubarb in the Catbird Seat*, 46–47; emphasis added.

12. Red Barber and Creamer, *Rhubarb in the Catbird Seat*, 245–46.

13. Quoted in Price, "Famed Broadcaster Is Interviewed," 17.

14. Data in this and the following paragraph are from Red Barber, *Show Me the Way to Go Home*, 52–56.

15. "Bill McCaffrey Now Managing Red Barber," *Variety*, October 11, 1944, 28; Creamer, RITCS, tape 10, side B.

16. "Red Barber—Here Is the Exception," *New York World-Telegram*, April 15, 1942, RBC, boxes 1–3, vol. 13.

17. Quoted in Richard Pack, "Fifteen Minutes of Woe," WOR Press Release, July 29, 1942, RBC, boxes 1–3, vol. 13.

18. Tom Meany, "Voice of Brooklyn Has Competition from Eye-Witness," *New York World-Telegram*, April 12, 1942, RBC, boxes 1–3, vol. 13.

19. Alton Cook, "He Fills-In Details," *New York World-Telegram*, July 6, 1942, RBC, boxes 1–3, vol. 13.

20. Irwin Robinson, "Old Gold Sales Zoom," *Advertising Age*, August 10, 1942, RBC, boxes 1–3, vol. 13.

21. Quoted in "Red Barber Delights the Tobacco Table," *The Tobacco Leaf*, June, 27, 1942, RBC, boxes 1–3, vol. 13.

22. Frank Chapman, "Cat Nips for Mr. Barber," RBC, boxes 1–3, vol. 13.

23. Quoted in Alice Hughes, "A Woman's New York," *New York World-Telegram*, May, 11, 1942, RBC, boxes 1–3, vol. 13.

24. John Hutchens, "Her Name in Lights," *New York Times*, September 24, 1944, 14SM; "LaGuardia," *Brooklyn Eagle*, January 10, 1945, 8.

25. "Chart of Celebrities' Favorite Drinks," *Sir* magazine, in the private collection of E. V. E. Joy.

26. Red Barber, *The Broadcasters* (1970), 179–80.

27. "New Sammy Kaye Show," *New York World-Telegram*, January 9, 1943, RBC, boxes 1–3, vol. 14.

28. "Old Gold Show," *Radio Daily*, January 29, 1943, RBC, boxes 1–3, vol. 14.

29. "Old Gold Show," Woody Herman, Red Barber, Allan Jones, RBC, audiotape cassettes, boxes 27–28.

30. "Red Barber Turns to Acting," *The Sporting News*, May 29, 1943, RBC, boxes 1–3, vol. 14.

31. "Gainesville Girls Find Red Barber," *Gainesville Sun*, October 14, 1943, RBC, boxes 1–3, vol. 14.

32. "Westchester Bulletin #1," *The Faith That Fits*, RBC, boxes 1–3, vol. 14.

33. Data in this and the following paragraph are from Red Barber, *The Broadcasters* (1970), 245–50.

34. Authors' interview with Tom Villante, April 13, 2018.

35. Red Barber. *The Broadcasters* (1970), 247.

36. Authors' interview with Tom Villante, April 13, 2018.

37. Edwards, *Fridays with Red*, 12–13.

38. Red Barber and Creamer, *Rhubarb in the Catbird Seat*, 59–61.

39. Quoted in Creamer, RITCS, tape 12, side A.

40. Red Barber and Creamer, *Rhubarb in the Catbird Seat*, 248.

41. Red Barber and Creamer, *Rhubarb in the Catbird Seat*, 250–51.

42. Data in this and the following paragraph are from Red Barber and Creamer, *Rhubarb in the Catbird Seat*, 251–56.

43. Red Barber and Creamer, *Rhubarb in the Catbird Seat*, 265.

44. "A and S Employees Aid Red Cross," *Brooklyn Eagle*, January 19, 1942, 3.

45. "Red Barber Doing Whale of a Job," *Signal Corps Message*, August 12, 1942, RBC, boxes 1–3 vol. 13; emphasis in original.

46. "Bond Sale Recipe," *Advertising Age*, August 24, 1942, RBC, boxes 1–3, vol. 13.

47. Vincent Callahan, "War Savings Staff News," October 1, 1942, RBC, boxes 1–3, vol. 13.

48. Kingsley Childs, "War Bond Drive Here," *New York Times*, June 6, 1943, 1S.

49. Quoted in Red Barber and Creamer, *Rhubarb in the Catbird Seat*, 79; see also "Donor Ceremony to Precede Game," *Brooklyn Eagle*, July 1, 1942, 16.

50. Red Barber and Creamer, *Rhubarb in the Catbird Seat*, 78–80.

51. "Asking for Blood Donations," *New York Times*, October 25, 1944, 38.

52. Paul Gould, "Red Barber off on Tour," *Brooklyn Eagle*, February 3, 1943, 18.

53. "Red Cross Leader Makes Blood Gift," *New York Times*, March 30, 1945, 13.

54. Red Barber, *The Broadcasters* (1970), 139.

55. Red Barber, "The 'Verce' of Brooklyn," *New York World-Telegram*, August 6, 1943, RBC, boxes 1–3, vol. 14.

56. Red Barber, *Show Me the Way to Go Home*, 59–60.

57. "Red Barber to Conduct Boro Red Cross Drive," *Brooklyn Eagle*, December 19, 1943, 1.

58. "Red Cross Sets $3,331,000 as Boro Share," *Brooklyn Eagle*, January 12, 1944, 3.

59. "Boro's $2,450,777 Tops Red Cross Drive," *Brooklyn Eagle*, April 1, 1944, 1; "Children's Pennies Spur Oldsters," *Brooklyn Eagle*, March 9, 1944, 3.

60. "Red Barber Named Head," *Brooklyn Eagle*, December 15, 1944, 1.

61. Harold C. Burr, "Shifts Credit," *Brooklyn Eagle*, March 9, 1945, 15.

62. "Brooklyn Can Be Proud," *Brooklyn Eagle*, April 20, 1945, 10.

9. On the Home Front

1. Quoted in Creamer, RITCS, tape 11, side A.

2. Lylah Barber, *Lylah*, 134.

3. Data in this and the following paragraph are from Lylah Barber, *Lylah*, 111–16.

4. Data in this and the following two paragraphs are from Lylah Barber, *Lylah*, 126–33.

5. "Liberty in New York City," RBC, audiotape cassettes, boxes 27–28, clip approximately halfway through tape. In the tape's first half, Barber welcomes U.S. Navy personnel to New York and introduces them to some of the city's attractions. Red's

fathering was award winning. In June 1945 he received the General Eisenhower plaque as "Sports Father of the Year" at an Ebbets Field ceremony. See "On the Air Lanes," *The Sporting News*, June 21, 1945, 18.

6. Data in this and the following paragraph are from Lylah Barber, *Lylah*, 134–38.

7. Lowenfish, *Branch Rickey*, 23.

8. Quotes in this paragraph are from Red Barber and Creamer, *Rhubarb in the Catbird Seat*, 267–68; emphasis in original.

9. Red Barber and Creamer, *Rhubarb in the Catbird Seat*, 269.

10. Lowenfish, *Branch Rickey*, 359–61.

11. Red Barber and Creamer, *Rhubarb in the Catbird Seat*, 269–70.

12. Lylah Barber, *Lylah*, 159–60.

13. Red Barber and Creamer, *Rhubarb in the Catbird Seat*, 273.

14. Red Barber and Creamer, *Rhubarb in the Catbird Seat*, 271–72.

15. Red Barber and Creamer, *Rhubarb in the Catbird Seat*, 275.

16. Red Barber, *1947*, 65.

17. Unless otherwise noted, data in this and the following two paragraphs are from Red Barber, *Show Me the Way to Go Home*, 76–81.

18. Red Barber to Virginia Barber, July 12, 1945; private collection of E. V. E. Joy.

19. Red Barber, *The Broadcasters* (1970), 137.

20. Red Barber and Creamer, *Rhubarb in the Catbird Seat*, 86.

21. Red Barber, *The Broadcasters* (1970), 133–39.

22. Red Barber and Creamer, *Rhubarb in the Catbird Seat*, 87–88.

23. Data in this and the next several paragraphs are from Red Barber, *Show Me the Way to Go Home*, 61–75.

24. "St. Barnabas Dedicates Its 4-Story Shelter," *New York Herald Tribune*, October 20, 1950, RBC, boxes 1–3, vol. 18.

10. "Oh, Doctor!"

1. Quoted in Creamer, RITCS, tape 10, side B.

2. Quoted in Creamer, RITCS, tape 10, side B.

3. Quoted in Red Barber, *The Broadcasters* (1970), 145.

4. Red Barber, *The Broadcasters* (1970), 148–49.

5. Red Barber, *The Broadcasters* (1970), 149.

6. "On the Air Lanes," *The Sporting News*, April 16, 1947, 36.

7. "John Derr Well Known in Radio Sports; Helps Red Barber," *The Bee*, November 20, 1952, 28; "John Derr, Pinehurst, North Carolina," https://www.legacy.com/obituaries/name/john-derr-obituary?pid=179373812.

8. "For the Record," *Washington Post*, December 30, 1991, https://www.washingtonpost.com/archive/sports/1991/12/30/for-the-record/c1212814-7d5a-45d0-9347-ef536558aef7/; "New Sports," *Broadcasting*, October 20, 1947, 79.

9. Quoted in Creamer, RITCS, tape 10, side B.

10. Quoted in Margaret Mara, "There's No Boss Like Her Own Boss, in Opinion of Red Barber's Secretary," *Brooklyn Eagle*, September 8, 1948, 21.

11. "Connie Mack Outlines Managerial Principles," *The Sporting News*, August, 20, 1947, 4.

12. "Babe Ruth Gives Tips on Playing the Outfield," *The Sporting News*, August, 27, 1947, 4.

13. "Red Barber's Club House," CBS press release, April 23, 1948, RBC, boxes 1–3, vol. 15.

14. "EQ Ratings," *Broadcasting*, February 23, 1948, 80.

15. Red Barber, *The Broadcasters* (1970), 146.

16. "CBS Seeing Double," RBC, boxes 1–3, vol. 17.

17. "New CBS Football Show," *Broadcasting*, November 1, 1948, 4.

18. "Cross-Country Grid Coverage Being Planned," *Trenton Times Advertiser*, May 8, 1949, RBC, boxes 1–3, vol. 15.

19. "Named Ace Grid Aircaster of '49," *The Sporting News*, December 28, 1949, 38.

20. "CBS Covers," *Broadcasting*, August 19, 1946, 33.

21. "Lever Brothers Sign Arthur Godfrey, Now Have 2-Hour CBS Block on Mondays," *New York Times*, July 22, 1947, 46.

22. Halberstam, *Sports on New York Radio*, 400.

23. Quotes in this and the following paragraph are from Lylah Barber, *Lylah*, 144.

24. Data in this and the following paragraph are from Lylah Barber, *Lylah*, 151–53; "Liberty in New York City," RBC, audiotape cassette, boxes 27–28; Sarah's solo starts about halfway into the cassette.

25. Data in this and the following paragraph are from Lylah Barber, *Lylah*, 144–53.

26. Advertisement, "You Can Stop the War," *Tallahassee Democrat*, October 23, 1972, 3.

27. Unless otherwise noted, data in this and the following paragraph are from Lylah Barber, *Lylah*, 140–41, 158–59, 160–66.

28. Lylah Barber, *Lylah*, 167.

29. Red Barber, "So Soon Death Follows," *Tallahassee Democrat*, October 29, 1972, 4D.

30. Lylah Barber, *Lylah*, 167.

31. Lylah Barber, *Lylah*, 175.

32. Lylah Barber, *Lylah*, 160.

33. Lylah Barber, *Lylah*, 174.

34. Walter Winchell, "Attention Jacksonville Citizens," *Pocono Record*, January 30, 1951, 4.

35. "Accident Fatal to Pedestrian," *Jacksonville Journal*, February 21, 1951, RBC, boxes 1–3, vol. 21; Red Barber, *Show Me the Way to Go Home*, 104–6.

36. "Jury Awards $3,500 in Auto Death Suit," *Orlando Sentinel*, June 7, 1951, 9.

37. "Red Barber Serves as Narrator," *New York Times*, December 11, 1953, 49.

38. Seth Livingstone, "The Top 100 Things That Impacted Baseball in the 20th Century," *Baseball Weekly*, January 5, 2000, 16–17, 21.

39. Red Barber, *1947*, 64–65; authors' interview with Tom Villante, April 13, 2018.

40. David J. Halberstam, "'42' Error: How the Jackie Robinson Movie Got Red Barber Wrong," *Bleacher Report*, https://bleacherreport.com/articles/1625574-42-error-how-the-jackie-robinson-movie-got-red-barber-wrong.

41. Gayle Talbot, "How Media Covered Jackie Robinson's Debut," APnews.com, January 31, 2019, https://apnews.com/2fae56ee1c2a46299604ee0deaaf04ab.

42. Spatz, *Team That Forever Changed*, 68.

43. Quoted in Sam Lacy, "Interracial Baseball No Problem to Red Barber," *Baltimore Afro-American*, RBC, boxes 1–3, vol. 22.

44. Quoted in Creamer, RITCS, tape 12, side B.

45. Red Barber and Creamer, *Rhubarb in the Catbird Seat*, 276.

46. Joe Bostic, "The Scoreboard," *New York Amsterdam News*, November 7, 1953, 1. Quotes in the remainder of this paragraph are also from this source.

47. Red Barber, *1947*, 317.

48. Red Barber, *1947*, 317.

49. Red Barber, *1947*, 317.

50. Red Barber, "Play by Play Highlights," RBC, box 40.

51. Quoted in Red Barber, *1947*, 318.

52. Red Barber, *1947*, 329.

53. Red Barber, "Play by Play Highlights," RBC, box 40.

54. Red Barber, "Sites of the Olympic Games Stir Some Memories," *Tallahassee Democrat*, April 29, 1973, 3D.

55. Pfeifer, *Gretchen's Gold*, 81.

56. Red Barber, "American's First Skiing Gold Took Everyone by Surprise," *Tallahassee Democrat*, February 24, 1980, 8F.

57. Pfeifer, *Gretchen's Gold*, 82.

58. "Red Barber, Stephen Laird, John Derr, Judson Bailey Assigned to Cover London Olympic Games for Columbia," CBS News Press Release, June 21, 1948, RBC, boxes 1–3, vol. 15.

59. Red Barber, "I Cover the Olympics."

60. "Red Barber Collapses Here," *Pittsburgh Post-Gazette*, July 24, 1948, 7; Red Barber, "A Book on Baseball Moguls," *Tallahassee Democrat*, June 13, 1976, 5D.

61. Quotes in this and the next two paragraphs are from Red Barber, *Show Me the Way to Go Home*, 85–87.

62. "Barber Flown to New York," *Philadelphia Inquirer*, July 31, 1948, 17.

63. Data in this and the following three paragraphs are from Red Barber, *Show Me the Way to Go Home*, 91–96.

64. "World's Busiest Barber," RBC, boxes 1–3, vol. 21.

65. Heinz, "The Two Red Barbers," 104, 106.

66. Reynolds, "The Two Lives of Red Barber," 104.

67. Sterling and Kittross, *Stay Tuned*, 864.

68. Walker and Bellamy, *Center Field Shot*, 24, 68.

69. Letter, Bob Pasotti to Red Barber, August 30, 1982, RBC, box 7, folder 1982. Pasotti specifically recalls the nitpicking over pencils and egg timers: "As you recollect, all was not juleps and yellow roses in our years together. Your demands on me seemed often so pointless (that damned egg-timer and No. 2 pencils in the day and No. 3's at night!)"

70. Harwell and Keegan, *Ernie Harwell*, 104–5.

71. Red Barber, "A Half-Century Cruise across the Airwaves," *Tallahassee Democrat*, March 8, 1981, 5F.

72. Branch Rickey, "Memorandum of Conference with Messrs. Virden, Lennen and Daughton," November 26, 1948, BRP, box 34, folder 1.

73. Red Barber, "My Ten Years with the Dodgers"; Red Barber, "How to Win a Pennant—By Two Who Did," *New York Times Sunday Magazine*, September 28, 1947, 22, 56–58; Walter Barber, "What to Look for at a Baseball Game"; Red Barber, "The Greatest College Football Player I Ever Saw, Jay Berwanger."

74. Heinz, "The Two Red Barbers," 107.

75. Cullen Cain, "Red Barber Calls New Task a Challenge," *Miami Sunday News*, April 23, 1950, RBC, boxes 1–3, vol. 22.

76. Red Barber, "That Misnamed 'Bonehead Play,'" *New York Journal-American*, March 15, 1950, RBC, boxes 1–3, vol. 23.

77. Red Barber, "As Klem Would Have Called It," *New York Journal-American*, March 17, 1950, RBC, boxes 1–3, vol. 23.

78. Red Barber, "Merkle Incident," *Christian Science Monitor*, February 26, 1987, 18.

79. Red Barber, "A Cinderella in Pants," *New York Journal-American*, May 6, 1950, RBC, boxes 1–3, vol. 23.

80. "Red Barber Sells All but Sleep; Grosses about 125G," *Billboard*, September 9, 1950, 8.

81. Michael Haupert, "MLB's annual salary leaders since 1974," SABR, https://sabr .org/research/article/mlbs-annual-salary-leaders-since-1874/; Paul Sullivan, "No End in Sight as Athletes' Salaries Skyrocket," *Chicago Tribune*, January 1, 2000, https://www .chicagotribune.com/news/ct-xpm-2000-01-01-0001010031-story.html.

82. "Red Barber's Big League Baseball Game" (ad), *The Sporting News*, December 13, 1950, 27.

11. Losing Control, Gaining a Purpose

1. Red Barber, "The Sports Vine," *Herald of Westchester*, August 18, 1950, RBC, boxes 1–3, vol. 21. In 2020 the COVID-19 pandemic forced radio broadcasters, in their home ball parks, to broadcast from the video feed of road games. They too were denied a full view of the field, resulting in the same problem Red Barber had encountered with television in 1950. Jeff Agrest, *Chicago Sun-Times*, July 31, 2020, 50–51.

2. Red Barber, "Turmoil behind the Baseball Telecast," *New York Times*, April 30, 1950, 60.

3. Bob Lanigan, "Red Barber's Job No Cinch Telecasting Dodger Games," *Brooklyn Eagle*, September 29, 1952, 20; authors' interview with Tom Villante, April 13, 2018.

4. Red Barber, "Turmoil behind the Baseball Telecast," *New York Times*, April 30, 1950, 58 and 60.

5. McCue, *Mover and Shaker*, 20–25.

6. Quoted in Creamer, RITCS, tape 1, side B.

7. Red Barber and Creamer, *Rhubarb in the Catbird Seat*, 279.

8. Red Barber to O'Malley, September 30, 1948, courtesy of walteromalley.com.

9. Red Barber to O'Malley, August 4, 1950, courtesy of walteromalley.com.

10. Red Barber to O'Malley, November 2, 1950, courtesy of walteromalley.com.

11. "Red's Blues: Barber May Quit Calling Play-by-Play," *Billboard*, December 16, 1950, 3.

12. "Branch Rickey Visits Red Barber," *Pittsburgh Press*, July 27, 1948, 21.

13. Red Barber to Rickey, November 2, 1942, BRP, box 33, folder 8.

14. Red Barber to Rickey, July 9, 1945, BRP, box 5, folder 1.

15. Red Barber to Rickey, January 3, 1946, BRP, box 5, folder 2.

16. Red Barber to Rickey, November 1, 1950, BRP, box 5, folder 5.

17. Red Barber to Rickey, May 7, 1951, BRP, box 5, folder 6.

18. Red Barber to Rickey, September 24, 1951, BRP, box 5, folder 6.

19. Rickey to Barber, November 6, 1952; Rickey to Mills, April 11, 1953; Mills to Rickey, April 14, 1953. All in BRP, box 60, folder Ohio Wesleyan University, Delaware, Ohio, Red Barber, 1952–53.

20. Telegram, Jim Bridge to Branch Rickey, May 18, 1953, BRP, box 60, Ohio Wesleyan University, Delaware, Ohio, Red Barber, 1952–53.

21. Jack O'Brian, "2 Plan New Sports Show," *New York Journal-American*, January 18, 1956, 40, BRP, box 21, folder 3.

22. Rickey to Rollins College, December 14, 1955, BRP, box 9, folder 9; Rickey to Lylah, Sarah, and Walter Barber, June 7, 1956, BRP, box 6, folder 6; Red Barber to Rickey, November 11, 1955, BRP, box 9, folder 9.

23. Quotes in this and the following paragraph are from Lylah Barber, *Lylah*, 177–79.

24. Lylah Barber, *Lylah*, 179.

25. Red Barber and Creamer, *Rhubarb in the Catbird Seat*, 285.

26. Lylah Barber, *Lylah*, 180.

27. Red Barber to Rickey, May 7, 1951, BRP, box 5, folder 6; authors' interview with Tom Villante, April 13, 2018.

28. Data in this and the following two paragraphs are from Lylah Barber, *Lylah*, 182–86.

29. Quoted in Robert Creamer, "The Transistor Kid," *Sports Illustrated*, May 4, 1964; https://vault.si.com/vault/1964/05/04/the-transistor-kid.

30. Quoted in Creamer, RITCS, tape 1, side B.

31. Quoted in Creamer, RITCS, tape 1, side B.

32. Quoted in Creamer, RITCS, tape 1, side B.

33. Authors' interview with Tom Villante, April 13, 2018.

34. Creamer, RITCS, tape 4, side B.

35. Quoted in Creamer, RITCS, tape 1, side B.

36. Quoted in Creamer, RITCS, tape 1, side B.

37. Authors' interview with Tom Villante, April 13, 2018.

38. Creamer, RITCS, tape 1, side B.

39. Jim Desmond to Red Barber, RBC, box 9, folder 1987.

40. Quoted in Creamer, RITCS, tape 6, side B.

41. Quoted in Creamer, RITCS, tape 6, side B.

42. Quotes in this and the following paragraph are from Barber, *Show Me the Way to Go Home*, 98–100; emphasis in original.

43. Barber, *Show Me the Way to Go Home*, 148–53.

44. Barber, *Show Me the Way to Go Home*, 142–47.

45. Lylah Barber, *Lylah*, 187–90.

46. Lylah Barber, *Lylah*, 191–96.

47. "Tele Topics," *Radio Daily*, September 7, 1950, 7.

48. Murray Robinson, "Red Barber's Homer Is Greek to Dodger Ginmill Illiterati," *New York World-Telegram*, October 6, 1952, RBC, boxes 1–3, vol. 25.

49. "Who's Who? Fifteen News Questions What's What?" *New York Times*, October 12, 1952, 2E and 9E.

50. Dick Young, "The Sports of Kings and Queens," *New York Daily News*, January 4, 1953, 31B.

51. Quoted in Bill Coleman, "RADIOpinion and TELEVISIONotes," RBC, boxes 1–3, vol. 22.

52. John Lardner, "The Incident at Fort Boggess," *Newsweek*, July 17, 1950, RBC, boxes 1–3, vol. 22.

53. Quotations in this paragraph are from Milton Gross, "Speaking Out," *New York Post*, September, 12, 1950, RBC, boxes 1–3, vol. 21.

54. Lester Rodney, "On the Scoreboard: Red Barber and the First Punch," *Daily Worker*, May 9, 1950, RBC, boxes 1–3, vol. 22.

55. Lester Rodney, "On the Scoreboard: Red Barber and the First Punch," *Daily Worker*, May 9, 1950, RBC, boxes 1–3, vol. 22; emphasis in original.

56. Quoted in Smith, *Voices of the Game*, 134.

57. Barber, *The Broadcasters* (1970), 173.

58. Creamer, RITCS, tape 10, side A.

59. Red Barber, *The Broadcasters* (1970), 174–75.

60. Oscar Ruhl, "From the Ruhl Book," *The Sporting News*, May 27, 1953, 22.

61. Unless otherwise noted, data in this and the following three paragraphs are from Creamer, RITCS, tape 1, side A.

62. Wolff, *Bob Wolff's Complete Guide to Sportscasting*, 86.

63. Howard Burr, "The Voice of Brooklyn Headed for Yankees," *Brooklyn Eagle*, October 28, 1953, 19; Howard Burr, "Yanks Take Everything," *Brooklyn Eagle*, October 29, 1953, 18; "Red Barber Will Be Missed Here," *Brooklyn Eagle*, November 1, 1953, 22; Tommy Holmes, "What the Dodgers Have Lost," *Brooklyn Eagle*, November 2, 1953, 17; Bob and Jean, "TV Mailbag," *Brooklyn Eagle*, November 2, 1953, 8.

64. Red Barber and Stein, *The Rhubarb Patch*; "Patterson in Dodger Fold," *Brooklyn Eagle*, August 3, 1954, 11; Tommy Holmes, "Heroes, Just Mortals," *Brooklyn Eagle*, August 16, 1954, 11.

12. Stadium Work

1. Quoted in Creamer, RITCS, tape 3, side B.

2. Red Barber, *The Broadcasters* (1970), 189.

3. Borelli, *How About That!*, 6–10.

4. Smith, *Voices of the Game*, 46. Smith's bluegrass music reference certainly reflects Red's Southern persona, but his musical tastes tended toward symphony, opera, and show tunes.

5. Quoted in Smith, *Voices of the Game*, 48; Jim Woods also claimed that Dodgers and Yankees owners, Walter O'Malley and Dan Topping respectively, both frustrated with their broadcasting "voices" and full of liquid courage at Toots Shor's, briefly entertained trading Barber for Allen. See Smith, *Voices of the Game*, 141.

6. Red Barber, *The Broadcasters* (1970), 191.

7. Quoted in Smith, *Voices of the Game*, 47.

8. Red Barber, *The Broadcasters* (1970), 193.

9. John P. Leonetti, "What Is Fenestration?" *Audiologyonline*, https://www.audiologyonline.com/ask-the-experts/what-is-fenestration-338.

10. Red Barber, *The Broadcasters* (1970), 193.

11. Jack O'Brian, "Red Barber in Hospital for Surgery," *Sidney News* (from International News Service), January 13, 1954, RBC, boxes 1–3, vol. 27; "Barber Undergoes Operation," *Broadcasting*, January 11, 1954, 72; "Barber to Undergo Hospital Operation," *Billboard*, January, 9, 1954, 6; "Air Lanes," *The Sporting News*, January 13, 1954, 20; "Air Lanes," *The Sporting News*, February 3, 1954, 26; Oscar Ruhl, "From the Ruhl Book," *The Sporting News*, February 17, 1954, 14.

12. Red Barber, *The Broadcasters* (1970), 197.

13. Red Barber, *The Broadcasters* (1970), 198.

14. Red Barber, *The Broadcasters* (1970), 196.

15. Herbert Kamm, "'Rebels' in the Yankee Camp," *New York World-Telegram and Sun*, August 20, 1956; RBC, boxes 1–3, vol. 28.

16. Quoted in J. G. Taylor Spink, "Looping the Loops," *The Sporting News*, July 31, 1957, 10.

17. J. G. Taylor Spink, "Looping the Loops," *The Sporting News*, July 31, 1957, 10.

18. Borelli, *How About That!*, 179.

19. Quoted in J. G. Taylor Spink, "Looping the Loops," *The Sporting News*, July 31, 1957, 10.

20. Quoted in Harrington, "Red Barber: An Interview," 23.

21. Quoted in Schoor, *The Scooter*, 182.

22. Red Smith, "Views of Sports," *Philadelphia Inquirer*, May 14, 1958, 46.

23. Quoted in Harrington, "Red Barber: An Interview," 23.

24. Quoted in DeVito, *Scooter*, 203.

25. Borelli, *How About That!*, 182.

26. Authors' interview with Marty Appel, April 6, 2018.

27. "Barber Fed Up with Desk Job," *Variety*, February 2, 1955, RBC, boxes 1–3, vol. 27.

28. Quoted in Herbert Kamm, "'Rebels' in the Yankee Camp," *New York World-Telegram and Sun*, August 20, 1956; RBC, boxes 1–3, vol. 28.

29. Red Barber, *The Broadcasters* (1970), 148.

30. "Red Barber Plays the Field; CBS Pact Meant Bypassing Lota Loot," *Variety*, February 23, 1955, RBC, boxes 1–3, vol. 28.

31. "Red Barber's 200G Freelance Kick," *Variety*, January 25, 1956, RBC, boxes 1–3, vol. 28; "Sponsor Hears," *Sponsor*, November 17, 1956, 84; "Red Barber Gets Post-Gillette Nod," *Variety*, April 13, 1955, 37.

32. U.S. Federal Income Tax Rates History, 1862–2013, Tax Foundation, https://taxfoundation.org/us-federal-individual-income-tax-rates-history-1913-2013-nominal-and-inflation-adjusted-brackets/.

33. "'Red Barber' Award to Honor Top UF Student Announcer," *Gainesville Times*, February 20, 1955, RBC, boxes 1–3, vol. 28; "Barber Award Is Given Goodwin, UF announcer," *Gainesville Sun*, March 6, 1955, RBC, boxes 1–3, vol. 28; "Red Barber Award to Goodwin," *The Sporting News*, March 23, 1955, RBC, boxes 1–3, vol. 28.

34. "Tuning In," *The Sporting News*, October 2, 1957, 60; "Yanks in Sgt. Bilko's Lineup," *The Sporting News*, October 9, 1957, 31.

35. "Tuning In," *The Sporting News*, January 22, 1958, 25; "Sponsor-Scope," *Sponsor*, March 8, 1956, 12; Val Adams, "Concert by Casals at U.N. on Oct. 24 Will Be on Radio," *New York Times*, September 26, 1958, 52; "Aqua-Spectacle," *Broadcasting*, October 8, 1956, 14.

36. "Red Barber on 'Open End,'" *Oakland Tribune*, March 4, 1962, 121.

37. "Air Lanes," *The Sporting News*, December 29, 1954, 29; "Football King at TV Box Office," *Broadcasting*, August 19, 1963, 36; "Red Barber Conducts New Sports Series," *Radio-Television Daily*, February, 23, 1962, 8.

38. "The Double Life of Red Barber," 62.

39. "Famed 'Redhead' Preaches Sermon in Cooperstown," RBC, boxes 1–3, vol. 27; Oscar Ruhl, "From the Ruhl Book," *The Sporting News*, August 25, 1954, 16; "Red Barber, Preaching at St. Mark's, Likens God to Good Sports Manager," *New York Times*, January 27, 1958, 18.

40. "The 'Old Red Head' Lives Two Lives," *Orlando Sentinel*, March 6, 1955, 9.

41. John Drebinger, "Tigers Check Yankee Rally in Ninth to Triumph before 35,660 at Stadium," *New York Times*, June 14, 1958, 16.

42. "Rollins Welcomes 250," *The Rollins Sandspur*, September 28, 1956, 1, OLRC.

43. Denise Kusel, "Treasured Social Activist," *Santa Fe New Mexican*, March 12, 2005, 4B.

44. McFarlane and Bashe, *Complete Bedside Companion*, 256; emphasis in original.

45. "Almost Meeting Red Barber," *Orlando Evening Star*, March 24, 1954, 14.

46. John Tiedke to Hugh McKean, March 8, 1954, OLRC, Barber, Walter "Red" file, 43A.

47. "Rollins 29th Animated Magazine," *Winter Park Sun*, February 23, 1956, OLRC, Barber, Walter "Red" file, 43A.

48. Lylah Barber, *Lylah*, 175.

49. Quoted in "Red Barber, Animated Magazine, February 26, 1956," 1, OLRC, Barber, Walter "Red" file, 43A.

50. Jim Locke, "The Locker Room," *Rollins Sandspur*, March 1, 1956, 6, OLRC, Barber, Walter "Red" file, 43A.

51. A. J. Hanna to Walter L. Barber, January 8, 1957; memo from "KL" to "AJH," OLRC, Barber, Walter "Red" file, 43A.

52. "Sarah Barber," *Flamingo* 34–44 (1957–61, Winter 1958): 19; OLRC.

53. Sarah Barber, "Greenwich Village," *Flamingo* 34–44 (1957–61), Fall 1957, 12–13, OLRC.

54. Sarah Barber, "A Sonnet for You," *Flamingo* 34–44 (1957–61), Fall 1957, 23, OLRC.

55. Sarah Barber, "As Days Pass," *Flamingo* 34–44 (1957–61), Winter 1958, 19, OLRC.

56. Lylah Barber, *Lylah*, 197.

57. Authors' interviews with Leslie Rich, December 12, 2019, and Judy Gomez, December 16, 2019.

58. Authors' interviews with Liz Bremner, December 3, 2019, and Judy Gomez, December 16, 2019.

59. In his article "Electroconvulsive Therapy," Jonathan Sadowsky, professor of medical history, explains that ECT was used in the mid-twentieth century as a "treatment" for homosexuality, "which was then considered by psychiatrists to be an illness. . . . Psychiatrists at the time who used ECT for that purpose believed they were trying to help sick people, which should serve as a warning about 'pathologizing' behavior, and assuming that the treatment will reduce stigma." Sadowski notes that the treatment was traumatizing for some gays and lesbians who received it. Using ECT for this purpose ended "in part because no evidence showed that it altered anyone's sexuality," but it survives in the social memory of the therapy (Sadowsky, "Electroconvulsive Therapy").

60. Lylah Barber, *Lylah*, 48; Red Barber and Creamer, *Rhubarb in the Catbird Seat*, 197.

61. Red Barber, *The Broadcasters* (1970), 193.

62. In early April 1958 Edward Murrow responded to a request from Red Barber for contacts in London who could help Sarah get admitted for some short-term study in or near Edinburgh, Scotland. Red's former boss provided three names and gave Red the address of Scotty Reston's son, who was studying at the University of Edinburgh. See Edward Murrow to Red Barber, April 10, 1958, ERMP.

63. Lylah Barber, *Lylah*, 197.

64. "Sarah Barber," UK incoming passenger lists, *Queen Elizabeth*, September 16, 1958; accessed through Ancestry.com.

65. "Sarah Lanier Barber," *Tomokan*, 1960, OLRC; "Poem by Rollins Senior," *Rollins Sandspur*, April 22, 1960, 3, OLRC, Barber, Sarah Lanier file, 150E.

66. "Sarah Barber," in directory of student addresses, *Tomokan*, 1960, OLRC.

67. Sarah Barber, "Awake Remembering," *Flamingo* 34–44 (1957–61), Fall 1959, 22–23, OLRC. The author is designated as "Anonymous" in this edition of *Flamingo*, but the poem was acknowledged as the work of "Sarah Barber" when it was accepted for publication in the 1959 edition of *American Anthology of College Poetry*. See "Poem by Rollins Senior," *Rollins Sandspur*, April 22, 1960, 3, OLRC, Barber, Sarah Lanier file, 150E.

68. Sarah Barber's grade cards, 1959–60, RBC, boxes 2–3, vol. 30.

69. Authors' interview with Judy Gomez, December 16, 2019.

70. McFarlane and Bashe, *Complete Bedside Companion*, 256.

71. Red Barber, *Show Me the Way to Go Home*, 113–14.

72. "Red Barber Does the Far East Bit," *Variety*, November 12, 1958, 18, 20.

73. Red Barber, *Show Me the Way to Go Home*, 115–16.

74. Data in this and the following paragraph are from Red Barber, *Show Me the Way to Go Home*, 117–23.

75. Red Barber, *Show Me the Way to Go Home*, 114–15.

76. "Red Barber," USO *Shows*, January 10, 1967, 1, RBC, box 17, folder 1.

77. "Surgery for Barber," *New York Daily News*, January 7, 1960, 70; "Caught on the Fly," *The Sporting News*, January 20, 1960, 31; Walter Winchell, "Man about Town," *Wilkes-Barre Times Leader*, January 11, 1960, 8.

78. Red Barber, *Show Me the Way to Go Home*, 130.

79. Edwards, *Fridays with Red*, 12.

80. "Maz' HR Miracle No. 1 Dazzler of '60," *The Sporting News*, January 4, 1961, sec. 2, 12.

81. Quoted in "Maris HR Assault Tabbed No. 1 Thrill," *The Sporting News*, January 3, 1962, sec. 2, 12.

82. Quoted in "Roger Maris 1961—61st Home Run as Called by Red Barber, WPIX-TV, 10/1/1961," https://www.youtube.com/watch?v=4hSNO_PhSnI.

83. Quoted in Richard Sandomir, "Maris's Big Moment: Deliveries Differed," *New York Times*, October 1, 1991, 9B; emphasis in original.

84. "Red Barber in Hospital," *New York Times*, February 25, 1964, 20; "Caught on the Fly," *The Sporting News*, March 7, 1964, 28; Til Ferdenzi, "Mikkelsen, Myer Pop Yogi's Optics," *The Sporting News*, March 28, 1964, 22.

85. Quoted in Creamer, RITCS, tape 2, side A.

86. "Barber Arrives for Yank Opener," *Fort Lauderdale News*, March 14, 1964, 19.

87. Quoted in Creamer, RITCS, tape 8, side A.

88. Quotes are in Creamer, RITCS, tape 12, side B. Barber enhanced the Cleveland doubleheader story a bit. In his telling of the tale, Barber broadcast three doubleheaders over three days. But *Baseball Reference* lists only two Yankees-at-Indians doubleheaders, on September 22 and 23, 1964. As Casey Stengel would say, you can look it up.

89. Lylah Barber, *Lylah*, 204–7. Perhaps most sadly for the readers of this biography, the 1963 move likely meant the loss of most of Red's and Lylah's personal files. Lylah Barber wrote, regarding the 1963 move, "Had it not been for the dispose-all we had installed in the basement when we built the house, I never would have made it" (Lylah Barber, *Lylah*, 206.) At the Walter Lanier "Red" Barber Papers and Book Collection at the University of Florida, there are few personal papers before 1965.

90. Quoted in Creamer, RITCS, tape 12, side B.

91. Coleman with Goldstein, *An American Journey*, 165–66.

13. Breakfast in Manhattan

1. Drebinger quoted in Borelli, *How About That!*, 198; authors' interview with George Vecsey, January 20, 2020; Faupel quoted in Borelli, *How About That!*, 198.

2. Borelli, *How About That!*, 198; authors' interview with Marty Appel, April 6, 2018.

3. Borelli, *How About That!*, 201.

4. Quoted in Red Barber, *The Broadcasters* (1970), 204.

5. Borelli, *How About That!*, 204.

6. Val Adams, "Yankee Schedule Omits Mel Allen," *New York Times*, November 25, 1964, 75.

7. Quoted in Creamer, RITCS, tape 12, side B.

8. Red Barber, *The Broadcasters*, 204.

9. Red Barber, *The Broadcasters* (1970), 206.

10. Quoted in Bill Bondurant, "Garagiola: .250 Hitter on the Air," *Fort Lauderdale News*, March 17, 1965, 5D.

11. Bill Bondurant, "Garagiola: .250 Hitter on the Air," *Fort Lauderdale News*, March 17, 1965, 5D.

12. Quoted in Creamer, RITCS, tape 13, side A.

13. Quoted in Red Barber, *The Broadcasters* (1970), 209.

14. Quoted in Creamer, RITCS, tape 13, side A.

15. Lylah Barber, *Lylah*, 209.

16. Despite Red's and Lylah's delight in Far Eastern design, when the Barbers put their house on the market six years later, their agent, perhaps thinking a Japanese farmhouse was not that appealing to the typical American buyer, marketed it as a "Celebrity's Magnificent Tropical Home." "Celebrity's Magnificent Tropical Home," advertising flyer, RBC, boxes 1–3, folder 1975 Clippings: *Tallahassee Democrat*.

17. Steve Seplocha, "Telebitting," *Fort Lauderdale News*, September 19, 1965, 61.

18. Larry King, "Introduction to the Da Capo Edition"; in Red Barber, *The Broadcasters* (1985).

19. Unless otherwise noted, quotes in this and the following two paragraphs are from Larry King, "[King] Interviews Red Barber."

20. Val Adams, "Steve Allen out of 'Secret' Show," *New York Times*, October 21, 1965, 95.

21. Quotes in this and the following paragraph are from Red Barber, *Show Me the Way to Go Home*, 22–23.

22. Red Barber, *Show Me the Way to Go Home*, 27.

23. Jim Ogle, "Mickey Mantle—Last of Yankee Super-Stars," *The Sporting News*, April 6, 1968, 8.

24. Red Barber, *Show Me the Way to Go Home*, 28.

25. Red Barber, *Show Me the Way to Go Home*, 24. In our review of newspapers from the 1966 season, we found no references to the Yankees' Sunday services. Red's partner, Bobby Richardson, offered a different timeline in a 1993 *Guideposts* article on Barber and the "Baseball Chapel." In Richardson's account, the idea for a Sunday religious gathering started when Barber saw Richardson, Tony Kubek, and Mickey Mantle rushing to get to a game in Minneapolis in August 1962. They were late because they had been delayed returning from a downtown Protestant Church service. Barber, writing in 1971, and Richardson, in 1993, differ on the location, time, and manager involved in the first service. It is possible that the initial discussion between Barber

and Richardson took place in 1962, but the idea did not bear full fruit until the 1966 season. See Richardson, "Locker-Room Legacy," 7.

26. Richardson, "Locker-Room Legacy," 8.

27. Richardson, "Locker-Room Legacy," 8.

28. A review of a May 1966 recording of Barber and Garagiola covering a road game with the Los Angeles Angels shows the pair working together smoothly with few interruptions by either broadcaster. "1966 05 08 Yankees at Angels," YouTube, https://www.youtube.com/watch?v=cJ61ULGai7g.

29. Quoted in Creamer, RITCS, tape 3, side B, RBC, box 41.

30. Creamer, RITCS, tape 13, side A, RBC, box 41.

31. Quoted in "Yankee Broadcasters Have Brighter Future," *Miami News*, September 21, 1966, 29.

32. Despite Topping's rebuke, Barber and the other Yankees broadcasters remained a team and the public voice of the franchise. When NBC's daytime show *The Match Game* featured the Yankees for the week of May 30, 1966, the broadcasting team members—Barber, Rizzuto, Coleman, and Garagiola—were contestants on one of the episodes. "Yankees on Game Show," *Ithaca Journal*, May 28, 1966, 24.

33. Red Barber, "Should Ballclubs Have Control over Announcers? No." *New York Daily News*, July 29, 1979, 9.

34. Quoted in Mann, *Decline and Fall of the New York Yankees*, 213; for baseball salaries at the time, see "Minimum Salary," *Baseball Reference*, https://www.baseball-reference.com/bullpen/Minimum_salary.

35. Red Barber, *The Broadcasters* (1970), 210.

36. Quoted in Mann, *Decline and Fall of the New York Yankees*, 213–14.

37. Burke to Barber, September 20, 1966, RBC, box 9, folder 1985.

38. Augie Lio, "Coleman, Barber on Way Out," *Herald-News*, September 17, 1966, 17; Barney Krememko, "Davis New Poppa Bear?" *New York World Journal*, September 17, 1966, RBC, boxes 1–3, Clippings 1961–65.

39. Cliff Sundberg, "Tension Cause of Dissension on Top Teams," *Boston Traveler*, September 10, 1966, 4B.

40. Quoted in Creamer, RITCS, tape 13, side A, RBC, box 41.

41. Quoted in "Yankee Broadcasters Have Brighter Future," *Miami News*, September 21, 1966, 29.

42. Data in the next several paragraphs are from Red Barber and Creamer, *Rhubarb in the Catbird Seat*, 322–29.

43. Quoted in Mann, *Decline and Fall of the New York Yankees*, 214–15.

44. Lawrence S. Ritter, "Connecticut Yankee," *New York Times*, November 18, 1984, 18BR.

45. Michael Burke to Lawrence Ritter; accessed on February 14, 2020. This letter was located originally on Ebay. The listing has since been deleted, but digital images of the letter were retained by the authors.

46. Authors' interview with George Vecsey, January 20, 2020.

47. Quoted in Red Barber and Creamer, *Rhubarb in the Catbird Seat*, 333.

48. Jack O'Brian, "Red Barber Gets the Yankees' Ax," *New York World Tribune*; Val Adams, "Red Barber Dismissed after 13 Years as Yankee Broadcaster," *New York Times*, September 27, 1966; Kay Gardella, "Yanks' CBS Bosses Fire Sportscaster Red Barber," *New York Daily News*, September 27, 1966; "Yankees Fire Red Barber," *New York Post*, September 26, 1966. All in RBC, box 4, folder 1966 Retirement Clippings.

49. Quoted in Bob Williams and Lester Bromberg, "Barber: I Like the Mets," *New York Post*, September 27, 1966, 88, RBC, box 4, folder 1966 Retirement Clippings.

50. Quoted in Lou Miller, "Red Barber Didn't Put Yankees in Cellar," *New York World Journal Tribune*, September 27, 1966, RBC, box 4, folder 1966 Retirement Clippings.

51. Red Smith, "Something Special Label Fits Barber," *Washington Post*, September 29, 1966, 8C, RBC, box 4, folder 1966 Retirement Clippings.

52. James A. Wechsler, "L'Affaire Red Barber," *Boston Globe*, October 1, 1966, 7.

53. Jack Gould, "Red Barber: Foul Ball at the Ball Park," *New York Times*, October 9, 1966, RBC, box 4, folder 1966 Retirement Clippings.

54. "Scorecard," *Sports Illustrated*, October 10, 1966, box 4, folder 1966 Retirement Clippings.

55. "Squeeze Play," *Newsweek*, RBC, box 4, folder 1966 Retirement Clippings.

56. Costas, "Costas Coast to Coast."

57. Quoted in J. Anthony Lukas, "How Mel Allen Started a Lifelong Love Affair," *New York Times*, September 12, 1971, 82.

14. A Developing Writer, A Darker Vision

1. Lylah Barber, *Lylah*, 216.

2. Tommy Fitzgerald, "The Frustrated Professor," *Miami News*, September 26, 1965, 4C.

3. Quoted in Matt Messina, "Barber and Baseball Teamed Again in Japanese Setting," *New York Daily News*, August 26, 1967, 10.

4. Walter Cronkite to Red Barber, April 9, 1971, RBC, box 4, folder 1971.

5. Barber, *Lylah*, 216.

6. "Still in the Catbird Seat," *Broadcasting*, October 3, 1966, 64.

7. Bill McCaffrey to Red Barber, May 15, 1967, RBC, box 4, folder 1967. Barber appears to have had some buyer's remorse in selecting Lewis as his new agent. A February 1971 letter from New York media insider Quincy Carter, apparently the son of Barber's lawyer and friend Raymond Carter, responded to Barber's concerns about Lewis. The handwritten letter acknowledges Barber's legitimate criticism of Lewis's "rude" behavior but lauds him as "honest" with a "reputation for it," something that should not be taken for granted with agents. Carter also believed that Lewis "[was] doing everything he [could] for [Red]" in a tough economic environment and "[was] in awe" of Barber. See Quincy Carter to Red Barber, February 21, 1971, RBC, boxes 1–3, folder 1971.

8. Red Barber, "Interview with Casey Stengel."

9. "Red Barber Has Declined an Invitation," *New York Daily News*, May 1, 1970, RBC, boxes 1–3, folder Clippings, 1970; Buck, *Jack Buck: "That's a Winner,"* 15.

10. Quoted in Costas, "Costas Coast to Coast."

11. Red Barber, "Interview with Bill Terry."

12. John McMullan to Red Barber, February 4, 1967, RBC, box 4, folder 1967.

13. Red Barber, "Interview with Paul Richards"; Robert B. Pearsall to Red Barber, November 4, 1970, RBC, box 4, folder 1971.

14. Data in this and the following two paragraphs are from Red Barber, "Dr. Naismith Wouldn't Believe His Tall World of Flying Elbows," *Miami Herald*, October 25, 1967, 5D.

15. Red Barber, "It Took Son's Arrest to Bow Jackie's Head," *Miami Herald*, March 10, 1968, 5C.

16. Red Barber, "Interview with Walter O'Malley."

17. Red Barber, "Frankenstein a Stranger at South Florida University," *Miami Herald*, June 16, 1968, 5G.

18. Red Barber, "Ali the Loser Still the Winner in Harlem," *Miami Herald*, April 4, 1971, 9F. In a taped interview with Lefty Gomez, Red tells him that his daughter has taught second grade for six years in Harlem. He adds: "That takes almost as much courage as Gomez facing Jimmie Foxx." See Red Barber, "Lefty Gomez at Rollins College."

19. Malcolm Reiss to Red Barber, July 10, 1969, RBC, box 4, 1971. While interviewing Jim Bouton about his recently published *Ball Four*, Barber readily acknowledged the importance of quality editing: "Jim, you can't write a book without a good editor. . . . I know the value of a good editor." See Red Barber, "Interview with Jim Bouton."

20. Red Barber, "Can Baseball Be Saved?" Barber's *Reader's Digest* contributions also included a much more personal reflection, a poignant profile of William Barber, Red's father. See Red Barber, "My Most Unforgettable Character."

21. Red Barber, "Confessions of a Broadcaster Studying His Typewriter, *Authors Guild Newsletter*," May–June 1971, 6–8.

22. Robert C. Parker to John Carlson, October 26, 1973, and John Carlson to Robert C. Parker, November 4, 1973. RBC, box 5, folder 1972–73.

23. Leonard Shecter to Malcolm Reiss, May 1. 1970, RBC, box 4, folder 1971.

24. Dick Young, *New York Sunday News*, July 7, 1968, RBC, boxes 1–3, folder Clippings, 1967–68; Mark Stuart, *The Morning Call* (Paterson NJ), May 13, 1968, RBC, boxes 1–3, folder Clippings, 1967–68. For other representative reviews of *Rhubarb in the Catbird Seat*, see Rex Lardner, *New York Times*, March 24, 1968, 10BR; Arthur Daley, *New York Times*, April 9, 1968, 59; Joe Halberstein, *Gainesville Sun*, April 8, 1968, RBC, boxes 1–3, folder Clippings, 1967–68; "Red Barber's Autobiography" *Variety*, September 18, 1968, RBC, boxes 1–3, folder Clippings, 1967–68; Jack Kofoed, *Miami Herald*, May 28, 1968, 9B; Bob Wilson, *Boston Sunday Herald Traveler*, April 21, 1968, 15; *Publishers Weekly*, February 12, 1968, RBC, box 17, folder 3.

25. Val Adams, "Red Barber Attacks Garagiola in Book," *New York Times*, March 21, 1968, 64.

26. Red Barber, *Walk in the Spirit*, dedication.

27. Red Barber, *Walk in the Spirit*, 116–18.

28. Malcolm Reiss to Red Barber, May 13, 1968, RBC, box 4, folder 1968.

29. Donald Hutter to Red Barber, September 11, 1968, RBC, box 4, folder 1968.

30. Red Barber, "Confessions of a Broadcaster Studying His Typewriter," *Authors Guild Newsletter*, May–June 1971, 6–8.

31. Larry King, "The Old Redhead Writes about the Human Spirit," *Miami Herald*, July 29, 1969, 8c; "Barber's New Morality Tales," *Variety*, July 8, 1970, RBC, box 4, folder 1970; "Inspirational True Stories in Sports," *Brandenton Review*, August 24, 1969, RBC, boxes 1–3, folder Clippings, 1969; Marley Soper, "This Unusual Book," *Library Journal*, September 1, 1969, RBC, box 17, folder 4. For another representative review of *Walk in the Spirit*, see Dick Friendlich, "Red's Sketches Had Spirit," *San Francisco Chronicle*, August 10, 1969, RBC, boxes 1–3.

32. Frank Sinatra to Red Barber, August 6, 1969, RBC, box 4, folder 1969.

33. For representative reviews of *The Broadcasters*, see Yardley, "'Once a Miracle': *The Broadcasters* by Red Barber," 33–34 (longer, richer version in *Greensboro Daily News*, January 31, 1971, 4–6c); Jack McCarthy, "Sports Fans, This Is Red," *Miami Herald*, September 15, 1971, 4D; Ben Luparello, "Sports Whirl," *New York Sunday News*, March 14, 1971, RBC, boxes 1–3, folder Clippings, 1971; Joel Siegel, "Red Barber's Memoirs Take Us behind the Sports Microphone, but Not Very Far," *Sports Illustrated*, May 10, 1971, https://vault.si.com/vault/1971/05/10/red-barbers-memoirs-take-us-behind-the-sports-microphone-but-not-very-far.

34. Donald Hutter to Red Barber, January 12, 1970; Malcolm Reiss to Red Barber, April 10, 1970, RBC, box 4, folder 1970, 1971.

35. Effie Virginia Barber to Red Barber, June 10, 1971, RBC, box 4, folder 1971.

36. For sales estimates of *Rhubarb in the Catbird Seat* and *The Broadcasters*, see Ken McCormick to Red Barber, April 15, 1968, RBC, box 4, folder 1968, and Malcolm Reiss to Red Barber, April 13, 1972, RBC, box 5, folder Jan.–June 1972. Malcolm Reiss assured Red that "all future arrangements shall be considered in the light of your monthly Social Security payments." November 27, 1972, RBC, box 5, folder 1972–73.

37. Marvin J. Berkman to Red Barber, May 19, 1972, RBC, box 5, folder 1972–73; College of Journalism and Communication, University of Florida, to Red Barber, July 5, 1972, RBC, box 5, folder 1972–73.

38. Data in this and the following three paragraphs are from the audiotape cassette, RBC, boxes 27–28, Europe: France.

39. Lylah Barber, *Lylah*, 217–20.

40. Quotes in this and the following two paragraphs are from Red Barber, *Show Me the Way To Go Home*, 177–92.

41. "USO Certificate of Appreciation to Red Barber," RBC, box 17, folder 6.

42. Quoted in Sidney Fields, "Touches All Bases," *New York Daily News*, March 14, 1967, 36.

43. Edward Heffelfinger to Red Barber, March 29, 1967, RBC, box 4, folder 1965–71.

44. Edward Gurney to Red Barber, June 15, 1971, RBC, box 4, folder 1971; Edwards, *Fridays with Red*, 198–99.

45. Robert Keedick to Red Barber, June 9, 1967, RBC, box 4, folder 1971.

46. Rev. Henry I. Louttit to Walter L. Barber, October 16, 1965, RBC, box 4, folder 1965.

47. Red Barber, *Show Me the Way to Go Home*, 59–60.

48. "Red Chides Radio Men," *Broadcasting*, April 13, 1970, 76.

49. "Veteran Sportscaster Red Barber Sharply Criticizes Radio," *Advertising Age*, April 13, 1970, RBC, boxes 1–3, Clippings, 1970.

50. Fred Ferretti, "U.S. to Enlist Television in Anti-Drug Drive," *New York Times*, April 8, 1970, 67.

51. Unless otherwise noted, quotes in this and the following two paragraphs are from Red Barber, typescript of "Summer Commencement Address," University of Florida, August 29, 1970, RBC, box 17, Memorabilia, folder 5.

52. Red Barber, *Show Me the Way to Go Home*, 43. Earlier in the year, when he was in France, Barber resisted going to the World War I memorial cemetery when he and Lylah visited the battlefields in Verdun because he thought cemeteries were "morbid and ghoulish." The most valuable component of each person had already departed before the empty shells were deposited there. See audiotape cassette, RBC, boxes 27–28, Europe: France.

53. Lylah Barber, *Lylah*, 124.

54. Edwin Pope, "MacPhail Sees Christian," *Miami Herald*, February 28, 1967, 2D.

55. Lylah Barber, Lylah, 124.

56. Edwin Pope, "MacPhail Sees Christian," *Miami Herald*, February 28, 1967, 2D.

57. Lylah Barber, Lylah, 222.

58. Red Barber to Effie (Virginia Barber), August 1, 1971, in the personal collection of Virginia's daughter, E. V. E. Joy.

59. Lylah Barber, *Lylah*, 223.

15. Hall of Fame Broadcaster

1. Red Barber, "The Catbird Seat," *Tallahassee Democrat*, February 20, 1972, 3D.

2. Our analysis is based on a review of 552 Red Barber's "Catbird Seat" columns published in the *Tallahassee Democrat* between February 20, 1972, and July 4, 1982, accessed at Newspapers.com.

3. Red Barber: "Racial Conflict Easily Forgotten," *Tallahassee Democrat*, July 24, 1977, 8D; "Troubled History of Dick Allen Reflected in Many Trades," *Tallahassee Democrat*, December 8, 1974, 3D; "Moves by an Aging Rickey Were Momentous Ones," *Tallahassee Democrat*, July 16, 1972, 4D; "Inductees Owe One to Rickey," *Tallahassee Democrat*, January 17, 1982, 8F; "Total At-Bats Tell Story on Aaron and Ruth," *Tallahassee Democrat*, July 9, 1972, 3D; "Replays Have No Place in Officiating Games," *Tallahassee Democrat*, November 23, 1975, 3D.

4. Red Barber: "The Catbird Seat," *Tallahassee Democrat*, March 19, 1972, 2D; "Baseball Fuss Really a Thirty-Year War," *Tallahassee Democrat*, March 7, 1976, 6D; "Players Bracing for War over Free Agent Dispute," *Tallahassee Democrat*, February 22, 1981, 9F; "A Storm Brewing over Baseball," *Tallahassee Democrat*, June 4, 1978, 5D; "Sports Talk on the Pacific," *Tallahassee Democrat*, August 15, 1976, 2D; "And You Thought Finley Was Tight," *Tallahassee Democrat*, January 8, 1978, 6D.

5. Red Barber: "The Catbird Seat," *Tallahassee Democrat*, March 26, 1972, 3D; "A View on Lack of Class in Sports Literature," *Tallahassee Democrat*, July 27, 1975, 3D.

6. Red Barber: "'Tradition' Is Surrendering," *Tallahassee Democrat*, October 31, 1976, 7D; "Baseball's New Financial Frontier Lies in Lucrative Hometown Rivalries," *Tallahassee Democrat*, August 17, 1980, 4F; "Johnny-Vicki Marriage Faced Long Odds," *Tallahassee Democrat*, March 28, 1976, 4D; "Title 9 Is Creeping Closer," *Tallahassee Democrat*, July 16, 1978, 3D.

7. Red Barber: "Thanksgiving Day News Recalls Memorable Gaither Interview," *Tallahassee Democrat*, December 1, 1974, 4D; "Ali—The Symbol," *Tallahassee Democrat*, May 21, 1972, 2D; "Nobody Loved Ali Back Then," *Tallahassee Democrat*, September 24, 1978, 9C; "Reagan Got a New Name, New Game and New Fame," *Tallahassee Democrat*, July 6, 1980, 5F.

8. Red Barber: "That Awful Day Decades Ago," *Tallahassee Democrat*, December 11, 1977, 8D; "America's First Skiing Gold Took Everyone by Surprise," *Tallahassee Democrat*, February 24, 1980, 8F; "Vocal Cords Are Valuable," *Tallahassee Democrat*, April 5, 1981, 10F; "Lance Richbourg Reflected Those 'Pleasing Skills,'" *Tallahassee Democrat*, September 28, 1975, 9D; "The Day Onli Son's Dinner Was Late," *Tallahassee Democrat*, March 23, 1980, 3F.

9. Red Barber, "League Presidents Pose Problem," *Tallahassee Democrat*, April 15, 1979, 4D.

10. Lee MacPhail to Red Barber, April 18, 1979, RBC, box 6, folder 1979.

11. Malcolm Reiss to Barber, May 1, 1972, RBC, box 5, folder January–June 1972; William H. Thomas to Malcolm Reiss, May 29, 1972, RBC, box 5, folder January–June 1972; Malcolm Reiss to Barber, November 22, 1972, RBC, box 5, folder July–December 1972.

12. Walker Lundy to Red Barber, July 6, 1982, RBC, box 7, folder 1982.

13. Authors' interview with Walker Lundy, October 3, 2019.

14. Red Barber, "Columns Were Heady Wine," *Tallahassee Democrat*, July 4, 1982, 8F.

15. Malcolm Reiss to Red Barber, September 23, 1971; October 7, 1971; and November 12, 1971; all in RBC, box 4, folder 1971.

16. Dick Carpenter to Malcolm Reiss, December 1, 1971, RBC, box 4, folder 1971.

17. Malcolm Reiss to Red Barber, April 4, 1972, RBC, box 5, folder January–June 1972.

18. Malcolm Reiss to Red Barber, November 8, 1973, RBC, box 5, folder 1973.

19. Donald Hutter to Malcolm Reiss, December 3, 1973, RBC, box 5, folder 1973.

20. Red Barber: "Robinson and Rickey to Be Honored Today," *Tallahassee Democrat*, October 15, 1972, 5D; "So Soon Death Follows," *Tallahassee Democrat*, October 29, 1972, 4D.

21. Red Barber, "*I Never Had It Made*," *New York Times*, November 12, 1972, 53BR.

22. Harold Goldberg to Red Barber, November 16, 1976, RBC, box 6, folder 1976.

23. Data in the remainder of this paragraph and the following one are from Red Barber, "Ernest Hemingway and the Tough Dodger," *New York Times*, November 14, 1976, 190.

24. Red Barber to Father Comer, May 5, 1975, LCPL.

25. Red Barber, "Two Giants of Baseball Go Down at 85," *Tallahassee Democrat*, October 5, 1975, 7D.

26. Information about Billy Barber was compiled from public records and the following articles: "Even Redder," *Broadcasting*, April 5, 1943, 34; "Around Town," *Tampa*

Tribune, May 30, 1948, 34; "Ad Firm Gets Service Award," *Tampa Times*, April 9, 1968, 25; "Obituary, Barber, Otti Lenuweit," *Tampa Tribune*, June 13, 2009, 18; "Obituary, Barber," *Tampa Tribune*, April 9, 1975, 44.

27. Authors' interview with E. V. E. Joy, December 13, 2019.

28. John McCarthy, "'Top Management' Plaques Presented," *Tampa Tribune*, November 2, 1967, 33.

29. Conchita Benito to Mr. and Mrs. Walter Barber, January 21, 1975, RBC, box 6, folder 1975.

30. Conchita Benito to Red Barber, February 8, 1975, RBC, box 6, folder 1975.

31. Barbara Stewart, "A Few Moments with . . . Red and Lylah Barber," *Florida Magazine*, September 16, 1990, 6.

32. L. S. MacPhail Jr. to Red Barber, February 10, 1978, RBC, box 6, folder 1977. This interaction was a year before his spat with the junior MacPhail during the umpires' strike.

33. Quoted in Red Barber, "It Was a Busy Week for Red, Baseball," *Tallahassee Democrat*, July 30, 1978, 5D.

34. Red Barber, "It Was a Busy Week for Red, Baseball," *Tallahassee Democrat*, July 30, 1978, 5D.

35. Quotes in this paragraph are from "Mel Allen, Red Barber First Winners of Ford C. Frick Award," news release, National Baseball Hall of Fame and Museum, Cooperstown, New York, July 22, 1978, RBC, box 6, folder 1977–78.

36. "Broadcasters to Be Honored at Baseball Hall of Fame," news release, National Baseball Hall of Fame and Museum, Cooperstown, New York, June 21, 1978, RBC, box 6, folder 1978.

37. George M. Steinbrenner III to Red Barber, August, 15, 1978; Gabe Paul to Red Barber, August 14, 1978; Bowie Kuhn to Red Barber, August 1, 1978; Ted Williams to Red Barber, November 1979. All in RBC, box 6, folder 1978.

38. Vin Scully to Red Barber, August 11, 1978; Mel Allen to Red and Lylah Barber, undated. Both in RBC, box 6, folder 1978.

39. Unless otherwise noted, data in this and the following two paragraphs are from Red Barber, remarks made at the National Baseball Hall of Fame and Museum, Cooperstown, New York, induction ceremonies, August 7, 1978, NBHF.

40. Robert J. Kennedy to Red Barber, RBC, box 6, folder 1978.

41. Peter O'Malley to Red Barber, September 20, 1978, RBC, box 6, folder 1978; "Attention Dodger Fans, Tune in Tonight to Hear Vin Scully and Red Barber" (advertisement), *Los Angeles Times*, October 12, 1978, 103; audiotape cassette, "Speeches— Campanella, Roy. Speech by R. B. at a Dinner," RBC, boxes 27–28; Martin G. Moed, dean of faculty, to Red Barber, March 13, 1979, RBC, box 6, folder 1978; Steve Cady, "Stadium Opener Glitters Despite Dissenter," *New York Times*, April 6, 1979, 21A; "Saturday Little League World Series with Mel Allen and Red Barber!" (advertisement), *Los Angeles Times*, August 24, 1979, 65; "'Newcomers' Show Promise," *Los Angeles Times*, September 1, 1979, 45.

42. Malcolm Reiss to Red Barber, December 4, 1973, RBC, box 5, folder 1973; Ken McCormick to Red Barber, December 29, 1980, RBC, box 7, folder 1980.

43. Edward W. Stack to Red Barber, January 26, 1979, RBC, box 6, folder 1978.

16. National Public Radio

1. Quotes are in Edwards, *Fridays with Red*, 18–20, 173–75. The figure for Red's salary is in "NPR Commentator Agreement," December 8, 1988, RBC, box 9, folder 1984–88.

2. Bob Edwards to Red Barber, January 30, 1981, RBC, box 7, folder 1979–83.

3. Quoted in Edwards, *Fridays with Red*, 193–94.

4. Edwards, *Fridays with Red*, 175; "The Ole Redhead," *HuffPost*, February 13, 2008, https://www.huffpost.com/entry/the-ole-redhead_b_86514.

5. Lisa Twyman, "His Words Let People See," *Sports Illustrated*, August 13, 1990, 77; see also Edwards, *Fridays with Red*, 172.

6. Leonard Fleischer to Red Barber, December 3, 1988, RBC, box 9, folder 1984–88.

7. Edwards, *Fridays with Red*, 29.

8. Edwards, *Fridays with Red*, 15.

9. Mark Schramm to Red Barber, April 1, 1991, RBC, box 34, folder April 1991–June 1991; Bob Edwards to Red Barber, March 15, 1991, RBC, box 34, folder February 1991–March 1991.

10. Edwards, *Fridays with Red*, 174.

11. Twyman, "His Words Let People See."

12. *Morning Edition*, program on January 1, 1991, RBC, cassette tapes, box 40.

13. Susan Butcher to Red Barber, October 26, 1988, RBC, box 9, folder 1984–1988.

14. "Stamberg, Susan, Interviews Red Barber," March 29, 1991, RBC, Cassette Tapes, Interviews, box 40.

15. Alexandra D. Sandler to Red Barber, December 16, 1984, RBC, box 9, folder 1984–88.

16. Mark H. Tucker to Red Barber, January 7, 1989, RBC, box 10, folder 1989; Reitz to Red Barber, December 22, 1989, RBC, box 10, folder 1989; Lynne Romans to Red Barber, June 7, 1990, RBC, box 34, folder November 1990–December 1990; George Griener, S.J., to Red Barber, December 6, 1991, RBC, box 34, folder December, 1991.

17. Joseph Villeneuve to Red Barber, January 9, 1991, RBC, box 34, folder January 1991.

18. Red Barber, book review of *Radios: The Golden Age*, *New York Times*, December 13, 1987, 27BR.

19. Red Barber, "The Worst Thing about a Spitball," *New York Times*, May 15, 1988, 9BR; Red Barber, "Get It Back to the Infield, Willie," *New York Times*, April 1, 1990, 12BR.

20. Red Barber, "Leadoff Man" (book review of *Baseball's Great Experiment*), 28–31; Jules Tygiel to Red Barber, July 3, 1983, RBC, box 7, folder 1979–83.

21. Quotes in this and the following paragraph are from Red Barber, "Biography of Red Smith Lives up to Its Subject," *Houston Post*, June 29, 1986, 12F.

22. Roderick Nordell to Red Barber, January 13, 1986, RBC, box 9, folder 1984–88.

23. Red Barber, "Pro Football from $25 Franchise to Gold-Plated Super Bowl," *Christian Science Monitor*, January 27, 1986, 16.

24. Red Barber, "Rickey Recognized the Invaluable Contributions of Baseball Wives," *Christian Science Monitor*, March 26, 1986, 18; emphasis in original.

25. Red Barber, "Mirror, Mirror on the Wall, What Do Sports Tell Us All?" *Christian Science Monitor*, December 3, 1986, 34.

26. Thomas Oliphant, "Nostalgia Hits One out of the Park," *Boston Globe*, July 20, 1982, 1; Red Barber, "Reunion of Ebbets Field Stars," *Christian Science Monitor*, June 5, 1987, 15.

27. Marshall, "Interview with Red Barber."

28. Joe Garagiola to Red Barber, November 27, 1988, RBC, box 9, folder 1984–88.

29. Don Freeman, "Point of View," *San Diego Union*, February 24, 1987, 7D.

30. Bill McGrotha, "Other Fellow's Game," *Tallahassee Democrat*, September 1, 1987, 1–2D; "Sportscaster Red Barber Guest on Today Show," *New York Times*, August 16, 1982, 15C. Doubleday to Red Barber, July 13, 1982, RBC, box 7, folder 1979–83; Lucy Scott to Red Barber, November 16, 1988, RBC, box 9, folder 1984–88; "Broadcast Excerpt," transcript, *Good Morning America*, October 29, 1984, 1–5, RBC, box 18, folder 3.

31. Lynn Novick to Red Barber, April 4, 1990, RBC, box 11, folder 1990; see also Ken Burns to Red Barber, March 26, 1990, RBC, box 11, folder 1990.

32. Burns and Novick, *Baseball*, "Inning 6: The National Pastime."

33. Charlie Rose interview with Ken Burn, September 23, 1994. In Burns and Novick, *Baseball*, "Extra Innings."

34. Bowie Kuhn to Red Barber, June 18, 1984; James Burris to Red Barber, May 30, 1984; RBC, box 8, folder 1983–84.

35. Patrick Buchanan telegram to Red Barber, October 9, 1986, RBC, box 9, folder 1984–88; Richard Waters to Lylah Barber, October 22, 1986, RBC, box 9, folder 1984–88.

36. Letter to Red and Lylah Barber from Mrs. Sealy's fourth grade class, November 26, 1990, RBC, box 34, folder November 1990–December 1990.

37. Planned Parenthood, "Commitment, Contribution, Challenge," September 11, 1985, RBC, box 9, folder 1984–88; Faye Wattleton to Red Barber, September 12, 1990, RBC, box 11, folder 1989–90.

38. George Flowers to Kimberly Morris, August 29, 1984, RBC, box 18, Memorabilia, folder 3; Kimberly Morris to Red Barber, September 5, 1984, RBC, box 18, Memorabilia, folder 3; "The Spice of the Day's Sports Menu," UPI press release, October 31, 1984, RBC, box 18, Memorabilia, folder 3.

39. "Red Barber a Hit with Fans," *Tallahassee Democrat*, March 25, 1984, 2G; see also Maggie Maples, "Easter Seal Awards Dinner Honors Red Barber," *Florida Times-Union*, March 28, 1984, 16D.

40. "Long Island University Presents the George Polk Award," April 3, 1985, RBC, box 18 Memorabilia, folder 3.

41. Dean Charles F. Sidman to Red Barber, September 23, 1986, RBC, box 9, folder 1984–88.

42. "Campanella Named to HOF Board, Barber, Harwell to Veterans Committee," press release, National Baseball Hall of Fame and Museum, August 3, 1987, RBC, box 18, folder 4.

43. Gary Fineout, "Happy Birthday to Red Barber!" *Florida Flambeau*, February 18, 1988, 12.

44. Quoted in Gerald Ensly, "Barber Pleased by Peabody," *Tallahassee Democrat*, April 3, 1991, 2B.

45. Bob Edwards to Red Barber, May 5, 1991, RBC, box 34, folder April 1991–June 1991. Barber received a wide range of other awards during the year before he died, including the DiGamma Kappa Distinguished Achievement Award in Broadcasting and an honorary membership in the national Camellia Society for his active cultivation of the flowering plant. The University of Florida also converted the annual Red Barber Best Student Broadcaster Prize to an endowed and generous Red Barber Scholarship.

46. Ruth Frazier from Futures for Children to Red Barber, August 1, 1986, RBC, box 9, folder 1984–88.

47. Rhonda Begaye to Red Barber, RBC, box 11, file "Letters from Rhonda Maye Begaye."

48. Joan Shattuck to Red Barber, May 6, 1990, RBC, box 11, folder 1989–90.

49. Tom Brokaw to Red Barber, undated, RBC, box 9, folder 1984–88.

50. Pee Wee Reese to Red Barber, undated, RBC, box 7, folder 1983.

51. Audrey Woods to Red Barber, February 23, 1988, RBC, box 9, folder 1984–88.

52. Harry Moorman to Red Barber, June 13, 1985, RBC, box 9, folder 1984–88.

53. Bob Pasotti to Red Barber, August 30, 1982, RBC, box 7, folder 1979–83.

54. Janet Murrow to Red Barber, June 19, 1988, RBC, box 9, folder 1984–88.

55. Jane Leavy to Red Barber, June 14, 1989, RBC, box 10, folder 1989.

17. A Closed Family

1. Elliot Carlson, "Remember the Baseball Announcers," *AARP News Bulletin*, May 1988, RBC, box 9, folder 1988, 5, 34.

2. Don Freeman, "Red's View Still Clear," *San Diego Tribune*, March 4, 1988, 6E; Gail Shister, "Age Has Not Benched Red Barber," *Philadelphia Inquirer*, November 10, 1983, 10D.

3. Thomas French, "The Voice of Baseball Is Happy," *St. Petersburg Times*, October 16, 1985, 1D.

4. Andy Lindstrom, "The Voice of the Dodgers Still Has a Few Things to Say," *Tallahassee Democrat*, September 12, 1982, 1G.

5. Thomas French, "The Voice of Baseball Is Happy," *St. Petersburg Times*, October 16, 1985, 1D.

6. Godfrey Smith to Red Barber, November 19, 1971, RBC, box 4, folder 1971.

7. Thomas French, "The Voice of Baseball Is Happy," *St. Petersburg Times*, October 16, 1985, 1D.

8. Marty Appel to Red Barber, February 14, 1989, RBC, box 10, folder 1989; authors' interview with Marty Appel, April 6, 2019.

9. Bill McGrotha, "Barber Heard the Cheers," *Tallahassee Democrat*, March 11, 1984, 14D.

10. Shister, "Age Has Not Benched Red Barber."

11. Quoted in Jon Nordheimer, "Growth Pains after Loss of Oblivion," *New York Times*, April 12, 1985, 12A.

12. Quoted in Bob Minzesheimer, "New Audience for Old Voice," *USA Today*, April 27–29, 1990, 1A.

13. Thomas French, "The Voice of Baseball Is Happy," *St. Petersburg Times*, October 16, 1985, 1D.

14. Elliot Carlson, "Remember the Baseball Announcers," *AARP News Bulletin*, May 1988, RBC, box 9, folder 1988, 5, 34; see also Lylah Barber, *Lylah*, 222.

15. Quoted in Elliot Carlson, "Remember the Baseball Announcers," *AARP News Bulletin*, May 1988, RBC, box 9, folder 1988, 5.

16. George Vecsey, "The Unforgettable Voice of Summer," *New York Times*, October 23, 1992, 132.

17. Edwards, *Fridays with Red*, 213, 196; authors' interview with Bob Edwards, January 29, 2020.

18. Quoted in McFarlane and Bashe, *Complete Bedside Companion*, 29–30. This text, written by psychotherapists specializing in gerontological care, informs caregivers for the elderly about strategies for coping with the demands of the job. Sarah Barber and other caretakers volunteered to be interviewed about their experiences looking after their aging parents who were facing serious physical and/or mental decline. The text includes extended portions of these authors' interviews with Sarah Barber.

19. McFarlane and Bashe, *Complete Bedside Companion*, 201.

20. Authors' interview with Liz Bremner, December 3, 2019.

21. McFarlane and Bashe, *Complete Bedside Companion*, 201.

22. McFarlane and Bashe, *Complete Bedside Companion*, 205.

23. Authors' interview with Bob Edwards, January 29, 2020.

24. McFarlane and Bashe, *Complete Bedside Companion*, 205.

25. Authors' interview with Bob Edwards, January 29, 2020.

26. Authors' interview with Leslie Rich, December 12, 2019.

27. Edwards, *Fridays with Red*, 213–19.

28. McFarlane and Bashe, *Complete Bedside Companion*, 30.

29. Edwards, *Fridays with Red*, 213–19; see also Gerald Ensley, "A Legendary Voice Falls Silent," *Tallahassee Democrat*, October 23, 1992, 1A.

30. McFarlane and Bashe, *Complete Bedside Companion*, 30.

31. Edwards, *Fridays with Red*, 213–19.

32. Edwards, *Fridays with Red*, 220–22; "Program," Red Barber's Funeral Service, personal collection of Barber's niece, E. V. E. Joy.

33. Quoted in Gerald Ensley, "A Fond Goodbye to the Ol' Redhead," *Tallahassee Democrat*, October 27, 1992, 1A.

34. Quoted in Gerald Ensley, "A Fond Goodbye to the Ol' Redhead," *Tallahassee Democrat*, October 27, 1992, 1A.

35. Edwards, *Fridays with Red*, 223; authors' phone conversation with Bob Edwards, July 27, 2020.

36. For these excerpts and more from other letters sent from Red's *Morning Edition* listeners after he died, see Edwards, *Fridays with Red*, 175–80.

37. Martin Merzer, "Voice of Baseball," *Miami Herald*, October 23, 1992. For a representative sample of Barber obits, see Maury Allen, "Red Barber Set the Standard," *White Plains Journal News*, October 23, 1992, 41; Scott Montgomery, "Legendary Sportscaster Dies," *Palm Beach Post*, October 23, 1992, 1; Robert Thomas Jr., "Red Barber, Baseball Voice of Summer," *New York Times*, October 23, 1992, 1A; "Red Barber dies at 84," Muncie *Evening Press*, October 22, 1992, 21; "Barber's Death Great Loss," *Rochester Democrat and Chronicle*, October 23, 1992, 1D; Bob Raissman, "Ol Red Head Is Gone," *New York Daily News*, October 23, 1992, 72; "Red Barber, Colorful Broadcaster," *Boston Globe*, October 23, 1992, 49.

38. George Vecsey: "The Unforgettable Voice of Summer," *New York Times*, October 23, 1992, 132, and "Every Inning a Late Inning," *New York Times*, October 25, 1992, 3E.

39. Quoted in Craig Basse, "Fridays Will Never Be the Same," *Tampa Bay Times*, October 23, 1992, 2.

40. Martin Fennelly, "The Voice of Baseball, Red Barber," *Tampa Tribune*, October 23, 1992, 1.

18. Legacies

1. Authors' interview with Pat Hughes, January 23, 2013; Harwell quoted in Smith, *Voices of the Game*, 28.

2. Authors' interview with Pat Hughes, January 23, 2013.

3. Hughes, "A Commemorative Tribute Red Barber Play-by-Play Pioneer."

4. Vin Scully, audio segment in "Remembering Red Barber."

5. Vin Scully, "Unforgettable Red Barber," 91–94.

6. Dick Enberg, "Tributes Red Barber."

7. Ernie Harwell, video segment in "Remembering Red Barber."

8. Bob Picozzi, audio segment in "Remembering Red Barber."

9. Bob Picozzi, audio segment in "Remembering Red Barber."

10. Michaels, *You Can't Make This Up*, 60.

11. Richard Sandomir, "Curt Gowdy, a Seminal Announcer of Big Games on Television, Is Dead at 86," *New York Times*, February 21, 2006, 11C.

12. Quoted in Corbett, "Red Barber," 288.

13. Chris Berman, video segment in "Remembering Red Barber."

14. Costas, "Costas Coast to Coast."

15. Miller, *Confessions of a Baseball Purist*, 163.

16. Miller, *Confessions of a Baseball Purist*, 252–53.

17. Miller, *Confessions of a Baseball Purist*, 254–55.

18. Quoted in Richard Sandomir, "CBS Emerges as the Biggest Winner: TV Sports," *New York Times*, March 1, 1994, 15B.

19. Authors' interview with Tom Villante, April 13, 2018.

20. Quoted in Edwin McDowell, "The Literati's Appreciation for Baseball," *New York Times*, April 8, 1981, 11B.

21. "He Created Broadcast Standards," *Florida Today*, January 25, 1987, 9F.

22. Richard Costa to Red Barber, May 18, 1989, RBC, box 10, folder 1989.

23. William Bell to Red Barber, May 14, 1990, RBC, box 11, folder 1990; Lelchuk, *Brooklyn Boy*, 91–93.

24. Quotes in this and the following paragraph are from Barbara Grizzuti Harrison, "Red Barber," 102–18. For other testimonies on Barber's influence upon fledgling authors, see Shein, "Mom and the Babe"; Lawrence Van Gelder, "Ex-Dodger Aspirant Now Bats Out Books," *New York Times*, April 13, 1980, 12L; letter to Red Barber from Don Honig, June 7, 1986, RBC, box 9, folder 1986; Bob Geller to Red Barber, March 24, 1988, RBC, box 9, folder 1988.

25. Florence Pennella, "New Book Compliments Bard Exhibit," *Poughkeepsie Journal*, March 4, 1990, 11C.

26. Denise Kusel, "Money Has Soiled Baseball Tradition," *Santa Fe New Mexican*, March 28, 2001, 23.

27. Denise Kusel, "Money Has Soiled Baseball Tradition," *Santa Fe New Mexican*, March 28, 2001, 26.

28. Sarah Barber, "Feminizing the Traditional Curriculum," 19–20; Sarah Barber, *Connections*, 3–6.

29. Jeanette Miller, "Grand Opening Gives Hope House Good Start," *Santa Fe New Mexican*, August 23, 1992, 42; "Community Foundation Elects New Officers," *Santa Fe New Mexican*, March 24, 1999, 30.

30. Authors' interview with Liz Bremner, December 3, 2019.

31. A. C., "Queer in the s.w," *Santa Fe Reporter*, July 15, 1998, 49.

32. Denise Kusel, "Treasured Social Activist Sarah Barber Dies at 67," *Santa Fe New Mexican*, March 12, 2005, 4B.

33. Quoted in Denise Kusel, "Money Has Soiled Baseball Tradition," *Santa Fe New Mexican*, March 28, 2001.

34. Quoted in Dottie Indyke, "Sarah Barber and Gloria Donadello," http://www.southwestart.com/articles-interviews/feature-articles/intimate_connections.

35. Quotes in this and the following paragraphs are from authors' interviews with Ellie Edelstein and Margie Edwards, October 14, 2019, and Liz Bremner, December 6, 2019.

BIBLIOGRAPHY

Archives/Manuscript Materials

BRP. Branch Rickey Papers. Library of Congress, Washington DC.

ERMP. Edward R. Murrow Papers. Tufts University, Medford MA.

LCPL. Lowndes County Public Library, Archives, Columbus MS.

NBC Archives. National Broadcasting Company Records, 1921–1976. Wisconsin Historical Society, Madison WS.

NBHF. National Baseball Hall of Fame. Giamatti Research Center, Cooperstown NY.

OLRC. Olin Library, Rollins College, Archives and Special Collections, Winter Park FL.

RBC. Walter Lanier "Red" Barber Collection, Special and Area Studies Collections, George A. Smathers Libraries, University of Florida, Gainesville FL.

SM. Sandford Museum. Sanford FL.

Audio/Visual Sources

Barber, Red. "Lefty Gomez at Rollins College." 1966. Red Barber serves as master of ceremonies for Lefty Gomez's speech. Audio recording (reel to reel), RBC, box 23. Accessible at https://ufdcimages.uflib.ufl.edu/AA/00/06/53/35/00001/5.7.mp3.

———. "Interview with Bill Terry." July 2, 1971. Audio recording (cassette), RBC, boxes 27–28.

———. "Interview with Casey Stengel." 1967. Audio recording (reel to reel), RBC, box 24. Accessible at https://ufdc.ufl.edu/AA00065343/00001.

———. "Interview with Jim Bouton." 1970. Audio recording (cassette), RBC, boxes 27–28.

———. "Interview with Paul Richards." 1968. Audio recording (reel to reel), RBC, box 24. Accessible at https://ufdcimages.uflib.ufl.edu/AA/00/06/53/41/00001/5.13.mp3.

————. "Interview with Walter O'Malley." 1968. Audio recording (reel to reel), RBC, box 23. Accessible at https://ufdcimages.uflib.ufl.edu/AA/00/06/53/40/00001/5.12.mp3.

————. "Play by Play Highlights." Audio recording (cassette), RBC, box 40.

Brennaman, Marty (narrator). "Red Barber: From the Catbird Seat." Compact disc. VXYOU Network, 1993.

Burns, Ken, and Lynn Novick (producers). *Baseball.* PBS Home Video, 1994.

Cosell, Howard. "Interviews Red Barber." Audio recording (reel to reel), August 29, 1968, RBC, box 41.

Costas, Bob. "Costas Coast to Coast." August 11, 1991. Audio recording (digital) in the authors' collection.

Creamer, Robert. "Rhubarb in the Catbird Seat Tape Recordings." [RITCS.] Tapes 1–13, Sides A or B, RBC, box 41. These reel-to-reel audio recordings have been digitized. The URLs for each recording can be accessed at "A Guide to the Walter Lanier 'Red' Barber Papers." http://www.library.ufl.edu/spec/manuscript/guides/Barber.htm. Cited as "Creamer, RITCS" in chapter notes.

Enberg, Dick. "Tributes—Red Barber, KMPC, LA, March 19–March 31, 1974." Audio recording (cassette), RBC, boxes 27–28.

Hughes, Pat. "A Commemorative Tribute Red Barber Play-by-Play Pioneer." Compact disc. www.baseballvoices.com.

King, Larry. "Interviews Red Barber." Audio recordings (reel to reel) 1–4, October 7, 1965, RBC, box 41.

"Remembering Red Barber, Feb. 17, 1908—Feb. 17, 2008. Columbus, Mississippi Celebrates the Centenary of One of Its Illustrious Native Sons, Walter Lanier 'Red' Barber." www.videoservicesinc.net.

Transcriptions: Oral Histories and Interviews

Austin, Dan. "Interview with Red Barber." November 16, 1990. National Baseball Hall of Fame, Giamatti Research Center, Cooperstown NY.

Burrows, Ted. "Interview with Walter L. 'Red' Barber." October 17, 1974. Samuel Proctor Oral History Program, University of Florida. https://ufdc.ufl.edu/UF00006882/00001.

Caudill, Orley B. *The Mississippi Oral History Program: Interview with Mr. Walter L. (Red) Barber,* vol. 44. Hattiesburg MS: University of Mississippi Press, 1974.

Gannon, Michael. "Interview with Walter (Red) Barber." September 27, 1983. Samuel Proctor Oral History Program, University of Florida. https://ufdc.ufl.edu/UF00006252/00001.

Klein, Stewart. "The Truth about Radio: A WNEW Inquiry." October 2, 1966. RBC, box 18, folder 3.

Marshall, William J. "Interview with Red Barber." June 27, 1987. RBC, box 11, folder January–February 1990.

Snyder, Tom. "Interview with Red Barber." October 16, 1978. RBC, box 17, folder 2.

Wymore, Fred. "Interview with Red and Lylah Barber." April 20, 1985. RBC, box 18, folder 3.

Published Works

Barber, Lylah. *Lylah: A Memoir by Lylah Barber*. Chapel Hill NC: Algonquin Books, 1985.

Barber, Red. *The Broadcasters*. New York: Dial Press, 1970.

———. *The Broadcasters*. New York: Da Capo Press, 1985.

———. "Can Baseball Be Saved?" *Reader's Digest*, April 1969, 155–60.

———. "The Greatest College Football Player I Ever Saw, Jay Berwanger." *Sport*, December 1948, 63, 91.

———. "I Cover the Olympics." *Sport*, August 1948, 38–40, 77–78.

———. "It Isn't Work—It's Fun." *Redbook*, August 1945, 35–37, 115.

———. "Leadoff Man" (book review of *Baseball's Great Experiment*). *The New Republic* 189, no. 1 (July 4, 1983): 28–31.

———. "My Most Unforgettable Character." *Reader's Digest*, May 1970, 161–68.

———. "My Ten Years with the Dodgers." *Sport*, March 1948, 52–54, 84–87.

———. "The Night the Lights Came on in Baseball." *Modern Maturity* 26 (October–November 1983): 36–40.

———. *1947: When All Hell Broke Loose in Baseball*. New York: Doubleday, 1982.

———. *Show Me the Way to Go Home*. Philadelphia: Westminster Press, 1971.

———. *Walk in the Spirit*. New York: Dial Press, 1969.

———. "We Were Making History—Flying Blind." *TV Guide*, August 24, 1974, 16–17.

Barber, Red, and Robert Creamer. *Rhubarb in the Catbird Seat*. Garden City NY: Doubleday, 1968.

Barber, Red, and Barney Stein. *The Rhubarb Patch: The Story of the Modern Brooklyn Dodgers*. New York: Simon and Schuster, 1954.

Barber, Sarah Lanier. *Connections: Using Multi-Cultural, Racial and Ethnic Short Stories to Promote Better Writing*. Dubuque: Kendall Hunt Publishing, 1991.

———. "Feminizing the Traditional Curriculum: Bringing Feminist Materials into a Remedial Composition Setting." *LaGuardia Review*, Spring 1977, 19–20.

Barber, Walter "Red." "What to Look for at a Baseball Game." *Redbook*, July 1947, 28–29, 70, 72–73.

Borelli, Stephen. *How About That! The Life of Mel Allen*. Champaign IL: Sports Publishing, 2005.

Buck, Jack. *Jack Buck: "That's a Winner."* Champaign IL: Sagamon Publishing, 1997.

Carlson, Charlie. *Show Biz: A History of Entertainment in Seminole County, Florida*. New Smyrna Beach FL: Luthers Publishing, 2011.

Coleman, Jerry, with Richard Goldstein. *An American Journey: My Life on the Field, in the Air, and on the Air*. Chicago: Triumph Books, 2008.

"Compliments of Wheaties et al." *Time* 33, no. 16 (April 17, 1939): 62–63.

Corbett, Warren. "Red Barber." In Spatz, *The Team That Forever Changed Baseball and America*, 287–93. Lincoln: University of Nebraska Press, 2012.

DeVito, Carlo. *Scooter: The Biography of Phil Rizzuto*. Chicago: Triumph Books, 2010.

DiMaggio, Joe. *Baseball for Everyone.* New York: McGraw-Hill, 1948.

"The Double Life of Red Barber." *Look,* July 9, 1957, 60–62.

Edwards, Bob. *Fridays with Red: A Radio Friendship.* New York: Simon and Schuster, 1993.

"First U.S. Sports Event Is Televised by NBC." *Life,* June 5, 1939, 70–71.

Flewellyn, Valada Parker. *Images of America: African Americans of Sanford.* Charleston SC: Arcadia Publishing, 2009.

Frankau, Pamela. *A Wreath for the Enemy.* London: Heinemann, 1954.

Genung, John F. *Practical Elements of Rhetoric.* Amherst MA: J. E. Williams Press, 1885.

Gibran, Kahlil. *The Prophet.* New Delhi: Praskash Books, reprint 2018.

Halberstam, David. "Better Than Ever." *Parade Magazine,* December 18, 1988, 4–15, 19.

———. *Sports on New York Radio: A Play-by-Play History.* Chicago: Masters Press, 1999.

Harrington, Denis J. "Red Barber: An Interview." *Media History Digest* 12, no. 2 (September 1, 1992): 19–23.

Harrison, Barbara Grizzuti. "Red Barber." In Nauen, *Diamonds Are a Girl's Best Friend.*

Harwell, Ernie, and Tom Keegan. *Ernie Harwell: My Life in Baseball.* Chicago: Triumph Books, 2005.

Heinz, W. C. "The Two Red Barbers." *Cosmopolitan,* May 1953, 104–11.

Hubler, Richard. "The Barber of Brooklyn." *Saturday Evening Post,* March 21, 1942, 60–64.

Indyke, Dottie. "Sarah Barber and Gloria Donadello, Intimate Connections: A Collection." *Southwest Art Magazine,* February 2000. http://www.southwestart.com/articles-interviews/feature-articles/intimate_connections.

Johnson, Speed. *Who's Who in Major League Baseball.* Chicago: Buxton, 1933.

Johnson, William O., Jr. *Super Spectator and the Electric Lilliputians.* Boston: Little, Brown, 1971.

King, Carl. *Model T Days: Florida or Bust.* Lakemont GA: Tri-State Press, 1983.

Lamb, Chris. *Blackout: The Untold Story of Jackie Robinson's First Spring Training.* Lincoln: University of Nebraska Press, 2004.

Lardner, John. "The Incident at Fort Boggess." *Newsweek,* July 17, 1950.

Lelchuk, Alan. *Brooklyn Boy.* New York: McGraw Hill, 1989.

Lowenfish, Lee. *Branch Rickey: Baseball's Ferocious Gentleman.* Lincoln: University of Nebraska Press, 2007.

Mann, Jack. *The Decline and Fall of the New York Yankees.* New York: Simon and Schuster, 1967.

Marshall, William J., Jr. "Baseball from the Catbird Seat: An Interview with Walter 'Red' Barber." *Kentucky Review* 10, no. 2 (Summer 1990): 23–44.

McCue, Andy. *Mover and Shaker: Walter O'Malley, the Dodgers, and Baseball's Westward Expansion.* Lincoln: University of Nebraska Press, 2014.

McFarlane, Roger, and Philip Bashe. *The Complete Bedside Companion.* New York: Simon and Schuster, 1998.

Medley, Mary L. *History of Anson County, 1750–1976.* Wadesboro NC: Anson County Historical Society, 1976.

Michaels, Al. *You Can't Make This Up.* New York: HarperCollins, 2014.

Miller, Jon. *Confessions of a Baseball Purist.* New York: Simon and Schuster, 1998.

Nauen, Elinor, ed. *Diamonds Are a Girl's Best Friend*. Winchester MA: Faber and Faber, 1994.

Norris, Michelle. "Six Words: 'You've Got to Be Taught' Intolerance." NPR, The Race Card Project, May 19, 2014. https://www.npr.org/2014/05/19/308296815/six-words-youve-got-to-be-taught-intolerance.

Otto, Annie. *The Parables of Kahlil Gibran*. New York: Citadel, 1963.

Pfeifer, Luanne. *Gretchen's Gold*. Missoula MT: Pictorial Histories, 1996.

Price, Harry. "Famed Broadcaster Is Interviewed." *The Witness*, August 6, 1942, 11, 16–17.

Reynolds, Quentin. "The Two Lives of Red Barber." *Reader's Digest*, August 1954, 102–6.

Richardson, Bobby. "Locker-Room Legacy." *Guideposts*, October 1993, 6–8.

Sadowsky, Jonathan. "Electroconvulsive Therapy: A History of Controversy, but Also of Help." *The Conversation*, January 13, 2017. https://www.scientificamerican.com/article/electroconvulsive-therapy-a-history-of-controversy-but-also-of-help/.

Sanford Historical Society. *Images of America: Sanford*. Charleston SC: Arcadia Publishing, 2003.

Schaal, Peter. *Sanford as I Knew It*. Sanford FL: Sandford History Museum, 1970.

Schoor, Gene. *The Scooter: The Phil Rizzuto Story*. New York: Charles Scribner's Sons, 1982.

Schuck, Raymond. "Media Authority, Sports Mythology, and Organizational Identity: Red Barber as the Voice of the Brooklyn Dodgers." *Journal of Sports Media*, Spring 2016, 193–215.

Scully, Vin. "Unforgettable Red Barber." *Reader's Digest*, April 1993, 91–95.

Shein, Arn. "Mom and the Babe." *Modern Maturity Magazine*, April–May 1990, 62–65.

Smith, Curt. *Voices of the Game*. Updated edition. New York: Simon and Schuster, 1992.

Spatz, Lyle, ed. *The Team That Forever Changed Baseball and America: The 1947 Brooklyn Dodgers*. Lincoln: University of Nebraska Press, 2012.

Sterling, Christopher H., and John Michael Kittross. *Stay Tuned: A History of American Broadcasting*. Mahwah NJ: Erlbaum, 2002.

Television's First Year. National Broadcasting Company, 1940.

Tygiel, Jules. *Baseball's Great Experiment*. New York: Oxford, 1983.

———, ed. *The Jackie Robinson Reader*. New York: Plume, 1997.

Vance, Mona K. *Images of America, Columbus*. Charleston SC: Arcadia Publishing, 2011.

Walker, James R. *Crack of the Bat: A History of Baseball on the Radio*. Lincoln: University of Nebraska Press, 2015.

Walker, James R., and Robert V. Bellamy, Jr. *Center Field Shot: A History of Baseball on Television*. Lincoln: University of Nebraska Press, 2008.

Warfield, Don. *The Roaring Redhead: Larry MacPhail—Baseball's Great Innovator*. South Bend IN: Diamond Communications, 1987.

Wolff, Bob. *Bob Wolff's Complete Guide to Sportscasting*. New York: Skyhorse, 2011.

"World's Busiest Barber." *Look Magazine*, August 1950. RBC, boxes 1–3, vol. 21.

Yardley, Jonathan. "'Once a Miracle': *The Broadcasters* by Red Barber." *The New Republic*, January 6, 1971, 33–34.

INDEX